From Battenberg to Mountbatten

E. H. COOKRIDGE

From Battenberg to Mountbatten

The John Day Company
New York

First American Edition, 1968

Library of Congress Catalogue Card Number: 68-11292

CONTENTS

ILLUSTRATIONS

ILLUSTRATIONS

PREFACE AND ACKNOWLEDGMENTS

To study the fortunes of the Battenberg and Mountbatten family is to understand how within a century a power élite was formed. Modern history affords hardly any parallel to their rise, within a comparatively short period of time, to influence, privilege, wealth and predominance in many centres of power.

Yet surprisingly there are only a few biographies of some of the family's many members. One reason may be that the Battenbergs and Mountbattens have not encouraged writers to produce a full story of their family. One or two authors have eulogised individual members in the style of 'authorized biographers'.

But the Battenbergs and Mountbattens deserve better than to be treated as cardboard figures. Most of them were—and are—vigorous, gifted, often controversial, sometimes eccentric, but never dull people. In this entirely unauthorized attempt at a necessarily condensed record of the creation, rise and destinies of this family, I have tried to emphasize just these aspects, rather than repeat well known details which can be found in reference books.

During my research work, which purposely covered the past rather than the present, I obtained generous help from many though I can express my special thanks to only a few here. I gratefully acknowledge permission to use some material given by H.M. Queen Alexandra of Yugoslavia, Marjorie, Countess of Brecknock, Sir Harold Nicolson, K.C.V.O., and Sir Arthur Bryant, C.B.E. For locating documents, sources of reference and books, I am greatly indebted to the librarians of the British Museum; Miss R. Coombes, Librarian of the Imperial War Museum; Mr Peter Spiro, Librarian of the Institut of Bankers; the directors and archivists of the State Archives of Hesse; the *Landesmuseum* in Darmstadt; the *Preussische Staatsarchiv* in Berlin; the Historical Commission of the State of Hesse; Hofrat Dr H. Pauer, director of the *National Bibliothek* in Vienna; and their staff members.

The Hartenau Achives (assembled by the late Prince Alexander of Battenberg), containing invaluable dossiers including the diaries of Prince Alexander of Hesse, many thousand letters and documents of Queen Victoria, Empress Frederick, Bismarck, the Tsars, and all members of the Battenberg family, and preserved for almost half a century by Prince Alexander's son, *Sektionchef* Dr Assen von Hartenau, were destroyed at the end of the war. Fortunately, I was able to obtain some of the most relevant transcripts of the originals.

The book could never have been completed without the unstinted help of Mr Cecil Porter who contributed to some chapters and skilfully carried out revisions. I owe a debt of gratitude to Mr F. George Kay for valuable advice and encouragement, and to Mrs Janet Bonham for her conscientious secretarial work.

I want to thank the following publishers for permission to quote from books published by them: Cassell & Co., Constable & Co., Robert Hale, William Heinemann, Hutchinson, Hodder & Stoughton, Jarrolds, Longmans, Green & Co., Macmillan & Co., Macdonald & Co., and John Murray; and the Editor of the *Sunday Telegraph* and Mr Ivan Rowan for permission to quote from his article in that newspaper.

E.H.C.

CHAPTER ONE

LORD LOUIS' CODE

The history of the Battenberg and Mountbatten family is one hundred years old. The title-name of Battenberg was devised to hush a romantic scandal; the name of Mountbatten was a gesture in anglicization when in 1917 anti-German feeling ran high in Britain. The operative name in the history of this ebullient family is Hesse, and the ancestry of the Landgraves and Grand Dukes of Hesse goes back to Charlemagne and Saint Elizabeth of Hungary.

On a cheerless November night in 1851, at his palace in Darmstadt, Grand Duke Louis III of Hesse created the title of Battenberg for Countess Julie Hauke, a young woman who had eloped with his younger brother, Prince Alexander.

From that elopement and a morganatic marriage emerged a succession of remarkable men and women who, by linking again and again with Queen Victoria's descendants, by good fortune, by great talents, by tenacious self-assertion, and occasionally by a bizarre chance deeply affected the destinies of Europe and the intrigues of royal Courts and political chancelleries for four generations.

The thin blood of the Hesse princes received many renascent transfusions: German and Polish, French and English, Greek and Hungarian, Jewish and Spanish. The Battenbergs and the Mountbattens have come a long, long way. In the pursuit of their family interest they either allied themselves with, or fought, the Tsars and the Kaisers, the emperors of France and Austria, Bismarck and the Sultan, gave a ruler to Bulgaria, queens to Spain and Sweden, a princess to Greece, a husband to a prima donna, two First Sea Lords to Britain, a Viceroy to India and a husband to the granddaughter of a Jewish financier, a salesman to a New York store, a wife to a London decorator – and, of course, the present Heir to the Throne of English kings.

Captain Lord Louis Mountbatten, RN, born to Europe's royal purple at Windsor Castle in 1900, and till 1917 Prince Louis Francis Albert Victor Nicholas of Battenberg, had a strangely mixed public image in the years before the war. A great-grandson of Queen Victoria, he was a brilliant young naval officer, had been an international playboy, married to the wealthy heiress Edwina Ashley, host of magnificent parties, a close friend of the abdicated King Edward VIII.

He knew how deeply the English respect a noble title, and that if there was one thing which transcends British prejudice against 'foreigners' in high places it is the admiration for ancient lineage. So one day in the spring of 1939 when he was recovering from an attack of jaundice at his home at Broadlands in Hampshire, he began to compose his elaborate family tree – a tree with branches in every royal court of Europe, past and present. His mother, Princess Victoria of Hesse, the Dowager Marchioness of Milford Haven, helped him to compile this private Almanach de Gotha in miniature.

He recalled in the preface to this genealogical tables – so ingeniously devised that they earned the respect of experts – how the idea arose: 'During recent visits to relations in Germany and Sweden I had been asked by our daughters[1] to explain the exact relationship of all those they met and also those they heard talked about. "Who are Missie, Mössie, Ducky, Toddy?" they asked. I had managed to answer most of their questions, but it was difficult to explain the double cross-relationships arising out of the frequent marriages between cousins, often of different generations. So, while I was laid up, my mother helped to pass the time by dictating to me the great majority of the Relationship Tables.' Many years later when Lord Mountbatten was Viceroy of India a few copies of the book, dedicated to his children, were printed.[2]

In producing the *Tables*, Lord Mountbatten put to good use

---

[1] Lady Patricia, now Lady Brabourne, and Lady Pamela, now Lady Pamela Hicks.
[2] Rear Admiral the Earl Mountbatten of Burma, *Relationship Tables*, printed by the Viceregal Press, New Delhi, 1947.

his knowledge of naval signalling. As a young Royal Navy officer he invented a new signal coding system and later wrote the standard book on the subject. His system enabled three flotillas of destroyers to acknowledge a radio message within 60 seconds. It used a two-letter call sign which all 27 ships of the flotillas had to answer in strictly alphabetical order. He applied a coding method, based upon his signalling system, to his genealogical research by allotting a 'signal letter' to each of the great families with whom the Battenbergs and Mountbattens were related, each family member having a letter-figure code.

He explained in the foreword to the *Tables*: 'Originally, we only dealt with those whom my mother either remembered personally or knew of in their lifetime. As she was born in 1863 this included all relations living in 1870 and later. The remarkable thing is that she remembered practically every member of all the families concerned, and many anecdotes about them without having to refer to any books of reference.'

In this foreword written in 1947, at the time of his nephew's betrothal to Princess Elizabeth, Lord Mountbatten said that while space precluded going back beyond the nineteenth century as a general rule, he thought 'it would be interesting to trace the direct male descent for a thousand years or so in a few cases'.

This he did with great skill for Prince Philip, whose descent is seen to go back to such figures of history as Charlemagne, Saint Elizabeth of Hungary, William Percy (ancestor of Hotspur), Henry of Brabant and Hugh Capet, King of France.

The claim of having Charlemagne among the Mountbatten ancestors is, perhaps, the most significant and intriguing. The picture of Charlemagne conveyed by early mediaeval chroniclers must have attracted Lord Mountbatten: 'A typical German leader, over six feet in height, of superb athletic frame, a great hunter and excellent swimmer; handsome, with clear eyes, fair hair and a merry disposition.' Very much a Mountbatten, in fact!

The *Tables* suggest the unbroken descent of the Mountbattens from some of the greatest dynasties of history, which would make them the oldest extant among the noblest families. Compared with such a lineage covering more than a thousand years, the Norman and Plantagenet kings, the Saxon and Sallian emperors, the Guelfs and the Capets of Burgundy would be junior, and the Bourbons, Habsburgs, Stuarts or Tudors just upstarts.

'It had been necessary to have a starting point, or rather several starting points from which to develop the various families,' he wrote. 'My mother selected fifteen Heads of Families, born in the early part of the last century. To each of these I allotted an easily remembered letter, thus:

A King Alfonso xii of Spain
B King Leopold of the Belgians
C Landgrave Frederick of Hesse-Cassel
D King Christian ix of Denmark
F Grand-Duke Frederick-Francis ii of Mecklemburg-Schwerin
G King George i of the Hellenes
H Grand Duke Louis ii of Hesse and by the Rhine
L Prince Ernest Hohenlohe-Langenburg
M King Nicholas of Montenegro
N King William iii of the Netherlands
P German Emperor Frederick iii, King of Prussia
R Emperor Nicholas i of All the Russias
S King Oscar i of Sweden
T Duke Alexander of Württemberg, founder of the Teck family
V Queen Victoria of Great Britain.'

The children of each head of family were numbered in order of their ages, 1, 2, 3 and so on. Thus, for instance, the fifth child of King George i of Greece became 'G–5'. He was Prince Andrew, the father of Prince Philip, the Duke of Edinburgh. If persons had only one symbol besides the family letter they must be brothers or sisters (thus Prince Andrew's brothers, King Constantine of Greece was G–1, and Nicholas G–4. In the next generation instead of figures letters were added in alphabetical order. Thus Prince Philip being the fifth child (after the births of four daughters) of Prince Andrew of Greece, had the code G–5–E, while Prince Charles, the Prince of Wales would be, taking his Greek descent into account, G–5–E–1.

The simplest example of the relationship between the Queen and her husband can be taken from their common descent from King Christian ix of Denmark, whose second child was Queen Alexandra, the wife of King Edward vii (and great-grandmother of our Queen) and whose third child William became the King of Greece under the name of George i (and was the grandfather of Prince Philip, the Duke of Edinburgh). The code table can be drawn thus:

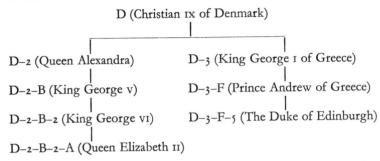

D (Christian IX of Denmark)

D–2 (Queen Alexandra) D–3 (King George I of Greece)

D–2–B (King George V) D–3–F (Prince Andrew of Greece)

D–2–B–2 (King George VI) D–3–F–5 (The Duke of Edinburgh)

D–2–B–2–A (Queen Elizabeth II)

which shows that the Queen and her husband are second cousins once removed.

However the system becomes more complex with descent from other Heads of Families. Both the Queen and Prince Philip are, of course, also descended from Queen Victoria, and thus they become third cousins:

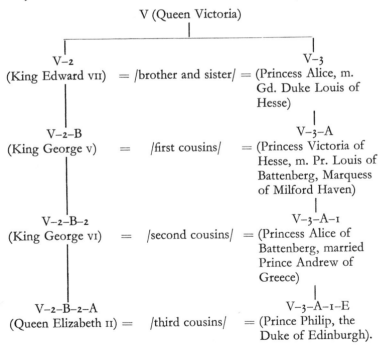

V (Queen Victoria)

V–2
(King Edward VII) = /brother and sister/ = V–3
(Princess Alice, m. Gd. Duke Louis of Hesse)

V–2–B
(King George V) = /first cousins/ = V–3–A
(Princess Victoria of Hesse, m. Pr. Louis of Battenberg, Marquess of Milford Haven)

V–2–B–2
(King George VI) = /second cousins/ = V–3–A–1
(Princess Alice of Battenberg, married Prince Andrew of Greece)

V–2–B–2–A
(Queen Elizabeth II) = /third cousins/ = V–3–A–1–E
(Prince Philip, the Duke of Edinburgh).

One can use other permutations, particularly for Prince Philip, taking into account his descent from King George III of England, his relationship to the family of the Tsar of Russia, and his direct lineage from the grand-ducal family of Hesse-Darmstadt. His codes then become, alternatively: X–(for George III)–5–A–3–A–1–E, R–(for Tsar Nicholas I)–5–B–6–E, and H–(for Hesse)–2–A–1–A–5.

On one table the Queen is her husband's 'second cousin once removed', on another (working out the descent from King George III of England), they are seen also as fourth cousins once removed and, while on the 'Danish' table the Queen is one generation younger than her husband, on the 'Georgian' table Prince Philip appears one generation younger than his wife.

The line of the Hesse family, the most relevant of all, can be traced without a break back to 750. My own research at the State Archives at Darmstadt produced documents about Giselbert, a landowner and patron of the Monastery of Kessling, showing that he had founded in 777 the Abbey of Priem. His son Reginardus was the Abbot of Echternach in 830. Giselbert II abducted the daughter of King Lothair of Lorraine and married her at Aquitaine. Through this marriage of Charlemagne's granddaughter, the Mountbattens can claim their link with the great Carolingian whose empire stretched from the Atlantic and the North Sea to the Mediterranean and the Danube. Another Giselbert married a daughter of King Henry the Fowler, the first Saxon emperor, who followed the East Frankish reign of the Carolingians.

The most important ancestor of the Hesse family in the Middle Ages was King Henry III the Magnanimous of Brabant (1207–48). His first marriage was to the granddaughter of German Emperor Frederick Barbarossa; the second to Sophie, daughter of Duke Louis IV of Thuringia and Elizabeth of Hungary. Elizabeth, 'the mother of the poor', performed the famous miracle of the bread-into-roses, cared for lepers and kissed their sores. After her husband died when she was only 20, her brother-in-law expelled her from the Castle of Wartburg. She entered the convent of the Third Order of St Francis and died four years later in 1231. She was canonized, and the Collect at the Masses said in Catholic churches on November 19 each year reminds mankind 'to think little of worldly prosperity and to be ever gladdened by heavenly consolation'. Although her descendants not always observed this tenet, the Mountbattens can claim to include a Saint in their family.

Worldly prosperity in abundance came to St Elizabeth's grandson, King Henry the Child. At the age of three he inherited the rich territories of Thuringia and Hesse from his great uncle, the German Emperor Henry Raspe, the man who had exacted an enormous ransom for freeing King Richard the Lionheart of England. Subsequent wars of succession to the German imperial crown left the family, however, only with Hesse, and Henry the Child had to content himself with the dignity of a 'Landgrave of Hesse', a title that exists to this day in the line of the princes of Hesse-Cassel. At times even the possession of the Hessian lands was in the balance, but Henry's descendants, who bore such appealing names as Hermann the Learned, Louis the Courageous and Louis the Peaceful, managed to maintain their hold. Since the fourteenth century many Hesse princes and princesses were named Louis or Louise and these names were later given to almost every member of the Battenberg and Mountbatten family. It is not by chance that two of the Queen's and Prince Philip's children have these names: Princess Anne as her fourth, and Prince Edward, born in 1964, as his second.

During the religious wars that followed Luther's 'Protest', Landgrave Philip of Hesse was one of the leaders of the Protestant Princes' League. When he and his allies refused to attend the Council of Trent and defied both the Pope and the Emperor Charles v, their lands were invaded by the imperial army and Philip was taken prisoner. One of Philip's sons-in-law, Prince Maurice of Saxony, who had originally espoused the Catholic cause, changed sides in 1551, turned against the Emperor, concluded a treaty with the king of France, and freed his father-in-law, restoring to him his possessions. On his deathbed in 1567, Philip of Hesse divided his territories between his four sons. Hesse-Cassel went to the eldest, William; Hesse-Marburg to Louis; Rhinefels to the third son, Philip, and Hesse-Darmstadt to the youngest, George. Both the Marburg and Rhinefels lines died out and these territories were merged with Hesse-Darmstadt. The two principalities of Hesse-Cassel and Hesse-Darmstadt lasted until the German Republic was proclaimed in 1918, at the end of the First World War.

Some of the Hesse-Darmstadt princes were wise and good rulers, such as Louis v who founded the university of Giessen. Others were wastrels and libertines who built magnificent palaces from exhorbitant taxes wrung out of the people. Two of the princes were closely linked with British naval history. Frederick (1616–82) commanded the galleys of the Knights of Malta against the Turks, became Captain General of Malta and built the palace now known as Admiralty House. Both Lord Mountbatten and the Duke of Edinburgh when stationed at Malta occupied the very same chambers as their seventeenth-century ancestor. George, younger son of Landgrave Louis vi (1669–1705) entered the English service, commanded the Royal Marines at the capture of Gibraltar and was made Governor of Gibraltar in 1704.

Louis ix of Hesse-Darmstadt restored some prosperity to his state, but the role of his wife Caroline was more important. She had come from the small and impoverished court of Zwei-bruecken, but had received an excellent education which she used to make Darmstadt one of the most important intellectual centres of late eighteenth-century Germany. Remembered as the 'Great Landgravine', she attracted to her court poets, philosophers, painters and sculptors. It was under her guidance that the palaces, still held today by some of Prince Philip's sisters and cousins, were restored and adorned. She was a patron of the German poet Klopstock who, influenced by Milton's *Paradise Lost*, wrote the *Messiah*.

If the southern principality of Hesse-Darmstadt was becoming peaceful, civilised and prosperous, in the northern area of Hesse-Cassel the greedy Duke Charles copied the mediaeval custom of hiring out his soldiers to foreign powers. His heir Frederic ii 'sold' 22,000 Hessian soldiers – mostly peasant lads captured by press-gangs – to be used by George iii of England as mercenaries in the American War of Independence.

During the Seven Years' War Hesse supported Prussia, but with the advent of Napoleon, Landgrave Louis x became one of the leaders of the Rhine League and promptly allied himself with Bonaparte. One historian wrote that 'the loyalties of the Hesse princes during the Napoleonic wars veered like a windcock in a whirlwind', but their manoeuvring between the cliffs of power politics certainly brought good results to themselves.

The Hesse ruler was rewarded by Napoleon with some of the sequestrated estates of the Church and several cities hitherto ruled by bishops, such as Mainz and Worms. For the first time Hesse-Darmstadt expanded her territories beyond the Rhine. Louis decided to mark this by proclaiming himself Grand Duke on 14 August 1806, discarding the lower rank of Landgrave.

But as soon as Napoleon's star began to decline, he changed sides once more. At the Congress of Vienna, where saints and sinners were sorted out and the German princes who had supported Napoleon punished with the loss of their thrones, Louis found himself on the side of the saints. He gained another strip of land and was confirmed by the Great Powers as Grand Duke Louis I of Hesse and by Rhine.

He was a liberal ruler and in 1820, long before the Revolution of 1848, gave Hesse a constitution which curtailed his own autocratic powers and provided for a limited electoral system to a parliamentary assembly. He even forced a similar course upon neighbouring German princes. When he died in 1830 he left his son, Grand Duke Louis II, a well-ordered little country with a number of fine towns and the proud capital of Darmstadt which, although having a population of only 40,000, was regarded throughout Germany as an important centre of arts and science. It was at Darmstadt that the first German Technological University was founded to produce some of the finest technicians and engineers of nineteenth century Central Europe. The first All-German trade and industry congress assembled there in 1820, lasting for two years and laying the foundation for Germany's industrial revolution.

The Grand Duke lived to the age of 77, and was succeeded in 1830 by his son Louis II, who was 53 years old. His biggest contribution to the history of Hesse, indeed of Europe generally, was that he sired four children who all made important marriages. His wife was Wilhelmina, daughter of Charles Louis Markgrave of Baden, a woman of considerable intelligence, who realised, much as Queen Victoria did, that dynastic power can be achieved, and probably best achieved, by clever match-making. Her sisters, the princesses of Baden, had all married well, ascending the thrones of Russia, Bavaria, Sweden and Brunswick. Wilhelmina had similar hopes for her three sons and only daughter.

She suffered from tuberculosis, although her protracted illness was either never recognised by her doctors or, more possibly, concealed from both her and her husband. When she was slowly dying in 1835, at the age of 46, the Court medical bulletins alternated between descriptions of her illness as pneumonia, lung congestion and intestinal trouble. She had been ordered by her Court physicians to take ice-cold baths to 'fight the fever and distemper', was weakened by continuous blood-letting and the application of leeches, and yet had the strength of mind to conduct a vast correspondence with her sisters and relatives at every European Court, to find suitable brides for her two elder sons and to plan a match for her little daughter Marie.

The Grand Duchess lived long enough to see her first-born, the later Grand Duke Louis III, marry Princess Mathilde, daughter of King Louis of Bavaria and sister of the later King of Greece. Mercifully, she was spared the shock of the scandal which soon afterwards rocked the Court of Munich. Her son's father-in-law, the Bavarian ruler, had at the age of 60 become hopelessly besotted with the Scottish-born adventuress Elizabeth Gilbert. As 'the Spanish dancer Lola Montez' she had taken Europe's capitals by storm, and soon after her debut in Munich became the king's mistress. He showered extravagant gifts upon her and raised her to the rank of a Countess Landsfeld. She asserted such a hold over her royal lover that she made and unmade his cabinet ministers. The role she played during the revolutionary movement in 1848 in Germany eventually led to King Louis' abdication and her flight to London.

The Grand Duchess of Hesse died before the scandal broke. She had the satisfaction of knowing that her family had not only linked themselves with the Bavarian dynasty but also that her second son, Charles, had become engaged to the granddaughter of King Frederick William II of Prussia. When she died her daughter Marie was 12, and her youngest son Alexander 13. Five years later Marie married the Tsarevitch of Russia, who became Tsar Alexander II. Her youngest son, however, was to make a very different alliance. After jilting a Russian grand-duchess, he was to elope with a poor orphan girl, and in doing so to found the Battenberg family.

CHAPTER TWO

THE DASHING GUARDS OFFICER

Prince Alexander of Hesse

TWELVE-YEARS-OLD Prince Alexander of Hesse stood in the park of the grand-ducal palace near Darmstadt, below the windows of the heavily-curtained room where his mother was slowly dying. With him was his sister Marie, his tutor, Captain Frey, and several courtiers and servants. They all stared apprehensively at the strange spectacle in the sky.

The day was Saturday, 10 October 1835. The comet, which the English astronomer Edmond Halley had predicted in 1705 almost to the very day, swept with an awsome, fiery trail across the heavens. Alexander took paper and pencil from a servant and began to draw the comet's curve in a childish scrawl. Bending forward, the boy's tutor whispered: 'This could be a terrible foreboding. Please God that it may turn into a good omen for your life, my dear Alexander . . .'

The boy looked up with a smile: 'Why not, Captain Frey? I should like to be a comet, flying so high and far.'

'You must not talk like that,' the tutor rebuked him; 'remember what I wrote for you "On Pride". You must be humble and pray for your dear Mama to regain her health.'

Frey was a well-educated and progressively-minded man, a trifle eccentric at times, but devoted to his two young charges. He instilled in both Alexander and Marie respect for humbler people and gave them hard physical training, sometimes ordering them to help the servants and gardeners, which was unusual at a German princely mansion of the nineteenth century. The tutor kept a detailed diary of his pupils' progress. Part of this record was a 'Register of Tears and Grimaces', in which he entered 'naughty outbursts' and tearful scenes. Each month he read out a 'balance sheet' to the two children, and, if Alexander had been more short-tempered or had shed more tears than his sister, he was severely reminded how unseemly this was for a young prince and an officer in the Grand Duke's army. For, as was the custom, Alexander had been made a lieutenant on his tenth birthday and wore a resplendent Life Guards uniform on State occasions.

There was a great difference in age between the two younger children and their two older brothers. The beautiful Grand-Duchess Wilhelmina had suddenly produced, in 1823 and 1824, the two new babies, when her two sons were already almost grown up. At Darmstadt and many German courts the whisper had gone round that the two younger children were not the Grand-Duke's but fruits of his wife's secret romance with her chamberlain, Baron Augustus von Grancy. If this was true, Lord Mountbatten's genealogical tables would make little sense. But nobody has ever proved the rumours of the Grand Duchess' alleged adultery. When Alexander was still a little boy, his eldest brother, Louis, was already married. Because of their mother's illness Alexander and Marie spent their childhood in the care of governesses and tutors, and brother and sister became very close.

Because of its geographical situation and its historical past, the Grand Duchy of Hesse occupied in spite of its smallness an important place among the thirty-nine states of Germany before unification. The Hesse family was well-connected with the great courts of Europe, mainly through the marriages made by Grand-Duchess Wilhelmina's sisters. The oldest, Elizabeth, Dowager-Empress of Russia (her husband Tsar Alexander I died in 1825 and was succeeded by his brother Nicholas) had always hoped that her nephew by marriage, Sasha, the Crown Prince Alexander of Russia, would one day marry her niece Marie of Hesse. After her sister Wilhelmina died, Empress Elizabeth was even more determined to arrange this match, even though the girl was then only 12. At Wilhelmina's funeral she discussed her plan with Marie's father. Three years passed, however, until in the summer of 1839 the 20-year-old Tsarevitch was sent to Darmstadt and met Marie, now a pretty but delicate girl of 15. Like her mother, Marie suffered from consumption, but this only made her features more appealing, with her large blue eyes, almost transparent skin and thin but graceful figure. She had been ordered to hide from the Russian cousin the fact that she suffered from obstinate coughing; was told not to get hot and flushed, not to dance too much which would have made her tired, and to try her best to make a good impression. She must have succeeded in all this, for the Tsarevitch fell in love with her during his first visit.

The delicate state of the Princess's health compelled her father to postpone the plan of an engagement, but negotiations between the courts of Darmstadt and St Petersburg continued, and in April 1840 the Tsarevitch paid his second visit to Castle Heiligenberg. The spark of his affection for Marie had been carefully fanned by the match-makers.

Sasha had brought her a magnificent present, a diamond bracelet from the Russian crown treasures, but the same day that he gave it to her she lost it in the rose garden; a most embarrassing event which was regarded as a bad omen. The loss was concealed from Tsarevitch for a day or two, but fortunately the daughter of one of the gardeners found the bracelet and Marie was able to wear it at the ball given in honour of the Russian guests. The Tsarevitch took a great liking to his 17-year-old cousin and namesake, Alexander of Hesse. He even so far fogot his dignity as to engage in a wrestling match with him, which the Hesse prince won.

The betrothal of the Tsarevitch to Marie was announced on 16 April 1840. The Russian Crown Prince told Alexander that he must accompany Marie to St Petersburg and stay for a year or so at the Russian court, so that 'your little sister will not be too lonely after the parting from her family and Darmstadt'. The Grand Duke was delighted; he thought that a sojourn at St Petersburg would do his youngest son a great deal of good. It was to be a fateful visit indeed.

In June 1840, Tsar Nicholas I and Tsaritsa Charlotte (the former Princess of Prussia) arrived in Darmstadt with their second daughter Olly, the lovely Grand Duchess Olga Nicolaievna, to take Marie and her brother back to St Petersburg for the wedding. Alexander fell in love as soon as he had set eyes on Olly, but she treated him with the slightly mocking condescension of a girl who though of the same age was much more mature and sophisticated. To Olga, accustomed to the panache of Russian Guards officers, Alexander was a country bumpkin who must learn the refined manners of a great court. But Olga was wrong. Even though Alexander had seen nothing of the world beyond the modest court at Darmstadt and the homely country house of Heiligenberg, he was at 17 a young man of quite remarkable intelligence, great aptitude for learning, a gifted amateur painter, handsome, nearly six feet tall, with an athletic and well-proportioned body, and with dark silky hair. He was gay and charming, always ready for fun yet certainly not empty-headed. Tsar Nicholas took an immediate liking to him. At the dinner table one night, glancing at Alexander's uniform, he commented that a lieutenant's rank was hardly good enough for the future brother-in-law of the Tsarevitch and thereupon made him a captain in the Imperial Russian Chevalier Guards.

Now it was time for the two Hesse children to leave for Russia with the Imperial Majesties and Grand Duchess Olga. Tearfully Captain Frey embraced Alexander and, regardless of his new rank, told him to watch his posture, keep his chin high and his chest out, and 'learn Russian so that you can talk to the common people, too, although at the Court of St Petersburg everyone talks German anyway. . . .' The long journey across Germany and Russian-Poland was made in a cavalcade of coaches, each drawn by eight horses, flanked by platoons of Cossacks and Dragoons. Marie shared her coach with Olga. There were stops at almost a dozen German courts – Cassel, Gotha, Weimar, Brunswick, Anhalt, Saxony, and Prussia – before they made the state entry on 8 September into St Petersburg where little Princess Marie saw with astonishment the roads to and through the capital lined with tens of thousands of troops of every kind, Hussars and Chevaliers, Uhlans and Dragoons, Cossacks, Circassian and Tartar warriors in Oriental dress. Guns thundered nonstop, church bells clanged out, band after band played the national anthem, the words being fervently intoned by the ragged multitudes held back at a distance from the road by the bayonets of the infantry and the flourished knouts of the Cossacks. The words? 'That God Almighty may preserve the right-believing and orthodox Tsar of all the Russias. . . .'

Alexander who had followed alone on horseback, visiting various relatives on the way, was reunited with his sister the day before. He, too, was awestruck by the splendour of the Winter Palace and the scene of the festivities that had already begun, merry-making that was in no way impaired by reports of famine in several Russian provinces following a drought that had ruined the harvest. The Court of St Petersburg was the most magnificent in Europe, if one that was gravely divided. Three successive German Empresses had filled it with scores of German princelings and hangers-on; this had in its turn produced a 'Russian Court Party' led by Count Orlov, which attempted to limit German influence.

Count Orlov, who stood high in Tsar Nicholas' favour, did not want yet another German Tsaritsa. Even before Nicholas paid his visit to Darmstadt, Orlov told him the story that Marie was not the legitimate daughter of the Grand Duke of Hesse, but of the chamberlain reputed to have been the lover of the Grand Duchess. Orlov showed the Tsar secret reports from his spies in Germany, pointing out that Marie and Alexander had been born within a year after a lapse of 17 years, and inferring that Grand Duke Louis had lost his virility many years before the births of the two younger children.

But the Tsar scorned these allegations. He told Orlov: 'That may be so. But who are you and who am I? We can only hope to be the sons of our fathers whose proud names we bear, but who on earth can prove it?' And he added: 'Now, it is my wish and my order that all this talk shall stop. I should not advise anyone to suggest that the heir to the Russian throne is marrying a bastard.'[1]

Tsar Nicholas I was popular with the Russian aristocracy despite his fondness for everything German. He had no time for the liberal ideas of his late brother, who had initiated the liberation of peasant serfs in the Baltic provinces, had abolished torture of prisoners, had proclaimed amnesties for political offences and repealed censorship of foreign books. Nicholas was a firm believer in autocracy. He scrapped most of his predecessor's reforms, drowned the Polish rebellion in blood, and exiled revolutionary agitators to the newly-conquered steppes of southern Siberia. His victories over Persia and Turkey had enhanced Russia's prestige, and his aim was to maintain the

[1] Count Karl Ludwig von Ficquelmont, *Memoirs*, Vienna 1928. Also cf. Corti, Egon Cesare, *Unter Zaren und Gekrönten Frauen*, Salzburg, 1936, p. 8 ff.

largest army in Europe. His powerful officers corps was recruited almost entirely from the sons of aristocrats and boyars. His omnipresent secret police controlled the people by oppressive measures.

He wanted his future daughter-in-law, young as she was, to assimilate the ideas of Russian autocracy and nationalism and the orthodoxy of the Russian church. He delayed the wedding until Easter 1841, so that she could get accustomed to the Court and Russia generally, and could be prepared for entry into the Russian Orthodox Church. He also insisted that both she and Alexander should learn at least some Russian.

But the severe winter was too much for the consumptive princess and she spent almost all January and February in bed, gathering strength again after the endless balls and banquets of the Christmas season, emerging even tinier, thinner, paler and more ethereally beautiful than before, and applying herself timidly to her many new duties.

Alexander of Hesse lived a very different life. Although he did not like everything he saw, remembering Captain Frey's progressive opinions, he was fascinated by the vigorous activities of the younger set at court. Even though many of the Russian courtiers and officers looked on the German prince with definite reserve, the ladies of the Court did not. Repulsed again and again by the Grand Duchess Olga, Alexander soon found all the consolation he could desire. He was soon entangled in a succession of gallant affairs with beautiful and willing women of the Court.

One thing annoyed him, however: Russian courtiers would address him as 'Prince of Darmstadt'. Dropping his cheerful grin, Alexander would make it known, distinctly haughtily, that he was a 'Prince of Hesse and by Rhine'. When the Russians were, understandably, confused by these petty German titles, Alexander emphasized that his title went back a thousand years, to the times of Charlemagne. But when on at least one occasion he added 'in those days nobody had ever even heard of the Romanovs,' he irritated the Russians although he delighted the Court of Vienna when the Austrian Ambassador, Baron von Meisenburg, promptly reported the remark to Metternich.

Alexander kept up a lengthy correspondence with Captain Frey back in Darmstadt. Before the wedding he had been promoted by the Tsar to the rank of a colonel in the Imperial Guards, and after the ceremony he was given the Order of St Andrew. To his old Tutor Alexander wrote sardonically, 'No one has ever earned an Order so easily, unless it can be considered a merit to have survived the wedding breakfast where the tables were bending under the weight of the gold plate loaded with exquisite foods and crystal filled with precious drink. . . .'

The wedding took place on 16 April 1841 at the Cathedral of St Peter and Paul with all the pomp of the Eastern Church. The ceremony began at 8 o'clock in the morning and lasted for several hours, with the Patriarch of the Russian Orthodox Church and the Metropolitan of Moscow officiating, surrounded by the entire Synod and several hundred priests. The wedding festivities lasted for a fortnight, an endless succession of military parades, banquets, State receptions, fancy dress balls and musical soirees. For one ball at the Winter Palace 42,000 invitations were issued; it began at 9 p.m., lasted through the night and until the afternoon of the next day. A few hours for sleep and the Court and many of the guests assembled again for another State banquet. Baron von Meisenburg reported to Vienna: 'Even diplomats accustomed to such spectacles were dazzled by the superb furnishings and decorations of the palaces, by the incredible luxury of the dresses of the ladies and the splendour of the uniforms, the display of priceless jewels, the abundance of viands and wines, and the profusion of exotic flowers'. He added: 'A little of the expense of this cornucopia would have been enough to allay the suffering of those Russians who at the same time perish of famine'.

The Tsar, so preoccupied with military matters, ordered that his army must stage the greatest show of all. One military display followed after another. At one parade there was a march-past by 40,000 troops, every soldier in brand-new uniform; on another occasion 40 regiments of cavalry charged at full gallop towards the marquee of the Imperial Family and their guests, reining suddenly at a few yards' distance with not one horse projecting from the lines by as much as a nose. For several months the revelry continued. In February 1842 Metternich's special agent Count Woyna reported: 'Balls, dinners, masked balls and soirees follow one another with such rapidity that nobody in Petersburg has time for politics'.

Caring least of all for politics was the 18-year-old Colonel of his Imperial Russian Majesty's Life Guards, Prince Alexander of

Hesse. He had other things to worry him by now. The sheer precision demanded of the Russian cavalry defeated him. At one parade he was leading his regiment on an unruly horse named 'Adonis'. As the massed bands crashed into a rousing march the horse shied and carried Alexander backwards, right past the Tsar. Furious, Alexander dismounted and changed to another horse, but this time his mount bolted straight into the Tsar's entourage, almost colliding with Nicholas himself. The Tsar, white with anger, rode up to the young Prince and, before the assembled thousands, snapped at him: 'See that you learn to ride properly. You are a disgrace to your regiment! Understand?' Alexander returned home that evening humbled and outraged at the public reprimand, but the beautiful Grand Duchess Olga came to see him, led him to a terrace overlooking the gardens and, for the first time, let him kiss her lips. She told him she would beg Papa to be less severe in future, but at that moment Alexander did not care for the Tsar's views. For a little while Olga was gentle, even affectionate up to a point with Alexander, who felt encouraged enough to put out feelers to see if he would be welcome as Olga's suitor. He decided to make a public gesture at a mediaeval tournament staged at the summer palace of Tsarskoe Selo. Every rider was to wear armour brought from the museums in Petersburg, Moscow, Kiev, Warsaw, and even from Germany. At one stage of the pageant each knight had to kneel in front of a lady to receive a silk scarf from her. Alexander chose Olga but to his dismay was told that the Tsaritsa had already instructed Prince Baryatinsky, the Tsar's handsome aide-de-camp to attend her daughter. Deeply hurt, Alexander turned to 'Bijouette', the Countess Barbara Sheremetyev, pretty, vivacious, only recently married, and quite amoral.

Olga may have been a little in love with Alexander, but her mother had warned her that the Hesse prince was no suitable match. The family had had one misalliance already – when the Tsar and Tsaritsa had unwillingly agreed to the marriage of their eldest daughter, Marie, to the dashing Duke of Leuchtenberg, son of Eugene de Beauharnais, Bonaparte's stepson. Nicholas and Charlotte of Russia had their eyes very firmly fixed on a really suitable marriage for Olga, with Archduke Stephen of Austria, a match that would have linked Russia with the Habsburgs and the Austro-Hungarian Empire and changed the history of Europe. Whatever instructions she may have had from her parents, Olga enjoyed her affair with Alexander and played it in a classically feminine manner, one day hot, another day cool. Perhaps some older and mischievous friend hinted to Alexander that making Olga jealous might produce results. It certainly did produce an unexpected one.

Alexander now openly flirted with any of the ladies at the Court on whom he could lay his hands. There was no particular *finesse* about it. He took whatever he could get, and there was no lack of beautiful and willing women. Apart from Bijouette, who was almost too bare-faced in her passion for him, there was Countess Vera Stolypin, the best dancer at court and noted in more than one diary as 'no prude'. There was a French lady-in-waiting, a Mademoiselle de Rehbinder, to whom Alexander had paid the usual attentions and who was compelled to make a sudden marriage with a minor Court official, Colonel Ponamarov. There followed a whole succession of not so young and married ladies who, whatever they did in private, treated him in public as a notorious Don Juan. Alexander found he had overstepped himself. He had intended to make Olga jealous; now there was grave risk that she might be really hurt and angry. Olga, however, showed no signs of anger, but no signs of affection either. She had decided to meet her parents' wish for her betrothal with the Austrian archduke.

In July 1842 the Tsar and Tsarina celebrated their silver wedding. It was another occasion for great festivities, including a tattoo of twelve-hundred trumpeters and drummers, but above all for serious talks with the two other members of the Holy Alliance. Both Prussia and Austria took the occasion to pay special tribute to Russia. The King of Prussia appeared in person, while the feeble-minded Emperor of Austria was represented by Archduke Charles Ferdinand with whom the Tsar once again discussed the plan of a marriage between Olga and Archduke Stephen. Archduke Charles could only promise to put the idea once more before Metternich.

Olga was not all that easy to marry. She had a will of her own which even the Tsar respected. When in 1840 he had tried to marry her to Crown Prince Maximillian of Bavaria, the high-spirited girl took one look at her suitor and ended the matter instantly with the loud and public assertion: 'I'll never marry a man who looks as stupid as that'. The prince left St Petersburg deeply hurt, and to the Tsar's apologetic letter the King of Bavaria replied that he had decided to make other arrangements for his son. A year later Archduke Albrecht of Austria, the son of the field marshal who had defeated Napoleon at Aspern, appeared as a suitor and courtiers said they saw 'the first raptures of a dawning passion'. But Olga treated him coldly and he, too, soon departed having, it seemed, heard gossip of Olgas' strange affair with Alexander of Hesse. Thus Olga had been rejected twice, by her own fault, and she began to realise that next time she would have to make up her mind. After the betrothal of her youngest sister, Alexandra, to Prince Frederick of Hesse-Cassel, she was now the only unmarried daughter of the Tsar.

In August 1842, Crown Princess Marie gave birth to a daughter. Alexander, deeply worried about his sister's health, forgot his amorous preoccupation and visited her daily. The 'Russian Party' at the Court rejoiced that the child was not a son, who would have been in direct succession to the throne. There was now open animosity against the Hesse members of the Tsar's family. The Tsar's negotiations for Olga's betrothal with the other Austrian prince, Archduke Stephen, made slow progress and Nicholas I began to blame his daughter's friendship with Alexander for this. Rebuking him for his 'licentious behaviour', he ordered Alexander to take a prolonged leave of absence and to go home to Darmstadt.

When he returned in the spring of 1844, he found the atmosphere improved. In September 1843 his sister had given birth to a son, which had pleased the Tsar greatly, even if it annoyed the 'Russian Party', and great celebrations had taken place in St Petersburg. On his arrival Alexander found, to his surprise, the widowed Grand-Duchess of Mecklemburg-Schwerin and her unlovely daughter Louise as guests of the Tsar. His surprise grew into consternation when his brother-in-law, the Tsarevitch, slapped his shoulder and, at first, seemingly jokingly and then quite seriously, suggested that Alexander should pay attention to Louise, adding that it was the Tsar's and the Tsaritsa's desire that he should marry the German princess.

Alexander realised that this was a scheme to end once and for all his bid for the Tsar's daughter. Olga herself now took a hand in matters. While she probably never had intended to marry

Alexander, she was annoyed at the arrival of Louise and decided to spoil her parents' too-obvious plan. She made herself especially pleasant to Alexander and insisted that he be invited to the palace of Gatchina where the Court was accustomed to spend some weeks of the autumn in 'the simple rural life'. From the moment of their arrival Olga monopolised Alexander, taking him hunting and on long rides until the Tsar forbade her to meet him without others being present. Olga defiantly ignored the order, and as winter set in went skating with the infatuated prince. On 28 December, after a family dinner, Olga took Alex out to a glassed-in and heated terrace which was bathed in moonlight. As he was about to take her in his arms for yet another of those half-satisfying embraces which was all Olga ever permitted, she drew back and told him that her mother had made a terrible scene earlier that evening and absolutely forbade her ever to see him alone again. Having said this, Olga threw herself into Alexander's arms and through her tears promised to meet him secretly again, a pledge she never fulfilled. For the next few days Alexander had to be content with seeing his beloved only under the full and mocking gaze of the Court. Just after Christmas Alexander gave Olga at a state dinner a sheet of music. This was a Gallop which he had composed for Olga's own Regiment of Hussars. With the music went a rather primitive water colour painting of Olga on horseback, escorted by an officer bearing a good resemblance to Alexander himself. It was all too naïve. The Tsar stretched out his hand for the sheet, glanced at the picture, and raising his head to scowl across the room at Alexander snorted, 'This gallop will never be played!'

By now, too, the Tsarevitch, who had invariably taken Alexander's side, was having second thoughts. It was not that he was opposed to a marriage between his friend and brother-in-law and his sister Olga, but he resented the fact that while Alexander was wooing Olga he was also carrying on blatant affairs with any woman who would permit him. One day the Tsarevitch said casually to Alexander: 'You know of the campaign against Shamyl in the Caucasus? Baryatinsky is going there. Have you ever thought of going with him?'

'Yes, of course,' stammered Alexander. If his friend Sasha felt obliged to drop such a heavy hint as that, more or less an instruction to leave the Court, things really must have become serious.

He went to Olga, hoping perhaps that she would stop him, and told her he had decided to ask the Tsar for a command in the campaign against the Circassians. Far from discouraging him Olga coldly gave him her blessing, adding 'It is, of course, your duty to go and fight for our country'.

Alexander's decision to go to the war put the Tsar in such a good mood that he bestowed on him the rank of a brigade-colonel. The night before his departure, on 6 April 1845, Alex wrote in his diary: 'I do not know whether Olly really loves me. She was little affected when I said goodbye. All she gave me as a farewell was to read every day the 19th Psalm as a memento of her . . .' Opening his Bible Alexander read: 'May the Lord hear thee in the day of tribulation. May He be mindful of all thy sacrifices. . . .' Alexander's passion for Olly began to cool off in the face of such a message.

When Alexander reached Tiflis and reported to the Commander-in-Chief, Count Vorontsev, he discovered that despite the Tsar's promise he was a general without a command. What was almost worse, the Tsar had ordered that Alexander's safety be preserved at all costs and that he must go nowhere without a dozen Cossack bodyguards, two adjutants, a doctor and a valet. General Vorontsev, who led the same rough life as his soldiers, always in danger of ambush from the half-savage Moslem followers of Imam Shamyl, was half-amused and half-enraged. He told Alexander that 'the gentlemen in the Winter Palace must have a strange opinion of how wars are fought in the Caucasus'. Alexander was suitably embarrassed, but by displaying not only keenness but also personal courage he soon gained the trust and friendship of Count Vorontsev. At first the Russian army was successful. Shamyl's wild warriors were put to flight and his capital Dargo was taken and sacked. Alexander was appalled at the Russian brutality: no quarter was given to man, woman or child, villages were looted and set afire, women raped. He then discovered that Shamyl's troops treated the Russians even worse. Prisoners who fell into the hands of the Circassians went through terrible tortures, their hands, noses and ears were cut off, tongues torn and eyes gouged out. It was an utterly merciless war on both sides. Early in July Imam Shamyl struck back, inflicted heavy losses upon Vorontsev's ragged army and recaptured Dargo. The Commander-in-Chief and his staff, including Alexander,

FAMILY GROUP IN 1868 AT HEILIGENBERG CASTLE
From left to right: Prince Alexander of Battenberg, Grand Duchess
Marie Alexandrovna of Russia, Princess Marie of Battenberg,
Grand Duke Paul Alexandrovitch of Russia, Grand Duke Sergius
Alexandrovitch, Prince Louis of Battenberg, Prince Francis Joseph
of Battenberg and Prince Henry of Battenberg.

FAMILY GROUP IN 1887 AT THE COURT THEATRE IN DARMSTADT
From left to right: Prince Henry of Battenberg, Prince Louis of
Battenberg, Prince Francis Joseph of Battenberg (standing), Prince
Gustav Ernst zu Erbach-Schönberg and his wife, Princess Marie
of Battenberg, Prince Alexander of Battenberg, and their parents,
Princess Julie of Battenberg and Prince Alexander of Hesse.

(After a painting by Granner.)

Prince Alexander of Hesse
(1823–1888) in the
uniform of a Russian
general.

Julie von Hauke
(1825–1895), Princess of
Battenberg, his morganatic
wife.

only just escaped capture and ghastly death. The Russians kept their hold on the lowlands, but it was a Pyrrhic victory.

Alexander wrote to his sister and brother-in-law: 'We are terribly depressed, our position is perilous . . . we cannot return the way we came and before us lie dark forests full of fanatical foes'. He added somewhat flippantly that 'according to reports of prisoners we have taken, Shamyl's wife has asked her husband to be given the German Prince (me) when he is captured'. He was clearly flattered that his reputation as a lover had come even to the notice of the Circassian lady in the dark forests of Daghestan. Eventually the Russian army withdrew to Tiflis and Alexander went to the spa of Kisslovotsk where the Tsarevitch waited for him, to give him the Order of St Andrew 'for heroic conduct'. Prince Alexander's first question was about 'dear Olly', but the Tsarevitch merely remarked that she was well and planned soon to depart with her parents for Italy. Alexander realised that he had only a slender chance of seeing Olly again. He was partly consoled by the great victory celebrations which had been staged for the Tsar, who reviewed the entire Black Sea Fleet at Sebastopol. Knowing too well how poorly-equipped the Caucasus army had been, Alexander was astounded by the great victory parade on land, with its 189 squadrons of cavalry with 22,000 horsemen and several infantry divisions from many garrisons of the empire.

Tsar Nicholas, well satisfied with the doubtful victory, praised Alexander fulsomely but told him not to return to St Petersburg, but to go to Darmstadt and 'enjoy six months of well-deserved leave'. Alexander understood that he was being kept away from Olly. The Tsar had good reasons for this: one last attempt was to be made to change the hostile attitude of the Vienna Court to the plans for Olga's marriage to Archduke Stephen. The Tsar still believed he could persuade Emperor Ferdinand and even Metternich. He first went to Prague where Archduke Stephen told him he could do nothing himself. Next, the Tsar went to Rome, joined now by the Tsaritsa and Olga, and tried to persuade Pope Gregory XVI of the advantages of a match, especially if Grand Duchess Olga became a Catholic. Nicholas had strongly hoped to find an ally in the anti-liberal Pope, but all Gregory was prepared to promise was to tell Vienna that the Vatican had no objections to such a marriage. In exchange, the

Pope received from Nicholas a promise of better treatment for Catholics in Russia. Feeling that he had gained some powerful support, Nicholas was disconcerted to be met at Pavia on his way to Vienna by the Austrian Minister of State, Count Ficquelmont, who told him diplomatically but very definitely that his journey was not really necessary. Nothing would change Metternich's decision that a link between the Russian and Austrian dynasties was inopportune. The Tsar decided to continue his journey to Vienna, but see neither the Emperor nor Metternich. When on 30 December he reached the Austrian capital, he told his old friend Prince Liechtenstein, sent by the Emperor to meet him:

'I am here incognito, passing through on my journey home. I do not want to see Ferdinand the Imbecile nor his rascally Chancellor.'

Metternich now felt he had gone too far and sent his third wife, Countess Zichy, another old friend of the Tsar, to appease him. Melanie Metternich did her best, and though she could not promise any results she did persuade him to meet the Emperor and attend a State dinner. Nicholas, who had a sense of humour, appeared at the dinner in the uniform of a Cossack general with silver dagger and silver cartridges in his belt, instead of wearing, according to etiquette, the uniform of the Austrian regiment of which he was the honorary colonel. He hardly spoke a word, apart from complaining in Metternich's hearing of the 'malicious and rascally rumours circulated from Vienna about tyranny in Russia'. Next day he sent Count Orlov to Metternich. The Austrian chancellor suavely said: 'Although the matter is extremely difficult, the Tsar's visit to the Pope might yet be a good beginning for further talks . . .', to which Orlov replied 'No, Excellency, the talks are not beginning, they have come to an end'. Metternich wondered what had made the Tsar change his mind so suddenly.

In fact, on his way to Italy the Tsar had prepared another scheme in case he failed in Vienna. He had told the Russian ambassador in Stuttgart to approach King William I of Württemburg and suggest a betrothal between his son, Crown Prince Charles, and Olga. The king was enthusiastic, and without delay sent his son to Palermo where Olga was staying with the Tsaritsa. On 22 January 1846, while Alexander was still on leave at Darmstadt, the following announcement was made in St Petersburg: 'His Imperial Majesty the Tsar has received the joyful news by the hand of a courier from Her Imperial Majesty the Tsaritsa that on the sixth of this month Her Imperial Highness, the Grand Duchess Olga and His Royal Highness the Crown Prince of Württemberg, following the dictation of their own hearts, have contracted an engagement of marriage'.

Alexander had in the meantime learnt all about the original plan to marry Olga to the Austrian archduke. He would have put up with it, realising the dynastic and political importance of such a marriage. But the news of the sudden engagement of his beautiful and beloved Olly to 'that flabby and insignificant Swabish princeling' deeply shocked him. He decided to go off and see something of Europe's capitals to forget his sorrow. In the spring of 1846 he wrote to his sister from Vienna: 'It seems that one should marry to please oneself and not to please other people. I grieve for Olly and I am not at all happy about your suggestions about Vivi (Louise of Mecklemburg-Schwerin). I am not at all disposed to tie myself down at the age of twenty and three. If I marry her I shall have to stay in Darmstadt with the prospect of doing nothing all the rest of my life, or in St Petersburg where I cannot live a married life at all without money. So you will not be surprised if I avoid the trap that is set for me so openly.' After meeting Emperor Ferdinand he wrote again to Marie. 'The Emperor is a pathetic object in the hands of Metternich. Indeed, to put it clearly, he is an idiot. He was very polite to me but his mumble is quite unintelligible. . . . The Empress speaks no German; she is a plain, insignificant woman. Nobody pays the slightest attention to the Emperor, even his valets are rude to him.'

From Vienna he went to Greece and the Bosphorus, then to Rome, and to Naples when he was sure that the Mecklemburg princesses had left the city. In Rome he had arrived at the time of Pope Gregory's death, and he attended the Requiem mass at St Peter's. He was greatly impressed by the display of ancient pomp, with twenty-six cardinals and sixty archbishops leading the procession, but he remarked in his diary that the religious ceremonies seemed to him as so much 'hocus pocus'. Although he conscientiously visited the Italian art cities and toured Rome's antiquities, his impressions were superficial. The glory of classic art had little appeal to his thoroughly practical mind.

After a brief visit to Darmstadt he returned to St Petersburg in September 1846, having overstayed his leave. He at once threw himself into the revelry, the gambling and drinking, and making love as indiscriminately with the ladies of the Court as with the gipsy girls of the taverns. Bitterly disappointed by Olga's betrothal, he defied the Tsar's displeasure for his extravagant conduct. At twenty-three, he was now deeply in debt and in the hands of money-lenders. Although the Tsarevitch was always ready to help with money, Alexander spent it faster than Sasha could replace it. So Alexander decided to find a way of earning some money for himself; after all, almost everyone at the Court of St Petersburg was involved in some dubious business, taking bribes for favours, or existing on the payroll of the secret service of some European power.

At that time, the five sons of Mayer Amschel Rothschild had established their dominion over the money markets of Europe. From their humble home in Jew Street in the ghetto of Frankfurt, they had progressed to their palaces in Paris, London, Vienna and Naples, and were financing, and dictating to, almost every European court and government. They had had a long connection with the Grand Dukes of Hesse (when the Elector of Hesse-Cassel fled from Napoleon in 1806, old Mayer Amschel had saved his fortune for him), and when the second Amschel Rothschild decided to conquer the last important capital of Europe, St Petersburg, he enlisted the help of Prince Alexander of Hesse. He despatched to St Petersburg one of his most clever negotiators, Moses Davidsohn, who offered Alexander a small fortune and a perpetual commission, if he could persuade the Tsar to let him establish a branch of the House of Rothschild in Russia and accept credits to finance the State budget and new railways.

Hoping to secure for himself the badly needed annuity, Alexander tried hard to win over the Tsarevitch and some of the Tsar's ministers and courtiers to the plan Davidsohn had prepared. The young man understood nothing of the financial details and the subtle implications of the deal, and he acted very naïvely. For a century the German banking family of Stieglitz had held a monopoly of all important financial transactions in Russia and they generously greased the palms of the Tsar's influential advisers. Alarmed by the Rothschild intrusion, the

Stieglitz group hit back. Alexander was told that Jews were forbidden by law to own or manage a business in Russia employing more than five clerks, and that no Jew was allowed to live permanently in St Petersburg or Moscow. Even Sasha was annoyed about Alexander's dealings with the Rothschilds, and the plan misfired. Moses Davidsohn returned to Frankfurt, and St Petersburg remained the only capital of a Great Power where the Rothschilds never did any business. They never forgave the slight. When the Crimean War broke out, 'the king of the Jews' offered Lord Aberdeen a million pounds free of interest to fight the Tsar. Only once did the Rothschilds advance a credit to a Russian government, the 'Liberty loan' in 1917, given to Kerensky after the overthrow of the Tsarist regime, a loan which was never repaid.

So Alexander had to manage without the Rothschild money, which did not worry him excessively, as long as the money-lenders were willing to make further advances. There were other unpleasant matters that weighed upon his mind. The Tsar sternly forbade him to pay attentions to his elder daughter Marie, Grand Duchess of Leuchtenberg, with whom Alexander had begun a pleasant flirtation, and had been repeatedly caught on dark terraces. Marie, though to all appearances happily married, had had no objections to an affair, even though, or maybe because, she knew that Alexander was also carrying on openly with Sophie Shuvalov and half a dozen others. Then the inevitable happened. During the carnival of 1848, Sophie told her mother she feared she might be pregnant.

That evening in January, as Alexander was seen to walk across the ballroom to ask Sophie for a mazurka, a slight, delicate girl with large sad eyes and a small, freckled face framed in dark hair, approached him and timidly gave him a message from the Countess Shuvalov. It was that if Alexander did not leave her daughter Sophie severely alone, and never even speak to her again, the Countess would make a formal complaint to the Tsar and Tsaritsa.

Alexander knew the little messenger only slightly as one of his sister's ladies-in-waiting. He had heard her called 'Julie', and he knew that she was the orphan of a Russian general killed during the Polish rebellion of 1830. Now, he just grinned after reading the *billet* from the Countess and, turning his back on

Sophie, took Julie by the arm and carried her off in a whirling mazurka.

This was his first dance with Julie Hauke, future Princess of Battenberg and great-great-grandmother of Britain's present Prince of Wales.

CHAPTER THREE

THE POLISH ORPHAN GIRL

Julie Hauke, Princess of Battenberg

IN HIS book on the lineage of his family, Earl Mountbatten devoted many pages to his Hesse ancestry, but gave only three lines to his grandmother, Julie Hauke, and none to her family. At the Court of St Petersburg the maid-of-honour to Crown Princess Marie was sometimes referred to as 'Fräulein von Hauke', sometimes as 'Countess Hauke'; more often by the matronly duchesses, who looked her up and down through jewel-encrusted lorgnettes, as 'that poor, sweet Polish orphan girl'.

In 1848, when Alexander first noticed her, Julie was 23, five feet two inches in height, shy though attractive in a docile way; she bequeathed to her descendants the long straight nose that has become famous.

Julie's great-grandfather had been a tradesman at Mainz, the ancient archbishop's city on the Rhine (which was later to belong to the Grand Dukes of Hesse). He had several children, but only one of his sons, Johann, made a success, having received a good education at the Latin school. He became a clerk in the State offices of the King of Saxony, and about 1755 was secretary to Count Aloysius Frederick Bruehl, whom King August III of Saxony, at that time also the King of Poland, had sent as his viceroy to Warsaw. After August's death in 1763, Russia and Prussia divided Poland between them and Count Bruehl hurriedly returned to Dresden. His young secretary changed over to the Tsar's side and remained in Warsaw as a Russian official. At the age of 39 he married a girl, fifteen years younger than himself, whom he had met on a visit to his family in the Rhineland. She was Maria Salome Schweppenhauser, daughter of the pastor of Sassenheim (whose predecessor at the rectory had been Pastor Brion, father of Goethe's immortal Frederica.) There were seven children of the marriage, the eldest was Moritz born in 1775.

Johann Hauck had changed the spelling of his name into Hauke, when his eldest son became an officer in the Tsar's army. When Napoleon restored an independent Polish kingdom, Moritz Hauck, now Maurice de Hauke, changed his allegiance, joined the Polish Legion under General Dombrowski and fought in Napoleon's campaigns in Italy, Germany, Austria and Spain, becoming a lieutenant-colonel in the Grande Armée. After Napoleon's downfall he returned to Poland, once again switched sides and secured the command of a brigade in Tsar Alexander's army. In 1820 he was appointed Minister of War in the Russian-controlled puppet government of Congress-Poland. In 1816 he had married 24-year-old Sophie Lafontaine, daughter of a French doctor who had settled down at Biberach-on-the-Riss, a small town near the Lake of Constance in Wurttemberg. The doctor was married to a Hungarian woman, Teresa Kornely. When their daughter Sophie married Maurice Hauke, he was fifteen years her senior; they had three children. The War Minister now resided at the Palais Bruehl, where his father once served the Saxon governor. By 1829 Tsar Nicholas had made Maurice a general and bestowed on him the title of Count.

A year later, in November 1830, the Poles rose against the Tsarist regime. Although the Tsar maintained Russian garrisons in Poland, many officers and soldiers were Poles and they made common cause with the revolutionaries, whose leader was the Polish general Chlopicki. The rebels marched on the Bruehl palace, dragged out the hated War Minister and hacked him to pieces before the eyes of his wife and children. Countess Sophie Hauke died of a broken heart in 1831, a few weeks after the Russians reoccupied Warsaw and avenged the insurrection in a terrible bloodbath among the Polish leaders. Tsar Nicholas did not forget the orphans of his loyal commander, and he ordered that they should be brought to St Petersburg.

Julie, the youngest, was five when her father was murdered and she was brought up with the daughers of aristocratic families at the celebrated Smolny Institute. Although born in Poland, she was German on her father's side and French-Hungarian on her mother's. Because she spoke German, she was chosen as a Maid of Honour to Marie, Princess of Hesse, when the latter became the wife of the Tsarevitch in 1841, and later one of her Ladies-in-Waiting. When she met Alexander of Hesse she was 23, parentless and poor, and probably resigned to spending the rest of her life as an old maid.

Little is known of her family from which she had cut herself off after her marriage. Her daughter, Princess Marie of Battenberg (who married Prince Gustavus of Erbach-Schönberg), wrote many years later in her memoirs: 'Mamma's extraction always had about it a halo of romance. Nothing interested me more than to learn something about her relatives, but she never spoke of them herself. As the youngest of her family, brought up in St Petersburg, she had less of the Polish element about her than the rest. Now and then she would mention a member of the Hauke family, and the events of which she told were always shadowed by the tragedy of her nation, for not only her father, but other family members, too, had died violent deaths.'[1]

Only once a relative of Julie visited the Battenbergs at Heiligenberg. His name was Alexander de Hauke and he was a Polish patriot who had come to study at Heidelberg university, being exiled by the Tsar. In 1863 he returned to Poland, took part in the anti-Tsarist rebellion and, apparently, was killed. For Alexander of Hesse, the family of his wife was a constant embarrassment: while he became the Tsar's brother-in-law, some of the Haukes fought against Russia and others were revolutionaries in other European countries. One of Julie's nephews, Count Josef von Hauke, abandoned his family name, proudly called himself 'Barefoot' (Boszak), joined Garibaldi's Legion and fought the Pope and the Austrians, when Prince Alexander was an Austrian general. He was killed at Garibaldi's side in the battle of Giacomo in 1867.

Alexander knew nothing of Julie Hauke when she brought him the warning from the Countess Shuvalov. After she had danced the Mazurka with him, Julie soon found herself in a strange position. She had fallen in love with the handsome prince, but

[1] Princess Marie zu Erbach-Schönberg, *Aus Stiller und Bewegter Zeit,* Brunswick, 1921.

he and Sophie Shuvalov continued to meet in secret, carried on their forbidden love affair and used her as their confidante. Julie carried their love letters to and fro and the books in which the enamoured pair underlined passages about love and devotion.

Life was pleasant at the Court of St Petersburg, though Europe was in turmoil. The year of revolutions and rebellions – 1848 – had shaken many great European states. A liberal Parliament had assembled at Frankfurt, and in France King Louis Philippe was swept from his throne. There were a few timid attempts at stirring up trouble in Russia but with an army of half a million – at that time the largest in the world – and a police force of 120,000 nobody at the Russian Court had need to worry.

Alexander concentrated all his attention on Sophie Shuvalov, and every afternoon at 5.30 he took his walk beneath her windows. From time to time the lovers were able to have secret meetings in the Chinese Garden of the Winter Palace, which Julie Hauke helped to arrange. At last the Shuvalov family made their long-threatened complaint to the Tsar who told Alexander to stop the affair or leave St Petersburg. But both Sasha and Marie pleaded with the Tsar, who softened and even went as far as to suggest that Alexander should marry his niece, Grand Duchess Catharine, the daughter of his brother Michael. The Grand Duke was one of the leaders of the 'Russian Party' and had always been hostile to the Hesse prince. Alexander disliked Catharine, probably because he detested her father, and, in any case, he was determined not to get involved with yet another Grand Duchess in need of a husband. He told this to his sister and his brother-in-law, but pretended to the Tsar that he was honoured and pleased about the suggestion to become Catharine's suitor.

Then, in June 1848, Alexander's father, Grand Duke Louis II of Hesse died shortly after his abdication enforced by the revolutionary movement. Alexander went to Darmstadt, where his brother Louis, already for some time his father's co-regent, had ascended the grand-ducal throne. The death of his father, from whom he felt estranged, did not visibly grieve Alexander. After his return he celebrated his 25th birthday on 15 July as gaily as ever, receiving presents with hidden verses and love notes from no less than ten young ladies. One of them was from Countess Julie Hauke, and in his diary Alexander noted with surprise her little poem which expressed admiration and affection for him. 'I really did not notice that the girl was in love with me,' he wrote.

Julie, in spite of her apparent docility, was persistent and intelligent, and Alexander, forced to ignore Sophie Shuvalov and worried about the Tsar's plan to marry him off to Grand Duchess Catharine, was now drawn more and more to the 'little Polish orphan'. His sister and brother-in-law, realising that Alexander would bring the Tsar's wrath upon his head, redoubled their effort to persuade him that Catharine was a most desirable match. It seems that Alexander almost yielded particularly after the Tsarevitch told him that the Tsar would offer him the throne of one of the Danube principalities, Rumelia or Servia, which, though still nominally parts of the Ottoman Empire, were under Russian influence.

Alexander might have married Catharine and become a Balkan ruler, had not Julie taken command of the situation and become his mistress. For a time they succeeded in keeping this liaison secret, even from the Tsarevitch and Marie. One day in the autumn of 1849 the Tsar, passing the Tsarevna's suite, opened a door which he thought led to his daughter-in-law's drawing room. In fact it opened into the room of her lady-in-waiting. An amazed and furious Tsar saw Alexander and Julie embracing passionately. This, coming on top of Alexander's many escapades and his hesitation over marrying Catharine, so enraged Nicholas that he raved at the pair for some minutes, calling them every foul name he could think of.

For the next few weeks Alexander was banned from all functions at the Court and Julie banished to her rooms. The Tsar told Alexander that he had forfeited his chance of an engagement to Catharine, and threatened that he would send him off to some remote garrison in Siberia. Once again Sasha and Marie came to Alexander's rescue, but the Tsar made sure that Alexander received his punishment. He told Sophie Shuvalov that she had lost her lover to her best girl friend and confidante, and also informed his brother, Grand Duke Michael, of Alexander's misdemeanour. Michael, the Commander-in-Chief of the Imperial Guards, now made the most of every opportunity to persecute Alexander, reprimanding him for alleged lack of discipline in his regiment, and removing from his entourage all the officers who were his friends. Life for Alexander became almost unbearable.

Although he received passionate love letters from Julie who was forbidden to see him it is unlikely that at that stage he reciprocated her feelings. He was still in love with Sophie Shuvalov, and when on the rebound Sophie became engaged in January 1850 to his old friend and war comrade Prince Bobrinsky, Alexander was in dismay. He wrote in his diary: 'I cannot bear the idea of Sophie belonging to someone else!' – almost exactly the same words he had written when he lost his beloved Olly to the Prince of Wurttemberg.

Now that he was in deep disgrace with the Tsar, he decided to leave St Petersburg. In August Nicholas granted him indefinite leave from the army and told him rudely that he was glad to see the back of him, at least for some months. Alexander went to Darmstadt to visit his elder brother, Grand Duke Louis III, who was becoming enormously fat and suffered from gout. Alexander left his depressing little court for Paris and for his first visit to London, a visit which was in many ways to change his entire attitude to life and his political thinking. The German Prince and Russian officer was staggered at what he called in his diary 'the liberal ways of life in England'. After a visit to the offices of *The Times* newspaper he wrote to Marie, 'It is utterly amazing how the journalists can write quite freely about the Royal Family, even about the private lives of Queen Victoria and her Consort in a newspaper which is being read by everybody. *The Times* is being printed on a steam press; it has two editions, one in the morning and another in the afternoon, and altogether 56,000 copies are sold every day!'

On a visit to the Bank of England he was shown £2,000,000 in gold bars and £14,000,000 in banknotes, and at his request was allowed to touch a bundle containing a million. Another enthusiastic letter went to Marie. While in London he carried himself off as a Russian General, rarely mentioning that he was also a German prince. He regarded himself by now almost as a Russian rather than a German. Although he made a formal call on the Prince Consort, conveying greetings from the Grand Duke of Hesse, he was not, to his chagrin, invited to meet Queen Victoria. One reason for this cold-shouldering in British Court circles was the ruthless suppression of the Hungarian rising by Russia and

Austria. Unfortunately for Alexander, Kossuth the leader of the Hungarian rebellion, who had escaped the scaffold, arrived in London about the same time, to be hailed everywhere as a hero.

At the beginning of 1851 Alexander returned to St Petersburg, only to find himself ignored by the Tsar and the Tsaritsa, while Grand Duke Michael immediately renewed his persecution. Within a few weeks, and this time quite unjustly, the Grand Duke lodged before the Tsar the complaint that Alexander's conduct and his 'scandalous affaire' with Julie Hauke had 'absolutely demoralised the Officer Corps and all the young A.D.C.s'. He demanded Alexander's removal from the command of the Imperial Guards brigade.

Alexander found support from his brother-in-law, but he soon found out that this was because the Tsarevitch's own conscience was now far from clean. Marie was in poor health and unable to satisfy her virile husband. Although the Tsarevitch loved her he had taken a mistress, the pretty Countess Eugenia Makov, meeting her regularly in a secluded hunting lodge. Realising that Sasha's friendly condescension arose mainly from an affair that was making his own sister desperately unhappy, Alexander decided to leave St Petersburg, this time for good. All this, and what he had seen in England, reinforced his resentment towards the rigid formality and autocracy of the Russian Court. He played with the idea of going to England and asking Queen Victoria for a commission in the British army. He had begun seeing Julie Hauke again and confided his plans to her. 'Take me with you, dear Alex,' she pleaded. It seems that his decision to ask her to marry him came quite suddenly, and in a mood of depression rather than in exaltation.

They agreed that he would publicly announce their engagement. But Julie was a ward of the Tsar, and Alexander had to go to him and ask for permission to marry her. He consulted Sasha and Marie. Both were greatly upset, and the Tsarevitch told him bluntly:

'This would be the end of your life in St Petersburg. My father will never consent to your marriage with a mere lady-in-waiting. Don't forget that your sister will one day be the Empress of Russia. You're being foolish. You've had your fun . . . but marriage . . . damn it all!'

If Alexander still wanted to reconsider his decision, it was too late. Julie, bursting with pride and happiness, had told her girl friends under a pledge of secrecy they broke within minutes. Soon all the Court knew that Alexander intended to announce his engagement to the 'little Polish orphan', and the Tsar's fury was boundless.

Neither the Tsar nor anyone else at Court could even dream of breaching the rigid rule that one married within one's own caste. On this sort of rule rested their authority, privileges and security in a world of rebellion against these very things. Apart from State policy and dynastic interest, the Tsar simply could not suffer such public insolence as Alexander's intended engagement. The mothers of the Court wanted the handsome prince, the brother of the future Empress, for one of their own daughters, certainly not for a penniless servant without a family. The girls themselves, so many of whom had shared his bed, regarded the choice as a personal insult; overnight Alexander and Julie found themselves in a welter of hostility and intrigue. Even Marie was angry. With her husband's unfaithfulness she saw her own future in jeopardy, and her brother's conduct could only worsen things for her.

Frantic messages were sent to Darmstadt, almost ordering Grand Duke Louis as head of the Hesse family to forbid the marriage. Louis, engrossed in his collection of coins and preoccupied with his gout, did not care what happened, but he did write a letter to his 'little brother', telling him not to be a fool. Apparently the Grand Duke never believed that Alexander was serious about his intended marriage to 'that girl', and he advised him rather belatedly to wed 'one of the girls of that big litter of Catharine the Great'. To Louis it was inconceivable that Alexander would sacrifice position, prospects of a brilliant career, perhaps a crown, indeed everything, for the sake of a little orphan. He did not know that to Alexander it had become a question of his honour.

When, after keeping him waiting for many weeks, the Tsar at last consented to receive Alexander in formal audience to present his request, he was still so angry that he hardly let the young man speak. He told him that if he did not immediately and publicly renounce his plan to marry Julie Hauke he would be banished from Russia and be deprived of his Russian general's rank. Without saying a word Alexander bowed and left the room.

In civilian clothes and carrying one suitcase, Prince Alexander

of Hesse left St Petersburg on 4 October 1851. Separately
Countess Julie Hauke left also, both in a thoughtful, not to say
sad mood. They met at Warsaw, continued together to Breslau,
and here, in the county town of Prussian Silesia, they were married
on 28 October. He was 28, she was two years younger. At once
Alexander wrote to Grand Duke Louis, and to Marie and Sasha
informing them of the marriage. Louis wrote back saying that
Alexander had been 'an unpardonable fool'. But he added his
good wishes, and, much more important, said that all the constitutional and dynastic consequences would be dealt with by his
Chief Minister, Herr von Dalwigk. Marie and the Tsarevitch were
appalled, and Marie seemed to be obsessed with the idea that it
was her fault that her brother had become infatuated with her
lady-in-waiting. The Tsar ordered his Commander-in-Chief to
announce that Alexander had been cashiered from the Imperial
Guards, refusing the Tsarevitch's pleas to retire him honourably
from the Russian service and grant him a pension.

By 3 November 1851, it had been raining for days in Darmstadt.
The banks of the Rhine and the Main were flooded, and that night
the streets of the little town were deserted except for one carriage
which rumbled slowly through the downpour. The mood of the
man inside the coach matched the weather. Herr Karl Friedrich
von Dalwigk, Grand Ducal First Minister, was sullen and
resentful. As he swayed on the hard horsehair seat, the coachman
could hear him muttering 'Why can't he conduct affairs of State
in daylight!' Across the Louisen Platz, into the Parade Platz and
into the drive of the palace the coach rolled on. Lights streaming
from almost every window of the ornate building lit the scene,
only serving to annoy Herr Dalwigk still more, and reminding
him that the creator of this sixteenth century extravagant palace,
Duke Philip the Magnanimous, had also been called Philip the
Wasteful.

Dalwigk stumped angrily up the great staircase to the Grand
Duke's library. This was 1851, and not an era when a Minister of
State could be treated with less consideration than a stableboy!
However, it was clear instantly that the ill mood of the First
Minister was as nothing compared with the vile temper of his
master. Louis III sat in a deep armchair, his gouty leg propped up
on a table, scowling into the fire. Slowly he turned his head, his

multiple chins emerging from the folds of his velvet dressing gown.[1]

Somewhat daunted Dalwigk could only say, 'Your Highness wished to see me?' making it sound as reproachful as he dared.

'Yes. And you took a long time in coming! Too busy plotting with your liberal cronies I expect,' snarled the Grand Duke. Without waiting for an answer he thrust a piece of paper at his reluctant visitor.

'Look at this!' he said. 'The idiot has married that Polish girl. The ungrateful, obstinate, stupid ass has married her!'

With barely concealed pleasure Dalwigk studied the paper. 'Your Highness,' he began smoothly, 'will recall that not only did I warn Your Highness that such a union was imminent, but even gave you the time when it would take place. Prince Alexander has chosen to disregard the advice of Your Highness, the advice of his brother, as he did the advice of his sister Her Imperial Highness the Crown Princess of Russia, and even the orders of the Tsar himself. But I must remind Your Highness that Prince Alexander has reached his majority. He can indeed marry whom he wishes – provided of course that certain constitutional prerogatives are observed, namely the law of succession.'

Dalwigk paused after this long speech, then resumed, very quietly. 'Prince Alexander told me of his decision, emphasizing that he was quite prepared to forego his privileges and his commission in the Imperial Russian Army for the sake of his love. Indeed, sir, if I may venture an opinion, this is to his credit . . .'

'*Blödsinnige Gefühlsduselei!*' the Grand Duke exploded. 'But of course, Dalwigk, I should have known that you would take the side of the silly boy, you with your liberal views and little regard for the dignity of thrones. You are probably happy that there now will be one German prince the less!'

After a moment spent in glaring resentfully at the portraits of his ancestors, pompous looking men staring down from their gold frames on the walls, Louis resumed in a more conciliatory mood. 'Unfortunately I need your advice. What are we going to do with Alex and that Polish girl? We can't have a "Fräulein Hauke" in the family. She must have some title, if only for their children's sake.'

[1] Cf. *Tagebücher des Freiherrn Karl Friedrich Reinhard von Dalwigk* (Diaries), Edit. W. Schüssler, Rostock, 1920.

'She is not exactly a "Fräulein Hauke", Your Highness. She is a Polish Countess, even if her grandparents were commoners. Her late father, Count Moritz von Hauke, was a general and at one time Poland's Minister of War . . .'

'Fiddlesticks, Dalwigk,' Louis retorted, angry once again. 'Count, general, minister . . . his people kept a shop in Mainz, they sold wurst and pickled herrings most probably. And what is more, he was a minister in that rebel government of 1830, a regime of seditious, illiterate peasants. The Tsar was quite right to have him strung up . . .!'

'With Your Highness's permission,' Dalwigk interrupted, exasperated with the Grand Duke's complete lack of historical knowledge. 'He was not strung up by the Tsar. He was cut down by the sabres of the rebels as a loyal servant of the Tsar. Indeed, the Tsar should have shown a little more gratitude and forgiveness at the present moment. Count Moritz was murdered before the eyes of his wife and his two little daughters, one of whom is now the spouse of Prince Alexander.'

'All right, all right, Dalwigk! Have it your way. What I want to know is how we can regularize this ridiculous marriage? All my relatives are livid. Here, read what Queen Victoria says. She is very, very angry. And the Tsarevitch writes as if his favourite brother-in-law were dead and buried rather than celebrating his nuptials. We must make a countess of that Polish girl or Alexander will have to eat with the footmen below the stairs if he ever visits St Petersburg, Osborne, or Schönbrunn again!'

Dalwigk waited a moment or two, as if for reflection. Then he admitted: 'I have thought about it. It's bad, but it would be quite in order to recognise the morganatic marriage. Prince Alexander could retain his title and rank, though it might be better if he resided abroad. His wife could be raised to the dignity and rank of a Countess of the Grand Duchy of Hesse-Darmstadt and by Rhine. The children, hm . . . hm . . . the children would however have to bear the mother's name. That is the legal position according to paragraph 17, clause four, sub-section . . .'

'Yes, yes, Dalwigk, I know all that. Have you thought out a name?'

'Well, Your Highness, one suggestion is that Fräulein von Hauke, I beg your pardon, I mean the princess . . . I mean the prince's wife . . .' Herr von Dalwigk was very much at a loss to find the correct description for the young woman, a fact which did not escape the Grand Duke who smiled for the first time as he remarked, 'You see Dalwigk, we just don't know what to call that girl. Now, we must find a decent name for her and for her brats to come'.

Diffidently Dalwigk suggested: 'I did think that Countess von Kellerburg might be a suitable title. There is a castle, dating from the fifteenth century . . .'

'Kellerburg?' the Grand Duke snorted. 'It sounds like a bottle of cheap Rhine wine. Think of something better!'

'Yes, sir. Another thought . . . a submission, if I may. There is a little hamlet near Wiesbaden called after an ancient knightly family. They fought in the Crusades. The family is extinct, the title defunct, but it could be revived by a grand-ducal edict, if Your Highness pleases, a proclamation according to clause 18 of the Act of 1820.'

'I know it can be done Dalwigk, but what is the name, is it decent?'

Herr von Dalwigk waited a moment, perhaps to give impact to his words. 'They were the Counts von Battenberg, Your Highness. They had a fine castle overlooking the river Eder at Battenberg. The ruined tower and bastions still stand on the eastern slopes of the Westerwald.'

A slow smile of relief spread over Louis's plump features.

'Battenberg? Battenberg . . . All right . . . Battenberg it shall be, Dalwigk! Prepare the necessary scribbles tomorrow morning, a decree making the Polish wench a countess. A Countess von Battenberg. But when my dear young brother comes home with his countess . . . publish the decree the day after tomorrow . . . I must talk to him about money. If he thinks his Battenbergs are going to scrounge on me he is mistaken! Good night, Dalwigk.'

The decree announced that His Illustrious Highness the Grand Duke Louis III of Hesse-Darmstadt and by Rhine had graciously elevated on this fifth day of November in the year of Our Lord 1851 Fraulein Julie Teresa von Hauke, daughter of Count Moritz von Hauke, deceased, and Countess von Hauke, née Mademoiselle Sophie de Lafontaine, to the rank, dignity and title of a Countess von Battenberg and that the issue of the morganatic marriage of His Highness the Prince Alexander Ludwig Georg Emil of Hesse-Darmstadt and by Rhine, third son of the late and lamented Grand Duke Louis II, and the said Countess von Battenberg would for ever enjoy the rank, dignity and title of Counts and Countesses von Battenberg, but would have no right or claim to the succession to the throne in accordance with the Act of Constitution of 1820.

The Prince of Hesse and the Countess von Battenberg were now entirely dependent on whatever money they could get from Grand Duke Louis and Tsarevna Marie. Louis sent a small sum, and Marie, very secretly, 20,000 roubles. Alexander had intended to go to Darmstadt, hoping that his brother would give him, at least for a time, some sinecure position, but a letter from Herr von Dalwigk settled that. Dalwigk's policy as Chief Minister was aimed at the so-called 'tri-partite' solution of the German problems, with Austria, Prussia and the 'real Germany' – the smaller kingdoms, principalities and dukedoms who were scared of Prussia – sharing power in central Europe. Dalwigk hoped that Hesse would play an important role in this trinity, but to accomplish this good relations were needed with both Austria and Russia, for only Russia could be an effective deterrent to the growing Prussian claim to dominate all the German States.

Dalwigk dare not offend the Tsar, and he told Alexander that his presence in Darmstadt would be most embarrassing. He also warned him that his wife, the Countess von Battenberg, must never call herself a Princess of Hesse. He advised Alexander to petition Emperor Francis Joseph of Austro-Hungary for a commission in the Austrian army, although he could not hold out hope that the Emperor would oblige. Relations between Russia and Austria had improved after the Tsar had visited Vienna, and Francis Joseph would be wary of giving offence to the Tsar. It was, therefore, not surprising that when Alexander wrote to the Austrian Emperor he received a long-delayed and cool reply, telling him that there were 'no vacancies' in the Austrian army.

So, Alexander and Julie travelled into exile to Geneva to wait until the tide of fortune turned. At first they lived in a small private hotel, ever worried over money. Then sister Marie from St Petersburg and brother Louis from Darmstadt sent modest funds, and Alexander could rent a pleasant villa. There Julie gave birth to their first child, a girl born on 18 July 1852 and named Marie.[1] A nannie, Adele Bassing, was engaged, and this good woman remained with Marie for 45 years, until she died in 1898, when her 'baby' was a mother of three grown-up children.

In the winter of 1852 the Tsarevitch and his wife visited Darmstadt and Marie implored her brother, Grand Duke Louis, to give Alexander the command of his army of 10,000 men. But Louis refused, even though the Tsarevitch assured him that Tsar Nicholas would not object to such a modest appointment. Sasha and Marie made another attempt to help during their visit to Vienna, a few weeks later, but Emperor Francis Joseph was still reluctant to risk the Tsar's displeasure. It seemed that poor Alexander and Julie would have to stay in their Swiss exile for a long time. However, the Tsarevitch's intervention moved Emperor Francis Joseph to say that he would give Alexander a commission in the Austrian army if the Tsar would forgive and restore the prince to his Russian rank. At Christmas Sasha and Maria found the Tsar in an amiable mood, and on 13 January 1853 Alexander's name was put on the 'retired list' of Russian generals. Moreover, the Tsar wrote a personal note to Francis Joseph to the effect that there was 'nothing dishonourable in the retirement of Prince Alexander of Hesse', but that it had become necessary simply because a one-time lady-in-waiting could not become a sister-in-law of the future Empress of Russia. The way for Alexander's entry into the Austrian army seemed to be clear, when an event intervened which brought about a new delay.

On 18 February 1853, a tailor named Lebenyi, a former Hungarian rebel fighter, made an attempt on the life of Francis Joseph. The dagger wound the Emperor received was not serious, but it was several months before he invited Alexander to visit Vienna. By then the relations between Austria and Russia had deteriorated. The Tsar had embarked upon expanding his power in South East Europe, where Sultan Abdul of Turkey had been losing control of the Danubian principalities, and the Russians encouraged the Serbs and Bulgars in their rebellion against the Turks. In the spring of 1853 the Tsar had a series of conferences with Lord Seymour, the British ambassador in St Petersburg, and asked him to submit to Lord Aberdeen, the Prime Minister, a plan to carve up the Ottoman Empire. Wallachia, Moldavia and Bulgaria would come under Russian

[1] The later Princess Marie zu Erbach-Schönberg.

protectorate, while Britain would take Egypt and Crete. Lord Aberdeen favoured this plan, but Lord Palmerston and most of the cabinet members opposed it, and the Russian proposals were turned down. Nevertheless, on 2 July 1853 the Russian army marched into the Danubian principalities and the troops were greeted as liberators. Turkish garrisons were disarmed and sent home. Austria was watching the Russian move in the Balkans with growing resentment and anxiety; the Tsar's high-handed action caused strong reaction also in Britain.

Emperor Francis Joseph was now prepared to welcome Alexander if only to spite the Tsar, though he did not show himself particularly generous. Alexander had secretly hoped to preserve his major-general's rank and receive the command of a division, but the Emperor told him that the best that could be done for him without causing resentment among Austrian officers was to give him the command of a brigade and the rank of a brigade-colonel.

Alexander, with his quick temper, which he passed on to his Mountbatten descendants, recalled in his diary that he 'almost walked out from the audience room of the Palace of Schönbrunn'. But he had managed to control himself and accepted the demotion. He was given the command in October 1853. His posting was a cunning choice: he was sent as a garrison commander to the Styrian town of Graz where the Emperor's uncle Archduke Johann lived. The Archduke had also made a morganatic marriage, with the pretty daughter of a village post-master, and, having renounced all his royal privileges, now resided in quiet retirement. Francis Joseph thought that Alexander and the Countess of Battenberg would find life there more congenial than in the formal atmosphere of Vienna. The provincial dignitaries of Graz had accepted the Archduke and his wife, while the Vienna Court society ostracized them; the same would apply to Alexander and his wife.

Alexander accompanied Francis Joseph to Olmuetz for a meeting with the Tsar. The meeting was the final attempt of the two monarchs to come to terms over the Balkans; but when Tsar Nicholas asked Emperor Francis Joseph for assistance against the Turks, and if necessary against Britain and France, the Austrian flatly refused, telling him that the Russian advance into the Balkans was a threat to Austro-Hungary. The Olmuetz meeting only worsened the relations between the two emperors; soon they were to become irreconcilable enemies. Alexander, pro-Russian at heart, found himself with divided loyalties in his new post.

When he returned to Graz life was quiet for a while. His military duties were light, and to dispel boredom in the sleepy provincial town Alexander and Julie found a new interest: Occultism, which had become a rage since Empress Eugénie had introduced 'spiritual seances' to her salons in Paris. Evening after evening Alexander and Julie sat at the Castle of Graz in the company of local worthies, the civil governor, the county judge, the police superintendent and a few aged aristocrats and retired generals, waiting for the spirits to knock on their table. Alexander filled pages of his diary with descriptions of the seances and clearly believed in the utterances of the medium, who managed to summon up the spirit of a butcher who announced that he had died 140 years earlier and showed great familiarity with the history of Hesse-Darmstadt. Julie was enthralled when the spirit predicted great fortune for Alexander, including crown and money. On another occasion the medium 'materialised' the spirit of Alexander the Great, all the way from his grave at Babylon. In a seance that lasted over three hours Alexander the Great predicted that his 'brother', Alexander of Hesse, would rise to great heights.

On 23 October Turkey declared war on Russia, and Alexander, more anxious than ever to look into the future, sought advice from the spirits almost every evening. The seances came, however, to an abrupt end when the medium added blackmail to his accomplishments. He permitted the spirits to reveal details of certain adulterous affairs among the dignitaries of Graz, having been refused payment for silencing the apparitions. Alexander was now greatly worried about a possible conflict between Russia and Austria. He certainly did not want to fight, as an Austrian officer, his former country of adoption, of which his sister was the Crown Princess.

When British and French warnings to the Tsar were disregarded, a British fleet was ordered to Constantinople to protect the Turkish coast, enraging the Tsar even more. In a final attempt to secure Austria's help, he wrote to Francis Joseph: 'Russia's war against the Sultan is a crusade in defence of Christendom, while France and Britain are committing the infamy of allying themselves with the Crescent', and he asked the Austrian Emperor: 'Do you want France and England ruling in Constantinople?' However, Francis Joseph remained unresponsive; fearing a dangerous increase of Russia's power he assured Paris and London that he was prepared to assist the Western Powers in their action against Russia. On 3 January 1854 British and French warships entered the Black Sea, and on 27 February an Anglo-French ultimatum demanded from the Tsar the evacuation of the Danube principalities. The Tsar replied by ordering his troops to cross the Danube, and on 28 March Britain and France declared war on Russia. The Crimean War had begun.

During these months Alexander maintained from Graz a correspondence with his sister and his brother-in-law in St Petersburg which bordered on high treason. Austria had mobilised her army on her Russian border in Galicia and threatened to occupy Montenegro, Albania and Bosnia if the Russians were to advance any further. Alexander could, at any moment, expect an order to command his brigade against the Tsar's forces. Yet at this very time he was writing to St Petersburg: 'The most unfortunate turns of Austria's incomprehensible policy may place me in a camp hostile to Russia, but they will never succeed in altering my convictions and my sacred feelings of loyalty to Russia'. Moreover, he reported to the Tsarevitch that most of the Austrian generals and the Austrian army were entirely in sympathy with Russia. To another letter in which Alexander bitterly complained about the Austrian Emperor's policy, the Tsarevitch replied: 'Your remarks about Austria's infamous policy seemed to me so right that I submitted them to the Tsar. Your feelings and those which you say animate the Austrian army have greatly pleased my father'.

In a letter written in June 1854, Alexander assured the Tsarevitch 'This, at least, is certain – that I shall never draw my sword against my erstwhile brothers-in-arms'. This letter was written a few days after the birth of his first son, in Graz on 24 May 1854. The boy was named Louis; he was to become Britain's famous First Sea Lord, the Marquess of Milford Haven and father of Earl Mountbatten of Burma.

Alexander and Julie were proud and excited about the birth of their heir, even though it was overshadowed by the war and the family's difficult position. Alexander's letters to St Petersburg were intercepted by the Austrian secret police and copied before being forwarded. His real sympathies were now well known to Emperor Francis Joseph and his ministers. Although the emperor showed forbearance, it was decided that Alexander's presence in Austria had become inopportune. He was transferred to the headquarters of the Austrian army in the Italian provinces of Lombardy and Venetia. Again Francis Joseph had shown shrewdness and a sense of humour: the Commander-in-Chief at Verona was 88-year-old Field Marshal Count Radetzky: a Czech by birth, he shared Alexander's sympathies with Russia.

During the Crimean War Austria remained neutral but helped the Western Allies by immobilising large Russian forces on her frontier. The Tsar was compelled to evacuate the Danube principalities, which were immediately occupied by Austrian troops. At the height of the battle of Sebastopol Tsar Nicholas I died after a bout of bronchitis at the age of 59. Alexander's brother-in-law and sister were now the Tsar and Tsaritsa of all the Russias.

Overnight the young Prince of Hesse became a person of considerable political importance. His close friendship with the new Tsar Alexander II, the fact that both shared liberal ideas, counted even more than that he was the brother of the new Empress of Russia.

The new Tsar wasted no time in asking Alexander to come to St Petersburg. He wanted to give him high office, but encountered strong opposition from his Ministers and court officials. The stumbling block was Julie; it was unthinkable that she should occupy a position in Court Society beside her husband. But the Tsar could, at least, entrust his brother-in-law with unofficial diplomatic missions. He wanted to make peace with Britain and France, and Alexander went to Vienna to ask the Austrian Emperor to act as mediator. Francis Joseph agreed, and Alexander brought the good news to the Tsar. But when he returned to Vienna to discuss the terms of a peace treaty, Francis Joseph did not want to pursue his own suggestion. After the Russian defeat at Sebastopol, he had decided to let the Tsar extricate himself from his predicament. The Tsar was compelled to yield to all the demands from Britain and France and to sign the humiliating peace treaty of Paris which ended the Crimean War.

Julie took a keen interest in her husband's discreet assignments. She had a distinct talent for political intrigue, and, although she deliberately remained in the shadow, many of her husband's successes as a diplomatist and secret negotiator must be put to her credit. When, in later years, Alexander became the Tsar's trusted emissary and conducted difficult and highly confidential negotiations with various European rulers and statesmen, he never failed to consult his wife. Julie of Battenberg's letters to her sister Sophie – preserved in the Schönberg archives – from Milan, Verona, and later from Heiligenberg, are full of shrewd political observations and comments. From the wings she watched the great affairs of the world; she was more interested in political events than in the upbringing of her children.

Her daughter Marie remarked in her memoirs that, when the family lived in Austria and the Italian provinces, 'I did not remember much of my parents in these years'. She wrote:

'We children lived entirely to ourselves with Adele and our maid, who at first was old Evi, and later a Swiss girl named Hortense, and then Harriet, an Englishwoman. We saw papa nearly always in uniform or on horseback. He was the sunshine in our lives . . . Of mamma we always stood a little in awe, because she was strict and made us speak French with her. She probably loved us all alike, but it was not her habit to be tender . . . and I remember how we elder ones would sometimes comment upon this among ourselves. Praise from her always made a great impression on us . . . Next to my father, the one I loved best was Adele Bassing, whose influence extended itself to all my brothers . . . To her I owe almost everything that made in the days of my youth for the training of my heart and intellect.'[1]

There are very few references to her mother in Marie's diaries, neither did Julie's only daughter pretend that she felt strong affection for her mother. Julie's four sons left their home very early to become cadets in the British navy and the armies of Saxonia and Prussia. If Julie of Battenberg was not a doting and affectionate mother, she certainly was a devoted wife, taking a passionate interest in her husband's affairs and sharing his ambitions. It must have been galling for her that, because of her

[1] Princess zu Erbach-Schönberg, op. cit.

ambiguous position, she was compelled to remain in the background for very many years.

Despite the humiliating end of the Crimean War, the Tsar's coronation on 29 August 1856 took place in Moscow with all the traditional pomp and splendour. Prince Alexander had been, of course, invited to the festivities, but his wife had not. The Tsar explained as gently as he could that it was still too early to receive at Court the former lady-in-waiting as the new Empress's sister-in-law. Assuring her husband that she understood and did not feel hurt, Julie herself urged him to go to Moscow.

Thirty golden coaches each drawn by six horses followed the imperial carriage to the Cathedral which housed the Miraculous Madonna of Vladimir, Russia's most revered ikon. Eight thousand bells tolled from Moscow's sixteen hundred churches when Alexander II and Tsaritsa Marie entered the cathedral. During the coronation ritual two incidents occurred which many of the distinguished guests regarded as the worst of omens for the future of the imperial couple. As four of the ladies of the Court tried to place the enormously heavy crown on Marie's head, it fell to the floor and rolled away. And when Prince Pludov and Prince Shakovskoy were about to hand the sceptre to the Tsar, they dropped the silk cushion upon which lay the collar of St Andrew.

In spite of the Russian army's war losses in the Crimea, eighty thousand infantry men and twenty thousand riders paraded before the Tsar and his guests. The Tsar had insisted that the people of Moscow should share in the festivities and innumerable tables, loaded with food and drink were erected in many squares. Three hundred thousand people feasted, served by men of several infantry regiments, with artificial fountains flowing with wine, vodka and beer instead of water. Although neither now a Russian officer nor a Tsar's subject, Sasha gave Alexander the Coronation medal with the words: 'I would have wished you could wear it on our uniform and not on an Austrian one, but I know that you have never ceased to be one of us.'

Alexander returned to Verona even more devoted to Sasha and Russia than ever before. He had promised the Tsar to keep him informed of all Austrian political moves which came to his notice. It seems that he was not too careful about his correspondence. He was now regarded in Vienna as the Tsar's secret agent, and it was therefore not surprising that when Emperor Francis Joseph and Empress Elizabeth visited Verona in November 1856, the Emperor was not only cool to Alexander but inflicted a calculated insult on him. He ordered that the Countess von Battenberg should stand among 'the ladies of lower birth', while her husband was given precedence as a prince of royal blood. When Francis Joseph and Elizabeth passed down the long line of the 'lower ladies', mainly wives of officers, they spoke graciously to some of them but did not even glance at Julie as she curtsied. Alexander was so deeply hurt that he wanted to resign his commission there and then. Once again Julie calmed him, but he asked the Emperor to be transferred from Verona to Milan. This the Emperor refused bluntly with no bones made about reason. He told Alexander that Milan was not the place for a man with his uncertain loyalties. It was full of Piedmontese rebels and Napoleon III's secret agents.

Alexander was now reporting regularly to St Petersburg about the growing danger of a conflict between Austria and France, and the Tsar asked him to put out feelers to find whether he could arrange a meeting with Napoleon. As yet another expression of his friendship, the Tsar offered to be the godfather to Julie's third child, born in Verona on 18 April 1857. The boy was christened Alexander; twenty-two years later he was to become the ruler of Bulgaria.

Alexander was determined to comply with the Tsar's request, but how could he accomplish his mission to Napoleon without openly working against Austria's interests? Fortunately, a letter arrived at the end of June 1857 from his brother, the Grand Duke Louis: 'The Russians are invading us on July 7. They will roll into Wildbad in a week. Come and help!' This was the Grand Duke's way of announcing a visit by their sister Marie and the Tsar to Darmstadt. At the age of 51, Louis III was becoming increasingly eccentric. He had grown enormously fat and, plagued by gout, he insisted on being carried about in a sedan chair. When he was Prince Regent he had sympathised with the liberal and revolutionary movements of the late 1840s, but by now he had become affected with a grand-seignorial way of life, a miniature 'roi-soleil' of an impoverished provincial court. Although his sluggish body housed a deft and alert mind, he had become increasingly reluctant to take part in public affairs.

Instead, he was completely engrossed in his large and valuable collections of coins, watches, snuff boxes, meerschaum pipes and cigar-holders. When he travelled from Darmstadt to his summer residences of Rosenhöhe or Heiligenberg, which were his only ventures abroad, he used a state carriage drawn by four horses, with flunkeys and outriders in faded liveries, preceded by several carriages with his personal cooks and servants and waggons loaded with food.

Alexander hurried to join Sasha and Marie at Darmstadt, from where they went on to take the waters at Wildbad and Bad Kissingen. He had heard that Napoleon III would spend a vacation at Plombières in the Vosges mountains at the same time. He wrote to the French Emperor asking for an interview and received a cordial assent by return. At Wildbad he had a long talk with the Tsar. It was not easy to find a place for a secret meeting of the two emperors, but Alexander had a bright idea. He suggested that the Tsar and Napoleon should meet at Stuttgart where his once beloved Olly, the sister of the Tsar, now lived as the wife of the Crown Prince of Wurttemberg.

Although the plan had been kept secret, Francis Joseph heard of it, probably through his spies in Paris, and Alexander received from him a confidential letter by special messenger, cunningly addressed 'My dear cousin and general', reminding Alexander that he was still in the Austrian Emperor's service and owed him allegiance. Francis Joseph, now well aware of his political isolation, asked Alexander if he could arrange to meet the Tsar before the Tsar met Napoleon, adding that he was 'most anxious to dispel the unfortunate misunderstandings between Austria and Russia', and to discuss a new *rapprochement*.

Thus the 32-years-old Prince of Hesse, still the youngest major-general of the Austrian army, found himself with the key role in a series of complicated manoeuvres on which the peace of Europe depended. He went to Bad Kissingen to report to the Tsar. He had by now grown a handsome beard and was an impressive figure. The Tsar congratulated him upon his appearance and good health, adding, 'My dear brother, you should be a prince in your own right and not a servant of that vile Austrian! I shall look for a crown for you . . . perhaps as the ruler of a new Rumania'.

Though Alexander could hardly conceal his delight at the

prospect, he replied modestly, 'I shall of course obey you, my dearest Sasha, whatever you decide. Should I be called upon to become the prince of a united Rumanian kingdom you know that I would be your most loyal and faithful liege'. As it happened, a new Kingdom of Rumania did come about, though Alexander never wore its crown, but by a strange stroke of fate he was instrumental 30 years later in securing the crown of neighbouring Bulgaria for his second son, Alexander.

Throughout that summer of 1857 Alexander was rushing between Bad Kissingen, Plombières, Vienna and Stuttgart, stage-managing the momentous parleys between the Tsar and Francis Joseph, and between the Tsar and Napoleon. The Tsar had decided that Francis Joseph would have to wait. 'I shall meet Napoleon first and show the Austrians that the tables have been turned.' The Tsar returned for a few weeks to St Petersburg, travelling back to Germany for the appointment with Napoleon at Stuttgart on 24 September. At this meeting the Tsar approved Napoleon's plan to unite the Italian States under the presidency of the Pope, with the explicit exclusion of Austrian influence. Both emperors were greatly pleased with Alexander's work. Shaking his hand warmly, Napoleon said, '*Adieu, mon prince*, and many thanks for your great help in bringing about this meeting. You have done much for the peace of Europe'.

In Vienna, however, Francis Joseph was furious, correctly assuming there was a conspiracy afoot against him. He was even angrier when Alexander told him the Tsar would receive the Austrian Emperor but only in Warsaw. 'Am I to go to Warsaw as a penitant, on a journey to Canossa?' he demanded. He suggested that the Tsar come to Vienna, an invitation that was flatly declined. Alexander's diplomacy did succed in bringing together the two monarchs, on the last day of September at Weimar. The meeting that was to be described by historians as a turning-point in relations between Austria and Russia, ended in dismal failure. The Holy Alliance was dead. Its two partners were to become bitter foes, and fifty-seven years later to meet on the battlefield.

Despite the failure of the Weimar meeting, Alexander was rewarded with high honours by both rulers. The Tsar gave him the Order of St Michael and restored him to the honorary rank of a Russian general; Francis Joseph went even one better, giving Alexander the Grand Cross of the Leopold Order, which admitted him to the Austrian nobility. He also granted him the long-coveted transfer to Milan and promoted him to the rank of major-general and commanding officer of the Austrian forces in Lombardy and Venetia under the Governor-General Archduke Ferdinand Max, the Emperor's brother.

A year later Alexander and Julie went from Milan to Darmstadt to spend Christmas with the Hesse family, taking their three children with them. They found the fat Grand Duke in high spirits. His marriage to Mathilde of Bavaria had remained childless, but he had formed an attachment to a pretty young member of the corps de ballet of the Darmstadt Court Theatre, a Fraulein Helen Appel. The young lady had recently given birth to a bonny boy, and the ageing Grand Duke was convinced that he was the father, although his belief was shared by only few other people.

Beaming at his 'little brother' the Grand Duke said: 'I've heard from the Tsar and "Bedinguet"[1] about your splendid work. You've got plenty of orders and medals, but I have a better present for you. I want to make Julie a princess, so that she can be received at every Court without trouble over etiquette.'

Alexander flushed with pleasure as the Grand Duke rumbled on:

'I remember how I asked Dalwigk, it's six or seven years now, that he should find a title for Julie, and that old fool told me about some old ruin called Kellerburg . . . Kellerburg, I beg you! We then found that name of Battenberg, which is a fine name. Dalwigk said we could make Julie only a countess then. But now she shall be a princess, and your lovely children will all be princes and princesses!'[2]

Alexander could hardly contain his delight. He embraced his brother, who had slouched down in his fauteuil, quite exhausted from his long speech. With the rank of a Princess went the title of 'Durchlaucht', which was almost as good as a 'Grand Ducal Highness'. Never again could Julie be snubbed.

---

[1] Nickname given to Napoleon III. It was the name of a mason in whose clothes he had escaped from the prison of Ham in 1846.

[2] The grand-ducal decree is dated 26 December 1858.

CHAPTER FOUR

THE CONFIDANT OF KINGS

ON HIS return to Milan in the autumn of 1858, Alexander of Hesse found the situation greatly changed. Hostility against the Austrians was now open: Austrian officers were spat upon in the streets, and when the Imperial Governor, Archduke Ferdinand Max, appeared in the royal box of the Scala Opera, he was greeted with shouts of 'Out! out!'

Despite ruthless suppression by the Austrian police and mass arrests of Italian patriots, street demonstrations and riots were frequent in Milan, Padua, Verona and Venice. Thousands of young Italians, including the sons of noble families, had entered the Piedmontese army or had joined the secret societies of Garibaldi and Mazzini. King Victor Emmanuel had defiantly declared: 'The hour of liberation of Lombardy and Venetia from the Austrian yoke has come at last!'

Austria had felt acutely the results of the Crimean War, which had undermined her international position and ruined her finances through prolonged mobilisation. In spite of the many provocations Emperor Francis Joseph tried to preserve peace, aware that any action against Piedmont would mean war with France. Napoleon had promised Victor Emmanuel immediate armed assistance in the event of an Austrian attack.

Distraught in his isolation, Francis Joseph sent emissaries to the king of Prussia to sound him for help, if only by mobilising the Prussian army as a warning to Napoleon. But in Berlin King Frederick William IV, a romanticist with liberal views, was in sympathy with the ideals of the Italian freedom movement and content to watch the conflict growing: war between Austria and France could only help Prussia. On 27 April 1859 Austria delivered an ultimatum to Victor Emmanuel, and when no reply was received, Austrian troops invaded Piedmont.

Prince Alexander of Hesse, in command of the Milan garrison, was ordered to cross the river Ticino. He drew his sword with reluctance. In his diary he wrote: 'The Austrians have taken the whole odium of the breach of peace upon their shoulders and have given Napoleon every pretext to send his whole army into Italy. We shall without any doubt be defeated.'

His first engagement with the Piedmontese was unsuccessful. The Austrian Commander-in-Chief, General Gyulai, proved ineffective, and when Emperor Francis Joseph arrived at the Verona headquarters to find matters in a state of chaos, he looked for someone he could trust. Strangely, his choice fell upon Alexander, the youngest major-general in his army, and he promoted him to the command of a division.

The battle of Magenta, at which French troops appeared for the first time, including fierce African Zouaves and Senegalese, went against the Austrians. On June 24, the French and Piedmontese won a decisive victory at Solferino. When Alexander of Hesse arrived on the battlefield, the Austrians were in full retreat, and, in a desperate bayonet charge to reverse the French onslaught, he led a battalion of Imperial Guards head on. His horse was shot from under him and he continued to fight on foot. A bullet hit his water bottle and it was only by sheer luck that he escaped injury. His division suffered heavy losses, but he managed to pull out his men in good order. They retreated towards Volta, where Alexander saw hundreds of abandoned cannons, vehicles and stores left behind by the fleeing Austrians.

The Emperor recalled him to headquarters, and ordered him to write to the Tsar asking him to mediate for an armistice. At Alexander's urgent request the Tsar sent an emissary to Napoleon advising him to make peace, and warning him that Prussia was mobilising and might attack across the Rhine. The French army had also suffered heavy losses at Solferino and Napoleon was ready to discuss peace terms, mainly because of the uncertain attitude of Prussia. The letter the Emperor received from the Tsar advised him 'to make contact immediately with my brother-in-law, Prince Alexander of Hesse'. On the following night

Prince Alexander of Battenberg (1857–1893), Prince of Bulgaria, (1879–1886), in the field uniform during his victorious campaign against Serbia in 1885. (*After a painting by F. Muller.*)

Princess Victoria of Prussia, grand-daughter of the German Emperor William I. Her secret betrothal to Prince Alexander of Battenberg caused Bismarck's wrath, led to the Battenberg Affair and hostility between Germany and Great Britain.

Johanna Loisinger, the operatic singer, whom Alexander of Battenberg married after his abdication from the throne of Bulgaria.

Queen Victoria with her
youngest daughter,
Princess Beatrice.

Prince Henry of
Battenberg, Beatrice's
Lohengrin and his wife
at their wedding in 1885 at
Whippingham, Isle of
Wight.

Napoleon's adjutant, Count Fleury, crossed the lines with a personal letter from the emperor and was conducted to Alexander's house. In his message Napoleon said that he had ordered the French fleet to bombard Venice if Francis Joseph refused to open parleys. Alexander hastened to headquarters and insisted that Francis Joseph should be awakened. There followed two days of almost uninterrupted discussions, the Austrian Emperor finally agreeing that Alexander should start negotiations with Napoleon. The French emperor welcomed him courteously: 'It is a great pity that I have to receive you as an enemy general, because I regard you as a friend'. He told Alexander he would accept the 'London Proposals' which the British Prime Minister had sent to both Napoleon and Francis Joseph, suggesting that Austria should agree to a confederation of Italian states under Piedmontese leadership, while Venetia would become autonomous under an Austrian archduke.

At first Francis Joseph rejected 'this insolent dictation', and Alexander unsuccessfully tried to persuade Napoleon to modify the terms. With revolutionary movements spreading throughout Austria, and waiting in vain for help from Prussia, Francis Joseph was, in the end, compelled to accept the 'London Proposals' and make peace with Napoleon. Austria lost Lombardy and Milan, but kept Mantua and Venetia. Alexander regarded the peace terms as just, but soon changed his opinion about Napoleon, who had promised to withdraw his troops from Italy, but, in fact, left them there and even occupied Rome. With French help Parma, Modena, Romagna and Tuscany were annexed by Piedmont in violation of the peace treaty. In a letter to the Tsar, complaining of Napoleon's 'two-faced policy', Alexander wrote: 'I have come round to your opinion – that Bedinguet cannot be trusted'.

The Austrian Emperor, although having accepted a humiliating peace treaty, felt that some reward was due to Alexander for his part in the negotiations. Wrongly, he decided to award him the highest Austrian order for gallantry, instead of a more conventional honour. The Maria-Theresa Cross was similar to the Victoria Cross – a reward for outstanding valour on the battlefield, regardless of rank.

The announcement of the award had an extremely bad reception in the Austrian army. It was only natural that Alexander was not popular with many high-ranking officers, who called him 'the Russian general' and envied his familiarity with the Emperor. Why was this foreigner given the highest distinction, asked the generals and politicians. Biting comments and cartoons appeared in Viennese newspapers, one showing a water bottle being struck by a bullet (a reference to Solferino), with the Maria-Theresa Cross pinned on the bottle. General Ramming published an essay in a military journal ascribing the Austrian defeat at Solferino to the late arrival of Alexander's division on the battlefield.

In vain Alexander tried to defend himself against the insinuations, even offering to return the Maria-Theresa Cross, but Francis Joseph refused to take the matter seriously. However, another incident occurred, which strengthened Alexander's decision to quit the Austrian army. Cavour, the chief minister of King Victor Emmanuel, died in 1861; and the loss of that 'architect of the unification of Italy' was deeply mourned by the Italians. Cavour had been hated in Austria, and when requiems were held in churches in Austrian Venetia police arrested many mourners. Alexander was at Stra, where the officers of the 62nd Austrian Infantry Regiment held a garden party. It was subsequently described as 'a service of mourning for Cavour' by Viennese nationalistic newspapers, who accused Alexander of being 'nothing but a traitor'.[1]

Exasperated by these vile attacks and becoming weary of his nomadic life, Alexander decided to quit the Austrian service. With the birth of his third son, Henry, in 1858 in Milan, he now had four children, and on 4 September 1861, his wife gave birth to yet another boy. Alexander and Julie longed to settle down in a place of their own. The Emperor tried to dissuade him from resigning, and as a compliment offered to be the new baby's godfather. The child was named Francis Joseph, and although Alexander appreciated the emperor's gesture, his intention to leave Austria remained. He wrote to the Tsar, broaching discreetly the problem of finance. With five children to support and educate, he must have a regular income. Could his brother-in-

---

[1] There is a remarkable similarity here with what happened to Alexander's son, Prince Louis of Battenberg, half a century later when, in 1914, as First Sea Lord, he was subjected to vituperative attacks in London newspapers, calling him a traitor.

law help? The Tsar and the Tsaritsa replied immediately, offering assistance 'should you decide to buy a good mansion in Darmstadt'.

In May 1862 Alexander induced his physician to certify that he had some uncertain internal complaint; he obtained a long leave from the Austrian army and took his family to Darmstadt. At that time his nephew Prince Louis of Hesse (later Grand Duke Louis IV) was betrothed to Princess Alice, second daughter of Queen Victoria. The Queen's eldest daughter, Princess Victoria, had shortly before married the Crown Prince of Prussia – later the German Kaiser Frederick III. The new link with the British royal family gave Alexander the idea of going to England, where he hoped to revive his connection with the Rothschilds and enter business. But he received interesting news from St Petersburg. The Tsar wrote that Count Otto von Bismarck was working to establish better relations between Prussia and Russia and he asked his brother-in-law to stay in Germany and to send him confidential reports about the situation there and also in Austria, which Bismarck had described as a stumbling-block to German unification.

In Frankfurt Alexander met for the first time Princess Alice, the newly married English wife of his nephew. The Hesse family had taken a great fancy to the princess and Alexander wrote to his sister and brother-in-law in St Petersburg that she was 'clever, friendly and better-looking than her photographs show, indulging in discussions about art, literature and science'. He added that Louis and Alice seemed happy, though ill-matched. 'She is an intelligent woman with great intellectual ambitions, very like her father, the Prince Consort . . . while Louis is a prosaic fellow, mainly interested in good food, hunting and horses.'

When Alexander was staying with his family in Germany, a revolution broke out in Greece and King Otto I, who had ascended the Greek throne in 1832 after the war of independence, was deposed. A new ruler was sought and the Greek crown was offered to Prince Alfred, Duke of Edinburgh, Victoria's second son. But Lord Palmerston, assessing the European tension, refused to allow Alfred to accept it, much to Queen Victoria's regret. Greek leaders put out feelers in the capitals of the Great Powers, and Alexander was both startled and flattered by a letter from Count Rechberg, the Austrian Foreign Minister, asking whether he would accept the Greek throne. Naturally, the Tsar supported this move, and so did Napoleon and the British government.

For several months Alexander lived in a rosy dream of anticipation, and the history of the Battenberg family might have taken a very different course had he become King of Greece. But Bismarck, who had shortly before become Prime Minister of Prussia, vetoed Alexander's candidature. In the eyes of the Prussian statesman, who was soon to exercise such dominating influence upon European politics, the Hesse prince was an exponent of Russian and Austrian interests, and totally unacceptable as a Balkan ruler. Bismarck brought strong pressure to bear against Alexander. First London and then Paris withdrew its support, and even the Tsar gave up this plan, anxious not to antagonize Bismarck with whom he was secretly plotting against Austria. Thus Alexander's dream of a crown dissolved in the haze of international intrigue, and the 17-year-old Prince George of Denmark was elected King of the Hellenes.

Queen Victoria, angered by Lord Palmerston's desertion of Alexander, invited the Hesse prince to London. This visit was to be much more exciting and pleasant than the one he had made twelve years earlier. It coincided with the birth on 5 April 1863, of a daughter to Princess Alice and his nephew Louis – a granddaughter for Queen Victoria, and named after her. Little did Alexander think that this new-born royal baby would one day become his daughter-in-law and the first Marchioness of Milford Haven.

At the christening at Windsor Castle, Alexander represented his brother, the Grand Duke of Hesse. The event was a turning-point in the destinies of the Battenbergs, for it not only forged a closer link between Alexander's family and British royalty, and eventually led to his first son's marrying the Queen's granddaughter, but to the marriage of the Queen's youngest daughter, Princess Beatrice, to his younger son, Henry of Battenberg. On his first visit he had been almost ignored by the British court, but this time he received a gracious reception.

His letters from London to Sasha and Marie in St Petersburg were full of enthusiasm, even though he knew of his sister's dislike of the English and their royal family. At that time there were persistent rumours that Queen Victoria had become mentally deranged after her husband's death, but Alexander reported that they were entirely groundless. He stated that the Queen 'with her pendulous cheeks', seemed a little eccentric in her widow's weeds, but that 'she was in full possession of her mental powers, quite alert and well-informed'. He wrote that at Windsor Castle he felt 'like being suddenly conjured into an entirely new world'. Although etiquette was not so stiff as at the Russian court, Queen Victoria enforced a strict 'no smoking' rule, not even permitting her guests to smoke in their rooms. However, Alexander, who loved a good cigar, discovered that there were rooms at the Great Tower which, though connected with the castle by a long passage and stairs, were remote from the main suites. He mentioned to the Queen that his rooms were rather cold, and was then given a suite in the Great Tower which had been recently equipped with better heating.

He could now smoke in peace, while at the castle – as the Prince of Wales told him – 'the death penalty was attached to the weed'. The heir to the throne began to visit Alexander regularly. The main reason for these visits was, as Alexander soon discovered, that the Prince of Wales also relished a good cigar and used Alexander's rooms to defy his mother's dictum.

In his letters to St Petersburg, Alexander expressed himself enthusiastically about the Princess of Wales: 'This Danish princess, whom all call Alex, is perfectly lovely, very natural and charming, as beautiful as her husband is plain. Bertie (the later Edward vii) is a funny little man. His features are not bad, he is a male edition of his sister Alice, but he is so broad for his height that he looks shorter than his wife. He is exceedingly friendly and cordial to me. The younger sisters, Helena (who later married Prince of Schleswig-Holstein) and Louise (later the Duchess of Argyll) are pretty and intelligent, especially the former. The Queen's youngest child, Beatrice, is a dear little girl with flying golden curls down to her waist, but she seems to be thoroughly spoiled by everyone. The boys are nice: Alfred, the Duke of Edinburgh, frank and jovial, is a typical naval officer; Arthur (later Duke of Connaught) is 13 and rather shy, so is 10-year-old Leopold (later Duke of Albany); they are strictly brought up – two little Scots in kilts, with blue knees, but they look intelligent . . .'

About his nephew, Louis of Hesse, husband of Princess Alice, he was less kind. He wrote to the Tsaritsa, 'Louis is rather a boor, though he tries to be quite the Englishman. He wears a Norfolk jacket, short breeches and multi-coloured garters, and is very fond of sherry and horses. But he hardly ever reads, and never writes at all; and he murders the Queen's English whenever he makes an official address. Nevertheless he is the Queen's confidant and she takes his advice on European matters – though his political ideas, if he has any, are those of the Duke of Coburg . . .'

Again, Alexander could not imagine that, in not too many years, his own son, Henry, would become the Queen's constant companion, confidant and adviser. After his visit at Windsor he stayed in London and had several meetings with Lord Palmerston and the Foreign Secretary, Lord John Russell. He reported to the Tsar: 'The British statesmen treat me as a colleague, they are well-informed through their secret agents about some of the negotiations I have conducted with Napoleon and Francis Joseph; they strongly dislike Napoleon and are extremely suspicious of his aims'. He added that Palmerston and Russell wanted to discredit the French Emperor in the Tsar's eyes, and that their comments were obviously made in the hope that they would be repeated by Alexander. He also mentioned, but discounted as 'quite ridiculous', Russell's 'highly secret information' that British secret agents had discovered Napoleon's preparations for a war against Russia, and his intention of sending a French fleet to the Baltic and bombard Kronstadt and St Petersburg.

Politics and secret conferences did not prevent Alexander having a good time in London. The Prince of Wales who, as Alexander noted in his diary, 'was being cruelly debarred by the Queen and her ministers from taking part in politics, is a connoisseur of pretty ladies and gay life, constantly involved in scandals'. The future Edward vii proved an excellent guide, taking Alexander to bawdy parties and dinners which ended round the card tables in the early hours, at which the Prince of Wales played for extravagant stakes. Alexander was introduced to some of the Prince's women friends, the 'professional beauties' of the English aristocracy and the music-halls; some of them were not disciplined to bestow favours on the handsome visitor from Hesse.

But at 40, the once dashing Guards officer, who had had so many love affairs before he married the insignificant 'Polish orphan girl', had become a model *paterfamilias* – unusual in an era when princes and noblemen kept at least one mistress, and most were inveterate gamblers and drinkers. Since his marriage no breath of scandal touched him, although he was not particularly shocked about his friends' indulgence and wantonness, and even resigned himself to the fact that his sister's husband, the Tsar, openly lived with Princess Catharine Dolgoruki.

From London, Alexander went to Paris. Despite his reservations about Napoleon and his allegiance to the Tsar, he got on extremely well with the French 'upstart'. Alexander could not keep off state intrigues; he imparted in great secrecy to Napoleon some of the information he had received from Palmerston and Russell in London.

Napoleon admired Alexander's keen brain and was very fond of him; he reciprocated by telling him of his idea of creating a new Kingdom of Poland. Like his great-uncle Bonaparte, the French Emperor regarded himself as the protector of the Poles, who had at that time risen in another revolt against their Russian oppressors. Growing anxious about the *rapprochement* between Russia and Prussia, which Bismarck was so skilfully engineering, Napoleon suggested to Alexander that he should ask the Tsar to make him governor-general in Warsaw, with a view of becoming the King of Poland under Russian suzerainty. The foxy Frenchman rightly assumed that a re-born, semi-autonomous Poland would become and remain a bone of contention between Berlin and St Petersburg and thus discourage Bismarck from turning against France.

Once again, for the third time, there seemed to be a chance of a throne for Alexander of Hesse. But Napoleon's suggestion had come too late. In Russia the nationalist party had forced the Tsar to quell the Polish rebellion in a bloodbath. Russification of Congress Poland was being carried out ruthlessly, the country was swamped by the Tsar's troops and secret police, and Polish leaders were being sent to Siberia. In any case, Bismarck would have never consented to Alexander's candidature for a Polish throne.

While after his return to Darmstadt Alexander was still nursing hopes, a crisis arose in an unexpected part of Europe. King

Christian IX of Denmark, taking advantage of the confusion which beset the relations between the Great Powers, had proclaimed a new constitution for his country, incorporating the Duchy of Schleswig and claiming for Denmark the Duchy of Holstein, a member of the German Confederation. The German Diet voted a federal 'punitive execution' against Denmark. Bismarck grasped the opportunity to proclaim that Prussia would uphold German unity and Austria joined in the alliance to punish little Denmark. King Christian had hoped for help from Britain and France, but none was forthcoming, and within a few weeks his army suffered a crushing defeat. But the victory won by Prussia and Austria only led to a conflict between these two powers competing for the domination of the German Confederation.

When the Austrians appointed a governor in Holstein and maintained troops there, Bismarck declared this as a hostile act against Prussia. He was determined on a war against Austria and was only searching for a pretext. In October 1865 he met Napoleon and dropped hints of compensation for France in the Rhineland in return for French neutrality; then with Napoleon's aid he concluded a treaty of alliance with Italy and made sure that Prussia's relations with the Tsar remained friendly. Then he ordered Prussian troops into Holstein and demanded Austria's ejection from the German Confederation. War had become inevitable.

Alexander and Julia, with their five children, were staying at the Castle of Heiligenberg, which had been lent to them by Alexander's elder brother, Charles. They were surprised to receive an urgent message from the Tsar, asking for hospitality for 'a gathering of all rulers of Europe in a meeting to preserve peace'. Although this was a highly flattering request, which showed how highly Alexander's diplomatic skill was regarded by the rulers and statesmen of the Great Powers, he was unable to accommodate so many illustrious guests at his home.

For the great meeting of crowned heads and their ministers he had, therefore, to choose Bad Kissingen. The meeting was abortive, and attended by only a few rulers, but before it took place Alexander entertained at Heiligenberg the Tsar and King William of Prussia, five German Grand Dukes and several princes. The Tsar brought an entourage of eighty-three ministers, officials and generals who had to be accommodated in Darmstadt.

Anxious weeks passed in protracted and fruitless conferences, and then the Tsar and Tsarina left for the south of France where their eldest son, the 22-year-old Tsarevitch Nicholas, was reconvalescing after a serious illness diagnosed as rheumatic fever. He was engaged to a Danish princess, but the wedding had been postponed because of his illness. Suddenly his condition became worse, and on Easter Sunday 1865 he had a cerebral haemorrhage. His parents were summoned from St Petersburg to Nice, and Alexander, too, hurried to the sickbed of his nephew. The real cause of the Tsarevitch's illness, tubercular meningitis, had either never been discovered, or had been concealed from the Tsar by the doctors.

Alexander telegraphed to Emperor Francis Joseph begging him to send the famous Viennese physician, Professor Oppolzer, and Russian doctors arrived with the Tsar. But the Tsarevitch was beyond their help. On 24 April 1865 he died in his mother's arms. His parents were heartbroken and Alexander tried to console them, as well as Princess Dagmar who had come from Copenhagen to the deathbed of her fiancé. 'Poor sweet child', Alexander prophetically wrote in his diary, 'who knows, she may yet become a member of our family'. She did, later marrying her fiancé's younger brother, who was to become Tsar Alexander III.

Although Julie had been elevated to the rank of a Princess, she still could not attend official functions in Russia. Alexander had to leave her behind when he travelled for his nephew's state funeral. The Tsar had apologised to Julie, explaining that for political reasons he was unable to admit her to his court.

In order to compensate his wife for this disappointment, Alexander decided after his return on a family visit to the little town of Battenberg from which she had taken her title. For some years they had received invitations from the burgomaster, but Alexander's preoccupation with international affairs and his many foreign travels had made such a visit impossible.

Battenberg was then a place of some 500 inhabitants, a picturesque village on the bank of the river Eder at the edge of the Westerwald Forest. It lay off the beaten track, though a bumpy road had been built to Wiesbaden. Ruins were all that remained of the castle, the home of the fourteenth century Battenbergs who had died out during the Crusades. Alexander and his family travelled there in a coach. They did not quite know what to expect, but their anticipation of a quiet and restful holiday was soon dispelled. They were received with truly German hospitality and were feted to the point of exhaustion. 'We had to earn our popularity by the sweat of our brows, in a temperature of 80 degrees in the shade,' Alexander wrote to his sister. The reception committee meticulously observed all traditions due to the lord of the castle, with interminable speeches and tributes by the burgomaster and local worthies.

At the entrance of the village they were met by mounted burgesses and transferred to an ancient state coach painted in the colours of Hesse and Battenberg. It was driven by the local postmaster under a succession of triumphal arches, gaily decorated with flags and bunting. The arches were somewhat unstable – they had been hurriedly erected of rough-hewn timber – and two collapsed just as the coach was passing underneath. No one was hurt, and the procession advanced shakily but joyfully, Alexander and Julie wearing fixed smiles and their children waving merrily to the crowds.

That was only the beginning – there was far worse to come, and the visit began to take on the atmosphere of an ordeal for the Battenberg family. They were expected to shake hands with the entire population including the inmates of an Old Folks' Home, and babes in arms. White-clad maidens served wine and pretzels, foresters and members of the rifle club fired continuous salutes, even during the recitals by several male choirs and the renderings of the fire brigade brass band; all the time the bells of Battenberg's three churches were pealing.

Alexander's head was spinning, and Julie was visibly wilting under the strain – but so far they had only come through the initial stages of the reception. After Alexander's brief reply to the burgomaster's hour-long address, the princely family entered the coach and drove slowly through the narrow, cobbled streets to the market place. Twice the coach almost collapsed, but everyone arrived without further mishap. The Gymnastic Society assembled in the market place, and for the next three hours the royal guests had to watch agile performances on the rack, trampoline, and vaulting horse. Alexander's family, now utterly worn out, had retired inside their coach to continue watching the spectacle. At the end of the display there was no let-up, as a male choir suddenly burst into song. This was too much for the terrified horses which bolted, knocking down several of the village maidens.

The second coach, carrying the prince's secretary and his children's governess and tutor, was even more unfortunate. The horses pulling it also shied, overturning the coach and spilling the passengers on to the cobbles. Little Sandro, who had joined his tutor in the second coach, was frightened and badly bruised. No wonder Alexander wrote afterwards in his diary: 'It was worse than the battle of Solferino'.

Almost a century later the people of Battenberg, which had trebled in size and become prosperous with a steelworks, again had occasion to greet distinguished members of the Battenberg family – though much less boisterously, if not less significantly.

On 2 May 1959, the grandson of Alexander and Julie, the Earl Mountbatten of Burma, visited the little town with his wife and one of his two daughters. It was the first visit paid by any member of the family since that triumphal reception in 1865. Two wars lay between these visits, and in both of them the descendants of Alexander and Julie had fought against the German Reich.

In the guest book of the Hotel Rohde, owned by Herr and Frau Lind, which has a handsome sign proclaiming 'Quiet Situation with Large Terrace affording a Wonderful View of the entire Valley of the Eder', there can be seen the following signatures:

'Mountbatten of Burma, A. F., Prinz von Battenberg.
'Edwina Mountbatten of Burma, Prinzessin von Battenberg.
'Pamela Mountbatten, Prinzessin von Battenberg.'

When Alexander and his family returned to Heiligenberg after that raucous and memorable visit to Battenberg, the Hesse prince needed income. He was now 42, with a large family to support. His general's pension and occasional allowances from St Petersburg were insufficient to provide for a livelihood according to his standing. He decided to enter business, having heard that British financiers had formed a syndicate to build a railway from Moscow to Sebastopol. He remembered his abortive dealings with the Rothschilds, and he knew that some of the international financiers who were fortune-making in Russia, Austria and Germany, would only be too happy to help. He exchanged letters with some of them and was invited to join several syndicates.

But this was not to be. The decision of the South German states against Bismarck's demand for the ejection of Austria from the German Confederation led on 15 April 1866 to Prussia's declaration of war on the Austrian Empire. During the weeks preceding the conflict, Alexander played a prominent role in the attempts made in Vienna, St Petersburg and London to prevent the war. But nothing could stop Bismarck in his determination to humiliate Austria and make Prussia supreme in Central Europe.

Shortly before the outbreak of the war, Alexander had gone to Vienna. He considered it his duty – as an Austrian general on the 'retired list' – to offer his services to the Emperor. Only a few months earlier he had entertained at Heiligenberg King William of Prussia, whom he liked and respected, but his scorn for Bismarck and Prussia's policy left him in no doubt where his allegiance lay.

Amongst Austria's allies were the kings of Hanover and Saxony and the South-German states, Bavaria, Wurttemberg, Baden, as well as the Landgrave of Hesse-Cassel and – very reluctantly – also Alexander's brother, the Grand Duke of Hesse-Darmstadt. Alexander was given the command of the Eighth Federal Army, a motley force composed of Hessian, Wurttembergian and Badensian troops, poorly trained and armed. He took his command very seriously, preparing his army for a long campaign.

But the war lasted for only seven weeks. In a *blitzkrieg* the Prussian army overran Hanover in two days and the king capitulated. Then the Prussians turned towards the south, occupying many towns of the Rhineland before even making contact with the Federal army. At Cassel Landgrave Frederick was taken prisoner and, when General Alexander of Hesse arrived with his troops in July 1866 at Grunberg, he heard not only of the capture of his cousin by the Prussians, but also of the utter disaster which had overcome the Austrian army at Koeniggraetz. By the end of July, without having fired many shots, Alexander's army began to melt away; one after another the German kings and princes sued Bismarck for peace.

Grand Duke Louis had never liked this whole bad business. His Chief Minister, Baron von Dalwigk, the man who had invented the name of Battenberg, had persuaded him to join the anti-Prussian alliance, although the Grand Duke pleaded with him that the Hessian army – all 10,000 of it – 'should stay peacefully at home'. When Alexander accepted his command, Louis had written to him:

'This damned business has absolutely spoiled my appetite for dinner. Is the devil after Dalwigk? It is a wretched business that we should be mixed up with it . . . It all pains and grieves me, not only as head of our family and Grand Duke, but also as an old soldier who, however, has never smelled powder. I do implore you, dear boy, to think once more whether there is not some way of counter-acting this whole damned fool trick . . . Sleep over it once more, and then tell me what you think to-morrow. Remember our House and our Hesse! Greatly troubled in mind and appetite,

I remain your devoted brother, Louis.'[1]

While Bismarck imposed harsh conditions on Emperor Francis Joseph and his uncertain allies, the Grand Duke of Hesse-Darmstadt was treated leniently. Austria was excluded from the German Confederation, Hanover, Nassau, Cassel, Frankfurt were annexed by Prussia; not only the king of Hanover but also the Elector of Cassel had lost their thrones, but Hesse-Darmstadt was allowed to survive.

Saddened and with a sense of almost personal humiliation, Alexander returned to Heiligenberg. The Austro-Prussian war and Bismarck's triumph had brought about a rift within the House of Hesse. Alexander was disgusted about the behaviour of his nephew Louis and his English wife, Princess Alice, who enthusiastically expressed their admiration for Bismarck, describing him as 'the greatest statesman in history'. In the case of Alice it might have been understandable: her sister was the wife of the Prussian Crown Prince. But Alexander was livid when his other nephew, Prince Henry of Hesse, arrived in Darmstadt in the uniform of the Prussian Guards regiment which he had joined during the war when his own country, if only nominally, had been Prussia's enemy.

It was only years later that Alexander came to understand – without ever quite approving of it – that the younger generation

[1] Original in the Hartenau Archives, a copy in the Hesse State Archives.

saw in Bismarck and in Prussia's hegemony the only way of realising the dream of a united German Reich. He also had, years later, good reason to regret his hostility towards Bismarck, who never forgave him and, eventually, took his vengeance on his son Sandro.

But, in 1866, seeing his brother, the reigning Grand Duke completely disinterested in politics and most members of his family 'mesmerised by Bismarck and prepared to barter Hesse to Prussia', Alexander once again thought of emigrating. He asked the Austrian Emperor for reinstatement in his army, but after the humiliating defeat, younger, ambitious leaders had emerged in Vienna and there was no room for a 'foreigner' in the Austrian army. All that Emperor Francis Joseph could do to reward Alexander for his loyalty was to make him an honorary General of Cavalry and increase his retirement pension.

As so often before, help came from St Petersburg. Prince Serge Dolgoruki, the brother of the Tsar's mistress, had become head of railway and mining finance syndicates. He invited Alexander to join him as a director. Alexander went to Russia, spent several months there, and his inherent shrewdness and skill as a negotiator contributed to the success of the enterprises.

His association with Prince Dolgoruki was, however, distasteful to him. He was greatly disturbed by what he saw in St Petersburg. His beloved sister Marie was in poor health and desperately unhappy about her husband's liaison with Catharine Dolgoruki, who now lived in a wing of the Tsar's palace and had borne him three children. The Tsar, with guilty conscience, tried to explain the situation to his brother-in-law and friend of his youth. At fifty, Alexander II of Russia was still a handsome, youthful-looking, virile man. He told Alexander that he still dearly loved 'our sweet little Marie', who had borne him nine children, but pleaded for understanding, saying that his marital relations with his ailing wife had long since ended, and that he needed a partner in love.

Catharine Dolgoruki's father, the extravagant Prince Michael, had squandered the fortune of his ancient family and his daughter had become the Tsar's ward. Alexander knew her from birth, but saw her only again when she was 16, a pupil at the famous Smolny Institute. At 18 she was received at Court and the Tsar fell head over heels in love with the beautiful girl, whose father he could have been. 'Do you understand, my dear brother, that I love them both, our Marie and my little Katie . . .?' the Tsar asked with tears in his eyes. All that Alexander could answer was that he understood and that he bore no grudge. As the years went by and his sister was slowly dying from tuberculosis, Alexander accepted the Tsar's love affair, and he eventually learnt to like and respect the beautiful and intelligent Catharine.

When Napoleon invited the Tsar in the summer of 1867 to the Paris World Exhibition, Alexander accompanied him. Catharine Dolgoruki was spending a holiday in Naples and arrived in Paris with her brother, Prince Serge, Alexander's business partner. The Tsar was staying as the Emperor's guest at the Elysée palace, but this did not prevent him from receiving Catharine there, an arrangement which shocked even Napoleon. Princess Julie of Battenberg was to join her husband in Paris, but Alexander wrote and begged her to stay at home: 'It would not be decent for a respectable woman to share the company of the Tsar's courtesan'. The dashing lover of yesterday had become a puritan.

The visit in Paris almost ended in tragedy. On June 6th when the Tsar was returning from a military review in the Champs de Mars, with Alexander following in the second carriage, a Polish emigré fired two revolver shots at the Tsar, shouting 'Long live free Poland', but the shots missed.

Alexander returned to the peace of Heiligenberg. Having been brought up by tutors and servants, he was anxious to devote as much time as he could to his children. His diplomatic travels and his war service had kept him for such long periods from home that he only slowly began to realise that his daughter was a young woman, now betrothed to the Prince of Erbach-Schönberg, and that his boys were also growing up. The eldest, Louis – the later Marquess of Milford Haven – was sent to England to join the Royal Navy as a cadet, the second, Alexander, called Sandro by all, was soon to join the military academy at Dresden.

In his diary Alexander noted: 'Louis was full of mischief and often failed to attend his lessons . . . he is leading his younger brothers to mischief and disobedience'. There were entries saying that 'I had to thrash the elder boys because there seems no other way to deal with their high spirits'.

He was, of course, a 'Victorian father', but his was a happy, closely-knit family, and the boys, if high spirited, were assiduous in their studies, spoke four languages and had exquisite manners. Their intelligence, quick wit and demeanour compared well with the qualities of many German princelings; most of them dull-witted and gauche youngsters.

Their foreign relatives were very fond of them and the Tsar had asked Alexander to send at least one of his boys to St Petersburg. When, much later, the choice fell upon Sandro, the result was tragic. Likewise, Princess Alice, 'the English princess' with whom Alexander quarrelled over Bismarck, was very fond of both Louis and Henry, and it was on her and her brother Alfred's insistence that the two boys entered the service of Queen Victoria.

His only daughter Marie was, in 1870, eighteen years old, an attractive and charming young woman, serious-minded and well-educated. The Tsaritsa had been looking around for a suitable match for her and discussed it with her parents when the Russian imperial family paid one of their annual visits to Heiligenberg. Alexander had arranged shooting parties for his brother-in-law, and invited the notorious medium Daniel Home – at that time the rage of London and Paris – to entertain the Tsaritsa, whose health had temporarily taken a turn for the better. Home was an accomplished ventriloquist and produced manifestations of 'spirits' which gave 'dictations', and the Russian imperial couple, with their hosts and a few guests attended such seances almost every evening.

While spiritualism provided a pleasant distraction from state affairs, the Tsar and Alexander discussed the new crisis in Europe's balance of power caused by Napoleon's insistence that Bismarck should fulfil his promise and cede to France territories on the Rhine – the price for French neutrality during the Austro-Prussian war in 1866. Bismarck denied that he had ever given such formal promises. After the Spanish revolution and the deposition of Queen Isabel, Marshal Serrano's government in Madrid was looking for a new ruler. Portuguese, Italian and German princes were lined up as possible candidates, when Bismarck appeared on the scene with Prince Leopold of Hohenzollern, a relative of the King of Prussia, as his candidate.

Napoleon declared that a Prussian prince on the throne of neighbouring Spain would be an insult to France. He exchanged letters with the Tsar, Queen Victoria, Emperor Francis Joseph and the King of Italy, trying to secure a coalition against 'the

Prussian nightmare which threatens Europe', and, without asking Alexander for his formal consent, proposed the Prince of Hesse for the Madrid throne. Once again a crown seemed to be within Alexander's grasp. But neither the Tsar nor London nor Vienna were prepared to rally with France against Bismarck. The Tsar, worried about the upsurge of revolutionary movements in Russia openly expressed his sympathy for Bismarck's policy, 'a safe-guard against the spreading of anarchy throughout Europe'.

Thus, when on 15 July 1870, the Franco-Prussian war broke out, Alexander watched with despair the rapid surge of the Prussian armies into France. Even at that moment he tried in great secrecy to induce the Austrian Emperor and the King of Italy to go to Napoleon's help, appealing to Francis Joseph to seize the opportunity and avenge Koeniggraetz. But Austria was already secretly committed with Prussia and, in any case, when these messages were exchanged the Prussians had crushed Napoleon's armies, and soon after the French Emperor became their prisoner at Sedan. There was no doubt in Alexander's mind now that Prussian militarism could, and one day probably would, dominate Europe.

When the King of Prussia after his victory over Napoleon was proclaimed Kaiser of the new German Empire, Alexander, after much heart-searching began to realise that he had to come to terms with the great changes in European balance of power, marked by the growing power of Germany, the weakness of France, the indifference of Britain and the revolutionary dangers developing in Russia. He consoled himself with the thought that, at least in one sense, the new German Reich would become a bulwark of European stability. Although liberal-minded, Alexander firmly believed in the established traditions and in the divine rights of crowned heads. Thus, after some hesitation, he accepted an invitation from the new German Crown Prince Frederick and his English wife to meet them at Bad Homburg. He knew that Crown Princess Victoria despised Bismarck as strongly as he did, and he was pleased that the invitation – in contrast to those extended by other royalties in the past – was offered not only to himself but also to his wife and his two elder children, Marie and Louis. Moreover, on the eve of his daughter's wedding to a German prince, he did not want to antagonize the Prussians.

Marie had fallen in love with the handsome Prince Gustavus Ernest of Erbach-Schönberg, whose family, once autonomous rulers of a tiny principality in the Rhine Palatinate, was very wealthy and of equal rank with ruling German princes. The Tsar and Tsaritsa had readily approved this match of her niece, and for a while politics were thrust aside for a happy family reunion at Darmstadt. The Russian relatives behaved in truly imperial manner. The Tsar provided Marie's dowry – 50,000 roubles – and gave her a splendid wedding present, a brooch of diamonds and pearls, whilst the Tsaritsa, whose godchild Marie was, presented her with a magnificent diamond tiara, a silver table set, and paid for her wedding dress of valuable lace.

At Marie's wedding, at which many of the Russian, German and English relatives had gathered, the project of a marriage between Prince Alfred, Duke of Edinburgh, Queen Victoria's 27-year-old son, and Grand Duchess Marie, the 18-year-old daughter of the Tsar, came up for discussion. Alexander persuaded his reluctant sister and brother-in-law to consider it favourably. Almost two years of discreet correspondence passed until Alexander's match-making succeeded. In July 1873, Alexander took advantage of a visit of the Tsar's family at Heiligenberg and invited Prince Alfred for another meeting with the Russians.

In the meantime Marie of Erbach-Schönberg, 'deliriously happy in her marriage', had given birth to a fine boy. With her husband and her baby she was amongst the guests. Although the Tsar, and particularly the Tsaritsa who strongly disliked Queen Victoria, were still reluctant, the display of their Battenberg niece's happiness apparently influenced their attitude towards the project of 'the English marriage' of their daughter. Power politics played, of course, an important part. Ever since the Russian advance in Central Asia and towards Afghanistan, relations between Russia and Great Britain were becoming more strained. The affection which had grown up between Prince Alfred and Grand Duchess Marie played only a secondary role in the considerations, which, in the end, induced both the Tsar and Queen Victoria to approve the link: it was a convenient means for a *rapprochement* between London and St Petersburg. Thus, as so often in the past, the diplomatic skill of Alexander of Hesse was triumphant. The marriage between Queen Victoria's son and the Tsar's daughter took place at St Petersburg on 28 January 1874, with all the pomp of the Imperial Court. The bride was given a magnificent dowry – a million roubles by the Russian government and 600,000 roubles by the Tsar, which secured for Prince Alfred, the Duke of Edinburgh, and his wife an annual income of £32,000, an extraordinary sum in those days, even for a son and daughter of emperors.

After the Tsar's visit to London, Queen Victoria expressed in a long letter to Alexander her appreciation for all his efforts, and she assured him that she would continue to take a motherly interest in his son Louis 'who is a dear boy and is doing extremely well in my Navy'.

In his retirement at Heiligenberg, Alexander, in spite of the many disappointments he had suffered in his personal ambition for a European throne, could justifiably nurse high hopes for the future of his Battenberg sons.

CHAPTER FIVE

THE MAKING AND BREAKING OF THE PRINCE OF BULGARIA

Prince Alexander of Battenberg

THE only Battenberg prince to gain a throne became a pawn of power politics in the Balkans. Four times his father, Alexander of Hesse, had been cheated of a crown; twice Bismarck thwarted him because he had served Prussia's adversaries. But his ambition of a crown was insatiable, and realising that it would never be fulfilled he succeeded in getting one, at least, for one of his sons.

His second son, Prince Alexander of Battenberg – known as Sandro because of the many similar names in the family – became the ruler of Bulgaria. Sent there as Russia's satrap he quarrelled with the Tsar and lost his support. Sandro's love for the daughter of the German Crown Prince Frederick made him the tragic hero of a woeful royal romance, created the 'Battenberg Affair' which envenomed relations between Britain, Russia and Germany, led to a clash of wills between Queen Victoria and Bismarck, caused a rift between the English-born Crown-Princess Victoria and her son, the later Kaiser William II, and ultimately enabled Bismarck to destroy him. Sandro of Battenberg, Prince of Bulgaria, was to die in exile, under an assumed name, finding solace in marriage to an Austrian opera singer, forsaken and forgotten, at the age of thirty-six.

The story of his Bulgarian crown begins in the mid-seventies, with the Balkans in turmoil. The oppression of the Christian peoples by the Sultan's officials and Mohammedan landlords had led to revolts in Bosnia and the Danubian provinces of the Ottoman Empire. Bulgar insurgents were suppressed with hideous brutality; in London Gladstone thundered against the 'Bulgarian atrocities', telling the Turks to get 'bag and baggage out of the provinces they had desolated and profaned', even though Disraeli feared Russian dominance if Turkey were weakened.

In 1878 the Tsar, influenced by Pan-Slav emotions spreading in Russia, stretching out his hand for Constantinople and a new Byzant, and anxious to divert attention from Nihilism proclaimed that he was 'coming to the aid of our oppressed Slav brothers'.

The news of the outbreak of the Russo-Turkish war was received with great excitement at Heiligenberg. At 18 Sandro of Battenberg was a lieutenant in the Dragoon Regiment of his uncle, the Grand Duke of Hesse, but service in sleepy Darmstadt was very uneventful. The suggestion from his other uncle, the Tsar, to join the Russian army was, therefore, welcome. His father, who had never faltered in his allegiance to Russia, gladly consented. The tall, handsome and bright boy had always been the Tsar's favourite nephew.

Sandro had received an excellent education, part of which he had gained at the Schnepfental boarding school, whose headmaster Dr Wilhelm Ausfeld was an educationist far ahead of his times. There were similarities between Schnepfental and the schools of Salem and Gordonstoun which Dr Kurt Hahn was to create half a century later, and where Sandro's great-nephew Prince Philip was to receive an education which stamped his personality. But whereas Hahn's ideas were of a cosmopolitan élite, Dr Ausfeld's aim had been to produce leaders of the new German Reich. Sandro's father came to dislike the 'Prussianism' of this school, and three years later sent the boy to the Dresden military academy of the King of Saxony who had fought Prussia in 1866.

During the campaign against the Turks Sandro took part in several engagements in Bulgaria, and his war adventures included the rescue of 800 Bulgarian women from rape and massacre at the hands of savage Turkish Bashi Bazouks. He learnt to love the Bulgars and in his letters to his father described them as 'unbelievably brave, honest and gay people'. When the Sultan was forced to sue for peace and Sandro entered Constantinople with his regiment, he heard from Russian generals that the Tsar would offer the crown of an independent Bulgaria to his father. He excitedly reported this to Heiligenberg, but it was no surprise to Alexander of Hesse who had already been summoned to St Petersburg.

At the Congress of Berlin, Britain and Austria, fearing Russian encroachments in the Balkans and the Near East, strongly opposed the Tsar's plans for a 'Greater Bulgaria'. Bismarck acted as a mediator and eventually a smaller Bulgaria was created, with the southern province of Eastern Rumelia remaining under the Sultan's suzerainty. British hostility to the Tsar's original plan – which Disraeli described as an attempt at establishing a 'Little Russia' in the Balkans – was fanned by a harmless incident at Constantinople, which had been wildly magnified in British newspapers.

The German ambassador gave a lunch for Sandro and his brother Louis, then a lieutenant in H.M.S. *Sultan*, one of the British ships sent to the Dardanelles as a warning to the Tsar. Louis took Sandro to his ship, where he was received with great courtesy by the captain – Prince Alfred, Duke of Edinburgh. Sandro was introduced to Admiral Hornby and was later shown over other ships, including the Royal Navy's newest ironclad H.M.S. *Temeraire*. When reports of Sandro's visit reached London, newspapers violently attacked 'the Russian spy', who had been allowed to see something as secret as the mechanism of a new Whitehead torpedo. Admiral Hornby and even Prince Alfred were not spared, an Admiralty investigation was demanded, Queen Victoria petulantly described her son's behaviour as 'anti-national', and the result was that Prince Alfred was relieved of his command and Louis of Battenberg was ordered to London for transfer to another ship.

Although, in the end, all was forgiven, the incident had poisoned Anglo-Russian relations, already strained by Disraeli's determination to bar to Russia the road to the Bosporus. The Tsaritsa, in her hatred of everything English, fizzed angrily about the insults offered to her Battenberg nephews. She wrote to her brother at Heiligenberg about Sandro: 'The poor boy is beside himself that the Queen [Victoria], that crazy old hag, made him a pretext for persecuting Alfred and more especially Louis'.

Having persuaded the Tsar at the Congress of Berlin to accept the compromise of a 'small' Bulgaria, and rejecting Alexander of Hesse as 'entirely unacceptable', Bismarck supported the Tsar when the 21-year-old Sandro of Battenberg was proposed for the

Bulgarian throne. Covetous for his family's fortune Alexander of Hesse had gone to Berlin, Vienna and St Petersburg in order to advance his son's chances. He told Bismarck: 'I did not expect that you would support me but I am grateful for your help for my son. Even though he is a Russian officer, he is a German prince. You know that neither I nor he would ever turn against the German Emperor or against Germany'. Bismarck accepted this statement from his old enemy with good grace. In Vienna Alexander of Hesse reminded Emperor Francis Joseph of his own war service in the Austrian army and assured him that Sandro would not be a Russian puppet. Disraeli, having robbed Russia of most of the fruits of her victory, willingly accepted Sandro, particularly as Queen Victoria was greatly in favour of the Battenberg's candidature. From St Petersburg, Alexander of Hesse could inform his son: 'Everything is arranged. The crown of Bulgaria is yours'.

But Sandro was not yet on the throne. Even when the National Assembly met at the ancient Bulgarian capital of Tirnovo to devise a constitution and elect the new prince, there were a score of candidates – German, Danish, Serbian and Montenegrin princes, rich bojars from Moldavia who offered bribes to the Assembly members – and Prince Dondukov-Korsakov, the Tsar's governor in Sofia, busy with intrigue against the 'German prince'. However, the National Assembly on 29 April 1879 elected Sandro of Battenberg by acclamation, 'the nephew of our beloved Tsar-Liberator, and the only one of the candidates who had fought on the battlefields for Bulgaria's freedom'.

A deputation was to go to Darmstadt where Sandro was waiting, but the Tsar insisted that the Bulgarian crown should be conferred by his hand in Livadia in the Crimea, and Sandro and the deputation travelled to the Tsar's summer residence. There, with tears streaming down his cheeks, the Tsar told the Bulgarian notables: 'From my hands receive your new prince and sovereign. Love him as I love him'. Sandro replied with a little speech his father had composed and rehearsed with him.

Before he set off for Bulgaria, Sandro visited Vienna, Berlin, Paris, London and Constantinople to pay his tributes. When he discussed with Bismarck the rivalries that beset Bulgarian politics and expressed some anxiety about his own future, the German Chancellor said with a wry smile: 'Do not worry, my dear Prince. Take your crown – one day it will be a pleasant souvenir'. It was a prophecy which was to come true earlier than Sandro expected.

Queen Victoria invited him to Windsor, acted most graciously and reiterated that 'the silly spy affair in Constantinople is forgotten and done with', but told him that he 'should not become too Russian, remember his allegiance to his family and not only to the Romanovs'. When the Tsaritsa heard about it from her brother, she wrote: 'I am pleased to hear that the Queen was friendly. It appears that Brown[1] has deigned to approve of the new Bulgaria and of Sandro'.

During the protracted international manoeuvres over Bulgaria, many events had taken place which affected the destinies of the Hesse and Battenberg families. In June 1877 the fat and eccentric Grand Duke Louis III died in Darmstadt and was succeeded by his nephew, Louis, who had married Princess Alice, Queen Victoria's second daughter. Within a year of becoming the Grand Duchess, Alice died at the age of 34. In Russia the Tsar had to abandon his plans for liberal reforms. Revolutionary movements were spreading, several governors and chiefs of the secret police were assassinated and an attempt on the Tsar's life was made in March 1879, the first of several to follow. But the saddest news received at Heiligenberg was that the Tsaritsa's health was rapidly failing.

Compared with the tension in Russia, Bulgaria appeared peaceful when Sandro reached Sofia. He had travelled, after a visit in St Petersburg, aboard a Russian warship from Odessa to the Bulgarian port of Varna where he arrived on 6 June 1879 during a heavy thunderstorm which many regarded as a bad omen. His reception by the people was genuinely friendly. Crowds cheered him all the way when he entered his capital on horseback, wearing the kolpak, the traditional Bulgarian peasant cap. But he was soon made to realise that Prince Dondukov, the Tsar's governor, regarded him as a mere puppet.

The Prince of Bulgaria found himself surrounded by Russian officers and officials. He was allowed to choose some of his Ministers, but was told that the Minister of War and the Minister of Interior and Police must be Russian officers. Bulgarian politics were extremely complex. In the first flush of newly-won inde-

[1] The Queen's Scottish gillie who was regarded abroad as her lover.

pendence, the National Assembly had given a most liberal Constitution to a country which was tribal, patriarchal and mostly illiterate. Its thinly spread intelligentsia and the handful of political leaders, educated in Western Europe or in Russia, were bitterly divided. The Conservatives strove for a 'Bulgaria for the Bulgars', the Liberals were incongruously aligned with Russian reaction, propounding Panslavist ideas and turning against the 'German' prince.

At the outset of his reign, Sandro suffered many humiliating pin-pricks. Embittered by having lost the chance of becoming ruler himself, Governor Dondukov vacated the Konak, the royal palace, but took all his furniture with him. Sofia was then a mere outgrown village of 20,000 inhabitants, with unpaved streets, open sewers, a few rows of streets around the ruins of the Byzantine St Sophia Cathedral (which, turned into a mosque under Turkish rule, had been almost completely destroyed in the earthquake of 1858), and wooden shacks where the poor lived. The National Assembly met in a gaming club established by a Frenchman for wealthy notables and landowners.

The Konak was a one storey house with an entrance leading to a hall with a shaky, wooden staircase to the Prince's private suite. It had been hurriedly enlarged, but the newly erected walls were of unplastered baked mud. The suite consisted of three rooms, a drawing room, a working room and a bedroom. The roof of the palace leaked, and a rough timber canopy had to be erected above the Prince's bed to prevent rainwater dripping onto his blankets. The Russian governor had removed even the enamelled bath-tub, which was replaced by a tin one; hot water had to be carried in buckets from the kitchen below. The kitchen staff consisted of an elderly Bulgar and his wife, whose gastronomic knowledge was limited to strongly spiced mutton dishes which Sandro, still suffering from after-effects of his war-time dysentery, could not stomach.

The 'State rooms' on the ground floor were large but bare, furnished with a few benches and chairs with cushions filled with wood shavings like in a peasant's cottage. The 'Throne Room', where the Prince was supposed to receive foreign ambassadors, contained a few card tables with vodka-stained green baize and chalk marks – mementoes of the Russian governor's gambling parties. Sandro brought three personal aides, all young German brother-officers; they became his Court Chamberlain, his ADC and his secretary, and were bitterly resented by the established Russian and Bulgarian officials. The aides were appalled by this royal residence, but Sandro, taking discomfort and humiliation with good humour, consoled them. He ordered furniture from a Vienna store and begged his mother to send him 'a few good pieces and ornaments from Heiligenberg, which would remind me of our comfortable home'.

For the Ministers he was allowed to appoint, he selected leaders of the Conservative Party who agreed with him that only an independent policy could avoid conflict with Austria and the Western Powers and prevent Bulgaria becoming a helpless satellite of Russia. But the first election for the Sobranie in October 1879 brought a crushing defeat for his Conservative Cabinet supported by only 30 of 170 members of the new parliament. The rest were Panslavists, Liberals and Radicals, almost all pro-Russian and exponents of the 'Greater Bulgaria' policy. However, a few of the new deputies, particularly the youngest and most brilliant of them, 22-year-old Stefan Stambulov, were sympathetic to the Prince's ideas of Bulgarian independence.

Had Sandro been more mature and less impetuous, he might have gained by playing off the ambitious politicians against each other. But he decided to dissolve the Sobranie, declaring that 'its composition made it impossible to carry out the business of government and safeguard law and order'. This brought about the wrath of his Russian Minister of War, a young, hard-drinking colonel, and his Russian 'political adviser', General Shepelev, who were plotting against him with Panslavist leaders. His father advised him to go to St Petersburg and put his troubles before the Tsar. He drafted for his son a sixteen-page memorandum, outlining the political difficulties in Bulgaria and suggesting the only solution – a dictatorship with ultimate power in Sandro's hands. Ironically, the autocratic Tsar advised, his nephew 'to be more sensible and adhere to the constitutional path'. Although formally observing the Berlin pact, the Tsar encouraged Panslav plans for a 'little Russia' in the Balkans. Hoping to dissuade him and to make him agree to the removal of Russian plotters, Sandro travelled in February 1880 to St Petersburg. His father, using a visit to his ailing sister as a pretext, hurried with his eldest son, Louis, from Darmstadt to take charge of the negotiations. The train which brought them from Germany on 17 February was late, and this delay saved the Tsar's life. Nihilists had placed several mines beneath the luncheon room and two salons of the Winter Palace, after months of tunnelling. The Tsar was greeting his brother-in-law and nephew when terrific explosions shook the palace. 'Everything was enveloped in a thick cloud of smoke and dust, the floor shook under our feet, the gas jets flared high for a moment and then all was covered in darkness', Alexander wrote to his wife at Heiligenberg. In the confusion Alexander and his son lost sight of the Tsar and believed that he was wounded or dead. Shrieks and groans were heard when they ran along the corridors towards the Tsaritsa's bedroom. The Tsar had remained unhurt and his first thought was not of his wife but of his mistress, Princess Dolgoruki, whose rooms were near the centre of the first explosion. Running towards them he shouted: 'Katia, my dearest Katia!' Neither she nor any member of the imperial family were hurt, but a little later a palefaced adjutant reported to the Tsar that eleven court officials, officers and guardsmen had been killed, and forty-four, mainly soldiers of the Finnish Guards, wounded in the outrage.

Under such circumstances neither the Tsar nor his Ministers were in the mood to think of Bulgarian problems. Sandro returned empty-handed to Sofia. 'I realised that in future I must stand on my own feet,' he later wrote to his father; 'I cannot count on the Tsar's help and protection.' He bitterly complained of 'treachery and corruption which pervaded Bulgaria'. With some of his father's financier friends he had tried to bring some order into the economy of his young state. But by bribery and influence, Russian speculators had gained control of financial and business enterprises. Prince Dondukov had founded the State Bank of Bulgaria, his friends had secured concessions for railway lines – either without or against the Prince's decisions.

In a stream of letters to the Tsar, Sandro described all this and, completely frustrated by silences and evasive replies, eventually told his uncle that he was thinking of abdicating and leaving Bulgaria. The Tsar replied: 'As long as I live it is your duty to keep the crown I gave you'. By then the Tsar was convinced that he had not long to live, and that any solution of the Bulgarian problem must be left to his successor. The revolutionary 'executive committee' had sentenced the Tsar to death; their leaflets announced that 'the avengers of the people would not rest until the tyrant and his henchmen lay dead'.

On 2 June 1880 the Tsaritsa died. During the last weeks of her life, emaciated almost to a skeleton, she had been barely conscious. No one was at her bedside when she died. The Tsar communicated his wife's death to her brother at Heiligenberg thus: 'The soul of our dear Marie is in heaven'. But less than six weeks later, on 18 June, he married Catharine Dolgoruki. It was a morganatic marriage, but the Tsar asked his Ministers and the Holy Synod of the Orthodox Church to make the marriage constitutional and his beloved Katia the Empress of Russia. He did not live long enough to see his wish carried out. Nihilist attempts had become ceaseless. Several governors and chiefs of the secret police were assassinated and the 'executioners' efforts were now directed against the Tsar. One plan involved the renting of a grocer's shop in the Sadovaya Street in St Petersburg and the digging of a tunnel under the street, the Tsar's usual processional route. Bombs were brought into the shop in butterkegs. After two abortive attempts, eventually four men and a woman, all carrying bombs, were placed at different vantage points along the route of the Tsar's return in a sledge from a review at the St Michael's Cavalry barracks on 13 March 1881.

On the Katherine Embankment a young man flung a parcel at the sledge. Though the assassin and some of the Cossack escort were killed, the Tsar remained unhurt. In the confusion which ensued another Nihilist, named Grinevitzky, calmly approached the sledge and threw a bomb only three feet from the Tsar. It tore off both the Tsar's legs below the knees and opened the left side of his body, splattering intestines on to his cloak. The assassin himself was blown to pieces. Despite his hideous wounds the Tsar remained conscious. To one of his adjutants he murmured: 'Quick, home . . . take me home to die . . . not here.' Thirty minutes later he died in his palace.

When Alexander of Hesse and Sandro joined the mourners at the lying in state, they knew that the Battenbergs had lost their friends in St Petersburg. The new Tsar, Alexander III, as coarse as his father had been gentle and cultivated, with strong Pan-Slav leanings and anti-German, had never approved of Sandro on Bulgaria's throne, having demanded it from his father for his

Danish brother-in-law, Prince Valdemar. Although he had often visited Heiligenberg with his parents, he was the only one of the Tsar's children who had never made friends with his Battenberg cousins.

The new Tsar lived in constant fear of assassination; he rarely left the Anitshkov Palace which he had turned into a fortress, surrounded by a deep moat to prevent it being mined by Nihilists. In order to divert his people's attention from revolutionary movements he encouraged the 'Black Hundred' organisation to stage Jewish pogroms. Although he never gave up the idea of Russia's conquest of Constantinople, he declared himself to be disinterested in the Balkans, trying to establish better relations with Austro-Hungary and Germany. However hostile he remained to Sandro, he agreed to recall some of the Russian 'advisers', and to replace them by men with some understanding of Sandro's high-minded ideas for reorganising his country and repulsing intrigues of venal Russian officials and speculators. One of the new men was General Ernrot, of Finnish-German origin. He became Chief Minister and arranged the elections for a new Sobranie. Sandro toured the country, arousing the peasants' enthusiasm for a 'really free Bulgaria', promising land reforms, farm modernization and better education. Although the election was conducted Balkan-fashion, with special commissars supervising the voting and the Prince's opponents put behind bars, there was genuine popular support for the new policy. The result was that all but fifteen members of the new parliament supported the Prince when he asked for special powers for the next seven years.

Sandro deprived the Sobranie of almost all its constitutional powers and made himself a *de facto* autocrat. Vainly the defeated leaders of the Liberals and Radicals appealed to Britain, France and the Tsar to end the Prince's dictatorship. The Tsar and his Foreign Minister, Giers, eyed the events in Bulgaria with undisguised hostility but decided for reasons of international policy to wait and see how far Sandro dared to go. Although Gladstone pursued a pro-Russian policy and was deeply concerned about Sandro's *coup d'etat* he could do little about it. At that time Sandro's elder brother Louis became betrothed to his cousin Victoria of Hesse, the granddaughter of Queen Victoria, and the Hesse and Battenberg families came once again into closer relationship with the British royal family and enjoyed the Queen's ardent support.

For some time Sandro's father and mother had been looking for a wife for him. Alexander of Hesse, that experienced royal match-maker, had found several suitable, wealthy, and more important, politically useful princesses. One was Helen of Mecklemburg-Strelitz, whose mother was Grand Duchess Catharine, a cousin of the Tsar. A marriage such as this promised to improve Sandro's strained relations with St Petersburg. Another was a Princess of Weimar, related to both the German and Russian dynasties, and through the Coburgs to the British royal family; a third the Austrian Archduchess Maria Antonia, a niece of Emperor Francis Joseph. The Mecklemburg princess was regarded as the most advantageous proposition, and for weeks Julie of Battenberg telegraphed her son daily, urging him to agree to this match. But Sandro knew that Princess Helen's brother and sister were 'complete idiots' and he asked his mother 'why should Helen be anything else?' The suggestion of a marriage with the Austrian archduchess he countered by declaring that it would only worsen his relations with Russia.

In fact, Sandro was in love and he was determined to win the girl for whom he felt a deep affection which was fully reciprocated. During his short service in the German Emperor's Garde du Corps while waiting for Bulgaria's throne, Sandro had met 16-year-old Princess Vicky, the daughter of Crown Prince Frederick and his English-born wife, Princess Victoria. The two young people – Sandro was 19 at that time – had fallen deeply in love and had vowed to wait for each other, whatever happend. Only the girl's mother, Queen Victoria's daughter, knew about it and favoured the match, even though she knew that Bismarck would never approve of it.

After Sandro became the Prince of Bulgaria, he continued a lively correspondence with his secret fiancée. Bismarck, whose secret police intercepted letters of every important personage, soon learnt about the secret understanding between the two. The Chancellor was working on a *rapprochement* between Germany, Austria and Russia – which was to lead to the Three Emperors Pact – and he did not want to antagonize the Tsar by a marriage with the out-of-favour Bulgarian ruler to a German princess. Personal spite against Alexander of Hesse and his sons was another motive for Bismarck's determination to foil this marriage project. The Battenbergs were aiming too high: one had married into the British royal family, another was betrothed to Queen Victoria's daughter Beatrice, the third was reaching for the German Crown Prince's daughter. When Sandro went to Berlin to ask Vicky's parents for their daughter's hand and the Emperor for his consent, Bismarck made it clear that such a marriage was out of the question. The Emperor blandly refused, and Vicky's parents told the young lovers to wait. Help came, however, from Queen Victoria to whom Sandro had confided at his brother Louis's wedding in Darmstadt. The Queen told him she would 'gladly and firmly support his proposal to her favourite grand-daughter', and Sandro returned to Bulgaria reassured that Queen Victoria would encourage Vicky's parents to give their consent.

The courtship was to become the notorious 'Battenberg Affair', which rocked European politics in the late 1880s, and because of Bismarck's and the Tsar's hostility accelerated Sandro's downfall. When Vicky warned him that their letters were being intercepted, Sandro persuaded his brother Henry, first in Germany and later in London, to act as a smuggling *postillon d'amour*. A correspondence also developed between the old Queen and the young Prince which was as touching as it was politically significant. In September 1884, Queen Victoria sent Major General Sir Howard Elphinstone, who had been her son's tutor and had become her trusted confidant, to Berlin in order to sound the aged Emperor William. She gave Sir Howard detailed instructions:

'He should know that Princess Victoria of Prussia is very much attached to the Prince of Bulgaria and *vice versa*; my daughter, the Crown Princess favours the project and the Crown Prince is not disinclined to it but the Emperor and Empress are violently against it, and they are very unkind, and the Empress especially won't look at or speak to the poor girl; and her brothers and sisters are also most unkind. Sir Howard should . . . put in a friendly word as he can say he knows the Queen is strongly in favour of it, having a high opinion of the Prince of Bulgaria and of his elder brother, Prince Louis of Battenberg, who is universally liked in England.'

But General Elphinstone did not succeed with the Emperor

and the matter came to a head when Henry of Battenberg married Princess Beatrice in July 1885. The German Crown Princess, greatly pleased about the marriage of her youngest sister, discussed Sandro's proposal to her daughter with her son William (the later Kaiser William II) and they had 'a terrible row'. The ill-tempered prince was furious: 'As usual, the Battenbergs cause trouble. Such a marriage would only result in a rift between Germany and Russia,' he said, added abusive remarks and declared he did not want a Battenberg in his family. When his mother checked him, he left Potsdam 'in a flaming mood'. The Crown Princess, now an active if clandestine accomplice of the young lovers, consoled them by saying that the Emperor was 88, that her husband would soon succeed him and that all would be well.

In the meantime great events were taking place in Bulgaria which for a while distracted Sandro from his personal affairs. Bulgarian nationalists had long been preparing a revolt in the Turkish-ruled province of Eastern Rumelia which had been excluded from a 'Greater Bulgaria' by the Congress of Berlin. Army officers, against Sandro's explicit orders, had formed 'free corps' which raided the province, and on 18 September 1885 the revolt broke out at Philippopolis. The Turkish governor was taken prisoner, his small garrison surrendered, and the revolutionary committee appealed to Sandro to occupy Eastern Rumelia by regular Bulgarian troops and to proclaim the annexation of the province which the Bulgars had claimed for so long as part of their country.

Although aware of possibly grave international repercussions, Sandro had to accept the appeal. When he arrived in Eastern Rumelia at the head of his troops he was greeted as a liberator. The annexation flouted decisions of the Great Powers, created the forbidden 'Greater Bulgaria', but passed without the dangers which Sandro had feared. Tsar Alexander III accepted it as a Panslavist victory, though he grudged Sandro his enhanced status and popularity. The Sultan, politically and militarily impotent, could do nothing, Austro-Hungary expressed displeasure but took no stronger measures, London and Berlin seemed content.

The only violent reaction came from Belgrade. King Milan of Serbia not unjustifiably regarded the Greater Bulgaria as a

Princess Ena of Battenberg at the time of her engagement in 1906 to King Alfonso XIII of Spain.

Prince Maurice of Battenberg (her brother), youngest son of Henry of Battenberg and Princess Beatrice, died at 23 of wounds received in action in France in October 1914. (*After a painting by de Laszlo.*)

ROYAL FAMILY GROUP IN OSBORNE IN 1898
From left to right: Prince Leopold of Battenberg, Princess of Anhalt with Prince Edward (now Duke of Windsor), Duchess of York (Queen Mary) with Princess Mary, Princess Margaret of Connaught, Prince Alexander of Battenberg, Duke of York (King George V) with Prince Albert (King George VI), Queen Victoria, Prince Arthur of Connaught, Duchess of Connaught, Princess Beatrice, Princess Patricia of Connaught (with dog), Princess Ena of Battenberg (Queen of Spain), Princess Victoria of Schleswig-Holstein, Prince Maurice of Battenberg.

Admiral Prince Louis of Battenberg, when Director of Naval Intelligence, with his two sons, George (later the 2nd Marquess of Milford Haven) and Dickie (the present Earl Mountbatten of Burma).

challenge. The Serbs and Bulgars had been traditional adversaries for centuries, vieing with each other for the leadership of the Christian peoples under Ottoman rule. Since the creation of Bulgaria, King Milan had increasingly leaned towards Austro-Hungary. Now Vienna encouraged him to check Bulgar aspirations in the Balkans. When his demands for a withdrawal of Bulgarian troops from Rumelia and his claim for compensation for alleged damage caused by raids into Serbia were rejected by Sandro, King Milan declared war, confident of Austrian help. There was none; the Serbian army was defeated in November at Slivnitza, when Sandro personally led his troops into battle, and the Bulgarians invaded Serbia, taking several towns. Only then Austro-Hungary intervened and Sandro had to order withdrawal.

Although the four-month war ended in a peace treaty which under pressure of the Great Powers restored the *status quo*, Serbia had suffered a humiliating defeat and Sandro had greatly strengthened his position. When he toured his country in the spring of 1886 he was enthusiastically cheered as a national hero. Many of his former Panslavist adversaries now supported him, amongst them the young leader of the Radicals, Stefan Stambulov. But Sandro's victory over the Serbs, his greatly enhanced stature and popular support caused alarm in St Petersburg. His assertion that Bulgaria had fully achieved her national independence was interpreted in Russia as a 'betrayal' by the Tsar's former satrap. Sandro was accused of conspiring with Austro-Hungary, with Germany, with Britain. These accusations were baseless: Austria had been hostile to him since the Serbo-Bulgarian war, and Bismarck was no less so. There was no conspiracy with London, but for the solace of royal sympathy in the affairs of his heart. But the Tsar and his ministers were determined to discredit the Prince of Bulgaria. Officially inspired attacks in the Russian newspapers stated that 'Sandro's shoes had grown too big for him', that 'he had a swollen head', that he was losing the support of the Bulgarian army, that his abdication was imminent.

Sandro's relations with Russian officers and officials and their hangers-on in Sofia became intolerable. At a dinner at the Konak, when the health of the Prince was proposed, his own Minister of War, the Russian Colonel Timmler, ostentatiously pushed away his glass, remaining seated and gazing insolently at Sandro when the toast was drunk. The Prince remained calm, but after the dinner told Timmler that he was dismissed and must leave Bulgaria within 48 hours. Several other Russian officers, known to have plotted against the Prince, were also expelled and relations between Sofia and St Petersburg reached breaking point. The Tsar's foreign minister remarked at a diplomatic reception in the hearing of the Bulgarian envoy that 'the hours of the Prince of Bulgaria are numbered, and the Tsar will replace him by Prince Valdemar of Denmark; if Sandro did not go voluntarily, he would be forced to abdicate'. Russian diplomats canvassed in Europe's capitals the plan of his deposition.

While Bismarck was cautious not to support this idea openly, he stated that 'as long as he was Chancellor, Sandro's marriage project would never materialise'. Bismarck's hatred is shown by some of the marginal notes he wrote on official documents dealing with the situation in Bulgaria. On a report from the German ambassador in Vienna, against the remark that 'the Prince of Bulgaria was now very depressed since the German Government had dropped him', Bismarck wrote: 'Yes, he is the skeleton at the feast. He is trying to climb by marriage', and where the ambassador suggested that Sandro should not be entirely abandoned, even though he 'was not a paragon', Bismarck pencilled: 'Why on earth not abandon him?', and beside the word 'paragon', he wrote 'hooligan' with two exclamation marks. In his reply to the ambassador, Bismarck wrote: 'Battenberg . . . is a climber and a disturber of the peace, whose efforts to make a marriage, which Queen Victoria favours, are a political threat to us, so long as he remains Prince of Bulgaria'.[1]

At Christmas 1885, Queen Victoria sent Sandro a letter in her own handwriting:

'Dear Sandro! I must follow the impulse of my heart and tell you how warm and fervent my sympathy and prayers have been for you. My admiration for your heroic conduct that was at the same time so dignified and moderate is great. But we have all endured sad hours full of anxiety on your behalf since . . . the outbreak of the war . . . I will not enter into political affairs in this letter, which is only intended to express my personal feelings for you, and to wish you both a happy new year and continued prosperity.'

[1] Cf. Lepsius J., Mendelssohn-Bartholdy A. (Ed.) *Die Grosse Politik*. Vol. III, pp. 342 et seq., Berlin, 1922-7.

The Prince of Bulgaria was certainly in need of comfort. Since the beginning of 1886 he was warned by his Ministers that the pro-Russian party was planning rebellion and that Russian Okhrana agents had arrived to organise it. Several conspirators were arrested at Burgos and Rustchuk and his police chiefs reported the discovery of plans for his assassination. But elated by the wide popular support, and underrating the determination of his enemies, Sandro brushed off the warnings. 'There will always be a few hotheads who will oppose my efforts, but they too will one day realise that I work for the greatness and prosperity of our nation and for a Bulgaria free from foreign dictation,' he told his friends.

At two o-clock in the morning of 21 August 1886, when he was asleep in his palace, his valet Dimitri burst into his bedroom and cried: 'Your Highness, you are betrayed, the Konak is surrounded, they will murder you!'

The Prince looked out of the window and saw officers and cadets with rifles and fixed bayonets in the forecourt. They shouted: '*Dolu knjaz*, down with the Prince! Kill him!' He hurried downstairs, trying to reach a door leading into the garden. Some officers burst into the palace, overwhelmed the few guards and ran after him, firing shots. There was nothing that Sandro, still in his underwear and with a cloak thrown over his shoulders, could do but surrender.

Brought back to his study he was faced by a group of wildly looking young officers, many of them drunk. Their leader, Captain Radko Dimitriev, tore a page from the Prince's visitors' book and scribbled a few lines. He was so drunk that he could hardly hold the pen. With a pistol at the Prince's ribs, he shouted: 'This is your abdication, sign it, Battenberg!' Without reading the 'document', Sandro wrote at the bottom of the leaf: 'God protect Bulgaria. Alexander'.

At that moment his brother, Prince Francis Joseph of Battenberg, who was on a visit at the palace, was brought into the room and asked: 'What is happening, where are your guards?' Sandro replied with a bitter smile: 'Yes, where are they?' The princes were ordered to dress and were taken to the building of the War Ministry. Dimitriev told them that the entire garrison, including the Guards regiment and the cadets of the military school, had joined the revolution, all public buildings had been occupied and the Cabinet arrested. The commandant of the Palace guards had gone over to the revolutionaries, which accounted for the fact that the conspirators had been able to enter the Konak without firing a shot. But this was not quite true; some troops had remained loyal to the Prince but, confined to barracks by orders of rebel officers, knew nothing of the night's events.

Sandro and his brother were taken to the St Michael Monastery twenty miles outside the capital. After 24 hours the journey continued in several carriages to Varna, where the conspirators hoped that their prisoners would be collected by a Russian warship. But none had arrived and they were taken to the small Danube harbour of Rasovo, put aboard the Prince's yacht and locked in two cabins on the lower deck.

The yacht sailed up the Danube and arrived on 24 August at Reni near Galatz. Prince Sandro tried to bribe a guard and escape with his brother to the Rumanian bank of the river, but Rumanian police officers, who watched his disembarkation, told him they had orders not to interfere. They gave him Bucarest and Viennese newspapers with sensational reports of fighting in Sofia, of a counter-revolution led by Stefan Stambulov and the setting up of a loyalist government in Rustchuk. But, it seemed, nobody abroad knew what had happened to the kidnapped Prince.

Helplessly, Sandro listened to his captors who told him he would be taken to Odessa and thence to St Petersburg. But later Russian officers arrived with news that the Tsar had ordered his release, on condition that he and Prince Francis Joseph would agree to travel under Russian escort to Lemberg in Austria. The party arrived there on the 27th and only then Sandro learnt of the world's reaction to his kidnapping, and of the events which had taken place in Bulgaria during the past few days.

In Lemberg his brother Louis was waiting for him. By Queen Victoria's special permission – he was a serving Royal Navy officer – Prince Louis had hurried from London across half of Europe to bring Sandro good news. Queen Victoria had sent strongly worded telegrams to the Tsar and the German and Austrian Emperors. The British ambassadors in St Petersburg and Constantinople had been recalled. Lord Salisbury, who a few weeks earlier had become Tory prime minister after Gladstone's downfall, contemplated military action against Russia.

The situation in Bulgaria appeared much better than Sandro dared to expect. Only a few army units had joined the officer's rebellion, although some of Sandro's own Ministers and the Archbishop Klement of Sofia were implicated in the conspiracy.

Stefan Stambulov and Colonel Mutrakov had put themselves at the head of the loyalists. A provisional government under Stambulov issued a proclamation recalling the Prince. The rebel leaders had fled or had been arrested. Soon telegrams began to arrive from Sofia. Stambulov and Colonel Mutrakov, who had become the Commander-in-Chief of the loyal troops, wired: 'The whole Bulgarian nation and the army has overthrown the traitors of the revolutionary uprising. They beg their Prince Alexander to return home, wherever he might be at present.' Another telegram from Stambulov assured Sandro: 'New Government and whole army for the Prince. Country quiet. Long live Prince Alexander.' Stambulov sent similar telegrams to the Prince's father in Darmstadt.

Delighted with the good news, Alexander of Hesse urged his son to return to Bulgaria. On 26 August he had received in Darmstadt a visit from Professor Langenbuch, an emissary of the German Crown Princess who had discovered through diplomatic sources in Berlin that the Tsar intended to send Prince Dolgoruki to Bulgaria to take over the reins of government, and, if necessary, to bolster this mission by sending Russian troops and warships. Sandro's immediate return was, therefore, imperative if he was to forestall the Tsar's action.

While Sandro and his two brothers travelled to Rustchuk and were received by Stambulov and loyalist leaders amidst cheering crowds of peasants and soldiers, sober notes were being exchanged between St Petersburg, Berlin, Vienna, London and Constantinople. The Tsar informed the Great Powers that he was sending Prince Dolgoruki as his commissar to Sofia 'to restore law and order'. Russian troops were massing in Bessarabia and a Russian fleet steamed out of Black Sea ports.

It soon became obvious that Sandro's return, however welcome to many of his subjects, could not solve the 'Bulgarian Question'. When the National Assembly met for an emergency session, deputies were not unanimous in favour of the Prince's restoration; they knew the threat of Russian armed intervention was very real and could lead to civil war. Sandro discovered that three-

quarters of the officer corps and the entire Orthodox clergy had
been implicated in the revolt. The Russian consul, who met him
in Rustchuk, partly succeeded in convincing him that Stambulov
had no support among the educated classes. Even with the support
of the peasants the Prince could not hope to re-establish his rule
without bloodshed. The Russian consul advised him to appeal to
the Tsar – the only thing that could save the situation was help
from St Petersburg.

All this seemed to be true enough. Sandro exchanged telegrams with his father who had tried to enlist help from the
German emperor. But under Bismarck's dictation, William I
curtly replied that a visit of Alexander of Hesse in Berlin would
be 'inopportune at the present moment'. Sandro was waiting for
advice from London and, in fact, a coded telegram arrived, signed
'Grandmama', apparently from Queen Victoria. But Sandro was
unable to decode it and did not learn its contents.

He had long discussions with his brothers. Eventually, with
the help of Louis, and 25-year-old Prince Francis Joseph, but
without consulting Stambulov, he composed in Rustchuk the
following telegram to the Tsar:

> 'I thank Your Imperial Majesty for the attitude taken by
> your representative in Rustchuk. His presence at my reception
> showed me that the Russian Imperial Government cannot
> sanction the revolutionary action taken against my person. I
> beg Your Majesty to instruct General Prince Dolgoruki to get
> in touch with me personally as soon as he arrives. I should be
> happy to give Your Majesty the final proof of the unchanging
> devotion which I feel for Your Majesty's illustrous person.
> As Russia gave me the crown, I am prepared to give it back
> into the hands of its Sovereign. Signed: Alexander.'

It was not clear for what Sandro expressed his thanks. The
message sounded far too servile; the last sentence proved
disastrous. As soon as Alexander of Hesse heard about it in
Darmstadt, he realised that his son had made a terrible mistake.
In London Lord Salisbury sighed with relief: by offering the
Crown back to the Tsar, Sandro had given up the fight. In
Berlin Bismarck rubbed his hands: Young Sandro had made a
blunder from which there was no escape.

The Battenberg brothers did not quite see it in this light.

Naïvely, they had hoped to touch the Tsar's heart. After all, he was Sandro's first cousin, he would forgive and allow the Prince to carry on. But the Tsar had no such intentions. Encouraged by Bismarck's attitude, sensing guarded support in Vienna, seeing Lord Salisbury's indecision, he was determined to administer the *coup de grace* to Sandro. He let him wait days for an answer, keeping the National Assembly on tenterhooks and creating more confusion and increasing doubt on the wisdom of restoring Sandro. Abroad, Russian diplomats spread rumours that many Bulgarian deputies had already abandoned the Prince and were secretly negotiating to replace him by Valdemar of Denmark. At last the Tsar's reply arrived:

'I have received Your Highness's telegram. I cannot countenance your return to Bulgaria as I foresee the disastrous results it entails for that sorely tried country. General Dolgoruki's mission appears now unnecessary. I will refrain from sending him in view of the unhappy situation to which Bulgaria is exposed as long as you remain there. Your Highness will understand what you have to do. I will reserve my judgment about it in respectful memory of my father, and in the interest of Russia and of peace in Europe. Alexander, Tsar.'

It was a coldly brutal order to abdicate, unrelieved by a single word of friendliness or comfort. Sandro's father was utterly distressed. He wired to his son:

'We were desperate reading the telegrams. A last attempt at reconciliation had to be made, but only after your entry into Sofia . . . your last sentence was terribly dangerous, apart from the fact that it was contrary to the Treaty of Berlin . . . You have cast your pearls before swine.'

When the exchange of the telegrams became known in London, Queen Victoria was extremely vexed. She had almost succeeded in bringing Lord Salisbury into action and now all her efforts had been destroyed. She wired to Sandro, trying to prevent his abdication:

'I am speechless and entreat you to cancel this step. After such a triumph this was unworthy of the great position you had won. You are being blamed for having telegraphed to the Tsar instead of asking advice here first.'[1]

[1] Telegram dated 4 September 1886, Hartenau Archives.

She followed it up by a letter from Balmoral Castle. Its remarkable wording is given here in verbal translation from the German original:

'My dearest Sandro! Words cannot express my feelings and my anxiety since the horrible August 21! Your parents could hardly have felt greater anxiety and fear and no one rejoiced more than I did when already on the third day the news of the counter-revolution arrived as well as of the great and heartfelt devotion of your people and of the great enthusiasm everywhere. But what you, poor dear Sandro, must have suffered, both mentally and physically! My resentment and fury against your barbaric, asiatic-like, tyrannical cousin[1] are *so great* that I can hardly control myself to write about it. But thank God! he had done himself very great harm in Germany, in Austria (especially) and, of course, *here*, the indignation is tremendous. My Government will make every effort to gain the support of the Great Powers against Russia and in your favour. If you want and can stay on, which I hope with all my heart, then you must make *your* own conditions and demand guarantees. You must appeal to the Great Powers (but not to Russia). I do not want to write any more today and I pray God, who has so *clearly* watched over your precious life, that He may continue to protect and bless you. Please give my greetings to dear Franzjos.[2] God grant that your health did not suffer. Ever your loving cousin and true friend,

VICTORIA, R.I.'

The Queen's telegram reached Sandro only after his arrival in Sofia, her letter several days later. Stambulov had preceded the three Battenberg brothers to the capital, and during his journey learnt of Sandro's blunder and the Tsar's reply. When he met the Prince, he cried: 'This means the destruction of all we had so carefully built up. This is the end of you!' He felt betrayed by the Prince and told his friends: 'This is the man for whom we roused the people of Bulgaria. We have put our necks into the Russian noose! He has taken a decision without even telling us beforehand. He had thrown away his crown at the feet of the Tsar, and he kept us in the dark about it.'

[1] Meaning Tsar Alexander III.
[2] Prince Francis Joseph of Battenberg.

The crowds greeting the Prince when he entered the capital did not know what lay in store. Greatly disillusioned, Stambulov told the Prince that his telegram to the Tsar had cost him much loyal support. With bitterness in his heart Sandro read reports of Bismarck's statement that 'Germany's interests would not be affected by a solution which would exclude Prince Alexander of Bulgaria from the throne'. The Chancellor had given a go ahead signal for any action the Tsar would care to take. When Crown Prince Frederick, prodded by his wife, tried to argue with the Emperor in Sandro's favour, Bismarck sent a memorandum which showed his malice:

'When Prince Battenberg became the ruler of Bulgaria in 1879, it was understood by all that he would attach himself and Bulgaria to Russia. As was to be expected from his character, which together with his qualities and faults he had inherited from his Polish rather than his German ancestry, he has given all the impression that no reliance can be placed either on his judgment or on his trustworthiness.'[1]

From Balmoral Castle Queen Victoria was flooding her Prime Minister with frantic notes: 'Prince Alexander was the guardian of Europe's peace . . . We lose one of the bravest and wisest rulers in him, if he is gone . . . We must not swallow that, meant as a slap in our face . . . Russia has undermined Bulgaria . . . it is a serious danger to Europe and peace . . . It will mean the Russification of the Balkans . . . The averting of a general conflagration in Europe is bound up with the maintenance of Prince Alexander's rule . . .'[2]

But although Henry of Battenberg had wired to Sandro that 'the Queen considers open hostility to Russia the best solution', it was mere wishful thinking. Lord Salisbury refused the Queen's demand to send a British fleet to the Bosporus. He was content to repeat his protests to St Petersburg, but he never intended to push the crisis to a danger point.

In Sofia, Sandro realised his ominous position. Stambulov had received identical diplomatic notes from Russia, Germany and Austria, warning him that captured revolutionary leaders must

[1] Corti, E. C., *Downfall of Three Dynasties,* and cf. Lepsius, J., *Die Grosse Politik,* p. 352 ff., Berlin, 1922–7.
[2] Queen Victoria, *Letters,* Third Series, Vol. I, London, 1928.

not be executed, nor their supporters victimised. Russia made it clear, with German and Turkish support, that an armed conflict in Bulgaria could only be avoided if 'the Prince confirmed the abdication he had already signed' – referring to the scrap of paper he had signed at pistol point during the night of the revolt.

On 4 September Prince Alexander of Bulgaria announced his abdication. 'I leave Bulgaria with only one wish,' he declared, 'that the country may be happy and free, and as a proof of this I am sacrificing myself.'

His last act of state was to appoint a Regency Council which included Stambulov and Colonel Murtakov. On 9 September he left Bulgaria and went to Darmstadt. He intended to stop in Berlin and see Vicky who during his long ordeal had become sick from worry and had sent him many messages affirming her love. But Bismarck, hearing of Sandro's intention from the German consul in Sofia, informed him that 'the Emperor was at present unable to receive him', and that in any case a visit to Berlin 'would be greatly misunderstood in other capitals'.

For a time Sandro shut himself off at Heiligenberg, pondering over his misfortune. His correspondence with Vicky and the Crown Princess continued, but Sandro began to realise that his courtship was becoming hopeless. Not only Bismarck but the whole German imperial family were now firmly set against him. Even the Crown Prince, slowly dying of cancer of the throat, seemed evasive and wavering. Sandro was still in love, but he had not seen Vicky for almost three years. The political struggle had exhausted him. He had lost his throne; he was an exile and no longer a suitable suitor for an imperial princess. He was embittered and felt humiliated; he was tiring of his intangible courtship of a bride so obstinately denied to him.

He found some comfort in the friendly reception in Darmstadt. His family was most considerate and the Hesse population treated him like a returning hero; he was hailed in the streets, and when he visited the Court Theatre the audience rose and shouted: 'Long live the hero of Slivnitza, the Prince of Bulgaria', and the orchestra played 'Shumi Maritza', the Bulgarian national anthem. Sitting embarrassed in the grand-ducal box, Sandro noticed a beautiful fairhaired girl, who clapped her hands in applause. He was told she was an Austrian singer, Johanna Loisinger, who had recently joined the Court Theatre.

It must have been love at first sight. From that evening on Sandro never missed a performance in which Fräulein Loisinger appeared on the stage. He sent her flowers but waited several weeks until he decided to be introduced to her. He knew that in provincial Darmstadt gossip would soon spring up about a liaison between the former ruler of Bulgaria and an actress.

For a year plots continued to be woven around Sandro's marriage project. Queen Victoria kept reminding him to press his betrothal. An emissary of the Crown Princess arrived in Darmstadt and then went to Vienna to contact Bulgarian leaders. The Crown Princess exchanged letters with Sandro's father who was deeply involved in these intrigues in which Sandro had become a mere tool.

The gist of it all was that when Crown Prince Frederick succeeded his father, he would dismiss Bismarck, sanction Sandro's marriage to Vicky, and smooth his road back to the Bulgarian throne. Even the Tsar would then hesitate to spite the new German Emperor's son-in-law. At 90, the ailing Emperor William was expected to die at any moment; Bulgaria had still no prince and was ruled by the Regency Council after Prince Valdemar of Denmark, frightened by Sandro's fate, had refused the throne.

Only Sandro was disinterested. When Stambulov asked him whether he would accept the crown again if it were offered to him, he replied that he felt honoured but had decided never to return to Bulgaria. Sandro was left in peace by his family conspirators only when he was laid up with a mild attack of smallpox during a holiday in the South of France. His romance with Johanna Loisinger blossomed through their love letters which they exchanged during his convalescence.

On his return to Darmstadt in June 1887, he received a surprise visit from Prince Henry of Prussia, the second son of the Emperor. 'There is only one question that raises a barrier between our families,' he told Sandro. 'I must speak frankly and I want you to answer equally frankly. My mother raves about you and she still wants you to marry Vicky. This unhappy story has been a nightmare to my family for years and has caused rifts and untold unhappiness. I must ask you – do you still want to marry Vicky?'

Sandro was deeply hurt. 'I do not know what right you have to call me to account like that,' he replied. 'I have not asked formally for the princess in marriage. I cannot understand why I am asked to renounce a marriage I could now not possibly enter into. Princess Victoria is free. She can marry whom she wishes. I shall be the first to congratulate Vicky if she becomes engaged to someone else.'

Impetuously, Sandro made a decision and burnt his boats. Henry of Prussia reported the conversation to his family and hinted that Sandro had found new happiness with a pretty operetta singer. A few weeks later two items of news reached Darmstadt: Prince Ferdinand of Coburg was elected the new Prince of Bulgaria; Emperor William was on his deathbed, but the condition of his son, Crown Prince Frederick, had also badly deteriorated.

At this juncture Sandro's mother, who had hitherto remained aloof from the intrigues, disturbed by his romance with Johanna Loisinger and anxious that he should yet make a good marriage, tried to convince Sandro that he was about to ruin his life. But it was too late; spending every free moment with Johanna, he had drawn away from his family.

Emperor William I, the founder of the German Reich, died on 9 March 1888, just before his 91st birthday. There followed ninety-two days of the reign of his son Frederick. Three weeks after his father's death the new Emperor wrote to Sandro, inviting him to Charlottenburg. Once again the telegraph wires vibrated with messages from Queen Victoria, from the new Empress Frederick, from Louis and Henry of Battenberg. Sandro hesitated. He told Johanna that he loved only her and did not want to marry Vicky any longer. But he would have probably yielded to his father's persuasion after the arrival of a telegram from Empress Frederick suggesting that Sandro's engagement to Vicky should be announced on April 12, during his visit in Charlottenburg. Queen Victoria's daughter was spoiling for a fight with Bismarck.

On his sickbed in Charlottenburg Emperor Frederick, unable to speak and communicating only by scribbled notes, had a conference with Bismarck. He told the Chancellor that he intended to discuss with Sandro the marriage project and also bestow on him the command of the Brigade of Guards. 'I want Sandro to live here so that the young people can see something of each other . . .' he wrote on the pad.

Bismarck read it slowly and then heaved his great bulk from the chair. 'If Prince Alexander of Battenberg comes here, I beg your Majesty to accept my immediate resignation,' he said.

The dying emperor lay still. Then his thin pale fingers gripped the pad and pencil and he wrote: 'No, no! What shall I do?' He knew he could not dispense with his Iron Chancellor.

'Countermand the invitation,' Bismarck ordered him. 'Battenberg must not come here, he must never see Princess Victoria again.'

The emperor nearly collapsed. 'Leave me alone,' he wrote on the pad.

After Bismarck had left, a telegram was sent to Sandro explaining that the emperor had had a relapse and had, regretfully to cancel the invitation. Bismarck quickly told his trusted newspaper editors that he had overruled the emperor. The 'Battenberg Affair' was nearly at its end.

Queen Victoria, then in San Remo, heard that her son-in-law was dying and decided to go to Berlin. Bismarck tried to prevent this visit too, but the Queen wrote: 'Bismarck's tyranny is unbearable. I will not give up my visit to the dear sick Emperor'. Before she set off she received news from London that changed her attitude to the proposed marriage. First her Prime Minister and then Henry of Battenberg let her know that Sandro was no longer anxious to marry Vicky. Gently, Henry broke the news: his brother was in love with another woman.

When the Queen arrived in Berlin she was almost heartbroken. She had the memorable conversation with Bismarck during which she told him that now neither she nor her daughter, the Empress, had any more interest in Sandro's marriage. Bismarck could hardly believe his ears; overjoyed he assured Queen Victoria of his great admiration and devotion – now that the terrible misunderstanding was over there was nothing that stood between Germany and Great Britain. From a table he took a picture of the Empress and in an almost ridiculous gesture pressed it to his heart – the picture of the woman who had hated him for years and whose feelings he heartily reciprocated.

Emperor Frederick died on 15 June. The news of Sandro's withdrawal and the Queen's conversation with Bismarck had been kept from him. In his testament he left a letter to his son, now

Kaiser William II. It was dated 18 April, two months before his death, and read:

'Should your mother or myself be suddenly called to depart this life, I hereby wish to state definitely that I give my full consent to the marriage of your second sister Victoria with the ex-Prince of Bulgaria, Alexander of Battenberg. I charge you by the love you bear your father to carry out this my last wish, which has been the hearts desire of your sister Victoria for many years. To avoid any suggestion of politics and to obviate any political difficulties, I give up my wish to grant the Prince, to whom I am greatly attached, a position in my army or any official decoration. I count on you to fulfil your duty as my son by complying with my wish and trust that, as a brother, you will not refrain from helping your sister. Your loving father, Frederick William.'

Kaiser William II did not intend to comply. He called his Minister of Justice and asked whether this letter was legally valid. It was not, the Minister servilely assured the young emperor: it was not a testamentary disposition, but a legally worthless document, obviously signed on the instigation of the late emperor's wife, when he was no longer in full possession of his faculties. The Kaiser seized upon this interpretation. He wrote a formal note to Sandro, informing him of the letter of the late emperor and demanding that he should make a solemn renunciation of the hand of Princess Victoria.

Sandro had long since decided to give up Vicky. He wrote farewell letters to her and her mother, saying 'I am renouncing the dreams of my youth', expressing good wishes for Vicky's future and closing the letter to her with the remark that 'it would be now impossible to continue further correspondence'.

His letter might have appeared cold and even cruel, but Sandro, telling Johanna Loisinger of his final break with Vicky, wrote: 'Behind locked doors I have allowed my tears to flow without being able to prevent it; they were for the grave of my youthful dreams, the collapse of all I had striven and hoped for many years, the failure of all my political and military plans.'

He was incensed about the Kaiser's coarseness and refused to reply. Eventually, it was Alexander of Hesse who wrote to the Kaiser, saying that, on his orders, his son had 'definitely broken off his engagement with Princess Victoria'. Surprisingly, in the same letter he asked the Kaiser whether Sandro could hope for an appointment in the German army. The letter came back unopened, although it is certain that its contents were communicated to the Kaiser by his secret police, even though the envelope was undamaged. Sometime later, the German envoy in Darmstadt informed the Grand Duke of Hesse that there was no place for Sandro in the German army, but that the Kaiser advised him to apply for an appointment to Emperor Francis Joseph of Austria.

Bismarck's victory was now complete. His revenge on Sandro's father had destroyed the son. Alexander of Hesse had been all his life in good health but, at 65, the worries of the past two years had greatly worsened a digestive trouble which only now was diagnosed as abdominal cancer. The proud schemer and warrior, who for a quarter of a century exercised such great influence upon Europe's politics, died on 15 December 1888.

After his father's funeral, waiting impatiently for news from Vienna about his appointment in the Austrian army, Sandro wrote to Johanna: 'I hope that soon you will belong to me with every fibre of your being . . . I am thanking God that such a sweet and precious being will belong to me for ever.' He told her he was determined to marry her and to emigrate with her to America if the Austrian army commission fell through. He had kept his decision from his dying father but when he told his mother about it, Julie of Battenberg replied that she would 'never consent to such a disastrous match'. It was said that she remarked she would 'rather see her son dead'. All her ambitions had been centred on that great marriage in Berlin; from her own bitter experience she knew what lay in store for Sandro, were he to marry beneath his station, and an actress at that. At last, news came from Vienna that Emperor Francis Joseph was prepared to offer Sandro the colonelship of the Austrian Infantry Regiment No. 27.

He decided to make a complete break with his past and asked the Grand Duke of Hesse for permission to abandon his name and title of a Prince of Battenberg and to call himself 'Count von Hartenau', after a village near the Castle of Battenberg from which his mother had taken her title.

In Vienna he met on 28 January 1889 Archduke Rudolf, the

Austrian Crown Prince whom he knew from childhood. Rudolf asked him: 'Would you like to come to my hunting lodge at Mayerling? I shall stay there next week and I want to introduce you to a very charming young lady.' Knowing of Rudolf's love affair with Baroness Vetsera, Sandro made his apologies, saying he had arranged to travel to Venice the next morning. Two days later Archduke Rudolf and Marie Vetsera were found dead with shot wounds at Mayerling.

From Venice Sandro went to Mentone where Johanna Loisinger joined him. Seven weeks after his father's death, on 6 February 1889, they were married there, with only two witnesses present and without notifying his family. The news caused a sensation throughout Europe. The curtain had fallen on the 'Battenberg Affair'.

The Mayerling tragedy delayed Sandro's appointment, but eventually he arrived in Graz where his regiment was stationed. The wheel of history had come full circle. In the sleepy county town of Styria, where his father had found refuge after his elopement and morganatic marriage to Julie Hauke, and where his eldest brother Louis was born, Colonel Count Alexander von Hartenau settled down with his beautiful young wife, the former opera singer, to the humdrum duties of a provincial garrison – exactly as his father had done almost forty years earlier. On 16 January 1890 their first child was born, a son whom Sandro christened Assen after a legendary Bulgarian hero.

Bulgaria had not forgotten him. Loyal Stambulov, who had remained prime minister under the new Prince, secured for Sandro an annual pension of 50,000 gold francs; his private estates, furniture and other possessions he had left behind realised two million Levas. Count von Hartenau could live in pleasant comfort and spend his leaves from military duties with his family abroad. But he was never again a guest in Europe's royal palaces.

For four years he found serene happiness in his marriage; a daughter Svetana, was born in 1892. Soon after her birth Sandro fell ill and his illness dragged on, diagnosed as an inflammation of intestinal tissues. On 16 November 1893, returning from a hunt, he felt unwell; two days later – eight years to the day after the battle of Slivnitza – he died at the age of thirty-six.

As in a Greek tragedy, all the main actors of the 'Battenberg

Affair' were doomed. Stambulov had remained loyal to Sandro's memory. He arranged a state funeral for the former Prince of Bulgaria, and tens of thousands mourned in the streets of Sofia when Sandro's coffin was taken with military honours to St George's Chapel for provisional burial. Later it was transferred to a marble mausoleum erected by public subscription in the centre of the city. Stambulov was Prince Ferdinand's prime minister until 1894, was never reconciled with Russia and resigned when the prince began to pursue a pro-Russian policy. Shortly afterwards, on 18 July 1895, he was assassinated by pro-Russian conspirators.

Bismarck, who had ruined Sandro's life, quarrelled with Kaiser William soon after his accession, was dismissed, and died in sulky seclusion in 1898.

Princess Victoria of Prussia, Sandro's beloved Vicky, probably never stopped loving him. In 1891 she married the Prince of Schaumburg-Lippe, a kind man who understood her heartbreak. After he died in 1916, Vicky became an eccentric. Her marriage at 60 to a young Russian adventurer, Alexander Zubkov, who relieved her of such fortune as she had saved from post-war inflation, provided sensational headlines for years. Her life, too, ended in tragedy. After Zubkov left her, and later went to prison, she died suddenly in 1929, some believed by her own hand.

Today, there are still Battenbergs living in Austria. Sandro's and Johanna's son Assen, who dropped his title of count and called himself Assen Hartenau, became an Austrian civil servant and retired as a Counsellor of the republic. In 1934 he had married Frau Berta Hussak (who had been married before) and adopted her son, now a 50-year-old Viennese physician, Dr Wilhelm Hartenau. From the latter's marriage to Baroness Marie Klein-Wiesenberg there are three children, Alexander, Elizabeth, and Francisca. Students of genealogy might, perhaps, regard them as cousins of the present Prince of Wales. Sandro's daughter, Svetana, married in 1925 Charles Boissevain and died ten years later at the early age of 42. Johanna Loisinger, Countess von Hartenau, survived her husband for nearly sixty years and died in Vienna in 1951 in her late eighties.

CHAPTER SIX

QUEEN VICTORIA'S FAVOURITES

Prince Henry of Battenberg
and his family

AT THE Castle of Schönberg, the ancestral home of the Princes zu Erbach-Schönberg, south of Darmstadt, a room preserved in memory of the first generation of the Battenbergs is crammed with souvenirs, family albums and letters which belonged to Marie of Battenberg, the first-born child and only daughter of Prince Alexander of Hesse and Julie von Hauke. In 1871, at eighteen, Marie had married Prince Gustav zu Erbach-Schönberg, and until her death in 1923 she collected everything concerned with her family.

Among hundreds of faded photographs, one shows a British officer being carried on a stretcher by four African natives along a jungle path in the Gold Coast. The handsome face, framed by a dark beard, is marked by death. It is the last photograph of Prince Henry of Battenberg on his home journey from the Ashanti campaign in January 1896, a homecoming he never completed alive.

His sister Marie, a great diarist, wrote on the back of this photograph 'This is the last picture of my dear merry brother Liko (Henry). His was a strange fate, he seemed in no way destined for the sorrows which hovered over our family'. His fate was, indeed, strange, for Henry of Battenberg had made the best of all the marriages of the sons of Alexander of Hesse, a match that elevated him to Queen Victoria's favourite and confidant and greatly advanced the destinies of his family. Yet, by a tragic fluke his life, holding every promise, was cut short at the age of thirty-seven.

Henry of Battenberg was born on 5 October 1858 in Milan, when his father was an Austrian general. He had never been 'Henry' to his family, always 'Liko': his Italian nurse had called him Rico (from Henrico), his little brother Sandro unable to pronounce the 'r' made Liko of it, and the name stuck. Like his sister and three brothers he spent his childhood at Heiligenberg, like Sandro he went to the progressive Schnepfental school and became a cadet at the Dresden military college. But after his eldest brother Louis had become a British naval cadet, and Sandro joined the Russian army, his father arranged for Liko to enter the Prussian Hussars – in an attempt at reconciliation with Berlin. When he was 25, before hostility between the Battenbergs and Bismarck became irreconcilable, the German Emperor gave him a commission in the famous Garde du Corps regiment, the Life Guards at Potsdam.

When her sons were growing up, Julie of Battenberg looked eagerly for a great marriage for each. For years, if unobtrusively, she shared her husband's political ambitions and dynastic schemes; her womanly instinct and her own hard experience of a morganatic marriage had made her determined to ensure suitable matches for her boys. She had ardently hoped – when Marie was only 14 – that the 20-year-old Tsarevitch (the later Tsar Alexander III) would take interest in the girl. In her diary of 1866, Marie noted: 'Sasha is always so nice to me . . . Yesterday I went to the drawing room and found him all alone. He threw himself on a sofa and wailed "*Je ne suis pas elevé pour être empereur*". I did not know what to say'. But the future Tsar cared little for his pretty cousin and even less for his Battenberg relations. After he succeeded his father he allied himself with Bismarck, destroyed Sandro and opposed Henry's English marriage. Marie married 'the boy next door', Prince Gustav zu Erbach-Schönberg. If in her mother's eyes this was not a 'great marriage', the Erbachs were wealthy and Marie lived with her husband happily until his death forty years later.

For her sons Julie of Battenberg had much higher ambitions. She fully approved of Louis' choice of Queen Victoria's granddaughter, Princess Victoria of Hesse, but bridal prospects in Europe's Courts for her other sons were unpropitious after Sandro had become Prince of Bulgaria and antagonized the Tsar and Bismarck. Sandro had made it all so difficult, having fallen in love with the German Emperor's granddaughter, having refused his mother's suggestions to marry a Wurttemberg princess or an Austrian archduchess, pursuing his hopeless suit with Vicky until it led to his doom.

Thus it was Liko upon whom his mother set her highest hopes. But the handsome young Guards officer was in no hurry; he enjoyed the gay life in Berlin, had become an accomplished sportsman, an excellent shot, mountaineer, skater, a gifted musician and elegant dancer, whom women of all ages pursued. For himself Liko wanted a marriage that would provide him with funds. Paris boulevard journals published indiscreet stories that he was 'on the books' of Madame Lacroix, the famous match-maker who had found wealthy brides, including some great American heiresses, for many an impoverished princeling. But, it seems, even Madame Lacroix failed to find him a wife who would be both rich and pass the scrutiny of his ambitious parents.

The great turning-point in his life and in the destinies of his family came in 1884, at his brother Louis' wedding to Queen Victoria's granddaughter. Headed by the old Queen almost the entire British Royal Family was present, including the Queen's youngest daughter, Princess Beatrice. She fell at first sight in love with Liko, six-feet tall, handsome, dark-moustached and glittering in his Garde du Corps uniform. At their first meeting, Beatrice must have seemed to Liko a pleasant, intelligent, but rather old-maidish 'blue-stocking', who had just become his elder brother's aunt by marriage; at 28 she was six years older than Louis' wife.

Beatrice had inherited the keen intellect of her father, the Prince Consort; she had received an excellent education, was widely read, and was interested in the arts and literature. But, having spent every moment of her life under her mother's sharp eyes, she knew nothing of the world. She had never been alone in a room with a man, not even with her brothers, lest she should hear a *risqué* word. Once on a walk in Windsor, when she was 25, she saw a corset in a shop; she turned away with a deep blush, shocked to learn that such discreet garments should be openly displayed and sold. For years she had been her mother's constant companion, dutifully attending her every whim, coping with her prodigal correspondence, straightening her cushions, adjusting her wraps, administering her medicines, accepting John Brown's rudeness, and reading to her such exciting books as Dean Stanley's *Life* in four fat volumes.

When she met Henry of Battenberg, she was attractive in a pale and shy way, inclined to plumpness, and very much 'on the shelf'. Liko could have hardly imagined himself as her suitor, particularly as Queen Victoria was telling everybody that 'my dearest little Benjamina will never marry but always stay with me'. But no sooner had Julie of Battenberg sensed that Beatrice was attracted to her handsome son than she began to plot. Liko was placed next to the Queen's daughter at every meal, was ordered to pay her special attentions, to ask her for every dance, and to take her for walks in the park of Heiligenberg. When he protested, he was told that it was important for his brother's future to win the favours of the Queen's daughter.

During that all-too-brief stay of the British guests, Liko discovered that he greatly liked Beatrice. In his company the shy princess had dramatically changed. Gripped by an awakening, unknown passion, she talked freely with him, as she had never done before. He found her warm-hearted and intelligent, and more knowledgeable about many things than himself. She had met, as a keen if silent observer, many famous people. Liko began to realise that here was an opportunity too good to be missed.

Queen Victoria, noticing her daughter's unusual elation and her interest in the young Battenberg, was not amused. She was determined not to lose 'Benjamina', her indispensable companion and helper; she spoke of her daughter as the only prop 'in my lonely old age'. When Beatrice excitedly confessed that she had fallen in love with Liko, the Queen told her that she was 'just a silly gel', that it was all a passing fancy and that there could be no question of a marriage which, besides everything else, was unsuitable and politically dangerous. And when Beatrice, for the first time in her life, tried to remonstrate, her mother became really angry. So angry that – although it must have almost broken her heart – she would not speak to her beloved daughter. After their return to England she continued her punitive silence; although mother and daughter spent their days together, commands or information would be scribbled by the Queen on little pieces of paper and pushed across the table during mealtimes. The Queen even cut out Beatrice from her *Journal* and letters;

between June and December 1884, her name vanished from the pages of the Queen's meticulous diary, and she was never mentioned in any of the many letters which the Grandmother of Europe so avidly wrote during these months to her innumerable correspondents. Her adored daughter 'Benjamina' was as good as dead for her.

The flame which the man she hardly knew had kindled in her heart almost overpowered poor Beatrice. She crept listless through her mother's apartments, left her meals untouched and spent sleepless nights sobbing into her pillows. Eventually, her eldest brother, the Prince of Wales – who could be quite firm with Queen Victoria when fighting someone else's battles – told his mother that she was 'entirely selfish and intolerable'. It all ended in a truly Victorian melodrama, with tearful reconciliation and embraces all round. Victoria's eldest daughter, the German Crown Princess, urgently intervened by letter, reassuring her mother that Liko Battenberg was 'a delightful young man', adding that Beatrice could hardly hope for a better match. Prince Louis of Battenberg, bringing to Osborne the good news that his wife, the Queen's granddaughter, was expecting a baby[1] also gently pleaded with the Queen – not, he said, for the sake of his brother but of Beatrice whom he 'loved and admired as if she were my sister'.

The Queen gave in, but on the strict condition that 'Benjamina' and Liko (who was to have British nationality and an Army commission) would after their marriage live with her. She invited Liko for Christmas, and found him warm and considerate – he agreed with everything she pronounced. She gave her consent to an official announcement of the engagement.

When Sandro heard about it, he wrote from Sofia to his father:

'Liko's engagement to Beatrice is of incalculable value! How the youngster managed to make Beatrice fall in love with him is a puzzle to me; for it must be admitted that Liko is not on a level with her intellectually. Of course I noticed in the spring that they were making eyes at one another, but I did not take it seriously, as I should never have thought that the Queen would agree . . . How strange the fate of our family is! I wonder how it will all end,' (and he added that his own hopes

[1] Princess Alice, the mother of the Duke of Edinburgh.

to marry Vicky of Prussia had greatly improved). 'The Crown Princess has sent me a most kindly letter and Vicky a heavy gold ring as a token of her love. Louis wrote and told me the Crown Princess had recently said to him the best thing would be if I would abdicate (as Prince of Bulgaria) and marry Vicky. I telegraphed to Louis at once that I would do so with the greatest possible pleasure if I could get Vicky. Now, if Liko married Beatrice, the German Emperor will give way too.'[1]

Liko was delighted with his reception at Osborne. He wrote to his father: 'The Queen is most gracious and kind. You can't think what a pleasant difference there is between the people of the Court here and in Germany . . . one feels at home at once.' He had long conversations with Queen Victoria and the Prince of Wales, took Beatrice for long walks, and had good advice from his brother Louis on how to treat British royalty and the Queen's entourage. He must have charmed them all and after he returned home, having promised to come back in March to accompany the Queen and Beatrice on a holiday in France, Queen Victoria recorded the events in her diary:

'Received a note from Liko Battenberg saying that my kind reception of him encouraged him to ask my consent to speaking to Beatrice, for whom, since they met in Darmstadt eight months ago, he had felt the greatest affection! I had known for some time that she had had the same feelings towards him. They seem sincerely attached to each other, of that there can be no doubt. I let Liko know, to come after tea, and I saw him in dear Albert's room. Then I called the dear child, and gave them my blessing.'

To Liko's parents, who had cautiously worked behind the scene, assuring the Queen of their gratitude for all her gracious help she had given to Louis and Sandro, she wrote to Heiligenberg:

'I found it very hard to give my consent, for Beatrice has been everything to me during these sad years, and I hoped that she would never marry. However, since Liko is prepared to live here with her . . . I yielded, and am glad to receive another dear son.'

[1] Hartenau Archives.

Everything seemed to go according to the Battenberg plan, but they did not reckon with Bismarck's violent reaction. As soon as the German Chancellor learnt of the engagement he vowed to prevent 'this new Battenberg intrigue'. He had regarded Louis' marriage as 'a move in Queen Victoria's subterranean plot against Germany', he was incensed about the Queen's and her daughter's (the German Crown Princess') support of Sandro's rule in Bulgaria and his marriage project to Princess Vicky, and now he described Henry's engagement as 'another move in London's finely woven plot to drive a wedge between Germany and Russia'. He had delusions about what was, in fact, a love match, and he sent his ambassador to the Tsar, urging him to use his influence to prevent 'yet another dangerous political Battenberg marriage'.

But in one of his rare genial moods, Bismarck agreed that there was no wonder that a woman would fall for a Battenberg. 'They are all extremely handsome fellows', he told Colonel Swaine, the British military attaché at a reception at the British embassy in Berlin and, noticing Liko standing nearby, he growled: 'Stop your ears for a moment, young Prince', adding with a belly laugh: 'Ja, ja, I have never seen a more handsome family than these Battenbergs!'

In March and April Beatrice and Liko accompanied the Queen to Aix-les-Bains and Geneva, her first holiday abroad since John Brown's death, and on the return journey stopped at Darmstadt, where she told Alexander of Hesse: 'Liko is like a dear son to me'. The wedding was arranged for 23 July, but in view of the sharp disapproval from Germany, Russia and even France, and some criticism in Britain towards yet another foreign marriage in the Royal Family, the Queen decided that it should be a quiet one, at Whippingham near Osborne. Space at this first royal wedding ever held in a village church was limited, so invitations could conveniently be restricted, thus avoiding political complications. Members of the German Imperial family were not present, and from the list of British dignitaries the name of Mr Gladstone – six times the Queen's Prime Minister, who had known the bride since her birth – was omitted.

But there was no lack of glittering uniforms, rich robes and tiaras. Henry of Battenberg wore the white and gold uniform of the Prussian Garde du Corps with silver breastplates and a silver helmet topped with the Prussian eagle, which prompted the Prince of Wales to grunt: 'Here comes Beatrice's Lohengrin!' The Archbishop of Canterbury officiated before the tiny altar, and ten of Beatrice's nieces, including the future Tsaritsa of Russia and the daughters of the Prince of Wales attended the bride.

On the evening of the wedding Queen Victoria noted in her *Journal*:

> 'A happier-looking couple could seldom be seen kneeling at the altar together. It was very touching. I stood very close to my dear child, who looked very sweet, pure and calm. Though I stood for the ninth time near a child and for the fifth time near a daughter at the altar, I never felt more deeply than I did on this occasion, though full of confidence.'

The newly-weds were allowed exactly two days for their honeymoon, at Ryde, a few miles from Osborne, before they were commanded to join the Queen. On the eve of the wedding the Queen had conferred the Order of the Garter upon Liko and raised him to the dignity of a Royal Highness, although in all that hurry it had been overlooked that he had not yet sworn the oath of allegiance and become a British subject. Busy weeks followed for Liko; he took his oath at the House of Lords, accompanied the Queen to the regatta of the Royal Yacht Squadron, and got used to wearing the kilt for dinner at Balmoral in September – on which Queen Victoria stubbornly insisted, in memory of John Brown. In winter his married life began in earnest at Windsor Castle, where he and his wife were given a suite adjoining that of the Queen.

Poor Liko! He had to adjust himself to a wife older than himself, much more mature and set in her ways. He had given up the life of a gay Potsdam guardee, had no career – his army commission was nominal – and had to spend most of the day in the Queen's company, helping Beatrice fuss around her mother. His leisure time was spent in tending Beatrice's aviary full of white doves and canaries, or admiring the peacocks bequeathed by Disraeli. Nevertheless, Liko, never brilliant but full of Battenberg charm and shrewdness, soon settled down, succeeding in overcoming the suspicions of some of the Queen's family and entourage. He became one of the very few people who could somehow influence the bundle of stubborn prejudices which was the Queen of England and Empress of India. He won his first battle over the ban on smoking in the royal homes. Queen Victoria hated tobacco so much that she could smell it with disgust even on a smoker's letter – which had to be burnt at once. But Liko received her permission to smoke in his own rooms, where he was joined by another nicotine-hungry refugee, the Prince of Wales.

What was much more important and significant, the Queen soon began to show him and to discuss with him State documents, barred to her own son, the future king. Liko never misused her confidence. Not interested in politics, he used his influence in this direction only when his brother Sandro got into trouble in Bulgaria, but never told his father or anyone else State secrets which had come to his knowledge. During the ten years of his marriage his family was always in the wake of Queen Victoria. Already in March 1886 he had arranged a Battenberg reunion at Windsor Castle. His sister Marie, one of the guests, noted in her diary:

'I am glad that since Liko joined her household, many of the Queen's peculiar habits have disappeared. She wears robes of lighter colour and she enjoys the company of guests and music. I have never felt more German than when with her, who is so proud of her German descent, and who knew how to foster the sense of kinship . . . The Queen has many German ways, for example she likes to soak cake in her coffee, which in England is absolutely forbidden. She speaks a quite classic German, without the slightest foreign accent . . . she always spoke German with me, and all the letters I possess from her are written in German. It was taken as a matter of course that . . . in the family circle we should all speak German, although I have been proficient in English since a child.

'The most interesting time is at breakfast: the Queen then generally discusses with us the latest political events suggested by ministerial dispatches, which are brought to her in steel boxes. I was then often able to convince myself what strong opinions of her own she holds . . .

'From half-past four till six the Queen drove out alone with me. She was very affable . . . The changing of the mantles and wraps during the drive, to which I had to see, went off quite well though I was a little nervous about it. On every change of temperature during the drive the Queen has to have a thicker or a lighter wrap as the case may be, put round her . . . In the evenings the Queen's orchestra is playing, which it has not done for a very long time. . . . The Prince of Wales came to dinner, and later smoked a long time in Liko's room, the only room where smoking is allowed . . . Today the Abbe Liszt came to luncheon and later played . . . I much appreciate the sight of the two figures as they stood facing each other: both little, both white-haired, both in black and dignified and a little embarrassed: she the ruler of the great British Empire, he the ruler in the realm of music.'[1]

To Marie Erbach this was an exciting experience, to Liko Battenberg it soon became routine. He draped the wraps around his mother-in-law's shoulders, supported her at the ordeal of a State Opening of Parliament, earnestly discussed with her the complexities of international and colonial events, dispelled her worries involving her hundreds of relations spread across Europe, and attended to trivial matters of the day-to-day running of her Household.

After her long seclusion, Liko was able to persuade her to show herself more often in public, to discard her widow's weeds at least occasionally, to open exhibitions, and take part in most of her Golden Jubilee festivities in 1887, even including a visit to Buffalo Bill's Wild West Performance at Earl's Court. He was always two respectful steps behind his Sovereign, never presuming the place due to her sons and, secure in the Queen's confidence and affection, if he was envied by them, he was not resented. In fact, the Prince of Wales, so pointedly excluded from secrets of State, preferred Liko to some of his brothers; of Prince Alfred he spoke of being a 'crashing bore', which Liko certainly was not.

What was of great importance to the Battenbergs was Liko's role as the Queen's companion and aide during her journeys abroad and visits to foreign capitals. He went with her in 1888 to Berlin, to the deathbed of Emperor Frederick, where he discussed with the Crown Princess the last, hopeless chance of

[1] Princess zu Erbach, op. cit., pp. 230 et seq.

his brother Sandro's marriage to her daughter. He met Maria Christina, the Queen-Regent of Spain, and this acquaintance later proved a stepping-stone to his daughter's marriage to King Alfonso XIII. There were meetings with the King and Queen of Italy, the Emperor and Empress of Brazil, the King and Queen of the Hellenes; on the railway platform at Innsbruck the old Emperor Francis Joseph waited to greet Queen Victoria, and at Munich the mad King Ludwig of Bavaria; when the Queen made her regular sojourns in Nice, there was always a procession of crowned heads and famous statesmen to her villa at Cimiez.

If the journeys abroad were important, so were visits of foreign potentates to the formidable Grandmother of Europe. Some of them embarrassed Liko – as when Kaiser William II arrived at Cowes in his yacht *Hohenzollern,* flanked by twelve German warships, behaving as if he had come at the head of an invasion force to conquer Britain. Neither Liko nor the Prince of Wales had ever forgiven the Kaiser for calling Sandro of Battenberg's marriage project to his sister a *mésalliance* and the Battenbergs 'those dangerous upstarts'. The later King Edward VII's memory went, of course, much longer back. He despised his Prussian nephew ever since, as a little boy at his wedding to Princess Alexandra, Willi had thrown his aunt's muff out of the carriage window, had screamed all through the ceremony and had bitten uncle Leopold of Belgium in the leg, just when the marriage vows were being exchanged.

Much more pleasant were the connections with the Russian relations. If Tsar Alexander III had been hostile, his son Nicholas II married Alix of Hesse, Liko's niece who had been a bridesmaid at his wedding. During the short ten years between his marriage and his death, Liko's family links with Europe's dynasties became through many marriages quite fantastic. The Battenbergs were now related to the reigning houses of Britain, Germany, Russia, Denmark, Norway, Rumania and Bulgaria – and soon afterwards also of Spain and Greece – and to almost every royal and princely family in the German Reich. Inter-marriages led sometimes to genealogists' nightmares: Liko's wife, when she was only 33 and had just given birth to her youngest child, had at the same time become someone's great-great aunt.

Although he appeared to the British public little more than a minor consort and the Queen's golden retriever, Liko was happy and, like all Battenbergs, took up new interests with zest. He was in the forefront of the 'penny-farthing' craze, drove the first wobbling, snorting motor-cars in England, rarely missed a good shoot, enjoyed sailing and yachting, and became an enthusiastic supporter of his wife's and her niece's (Princess Louise, the Duchess of Fyfe) preoccupation with the theatre. He brought about a revolution in Queen Victoria's life by arranging theatrical performances at Windsor Castle, with Eleanora Duse, Ellen Terry, Beerbohm Tree and John Hare in leading parts, and organized visits of Italian opera singers and the Comédie Française – though he confessed that his first preference went to Mr Gilbert's and Sir Arthur Sullivan's *The Gondoliers*. Queen Victoria attending these performances for the first time for thirty years – since the death of her beloved Albert – became herself so enthusiastic that she encouraged Liko to take part in amateur dramatics arranged by Princess Beatrice at Windsor. He was a great success as Saladin in a *tableau* entitled 'King Richard among the Saracens', the latter acted by the Queen's Indian servants.

There was some criticism of 'the idle prince' and, whilst news-paper comments were usually mild, *Punch* published some biting cartoons, implying that in return for his Civil List annuity, Prince Henry of Battenberg's main national service was playing billiards with Sir Frederick Ponsonby, the Queen's private secretary. This was quite unfair; Liko never shirked duties of innumerable minor royal engagements, opening bazaars, presiding over charity committees and often deputising for the Queen and his wife. Indeed, he had endeared himself to the British public. People liked his dash, his good looks, his interest in everything new and progressive, his keenness for sports of every sort. They appreciated that he eschewed pomposity and liked to talk freely and simply with them. He and Princess Beatrice were the first member of the Royal Family to go down a Welsh coal mine, where he tried his hand at hewing. Above all, the puritanical middle-classes, for years shocked about the stories of the love life and gambling excesses of the Heir to the Throne, approved of Prince Henry's and Princess Beatrice's exemplary family life.

When their first child, a boy christened Alexander Albert (Drino) – after both his grandfathers – was born on 23 November 1886, Queen Victoria had already thirty-six grandchildren and several great-grandchildren, but this new addition to her family pleased her like none before. Ever since her widowhood she used to spend Christmas at Osborne; wars, international crises, colonial troubles never altered this unwritten law. The arrival of little Drino, however, prompted her for the first time to break with her habit. She decreed it would be unwise for the baby to undertake a sea journey in winter and so, a little upset and uncomfortable, she spent her Christmas at Windsor.

The frosty-faced old Queen unbent and became almost light-hearted. A petrified Court official one day found her with Liko, sitting on a sofa, and 'actually roaring with laughter'. On a drive she ordered the coachman twice to halt and give a florin to a poor woman with a child in arms and again to a blind beggar. She crowned it all with engaging the Royal Box at Drury Lane for a Gilbert-and-Sullivan performance at Christmas, her first visit to a London theatre in living memory.

In quick succession three more little Battenbergs arrived: eleven months after Alexander, a girl was born on 24 October 1887 at Balmoral Castle. The former French Empress Eugénie, now blind and living in exile in England, whom Queen Victoria greatly liked and admired, was invited to be one of the child's sponsors and, accordingly, the baby was christened Eugénie Victoria Julia Eua – the last name having been chosen by her high-brow mother from Gaelic mythology. Sir Cameron Lees, minister of St Giles's Cathedral in Edinburgh, misread the 'u' for an 'n' and thus the future Queen of Spain became 'Ena' – as a family joke.

Their third child, Leopold, was born on 21 May 1889, three days before Queen Victoria's 70th birthday, at Windsor Castle; the baby had a slight dislocation of a hip which led later in life to lameness. Seventeen months later another boy was born at Balmoral Castle on 3 October 1891 and in a tribute to Scotland, Donald was added to his two other names: Maurice and Victor. Liko's family was now complete and with the children of his brother Louis, there were now seven bouncing Battenbergs–the eighth, Louis, the later Earl Mountbatten of Burma, was still to arrive. Strictly speaking, there were, of course, two more Battenberg children, those of Sandro, ex-Prince of Bulgaria, from his morganatic marriage with Johanna Loisinger, but their name was Hartenau, while Marie Battenberg, Princess zu Erbach, had, between 1872 and 1883, given birth to two boys and a girl.

The wailing of Beatrice's babies and later their fresh voices and laughter were music in Queen Victoria's ears. She spent every moment she could spare from State affairs with her grandchildren, who called her 'Gangan'. Though she had become very frail and her sight was failing, she never minded the children bursting into her apartments. Important visitors having an audience of Her Britannic Majesty were sometimes taken aback to see a worn golliwog or a spinning top lying on a chair in the audience room. By the Queen's order the children had miniature carts and ponies for exploring the royal gardens, where their grandmother spent her happiest hours watching them play and talking to them. Golden-haired Ena, she insisted, was the image of her beloved 'Benjamina', while baby Leopold 'was so alike in his ways and looks to my dear Leopold' – her son whose death at 30 in the year of Beatrice's engagement she still deeply mourned.

The childhood of these Battenbergs was happy, but their up-bringing in the hands of their grandmother was restricted. They grew to maturity without the widening influence of their father. Thus they did not develop the typical qualities of independence, talents, and faults, so much more apparent in the children of Louis of Battenberg, reared in greater freedom.

For a long time Liko had envied his brother who, rising in naval rank, had travelled the world, often accompanying the Prince of Wales, while he had been confined to the matriarchal households of Windsor, Osborne or Balmoral. When, in 1895, the British Government decided to send an Expeditionary Force to the Gold Coast – where King Prempeh of the Ashantis was raiding the British colony, stealing cattle and taking the Queen's black subjects into captivity and selling them as slaves – Liko decided that this was an opportunity to escape his apron-string life. The Queen had given her 28-year-old grandson Prince Christian Victor (the son of her third daughter Princess Helena who was married to Prince of Schleswig-Holstein) permission to join the African expedition, and Liko begged her to be allowed to go, too. At first she demurred but eventually agreed, when Princess Beatrice firmly supported her husband's request. 'All his brothers had distinguished themselves in military careers', she told her mother, 'we all admired Sandro when he led his troops in battle in Bulgaria; Louis is a splendid naval officer, even young Franzjos had seen military service. The

Ashanti campaign will be a wonderful opportunity for our dear Liko . . .'

The Queen still hesitated, having heard that the fatal climate at the Gold Coast was taking a heavy toll amongst British soldiers and colonial servants. But when Liko told her: 'I want to volunteer because I hope to prove in this way my devotion to my adopted country', she had to agree. The announcement of his appointment as a colonel with the Ashanti Expedition produced some ironic comments in London newspapers. Liko forcefully replied by having his application to Field Marshal Lord Wolseley published:

> 'I am an Englishman and I want to show the people of England that I am ready to take the rough with the smooth. I know there is no glory and honour to be got out of it, and I know the danger of subsequent ill health and perhaps death from malaria, which I know is so grave in that country.'

He went in May 1895 to Aldershot for training and sailed on December 7 to Africa. He was under the command of Colonel Sir Francis Scott, and immediately after his arrival at Akroful led his battalion through dense jungle forests towards Sula and thence towards Kumasi. At Prahsu his troops struck camp. In spite of the oppressive heat, he felt well and that evening he went for a stroll with Major Ferguson, who later complained of faintness. Two days later the major was dead. Liko sent a few telegrams home, lamenting his comrade's death and mentioning that 'the climate was beginning to tell on the troops'. The next message which reached Queen Victoria and Princess Beatrice was from the War Office, containing a report from Surgeon-Captain Hilliard, that 'Prince Henry of Battenberg has had a slight attack of fever and has gone back to base'. This was on January 12, and three days later a laconic dispatch arrived: 'Battenberg arrived at Prahsu. State of health worse'. On 17 January he was brought by stretcher to Cape Coast Castle and, although he protested that he wanted to stay until Kumasi was occupied and King Prempeh captured or dead, he was taken aboard H.M.S. *Blonde* which steamed for England. On 20 January he died in the ship's cabin, almost at the very hour when the Ashanti king capitulated at Kumasi. Liko's African campaign, in which he gave his life, had lasted exactly 20 days. His last message

Sir Ernest Cassel, the
German-Jewish financier
and friend of King Edward VII,
grandfather of Countess
Mountbatten of Burma.

Mrs Anette Cassel, born Miss Maxwell, of Darlington. Cassel's
'English Rose', who died three years after their marriage.

Maudie Cassel (1880–1911), Sir Ernest Cassel's only daughter,
married Colonel Wilfrid Ashley (later Lord Mount Temple); mother
of Edwina, who became Countess Mountbatten of Burma.

Princess Alice of Battenberg
(born 1885), at the age of 18, at
the time of her engagement to
Prince Andrew of Greece.

Prince Andrew and Princess Alice of Greece, parents of Prince
Philip, the Duke of Edinburgh, in exile in London after the Greek
revolution in 1922.

for his wife was typical of a Battenberg: 'If I die, tell the Princess from me that I came here not to win glory but from a sense of duty'. His death was shattering to both Queen Victoria and his wife, who had become a widow at 38, at the same age as her mother.

Liko's four children grew up fatherless, but they remained the Queen's favourites during the last five years of her life. The eldest, Drino (the later Lord Carisbrooke), once said that when he went to Wellington College he missed his grandmother more than his mother. Drino joined the Royal Navy, but in 1908 transferred to the army, and in the first world war served with the Grenadier Guards in France. In May 1917 it was announced that he, with other members of his family, had assumed the name of Mountbatten; on 17 July King George V raised him to the peerage as Marquess of Carisbrooke, Earl of Berkhamsted and Viscount Launceston, and two days later he married Lady Irene Denison, the only daughter of the second Earl of Londesborough.

He had the Battenberg initiative: although he could expect high promotion in the army and perform the duties of a minor member of the Royal Family – as did his mother for the ensuing quarter century almost until her death at 87 in 1944 – he went instead into business. Although he was 33, he trained as a junior clerk with the banking house of Lazard Brothers and soon was offered directorships of several important companies, including Eagle Star Insurance and Unilever. He took interest in some unusual institutions, such as the Bribery Prevention League, of which he became the president, and it must have been another streak of Mountbatten originality that, instead of turning to the 'Sport of kings', he took up a much more democratic pursuit, becoming Senior Steward of the Greyhound Racing Club. At the outbreak of the second world war he insisted at 53 on serving, and joined the R.A.F. as a non-flying Pilot Officer. He died in 1959, three years after his wife. There was only one child of the marriage, Lady Iris Mountbatten, born in 1920, of whom mention is made elsewhere in these pages.

The two other sons of Liko and Beatrice both died young. Leopold, although he dreamed of becoming a soldier, was through lameness and delicate health unfit for military service. He went to Magdalene College, Cambridge, remained unmarried, lived with his mother at Kensington Palace and travelled widely, visiting Canada, Australia, India and Japan. He was the scholar and intellectual of his family, but he did not lack the Mountbatten gumption. In 1914, lame as he was, he pestered everybody, from the King and Lord Kitchener downwards, to be allowed to join the Forces. Suffering continuous pains from chronic sciatica and inflammation of hip muscles and often in hospital, he nevertheless went with the King's Royal Rifles to France and, being unfit for combatant duties, served as an A.D.C. with an advanced divisional staff, being mentioned in dispatches and achieving the rank of Major. He fell seriously ill, underwent surgical treatment after the war, and on 22 April 1922 died during an emergency operation at Kensington Palace, at the age of 33. His mother who had devotedly nursed him was on a brief holiday in Sicily, and only nurses and servants were at his bedside.

The youngest, Maurice, was the liveliest of Liko's sons. From Sandhurst he passed out in 1911 to the King's Royal Rifles, and during the following three years he proved himself an ardent sportsman, particularly interested in aviation, making many solo flights from Hendon in string-and-canvas machines, and hoping to become a pilot in the new Royal Flying Corps. But dutifully he went with his regiment to France and from the very first engagement fought in the front-line. One of his surviving N.C.O.s, Corporal John Jolly of Newport (Mon.), gave the following brief description of young Prince Maurice Battenberg's gallantry: 'It was after the retreat from Mons that an order came to our company that a bridge must be taken at once. It was blocked with carts, broken furniture, glass and barbed wire. Lieutenant Battenberg told us that we must get through. He was first man over it, during a murderous enemy bombardment, a brave act for a young officer to go alone and thus inspire his men.'

For this he was mentioned in dispatches, but on 27 October 1914, less than three months after the beginning of hostilities, leading his company in an attack he was struck by a piece of shrapnel and died almost immediately, a few days after his 23rd birthday. Like many other brave British soldiers he was buried at the great war cemetery at Ypres. It was an ironic twist of Fate that his death from a German bullet coincided with the triumph of those behind the anti-German hate campaign in Britain who on 28 October, forced his uncle, Admiral Prince Louis of Battenberg, to resign as First Sea Lord.

The only daughter of Liko and Beatrice, golden-haired Ena, had many years earlier been removed from the scene of Europe's power politics which had led to the war in which her family was so grievously to suffer. After Queen Victoria's death, Beatrice's silken thraldom ended; at last she could devote more time to her daughter who in 1905 'came out' at 17, at a modest occasion, the Infirmary Ball at Ryde. But King Edward VII had not forgotten his mother's favourites: 'The King invited my mother and myself to stay afterwards at Buckingham Palace, as he wished me to come out officially', Ena later recalled. She accepted that a husband, carefully chosen for her by her mother, would be a minor German prince or, perhaps, one of the many Russian Grand-Dukes.

In June 1905, King Edward invited the 19-year-old King Alfonso XIII of Spain to London. Born posthumously, a king in his cradle already, he was thin and unprepossessing, with the thick lip of the Habsburgs inherited from his Austrian mother, Queen Christina, who had been Spain's Regent during his minority. But he was an intelligent and well-educated young man who as a boy had often rebelled against the stiff etiquette of the Spanish Court. Once, when his mother punished him by locking him in his study, he opened a palace window and cried: 'Long live the republic!'

It was no secret that his mother was looking for a bride for him, and the possibility of a political marriage to an English princess was not discarded, in spite of the difference in religion being at first regarded as an insuperable handicap. There were rumours that Alfonso XIII might become engaged to Princess Margaret of Connaught, King Edward's niece and four years older than the Spanish monarch. On his journey to London, Alfonso had narrowly escaped death when a Spanish anarchist threw a bomb at his carriage, but he was fearless and arrived the next day at Buckingham Palace quite undisturbed. In London he felt rather lost; it seemed all the young princesses invited to festivities in his honour avoided him. Princess Margaret was certainly not interested, she had fallen in love with the Crown Prince of Sweden, whom she soon afterwards married.

When Alfonso was asked by the Princess of Wales (the later Queen Mary) whether he liked any of the young ladies he had met at Buckingham Palace, he replied: 'Only one, the fair-haired, but I do not know her name.' Told that she was the King's 18-year-old niece, Princess Ena of Battenberg, he began to pay her great attention.

Princess Beatrice knew his mother, whom Queen Victoria had greatly admired, and a correspondence ensued. Soon Beatrice told her brother: 'Alfonso wants to marry Ena, Queen Christina is in favour, but the hitch is the question of religion, a Spanish queen must, of course, be a Roman Catholic.' King Edward VII was pleased about his niece's great prospect and discussed the tangled problem with his ministers and the Archbishop of Canterbury, Dr Davidson.

In January 1906 Queen-Mother Christina suggested that Princess Beatrice and Ena should go to Biarritz, where Alfonso could visit them without too much publicity. In his high-speed Panhard, he crossed the frontier from his summer palace at San Sebastian almost daily for several weeks, and later took Ena to his mother. It was agreed that no announcement of an engagement would be made until the religious problem could be solved. King Edward showed a very real concern for his Battenberg niece. With his Foreign Secretary, Sir Edward Grey, and ecclesiastical advisers he arrived in Biarritz on 5 March and had long conferences with Alfonso and Spanish ministers. All was meant to be secret, but newspaper reporters had trailed him from London and the news leaked out.

Immediately violent opposition sprang up in Anglican circles. In letters to *The Times* it was pointed out that the Royal Marriage Act forbade marriages with Catholics – although its provisions could hardly apply to Princess Ena. Protestant organisations staged protest meetings and issued appeals to the King and Princess Beatrice, reminding them that Queen Victoria had been a staunch upholder of the Protestant creed and would have never consented to a marriage of her granddaughter to a 'papist'. Kaiser William II harshly registered his disapproval of the marriage project, less because he was a good Protestant but because he wanted to prevent yet another 'great political marriage' of a member of the despised Battenberg tribe.

King Edward VII, on this occasion strongly supported by his son, the later King George V, firmly cut short the opposition. After a somewhat stormy session with the Archbishop of Canterbury and leading ecclesiastics, he gave his consent, declaring that 'Princess Victoria Eugénie of Battenberg will sign a document formally renouncing all her and her descendants' rights to the English throne on becoming a Roman Catholic'. Even by the wildest stretch of imagination, Princess Ena could hardly be considered as in line of succession, anyway.

The protests were not altogether silenced but Ena could now go to France in order to receive instruction for her conversion. Her godmother, the former French Empress Eugénie, invited her to stay at her villa at Cap Martin on the Riviera. There and later at Versailles Monsignor Pringle, the Roman Catholic Bishop of Nottingham, introduced Ena to the dogmas of his church. In April 1906 King Alfonso came to see her at Osborne, where in the bark of an old tree they cut a heart and their names.

On 24 May Princess Ena, with her mother and her three brothers, travelled to Madrid. By then the animosity against her wedding had subsided; demonstratively, King Edward VII and Queen Alexandra bade them farewell at Victoria Station. Ena's married life began with drama. The wedding was held with all the pomp of the Spanish Court, the Cardinal of Toledo saying the nuptial Mass and blessing the bridal couple with the words 'Go in Peace', as they left the cathedral. A long procession moved through Madrid's streets bedecked with flags and flowers towards the main square, the Puerto del Sol, and the Royal Palace. When it reached Calle Major, the king ordered the coachman to halt for a moment, so that he and his bride could acknowledge the wild cheering. This saved their lives. On the balcony of No. 88 stood the anarchist Matteo Moral. Seeing the carriages approaching, he threw a bomb, just a few seconds too early.

The Prince of Wales (the later King George V) who was in a carriage in front, together with Ena's eldest brother Drino, gave perhaps the best eye-witness description:

'Our carriage was just in front of the one in which Queen-Mother Christina and my aunt, Princess Beatrice, were driving, and they were just ahead of Alfonso and Ena . . . we heard a loud report and at first thought it was the first gun of salute. We soon learned that a bomb was thrown at the carriage of the King and Queen. It burst between the wheel horses and the front of the carriage, killing some 20 people and wounding about 50 or 60, mostly officers and soldiers. Alfonso and Ena were not touched, although covered with glass . . . The Marquesa Torlosa and her niece were killed, standing on a balcony just below that from which the bomb was thrown . . . Sir Maurice Bunsen (the British ambassador) and Colonel Lowther (the British military attaché) and four officers of the 16th Lancers, who stood nearby, rushed to the carriage and assisted Ena out of it; both she and Alfonso showed great courage and presence of mind. They got into another carriage at once and continued the drive to the Palace amid frantic cheering . . . The assassin was allowed to escape. I believe the Spanish police and detectives are about the worst in the world. No precautions whatever had been taken; they are the most happy-go-lucky people here . . . Eventually we had lunch at 3 p.m. I proposed Alfonso's and Ena's health, which was not easy after the emotions caused by this terrible affair.'

The two young people had certainly showed courage. With scores of killed and wounded lying around their carriage, and frenzied Spanish officials trying to drag their king and queen into the building of the Italian embassy opposite the scene of the outrage, Alfonso ordered them to calm down and said to his wife: 'Come on, Ena, we shall drive on in another carriage', to which she immediately agreed.

It could not have been easy for Ena of Battenberg to settle down to her new dignity as Queen of Spain. The etiquette of the Madrid Court was the most formal in the world. Her stern mother-in-law was still very much the real ruler, and Spanish courtiers and grandees did not altogether take kindly to their English and ex-Protestant queen. She had changed from modest surroundings to a life of great luxury, splendid palaces, great balls and state visits, always surrounded by watchful eyes of hundreds of officials and servants. But her mother, Princess Beatrice, stayed with her for some time; even for their honeymoon at the magnificent palace of La Granja she went with the young couple.

Within eleven months Queen Ena gave birth to her first child; it was important that it should be a male heir to the throne. It was, and the birth was celebrated with all the ancient pomp, King Alfonso carrying the child on a golden, lace-covered tray into the throne room to prove to assembled ministers, courtiers and nobles that an heir had been born. The Pope, who became one of the child's godfathers, sent Ena the Order of the Golden Rose, and Spain celebrated *fiestas* for a week.

But little Alfonso was a frail child and it was soon discovered that he suffered from haemophilia, the incurable 'bleeding disease' which prevents the clotting of the blood so that a minor injury, even a harmless tooth extraction, may cause a fatal haemorrhage. Queen Ena gave birth to six more children. Her second son, Infante Jaime, was born deaf and dumb, the next child was stillborn, but the three following, two daughters, Infanta Beatriz and Infanta Maria Christina – named after their maternal and paternal grandmothers – and a third son, Don Juan, were healthy. Then the youngest son, Don Gonzalo, born in 1914, also had haemophilia.

Congenital illness in the Spanish royal family made many influential people, particularly among the ultra-conservative and clerical elements, turn against the 'foreign Queen'. They disliked her former Protestantism – some indeed blamed it for her children's sickness – her fondness of dancing, tennis and golf, which was regarded as undignified for a Queen of Spain, and also the royal couple's frequent travels abroad, particularly their visits to the British Royal Family and the Battenbergs. Moreover, persistant rumours sprang up that the haemophilia of the royal children had been inherited from their maternal ancestors. There might have been some truth in this. Many years later, in 1962, medical experts in Britain expressed the opinion that Queen Victoria's mother (the Duchess of Kent, born a Princess of Saxe-Coburg) had passed the disease to some of her descendants.[1] It is a fact that it is always passed from the women to the men, never affecting women and often bypassing one or two generations. Tsarevitch Alexei of Russia (the only son of the last Tsar) also suffered from haemophilia, whilst all his sisters were free from it. He, too, was a great-grandson of Queen Victoria, like the Spanish princes. On the other hand, none of her grandsons and great-grandsons in direct male descent in the British Royal Family were affected, although it was rumoured that Princess Beatrice's son Leopold, who died under a surgeon's knife, might have suffered from it.

[1] Cf. *Sunday Telegraph*, London, 2 December 1962.

Queen Ena's marriage went through many personal and political upsets. In the first world war, with Spain remaining neutral, the sympathies of the Court were divided: Queen-Mother Christina an Austrian, Ena pro-British, and Alfonso, though inclined towards the Allies, careful never to annoy his formidable mother. Although Spain was spared the horrors of the world war, its after-effects made themselves felt. The revolutions in Germany, Austria and Russia encouraged socialist and anarchist movements; saddled with a disastrous war against Abdel Krim's Riff Kabyls in Morrocco, and on the verge of economic collapse, Spain went through a succession of army mutinies, rebellions and general strikes until the rise of the dictatorship of General Primo de Rivera.

In 1931 a period of renewed turmoil led to a bloodless revolution after the republican parties gained an overwhelming victory in municipal elections. King Alfonso and his family were forced to leave Spain without his formal abdication. The revolutionary junta proclaimed the republic, declared the king 'guilty of high treason' and confiscated all royal property. Once again a crown had slipped through Mountbatten fingers: Queen Ena's life in Madrid began with a bomb, it ended with a palace backdoor exit into exile.

Her life in many ways had been tragic. Alfonso was gifted, intelligent and charming, but like many Bourbons undecided and distrustful; his zest for life led him to superficial distractions and amusements, he devoted much of his time to motoring and polo-playing. Prophetically his wife once said: 'He is quickly tiring of everything, one day he will tire of me'. In exile in Rome he was at the bridge tables, while his wife spent long holidays in England with her Mountbatten family. King Alfonso died in 1941 at the Grand Hotel in Rome, at the age of only 55; his wife, after thirty-five years of marriage, never left his bedside during his last short illness.

The story of their children – 'quarter-Mountbattens' – is present history. The eldest son, Alfonso, married a Cuban lady of humble origin and renounced all rights to the throne. Gonzalo, the youngest, died from the bleeding sickness, Jaime, deaf and dumb, was hardly eligible as a Pretender to the Spanish throne, and thus the third son, Don Juan, the most 'English' of Queen Ena's children, was proclaimed by the Monarchist Party the rightful claimant.

Don Juan was Spain's first sailor-prince for many generations, having been a cadet at Dartmouth and having served as an honorary Royal Navy midshipman in H.M.S. *Enterprise*. The only one of Ena's sons enjoying good health, he had married a cousin, a Princess of Bourbon-Sicily, and lived in exile in Italy, France, Belgium, Switzerland and Portugal, acquiring university degrees in engineering and political science. Although General Franco had often reiterated that monarchy would one day be restored, Don Juan, partly because of his 'English past', was unacceptable, and his eldest son, Don Juan Carlos, born in 1938, was groomed for the Spanish throne.

After a secret meeting between his father and General Franco, Prince Juan Carlos, entered in 1957 at nineteen, the Military Academy at Saragossa and in due course became an officer in the Spanish army – the only member of King Alfonso's and Queen Ena's family who returned from exile. When he reached marriageable age, his grandmother, with all the inimitable skill of the Battenbergs for match-making, began to look for a suitable bride for him. It is said that at her Swiss home, at No. 24, Avenue de l'Elysée in Lausanne, Queen Ena had been presiding over many secret conferences, until her choice fell upon Princess Sophia of Greece, the daughter of the German-Danish King Paul of the Hellenes and his astute Prussian Queen Frederika, closely related to the Mountbattens. In 1962 the then 75-year-old ex-Queen Ena spared no effort to make this marriage possible. She travelled to Rome, assured the Pope that although Princess Sophia was of Greek-Orthodox faith, children of her marriage to Prince Juan Carlos would be Catholics, thus smoothing away a handicap for her grandson's claim to the Spanish throne. At the wedding in Athens in May 1962, she could rejoice in greeting many of her Moutbatten relatives, although the Duke of Edinburgh – who three years later, together with his two eldest children, the Prince of Wales and Princess Anne, attended the wedding of his nephew King Constantine and Princess Anne Maria of Denmark – was absent for obvious political reasons.

Queen Ena later also healed a threatening family rift when one of her granddaughters, Princess Sandra Torlonia (her daughter Infanta Beatriz had married in exile Prince Torlonia) insisted on marrying an Italian commoner, a Signor Clement Lecquio. She also reconciled her family to the marriage of Sandra's sister,

Princess Olympia Torlonia, who in 1965 wed an Englishman, Mr Paul Weiller, stepson of Sir John Russell, a British diplomat. When these lines were written in the winter of 1965, ex-Queen Ena, at 78, still took an active part in the destinies of her family and preserved a lively interest for all her Mountbatten relatives, paying regular visits to London.

Given political skill and favour, a sixth-generation Mountbatten descendant of Queen Victoria's favourite Henry of Battenberg, may wear, albeit precariously, the crown of Spain.

CHAPTER SEVEN

THE FIRST SEA LORD

Prince Louis of Battenberg,
First Marquess of Milford Haven

THE armies and navies of Europe in the nineteenth century had a long tradition of cosmopolitan command, mainly because frontiers meant little to the interrelated royal families. German princes served the Austrian emperor, Austrians fought in the service of German kingdoms and principalities, Frenchmen and Germans officered the Tsar's army, Russians served the Balkan princes. Only Britain stood firm in her traditions of material, moral and strategic separation: 'abroad' was full, at best, of wily politicians, at worst, of bloodthirsty anarchists. Despite their German royal house, or perhaps because of it, Continental ideology, customs, food and fashions were suspect, even spurned by the islanders. The fog might end at Dover, but the wogs began at Calais.

Britain's navy and army owed nothing to Continental traditions. After Abukir and Trafalgar, the Royal Navy emerged as the mightiest, the only, fleet to rule the oceans, a guarantor of the British Empire and the world-wide Pax Britannica. What more remarkable, then, that a German youth, the son of a Hesse prince and a nephew of the Russian Tsar, should reach the highest rank in Britain's seapower and serve his adopted country loyally and devotedly for half a century?

The story of Admiral Prince Louis of Battenberg, the later first Marquess of Milford Haven and father of Earl Mountbatten of Burma, so closely connected with such men as Lord Fisher and Lord Beresford, who had revolutionised naval technique and strategy, is the story of the growth of the Royal Navy in

size, equipment, efficiency and power and of its rapid technical
modernisation.

Prince Louis, whose father Alexander of Hesse was first a
Russian colonel fighting the Moslems in the Caucasus, then an
Austrian general against France and Italy, and finally a general
commanding South-German troops against Prussia in the war of
1866, was born on 11 September 1854 in Graz in Austria, and
spent his childhood in the many Italian garrison towns where his
father was stationed. He grew up against a cosmopolitan background, meeting during his childhood princely relations from
half of Europe's royal courts, even though his sister[1] insisted
that 'there was no more truly German home than ours . . . and
that our mother, a Russian-Pole and a Catholic, had only a good
influence on our German upbringing and on the Protestant spirit
of the family.' When by 1862 his family settled down at Heiligenberg, his father's sister and her husband, the Russian imperial
couple, and their children were frequent visitors. As a small boy
Louis invariably wore a Russian costume of a crimson or sky-
blue blouse, black velvet breeches, high leather boots and a
cockaded fur cap. His cousin, the later Grand Duke Louis IV of
Hesse-Darmstadt, seventeen years his senior, had in 1862 married
Princess Alice, Queen Victoria's second daughter; she and her
brother Prince Alfred of Edinburgh (through his own marriage
to the Tsar's daughter closely related with the Hesse and Battenberg families) were likewise regular guests at his parents' home.

Louis was a beautiful and extremely bright child. His sister
later wrote: 'We were one heart and soul, inseparable by day and
night. Louis had a sunny nature. He looked like a Raphael when
he was a little boy, like a Velasquez when he was older. It was as
if Nature, in addition to outward beauty, had showered her
gifts in profusion on this, her favourite . . . he learned quickly and
easily and all his talents seem to have fallen into his lap in the
same measure'.[2] At the age of four he could read German and
soon write it, and had begun to draw so well that the difficulties
of perspective did not exist for him. His gift for languages was
equally striking: apart from his native German, he knew Russian,
Italian and some French, and rapidly acquired a good knowledge

---

[1] Cf. Princess Marie zu Erbach-Schönberg, *Aus Stiller und Bewegter Zeit,* Brunswick, 1921.

[2] Princess Marie zu Erbach-Schönberg, op. cit.

of English before reaching his 'teens. He also became a gifted musician.

His family were mystified when at twelve he felt the call of the sea. Apart from a brief stay at Venice when he was still a toddler, he had hardly ever seen the sea; his passion was fostered by the books of naval battles and adventures he devoured, and by the stories his uncle Alfred of Edinburgh – then a Post-Captain in the Royal Navy – used to tell him. Soon he was determined to go to England and become a British sailor. The boy had to fight hard battles. His parents, in the words of his sister, 'were frightfully against making an Englishman of him', but in the end, with the help of his English aunt and uncle, he won. A tutor, a Mr Everett from Magdalen College, Oxford, was summoned to Heiligenberg and within a few months young Louis was not only proficient in the spoken and written language, but acquired sufficient knowledge of English and history to be able to look confidently towards the entry examinations prescribed for British naval cadets. On 25 September 1868, accompanied by his father and his tutor, he went to England. The next day he was taken to Dr Burney's school at Alverstroke; three days later he was formally entered as a naval cadet and placed on the books of H.M.S. *Victory*, Nelson's old flagship, flying the flag of the Commander-in-Chief at Portsmouth.

It had almost been overlooked that he also had to become a British subject. On 14 October Dr Burney hurried with him to a public notary at Gosport, where Prince Louis of Battenberg, aged 14, swore 'by Almighty God that I will be faithful and bear true allegiance to Her Majesty Queen Victoria, Her Heirs and Successors, according to law'; an oath he honourably kept all his life. Years later he remembered that hurried ceremony, the old notary in a greasy frock coat and the 'very dirty Bible', upon which he was told to lay his hand when swearing the oath. On 14 December he sat for his examination. He was quite confident he would pass, but he was worried, being a little short-sighted, that he would be asked to read the time by the clock of the Dockyard. He set his watch carefully by that clock and, giving a furtive look at his watch when the question was asked, passed this test, too, with flying colours.

His first seagoing experience early the following year was to be aboard H.M.S. *Bristol* under Prince Alfred, Duke of Edinburgh, but when the Prince of Wales learnt about it, he ordered that Cadet Louis Battenberg be appointed to the frigate *Ariadne,* which had been specially fitted out to take the future King Edward VII and Queen Alexandra for a Mediterranean cruise. Although when the Prince and Princess boarded the ship, Louis was invited with the officers to dine with them, from then on he was treated like any other midshipman and cadet on board. Life in the Navy was tough and the food appalling by modern standards. All the youngsters slept in hammocks in the small stuffy gun-room on the lower deck. The 'middies', like the men, had to eat the notorious, brick-hard ship's biscuits, bored into by maggots and weevils. When the maggots fell out they were sometimes put into pill-boxes and reserved for the 'Maggot Derby', a race – with bets – of the insects along the gunroom table, pencils being used as 'whips' to prod them on.

Life on the upper deck was very much more regal. When the Prince of Wales and his retinue later embarked on a flotilla of yachts for a journey up the Nile, 1,000 bottles of champagne, 3,000 of claret, 10,000 of beer and 20,000 of soda-water were loaded on escorting barges, with corresponding quantities of rich foodstuffs. Louis was allowed to join the party, was present at the great festivities staged in Cairo by the Khedive in honour of the British royal visitors, met Dr Lesseps, the creator of the Suez Canal, which was nearly completed and, when the Prince of Wales's retinue were showered with Orders and medals, the little cadet was not forgotten; he was as astonished as he was proud to receive the Medjidieh Order, Fourth Class. Later the Ariadne sailed to Constantinople and Athens. When at Pireaus Louis met King George I of the Hellenes, he could hardly imagine that one day one of the king's sons would become the husband of one of his daughters.

There followed five years' training on H.M.S. *Royal Alfred,* flagship of the North America and West Indies station, and a journey to India, once again with the Prince of Wales, on board the troopship *Serapis.* The young man's horizon had greatly widened. In India he travelled 7,000 miles with the Prince, hunting elephants and tigers, taking part in a Durbar and being entertained by maharajas, one of whom lodged the Prince of Wales in a bed of solid gold and insisted that he should have a silver bath-tub as a souvenir. It was the high noon of Imperial power in India. Again, could Prince Louis have guessed that his son would reign, briefly, as a Viceroy in its sunset?

When during these journeys the official artist, Mr Brierly, fell ill Louis put his drawing talent to good use: he produced many admirable sketches, some being published in the *Illustrated London News,* no mean achievement for a 17-year-old amateur. In 1876, now a Sub-Lieutenant, Prince Louis joined H.M.S. *Sultan,* captained by Prince Alfred of Edinburgh, and the following year the famous 'spying incident' occurred, when the British fleet was anchored off Constantinople and Louis's 'Russian' brother Sandro was entertained aboard the British ships.[1] This incident, wildly exaggerated by London newspapers, nearly cut short Louis's naval career. In the next few years he enjoyed long sea voyages, particularly in the Pacific, culminating in visits to the king of Fiji, a giant nearly 7 feet tall, and to the Mikado of Japan in 1881. In the meantime he had, during spells at home stations, passed several examinations and, although he had had little time to prepare himself, he passed them all with first class certificates. The results of his gunnery examination were described by the Board as the best ever recorded, which must have been partly due to the excellent drawings, plans and charts he had made.

In 1882 he was on half-pay leave and went home to Heiligenberg for his first long holiday. He spent most of it in the company of his cousin, the 19-year-old Princess Victoria of Hesse. Her mother, Queen Victoria's daughter, had died three years earlier at the age of only 35, and the young princess had been often invited to England, where Prince Louis had been meeting her at Osborne and at Marlborough House. He now stood high in the regard of both Queen Victoria and the Prince of Wales; the Queen had written to his father, praising his 'excellent conduct and devoted naval service'. For some time it had been no secret that the handsome Prince and Queen Victoria's granddaughter had fallen in love. Louis could expect to be accepted as a suitor, and during his stay in Darmstadt he asked his uncle for Victoria's hand. The Grand Duke was greatly pleased; Queen Victoria's consent was requested, speedily received, and the engagement announced. But it was decided that the young people should wait until Louis's expected promotion would enable him to set up a home and rear a family. When later Princess Victoria travelled to

[1] See *supra* page 76.

London, Louis's sister Marie, (Princess zu Erbach-Schönberg) accompanied her and stayed at Clarence House with the Edinburghs. At a ball at Lord Carrington's the Prince of Wales danced the first waltz with her. The Battenbergs had become personalities at the English Court. Soon Henry was to marry the Queen's youngest daughter.

At his wedding in Darmstadt on 30 April 1884, almost the entire British Royal Family was present: Queen Victoria with Princess Beatrice, the Prince and Princess of Wales, Prince Alfred of Edinburgh and his wife, the Queen's eldest daughter Victoria and her husband Crown Prince Frederick of Germany. All the Hesses and Battenbergs were there, of course; Sandro, the Prince of Bulgaria, had come despite his troubles with the Tsar, who had spurned his cousin's invitation but was represented by Grand Duke Sergius, who was married to a Hesse princess.

The wedding was a great royal occasion, but it was marred by the unpardonable indiscretion of the bride's father, Grand Duke Louis IV of Hesse. Queen Victoria expected her son-in-law to be still deeply mourning his wife. Instead, he had chosen the occasion to marry secretly and morganatically his mistress, Madame Kolemin, a divorcée of Polish origin. Shortly before his daughter's wedding he admitted to his family that he had promised his mistress to marry her then, because she hoped to be invited to the great festivities.

'A terrible prospect', wrote Louis's father in his diary. 'The Grand Duke seems to have lost his head completely. He says that stories of the bad reputation his flame bears all over Europe are malicious inventions! Julie is quite beside herself and so am I. The Queen [Victoria] has no idea of it, and for the present no one dares tell her.' The infatuated Grand Duke completely spoiled his daughter's wedding. The young princess looked pale, thin and ill, her eyes red-rimmed from crying, with most of the guests in a state of agitation. The Prince of Wales eventually broke the news to his mother.

On the following morning the Queen asked Prince Alexander of Hesse to come and see her and told him angrily: 'The situation seems to be even more serious than we thought. It appears that the Grand Duke is already married'. Prince Alexander had to confirm that Grand Duke Louis had, in fact, contracted a civil marriage on the day of his daughter's wedding. 'This is quite outrageous,' the Queen exclaimed. 'I can only say that I am beside myself, utterly crushed! I loved him as my own son. To do this, at this moment, on the very day his dear daughter married your dear son, when we were all happily gathered together here . . . it is simply beyond all expression!'[1]

Having recovered breath and composure, the Queen commanded Prince Alexander 'to do all you can to collect proofs of that woman's badness and to discover whether this unspeakable marriage was at all legal'. Queen Victoria's rigid principles of morality and decorum led her to condemn Madame Kolemin as 'a horrible and abominable woman', and she was determined that the marriage must be annulled. As usual, the Grandmother of Europe was busybodying herself, even though on this occasion she was justified in resenting her son-in-law's stupid behaviour. But even Prince Alexander's diplomacy was fruitless. Both the Grand Duke and Madame Kolemin insisted they were quite legally married and that they were determined to remain so.

The Prince of Wales then decided to bring the Grand Duke and his morganatic wife to their senses, 'if only for the sake of poor Victoria and Louis'. He went to Madame Kolemin and held a document under her nose, asking her to sign it there and then. It read: 'I admit that I agreed too hastily to the civil marriage on 30 April. I promise on my word of honour to retract it and to regard it as null and void'. Such a declaration, hurriedly composed by the Prince of Wales and Alexander of Hesse, had of course no legal value whatever. At another stormy interview, which lasted for two hours and during which Madame Kolemin went repeatedly into hysterics cursing the entire English royal family, she declared that she would sign nothing, before seeing 'my husband, the Grand Duke'. The latter had gone into hiding in fear of his formidable mother-in-law, but when he and Madame Kolemin met the Prince of Wales again the next morning, there was another terrible scene, the lady threatening to kill herself and produce 'a scandal which you and Queen Victoria will remember all your lives . . .'. Indeed, she gripped a paper knife and tried to stab herself in front of the Prince of Wales and was prevented only with difficulty from doing so.

The wedding guests dispersed in a very gloomy mood. The members of the British Royal Family and also the German Crown

[1] Corti, E., *Unter Zaren und Gekrönten Frauen,* Salzburg, 1936.

Prince told the Grand Duke that they would break off all personal relations with him and never speak to him again. In the end, the Grand Duke's marriage was dissolved by mutual consent by the Darmstadt civil court, and Madame Kolemin departed from Hesse with a handsome 'golden handshake' from her temporary husband.

If their wedding was overshadowed by this scandal, the married life of Louis of Battenberg and Victoria began in England under the happiest auspices. Louis found Princess Victoria a most understanding wife. To a close friend he wrote in 1885, not long after the birth of his first child, Princess Alice:

> 'She is really more English than German, and we invariably speak English together, which may seem strange at first sight. She is a regular sailor's wife, and takes an immense interest in all naval matters. She knows all my naval chums and all about them, including yourself, of course . . . I am more keen than ever about serving on, and she is ready to go anywhere with me. We are not blessed with earthly goods, and have to live in a small way, though we are all the happier for it, I believe.'[1]

Prince Louis received his first independent command in 1889 – the year when his daughter Louise, the later Queen of Sweden was born – in the destroyer H.M.S. *Scout*, but his big promotion came three years later, when as a Captain he was recalled to the Admiralty as Assistant Director of Naval Intelligence, Head of the Mobilisation Department and Chief of Staff to the Second Sea Lord. Soon afterwards he was also appointed naval adviser to the War Office. Inter-service co-ordination has always been an irksome and thankless job, requiring much diplomatic skill. The amount of effort needed was shown by his sitting on seven important committees dealing with such divergent matters as 'problems of enemy invasion of Great Britain', the role of Royal Artillery and Royal Engineers in forts and minefields, torpedo equipment, the introduction of electric light aboard ships and in shore installations, matters concerning colonial defence, submarine mining, general armament. He became chief secretary to the joint naval and military Committee of Defence – in a sense an embryo of the organisation to which his son was to devote much work and thought sixty years later.

[1] Kerr, M., *Prince Louis of Battenberg,* Longmans, London, 1934.

Working from rooms in the Horse Guards, once used by the Duke of Wellington, he settled many inter-service rivalries with great skill and good humour, giving offence to no one. When he left at the end of 1894 for a three-year tour at sea, in command of the cruiser *Cambrian*, the Duke of Cambridge, Commander-in-Chief of the Army, paid him this compliment, even more remarkable as it came from a soldier to a sailor: 'You have produced a mutual feeling of goodwill and unanimity, which I have always wished to see established, and which by your tact and sound judgment you have brought about to the fullest extent'. And from the War Office, General Sir Redvers Buller wrote: 'I suppose you like a ship more than a joint Secretaryship . . . but whatever I may have done, I feel I owe greatly to your ability and energy, and the very conciliatory spirit you have enthused into all differences'.

Prince Louis was rising not only in rank but in status. His family connections helped, of course. With his family growing – in 1892 his first son, George, was born – he had rented a house at Walton-on-Thames, and when his brother-in-law and his wife, Tsarevitch Nicholas and Alix of Russia, came to England, they spent three weeks there, after their state visit with the Queen and the Prince of Wales. Tsar Alexander III, who had not been friendly to the Battenbergs, was at 48 dying from Bright's disease. When his son succeeded him and Prince Louis went to St Petersburg in April 1896 for the new Tsar's Coronation, he was entrusted by Lord Salisbury with a delicate mission: to discuss with prime minister Lobanov-Rostovsky Russia's demand that the Suez Canal should be open to Russian warships. It was another facet of the eternal Eastern Question which had worried British governments for generations. Prince Louis succeeded in assuaging the Russians.

He was happy to be at sea again, but was to suffer two family bereavements which greatly affected him: in September 1895 his mother, Princess Julie of Battenberg, that 'poor Polish orphan' who had risen to such great heights, died at Heiligenberg at the age of 70, and shortly afterwards, in January 1896, his brother Henry died during the Ashanti campaign on the Gold Coast.

It was also the period when the first jealousies over Prince Louis became evident among some of the chairborne admirals.

Despite his many preoccupations he had found time for serious study of new naval techniques and had invented a course indicator, which was adopted as a standard instrument and, in spite of radar, is still being used by the world's navies. Prince Louis had been given the command of the *Cambrian*, one of the Royal Navy's most modern ships and Queen Victoria's escort ship during her travels to France, and naturally her captain, in the Queen's company, was meeting foreign royalties, statesmen and naval commanders. All this was, of course, galling to some of the senior officers in London. On one occasion the editor of a London newspaper wrote to Prince Louis, enclosing an article sent to his paper by a well-known admiral. The article (whose author wanted to remain anonymous, but whose name the editor told the Prince) drew attention to Prince Louis's German birth, referred to H.M.S. *Cambrian* as 'Battenberg's private yacht', questioned whether he should hold naval rank at all, suggested that he should resign, and spitefully belittled his work. The editor refused to publish the article, and it was also rejected by all other journals which the author later approached.

Ironically, when the anonymous admiral later quarrelled with a distinguished personage, Prince Louis interceded for him, ending the dispute and saving his enemy's position. Prince Louis was a man without guile and never vindictive. Yet, when the war broke out in 1914, the same admiral led the pack which was let loose against the man who had forgiven and befriended him.

Other naval leaders fully acknowledged Prince Louis as an officer of distinguished patriotism, great ability and practical foresight. The redoubtable and tempestuous Admiral 'Jacky' Fisher, who had been predicting a war with Germany for twenty years before its outbreak, got him to write memoranda on subjects connected with the organisation of naval Intelligence and naval staffs, needed to keep the Royal Navy ready for a war at short notice. In a memorandum dated 25 February 1902, when Prince Louis held the command of the new battleship *Implacable*, he wrote:

'It is thought by many who look around and see what is done by other maritime Great Powers, that the business of "Preparation for War", as carried out by the "Chief of the

Admiralty General Staff" of continental nations, does not occupy that prominent, not to say paramount, position at the Admiralty, which its importance seems to demand.

'The machinery, in the shape of the (miscalled) Intelligence Department, is there; it requires enlarging and strengthening and above all it requires someone at its head of sufficient power and influence. Everything points to the First Sea Lord as being the proper person to be its real head.'[1]

He added a number of extremely lucid suggestions for re-organising the Admiralty's administrative and Intelligence services. A few months later he was appointed Director of Naval Intelligence and, mindful of the growing threat from the Kaiser's naval ambitions, he began his long campaign to modernise organisation and improve strategic plans, in order to prepare for modern warfare, whilst many admirals were still thinking in terms of the Crimean War. He awakened the Government and the Admiralty to the new, unthought-of dangers to merchant shipping arising from the submarine, the torpedo boat and the lone commerce raider. He wrote a memorandum on 'Commerce Protection in War', the first thorough guide to this subject since sail had given way to steam. Indeed, it was the first step towards the organisation of the convoy system, which proved vital to Britain's survival in two world wars.

He was a clear thinker with no time for those who could not adapt themselves to new conditions and he did not mince his words. He pointed out that the Royal Navy's Whitehead torpedo practice was antiquated; he advocated long-range firing from fast-moving ship at another fast-moving vessel – and Germany's naval rearmament had provided her with many fast ships. He sharply objected to the complacent attitude of the War Office, responsible for Britain's coastal defences. 'Why could not men of the Royal Garrison Artillery be well trained to attack enemy ships with shore guns?' he asked. 'Why could they not be made really competent with special weapons?' He was equally critical of antiquated Intelligence methods: 'What especial opportunity have the officers and men of the new Channel Fleet of becoming familiar with foreign ships? They largely rely on the information that the Naval Intelligence Department supplies them in the

[1] Kerr, op. cit.

shape of pictures, plans and descriptions. But they have other things to learn, while the Royal Garrison Artillery officers have nothing else to learn. How can people be so helpless! When have they ever seriously attempted to educate themselves . . .? All they [the army] ask for is that when war is upon us we should detail hundreds of sea officers to join their batteries and stand behind the battery commanders with a spy glass and point out the enemy ships . . . and advise as to what to aim at and when to fire. It is childish. There is no other word for it.'[1]

This sort of lucid, outspoken comment obviously did not endear Prince Louis to some admirals and generals. He had the photographic memory, the passion for detail, the ancestral Teutonic thoroughness that his son Louis – then a boy of two or three – was also to show when he in turn held high rank. But he was not a stick-in-the mud; he had kept the 'sunny nature' of his childhood, he had a keen sense of humour, he devoted as much time as he could spare to his family and friends. At 50, still strikingly handsome, he was an excellent dancer and a lover of music and the theatre. Neither was he against some innocent fun, though he rarely had time for it. Once, with King Edward VII, who was a frequent visitor to the South of France, he put a modest stake on the roulette table at the Casino of Monte Carlo, and repeated it 448 times on *rouge*, winning every time and being pleased about his fantastic luck like a little boy.

Before Prince Louis left Whitehall once again in 1905, as a Rear-Admiral, commanding the Second Cruiser Squadron, one of his Assistant Directors of Intelligence wrote of him:

'It was a pleasure to take papers to Prince Louis for a decision or for an opinion, and his wonderful memory was an endless cause of astonishment. When a document was brought to him, with its accompanying memoranda . . . he always instantly remembered the full particulars . . . and the many views that had been expressed with regard to the subject, and this, although he might not have had it before him for a long time, and meanwhile had been overwhelmed with lots of other important matters requiring great consideration.'

However, there were times when uncomplimentary things were said about Prince Louis. All his life he was able to smile over a

[1] Kerr, M., op. cit., p. 183.

letter, to which he gave a special page in his scrap book. It was
sent to him by an Irish-American from Chicago, when his
squadron was visiting the United States and Canada, and it was
brief and to the point: 'I am hoping for an opportunity to plaster
your Royal Puss with rotten eggs!'

When he was Director of Naval Intelligence he was granted a
short leave to give away his daughter Alice at her wedding at
Darmstadt to Prince Andrew of Greece. It was a great event with
many members of the British Royal Family and the Tsar and
Tsaritza of Russia present.[1] Another even more exacting royal
occasion, because of its political and personal implications, was
the visit of Kaiser William II at Gibraltar, shortly after King
Edward VII had visited Prince Louis's flagship H.M.S. *Drake*.
The Kaiser had pompously announced that he was coming as
'the Grand Admiral of the German Imperial Navy', and Prince
Louis therefore decided, with a twinkle in his eye, to treat his
awkward cousin as an admiral and not as the German Emperor.
The Kaiser was greeted with only a 19-gun salute, due to a
commanding admiral, instead of a 21-gun salute which honours
a monarch. The Union Jack was hoisted beside the German
Naval Flag and not beside the German Imperial Standard. The
Kaiser was peeved about 'that Battenberg cheek', but said nothing
in public.

In 1908 Prince Louis, promoted Vice-Admiral, was Commander-in-Chief of the Atlantic Fleet, in 1912 he was made
Second Sea Lord, and on 9 December 1913 achieved his life's
ambition, alas, for too brief a period: he was appointed First
Sea Lord.

The menace of Germany was now plain to see. Prince Louis
had less than a year to make the final preparations for the greatest
challenge the Royal Navy had to meet since the days of Napoleon,
when in the words of Admiral Mahan 'a distant line of storm-
battered British ships, upon which the Grande Armée never
looked, stood between Napoleon and the domination of the
world.'

The Royal Navy was the focus of intense pride and patriotism
in Britain and the Empire; one British boy in three wore a sailor
suit. It represented the culmination of many years of intensive
research, building, development and training to which Prince

[1] See *infra* page 231.

Louis had made a very great contribution. It was greater in size, more devastating in fire power than the fleets of all the other great maritime nations combined. Air power had not yet risen sufficiently to shatter the towering dreadnoughts and battleships cased in armour plate and mounting 15-in guns.

Prince Louis worked ceaselessly, studying, writing, organising, inspecting, prodding, considering new ideas, making fresh plans to strengthen and develop the new modernised navy, not only at sea but in the long lines of supplies and shore communications. Every day, often deep into the night, he studied and improved the dispositions of all his ships in case war should suddenly break out.

At the Admiralty he had an understanding friend: Winston Churchill. It was thus that Prince Louis could take a crucial decision during the last few days before that memorable 4 August 1914. After the assassinations at Sarajevo, Austro-Hungary ordered on 24 July mobilisation against Serbia. On the following day, a Saturday, Prince Louis remained at his desk at the Admiralty, when the Prime Minister and Cabinet members had gone for their week-end in the country. In London the crisis in South-East Europe was not yet regarded as a danger inevitably leading to a world conflict. Certain military precautions had been taken, but the Home Fleet at Portland had been ordered to disperse. Prince Louis recorded the events during that week-end thus:

'Ministers with their week-end holidays are incorrigible. Things looked pretty bad on Saturday . . . but Asquith, Grey, Churchill and all the rest left London. I sat here (at the Admiralty) all Sunday, reading all the telegrams from embassies as they arrived. On Monday morning the big fleet at Portland had orders to disperse, demobilise, and give leave.

'I took it upon myself to countermand everything by telegraph on Sunday afternoon. When the Ministers hurried back late that evening they cordially approved my action, and we had the drawn sword in our hands to back up our urgent advice. I breakfasted with the King on Monday morning to report the action taken.'

On that day Austro-Hungary had declared war on Serbia; the First World War had started. Winston Churchill worked in closest harmony with Prince Louis during the last months of peace and the early weeks of the war. He could not have wished to have a better, a more enlightened, more pugnacious First Sea Lord, so much in agreement with his own bold naval strategy. But Churchill himself was being frustrated by timid Cabinet members, and Prince Louis's enemies – mainly a handful of retired and disgruntled admirals jealous of his abilities and advancement – soon began a 'patriotic' whispering campaign in the Service clubs against him, the German-born First Sea Lord.

The British were the most unwarlike people in the world. But the German attack on 'little Belgium' and the ensuing irresponsible anti-German hate campaign in the British Press engendered a jingoistic frenzy. It was a time of incredible gullibility and overheated imagination about everything and everybody German or even suspected to be German. Shops bearing German-sounding name signs were smashed up, a spy mania developed that led to absurd incidents. For instance, a young amateur aviator, named Gustav Hamel – whose father had come to England more than half-a-century earlier from Schleswig when it was still a Danish province, and who was born in England and never even learned to speak German – was killed some weeks before the war, when his little 'plane crashed in the English Channel. Now, newspaper reports and gossip in the clubs and pubs turned this unfortunate young man into a German spy, 'flying a German aircraft over Royal Navy bases in the South of England and taking photographs of British warships and port installations'. The gossip broke his father's heart and killed him.

The type of people who embroidered on the story of the 'sinister spy Hamel' said they had 'seen with their own eyes a letter from Germany, revealing that Prince Louis of Battenberg was a German spy, too'. They had conveniently forgotten that his entire family had a distinguished record in the service of the British Crown. His brother Henry, the husband of Queen Victoria's daughter, had died on active service in Africa. His nephews Maurice and Leopold of Battenberg were in France with the British Expeditionary Force; Prince Leopold serving in spite of his lameness and ill-health, and Prince Maurice soon killed by German shrapnel during the retreat from Mons. His own two sons were in the Royal Navy, George as a young sub-lieutenant, Louis as a cadet at Osborne. But what was remembered and maliciously worked up in newspapers was that Prince Louis of

Battenberg, who had given 46 years of loyal service to the Royal Navy, had been an honorary general in his uncle's grand-ducal little army of Hesse, and therefore 'a German officer'.

When Admiral Cradock's puny fleet suffered a defeat at the Battle of Coronel Prince Louis was blamed at once for 'this humiliating naval disaster'. But in fact, it was he who, realising the danger of the German Admiral Graf Spee's Far East flotilla crossing the Pacific and attacking Cradock's force off the coast of Chile, had pleaded that reinforcements should be sent to Cradock. But neither the Cabinet, nor the Admiralty, nor the Commander-in-Chief of the Grand Fleet were prepared to send two large battleships to Cradock's assistance, to match the firing power of Graf Spee's modern guns. In the end, when Prince Louis's advice was accepted, Graf Spee's fleet was completely destroyed in the Battle of the Falkland Islands on 8 December 1914, but by then he had already been compelled to leave his post at the Admiralty.

Thus, although Churchill had supported him and although most of his colleagues at the Admiralty and, certainly, the officers and ratings of the Royal Navy had the deepest respect for him and trusted him, the discreditable attacks and malicious inuendoes gained in strength. One of the London newspapers, the *Globe*, given to sensational, irresponsible reporting, excelled in baseless stories, dragging the First Sea Lord's name through the mud. Anything could have happened in a political climate when playing Beethoven's and Mozart's music was regarded in Britain as unpatriotic or outright treason, when wounded officers on short home leave from the front were given white feathers by young Society ladies, and little dachshunds were kicked in Kensington Gardens by ruddy-faced retired colonels.

On 26 October 1914 Prince Louis wrote to an old friend, a distinguished senior naval officer, who had expressed his indignation at the smear campaign:

'My responsibility and constant anxiety in this great office are very heavy, and being continuously attacked and yet quite helpless – although assured afresh of the Government's confidence – I feel sometimes that I cannot bear it much longer.'

Two days later he had made up his mind and wrote to the First Lord of the Admiralty, offering his resignation:

'Dear Mr Churchill,

I have lately been driven to the painful conclusion that at this juncture my birth and parentage have the effect of impairing in some respects my usefulness on the Board of the Admiralty. In these circumstances I feel it to be my duty, as a loyal subject of his Majesty, to resign the office of First Sea Lord, hoping thereby to facilitate the task of the administration of the great Service, to which I have devoted my life, and to ease the burden laid on H.M. Ministers.'

King George v learnt of his cousin's resignation only when Churchill told him the next morning. Prince Louis had used no backdoor or family connections to seek protection or favours. He had acted as honourably and dignifiedly as always, even though his decision had almost broken his heart. When on the same afternoon he came to see the King at Buckingham Palace he was, however, unable to conceal his emotions. The King noted in his diary, in his usual dry style:

'Spent a most worrying and trying day. At 11.30 a.m. saw Winston Churchill who informed me that Louis of Battenberg had resigned . . . The Press and Public have said so many things against him being born a German, and that he ought not to be at the head of the Navy, that it was best for him to go. I feel deeply for him. There is no more loyal man in the Country.

'. . . At 4 p.m. I saw poor Louis. Very painful interview, he quite broke down. I told him I would make him a Privy Councillor to show the confidence I had in him . . .'[1]

Churchill had accepted Prince Louis's resignation. In his official letter of reply, he expressed his regrets in guarded words, which some of Prince Louis's enemies tried to interpret as acquiescing in their campaign against the First Sea Lord:

'My dear Prince Louis,

This is no ordinary war, but a struggle between nations for life or death. It raises passions between races of the most terrible kind. It effaces the old landmarks and frontiers of our civilisation.

I cannot further oppose the wish you have during the last few weeks expressed to me to be released from the burden of

[1] Nicolson, H., *George V*, Constable, London, 1952, p. 251.

responsibility which you have borne thus far with so much honour and success. The anxieties and toils which rest upon the naval administration of our country are in themselves enough to try a man's spirit; and when to them are added the ineradicable difficulties of which you speak, I could not at this juncture in fairness ask you to support them . . .

I must express publicly my deep indebtedness to you, and the pain I feel at the severance of our three years' official association. In all the circumstances you are right in your decision.'

Lord Selborne, a former First Lord of the Admiralty in two Tory cabinets, declared: 'I would as soon mistrust Lord Roberts (the famous Field-Marshal) as Prince Louis, and that anyone should have been found to insinuate suspicions against him is nothing less than a national humiliation.'

In a remarkable letter to *The Times,* Mr J. H. Thomas, the Labour Party leader wrote:

'I desire to express my extreme regret at the announcement that Prince Louis of Battenberg has, by his resignation, pandered to the most mean and contemptible slander I have ever known . . . I am afraid that his action will simply be looked upon as a triumph for the mean and miserable section of people who, at a time of national trial, is ever ready to pass a foul lie from lip to lip without a tittle of evidence. I know nothing of Prince Louis except that I have never met anyone, either in Parliament, or connected with the Navy, but who spoke in the highest terms of his great ability and usefulness in our Navy; and if a man's honour is to be impugned in the manner and method as adopted in this case, then it will be difficult for public men to endeavour to serve their country in a manner we have a right to expect.'

The Commander-in-Chief of the Home Fleet telegraphed: 'We look to you with the greatest loyalty, respect and gratitude for the work you have accomplished for the Navy'. That this admiral spoke also for the lower deck was proved by a touching incident. Prince Louis's elder son, George, was serving in H.M.S. *New Zealand* and the news came when the ship was at sea. His turret's crew asked to see him. The petty officer, a dour Scot of few words, told him that all they wanted to say was that 'it was quite terrible that your father, sir, has been treated like that, and that we are all very sorry indeed . . .'

His younger son, Louis, was at that time a 14-year-old cadet at Osborne. Many years later stories – most of them apocryphal – were told that the boy had wept beneath a flagpole flying the Naval Ensign, when he heard the news. One thing, however, is true: it certainly gave him an impetus to get to the top. At Osborne he had hitherto not been the most assiduous of cadets, passing out thirty-fifth of eighty; but a little later at Dartmouth he was in the first sixteen of eighty. It might well be true that he had already vowed to attain the office of First Sea Lord, from which his father had been so meanly ousted.

When Prince Louis left the Admiralty, he retired to the seclusion of his home, Kent House in the Isle of Wight. Many of his former colleagues sent him invitations to visit their ships, but he replied that he did not want to get them into trouble. He even declined the invitation by Rear-Admiral Moore to come aboard H.M.S. *New Zealand* at Rosyth, before she sailed off on 24 January 1915 to the Battle of the Dogger Bank with his son, George, on board, although he later said that it was the hardest decision he ever made, not knowing whether he would see his boy ever again.

In 1917, when King George V, under pressure of the anti-German hate campaign, decided to change his dynasty's name of Saxe-Coburg-Gotha to Windsor, he suggested that the Battenbergs should also change their name, and the anglicised version of Mountbatten was devised. Prince Louis was created Marquess of Milford Haven, an old Royal title dating back to 1706, his son George became the Earl of Medina, the name of the river at Cowes, and his younger son was now known as Lord Louis Mountbatten; while his nephew Prince Alexander, Henry of Battenberg's eldest son, was created Marquess of Carisbrooke.

After a life-time of hard work, the new Marquess of Milford Haven devoted his enforced retirement to the study of naval history and to his collection of naval medals. A gift of a few old naval commemorative medals, when he was a young Commander, had started this hobby and over the years the collection grew to be the best in the world. Eventually he wrote a History of Naval Medals, which was published in three volumes, with magnificent illustrations.

The last years of his life were overshadowed by a series o
family tragedies. His brother-in-law, Tsar Nicholas ii, had been
deposed by the Russian Revolution and on 16 July 1918 he and
his entire family were murdered in a sordid massacre in the cellar
of their Ekaterinburg prison. Another of his wife's sisters, who
had been very close to her, Grand Duchess Sergius (Elizabeth of
Hesse-Darmstadt) was executed by the Bolsheviks; the authentic
news of their deaths being received in London only in 1920. A
cousin, Grand Duke Michael Alexandrovitch and a nephew
Grand Duke Igor Constantinovitch, also fell victims to the
Bolsheviks.

The Hesse family, to which he belonged and into which he had
married, were now war enemies, even though his wife's brother,
Grand Duke Ernest, so deeply detested the Kaiser's war that he
refused, and was officially 'excused', German military service.
His beloved sister, widowed Princess Marie zu Erbach-Schönberg,
had remained in Germany and communications with her were
only sporadic through neutral channels. His daughter Alice
was with her Greek husband and their children in Athens and,
in 1917, they became quite innocently involved in King Constantine's alleged pro-German activities.

Thus 'P.L.'s' (Prince Louis, as his close friends continued to
call him) evening of life was troubled and, having retired on a
modest pension of £2,000 a year, he, his wife and his unmarried
daughter Louise had to live frugally. In 1919 he had to give up
his home on the Isle of Wight, for financial reasons, and for a
time stayed in a small house at Fishponds, which belonged to the
family of his old friend, the late Admiral Lord Walter Kerr.
Later he and his wife went for some months to Corfu, where they
were reunited with their other daughter, Princess Alice of Greece
and their three granddaughters.

He never complained publicly or privately about the way he
had been treated and never sought commiseration, though in
1921, a few weeks before his death, he had some consolation in
being made Admiral of the Fleet – on the spontaneous request to
the King by Lord Lee of Fareham, then First Lord of the
Admiralty. He was only the second admiral on the retired list
thus honoured.

His resignation had not only been a personal tragedy; too late
it was recognised that it had deprived the Admiralty and Britain's

war leaders of one of the keenest strategic brains. It is certain, for instance, that if he had remained in office as First Sea Lord, not only would Britain's naval warfare have been far more successful but the convoy system against the U-boat menace would have been adopted very much sooner, with an immense saving in human lives, ships and treasure.

He died quite suddenly in London on 11 September 1921. In August he had spent with his wife and daughter Louise a holiday in England and then went to Scotland for a cruise with his son Louis, on board the *Repulse*, intending to travel in the autumn to Constantinople where his eldest son, George, was with his ship, H.M.S. *Cardiff*. On his return from Scotland he stayed in London at the Naval and Military Club, Piccadilly, having put up his wife and daughter in a nearby hotel. On that Sunday afternoon he felt unwell and decided to rest. The club housekeeper went to his room to collect the tea tray she had brought him a little while earlier, and found him dead on his bed.

Admiral of the Fleet the Marquess of Milford Haven, P.C., G.C.B., G.C.V.O., had an impressive naval funeral at Westminster Abbey, his coffin having been placed by the King's command in the private chapel of Buckingham Palace, where members of the Royal Family assembled for a private service, and then carried in a great military procession along The Mall and under the Admiralty Arch, passing his old office in Whitehall. Seven admirals and a major-general of the Royal Marines were the pall-bearers and the Abbey was thronged by royal representatives and high dignitaries of the State and the Services. His wish to be buried in the little cemetery of Whipingham on the Isle of Wight, near the place where he had spent happy days of scant leisure and sad years of enforced retirement, was respected.

Although he said that in his retirement he could, at last, devote himself to his family and 'live on in the lives of my two boys in the Royal Navy', he was not spared to see his eldest daughter marry in 1923 the Swedish Crown Prince and later become the Queen of Sweden; neither did Fate grant him to see the happiness of his younger son Louis, soon to marry Edwina Ashley, the heiress to Sir Ernest Cassel's fortune, and to build a great career upon the vindication of his father's memory.

To his eldest son, George, he left the title but no earthly goods. When his Last Will was proved, his entire estate in England amounted to £6,500. He had had possessions in Germany and Russia, but his share in a Siberian platinum mine was confiscated after the Russian revolution, and the disastrous inflation in Germany had taken a heavy toll of his property there. Heiligenberg Castle, where he and his sister and brothers had spent their youth, and which he had inherited in 1888 from his father, Prince Alexander of Hesse, was sold but the capital obtained – amounting to some £30,000 – was badly invested and most of it lost through the devaluation of the German currency.

The second Marquess of Milford Haven, who had inherited much of his father's ability and charm of manners, had a brilliant career in the Royal Navy, gifted with great intelligence and an easy grasp of modern technology. He gave every promise of rising high, if he had remained in the Service. But, with his private means reduced and with his responsibilities for bringing up two children, he decided in 1930 to quit the Navy, in which he had seen war service in the sea battles of the Heligoland Bight, Dogger Bank and Jutland under Jellicoe and Beatty, and to go into business. At first he worked in a finance house in New York's Wall Street, and after his return home became managing director and later chairman of the Sperry Gyroscope Company, making an important contribution to the rise of the British aviation industry. He was also a director of other companies, including Marks & Spencer and Electrolux. He had married in 1916 Nadejda, younger daughter of Grand Duke Michael of Russia and the Countess Merenberg-Torby, and had a son and a daughter.[1]

Having become the head of the Mountbatten family, the second Marquess took great interest in its younger members, particularly in the children of his sister Alice of Greece. When her small son, Prince Philip, after the stormy and hard days of his early childhood arrived in England as a pupil first at Cheam and then at Gordonstoun, uncle George became his guardian and the boy spent most of his vacations with him and 'aunt Nada' at their home near Maidenhead. It was uncle George who encouraged his nephew to enter upon a naval career, and it was a great blow to Prince Philip when the Marquess of Milford Haven fell seriously ill and died from cancer on 8 April 1938 at the early age of 46.

His mother, Princess Victoria, the Dowager Marchioness, sur-

[1] See *infra* page 284.

vived her husband and eldest son for many years. She died in London on 24 September 1950 at the great age of 87. From her apartments at Kensington Palace her son Louis, her daughter Louise and also her grandson Philip married, all making 'great marriages', such as the very first Princess of Battenberg had always dreamed for her descendants.

CHAPTER EIGHT

THE CASSEL EMPIRE

Sir Ernest Cassel.

A DISTINGUISHED congregation filled the Church of the Immaculate Conception in Farm Street, Mayfair, on the grey morning of 26 September 1921. There were courtiers, statesmen, aristocrats, men from the world of arts and the legal and medical professions, artists, and heads of the great companies and finance houses of the City of London. They had come in sorrow and homage – and out of curiosity.

'Grant him, O Lord, to pass from death unto life, which Thou promised to Abraham and to his seed,' Father John Ryan intoned the solemn words of the Offertory, and the choir sang Niedermeyer's *Pie Jesus*. The Requiem Mass was sung *in die obitus* for God's humble servant, Ernest Cassel. The priest prayed that 'God should not deliver him into the hands of the enemy, not forget him for ever, but command that he be taken up by the Holy Angels and borne to our home in Paradise . . . that, having put his hope and trust in God, he may not undergo the pains of Hell, but may come to the possession of eternal joys'.

Before the altar lay the silver coffin containing the earthly remains of Sir Ernest Cassel. Among the congregation were many who were astonished to be invited to the Requiem Mass. Even those who knew Sir Ernest intimately – and only a handful could claim his friendship – were surprised to learn that he was a Catholic. Chopin's *Marche Funèbre* closed the Mass and the congregation began slowly to file out. Ushers made way for the officers of the Royal Household representing King George v, Queen Alexandra the Queen Mother, and the many other official mourners.

Inquisitively but not unkindly, the crowd gazed at the small group of principal mourners. Everybody had heard of Sir Ernest Cassel, that immensely rich Jewish financier who had been the closest friend and adviser of King Edward VII, but comparatively few knew anything of his private life, or his family. Indeed, since the death of Edward VII eleven years earlier, the Midas-touch financier had fallen into obscurity, retired to comfortable seclusion. So the public wondered.

'He must have left many millions,' whispered one lady to her neighbour. Who would inherit his many fortunes reaped from Britain to Argentina, from Sweden to Turkey, from Mexico to Egypt, from America to Germany?

Politely the congregation made room for the small group of men in frockcoats and women with deep veils. Mr Asquith, Mr and Mrs Winston Churchill, the Earl and Countess of Shaftesbury, the Earl of Iveagh, the Earl of Verulam, and all the other bearers of great names whom Ernest Cassel had, at one time, so lavishly entertained in his great Mayfair home and at his several sumptuous country houses, stepped back and the men bowed their heads as the relatives passed.

There was 'Auntie Grannie', petite and aged Minnie Cassel, the sister of Sir Ernest, who after half-a-century spent in England still spoke the language haltingly and now tearfully accepted the condolences, murmuring, 'My por bruzzer, he was such a good mann'. Supporting her was her son, the celebrated King's Counsel, Sir Felix Cassel, and just behind her was her daughter Mrs Anne Jenkins, on the arm of her husband Colonel Albert 'Teddy' Jenkins, and Lady Cassel, the daughter of the Earl of Verulam and Sir Felix's wife. Next to her was her daughter Marjorie, Countess of Brecknock, escorted by her husband, the Marquess of Camden's heir. In another little group were the Ashley's, Sir Ernest's son-in-law, Colonel Wilfrid Ashley, M.P., soon to become a Cabinet Minister and a Peer, his second wife and his daughter Edwina. It was Edwina, however, who now commanded all the attention.

It was not idle speculation that this attractive girl of twenty would have most of her grandfather's enormous fortune. Some of the mourners had already heard a rumour that she had fallen in love with the penniless, though high-born naval officer Lord Louis Mountbatten. But Edwina, pale and composed, scarcely noticed the appraising glances, for her thoughts were concerned only with her grandfather to whom she had been so close. His death had come swiftly and in loneliness while Edwina was away from home. Perhaps then, the curious-minded could be forgiven if they saw more than sadness on Edwina's countenance – a look of disappointment that she had not been beside him at the end.

Lonely did her grandfather die, but to loneliness he had been accustomed most of his life. Great wealth, great influence, some affection, more suspicion and much unhappiness had marked his life. As *The Times* obituary said, he was proud of his achievements, proud of the quickness of his wit and his hard work that had gained him millions, but he rarely displayed emotions and he was sensitive to criticism, resentful of opposition, and often domineering towards those who depended on him—characteristics that rarely make for close friendships.

He was neither gregarious nor 'clubbable', attributes that were important to social and business success in the England of his times, particularly for a man without the right sort of background. Of course, such social contacts as a young Jewish immigrant, working for one of the City's leading banking houses, Bischoffsheim & Goldschmidt, could have made were strictly limited, but Cassel did not, it seems, ever attempt to establish them with London's well-to-do Jewish business community where he would have been welcomed as one of Bischoffsheim's 'brilliant young men', and within which he could have 'married money'. He never sought intimate friendships, perhaps because he could never open his heart to anyone. Although his business career was to bring him later into contact with a vast number of influential people, he was from the outset determined to work alone. After he left Bischoffsheim at the age of 28, he never went into partnership. 'A partner,' he said, 'is a man who can commit you to things and I don't ever mean to be committed by anyone.' Benson once said that there was about Cassel something of that strange and barren inhumanity which is not rare among those whose abilities have been long and exclusively devoted to the acquisition of wealth.[1] But however hard and ruthless Cassel could be in business, he was extremely gentle and unselfish to those he loved. His

[1] Cf. Benson, E. F., *As We Are,* Longmans, London, 1932.

devotion went hardly beyond the small circle of his family and it was usually expressed through bountiful gifts.

Ernest Cassel's life began on 3 March 1852, in Cologne. And that day no fairy by his cradle could have predicted that his granddaughter would become the wife of a scion of Charlemagne. Ernest was the youngest child of Jacob Cassel, a Jewish money-lender who earned a modest living from his transactions with the merchants and craftsmen of the Rhineland, where Jews enjoyed a greater measure of freedom than anywhere in the German Empire.

No jewish father was ashamed if his children were at work when those of his Gentile neighbours were still at school. At an early age, young Ernest had shown a quick, razor-sharp mind, perhaps best expressed in his prowess as a chess player. A child prodigy at chess, he was only eight when he took part in local tournaments against well-known players. He was also a gifted violinist and, deep in his heart, he must have dreamed of one day becoming a concert virtuoso. Musical talent ran in his family; his nephew Francis was to become a famous concert pianist and conductor. But the uncertainty of an artistic career did not appeal to Ernest's father, so he gave his son the choice of either becoming a professional chess player – there was good money in it then – or to go into banking.

There was little future for him in his father's business in Cologne, and when Ernest decided at the age of fourteen to enter the world of finance, he was apprenticed to the banking firm of Elzbacher & Co. as an office boy with prospects of promotion to leger clerk.

In the mid-nineteenth century many German-Jewish business men had responded to the Prince Consort's invitation and emigrated to England where they achieved positions barred to them on the Continent. The success of Disraeli, the exploits of the Rothschilds, were examples of what a determined young man could achieve. So when Ernest expressed his desire to try his luck across the North Sea, there were no parental tears but a word of encouragement. At fifteen he arrived in Liverpool, with a recommendation from his employers to the firm of Belssig, Braun & Co., grain merchants of German origin, who had attained prosperity in Victorian England. He used to rise at 6.30 a.m. in order to walk to work from his tiny, dark room where he lodged with a kindly widow, in order to save the penny fare on the horse tram. Work that started at 8 a.m. usually ended at 7 in the evening. The rest of his evenings were spent learning English, either from a primer borrowed from a neighbour's children, or by attending classes at the Mechanical Institute, where immigrants received instruction for a fee of threepence.

Ernest learned quickly, but could never master pronunciation. All his life, the man who later became a member of His Majesty's Most Honourable Privy Council, spoke perfect grammatical English, but with a harsh and gutteral German accent.

Once, when asked how his great fortune had been amassed and about the far-reaching part he had played in transactions of world-wide political and economic significance, he declared: 'My decisions have never been made by a conscious process of reasoning. Hard work, good and timely information and instinct are the real key to success'. And he added that the realisation of one's own ability and worth is another. 'It has sometimes been said that I started life as a clerk on 15s. a week. I never got less than £2. I was not so cheap as all that.'[1]

Soon Ernest Cassel determined to widen his horizon. He applied for a post as a clerk with the Anglo-Egyptian Bank, which advertised a vacancy in its Paris office. The firm received more than 200 applications, most of them of many pages, florid with self-appraisal. Ernest's two-line application said: 'I apply for the position in your office and I refer you to my former chiefs, the banking house of Elzbacher & Co., of Cologne'.

He got the job, but stayed for only a year in Paris, returning to England in 1870, having just escaped the siege of the capital during the Franco-Prussian War. But his brief employment in Paris was to become the stepping-stone to his life's success. There he met Moritz Hirsch, a man of humble Jewish origin like himself, born in Munich, who at the age of 30 had become one of Europe's great financiers. He had received concessions from the Ottoman Empire in Egypt and the Middle East; he was the leading banker of the Austro-Hungarian Empire and was created a baron in 1869 by Emperor Francis Joseph. Hirsch had built railways in the Balkans and Turkey, and had his fingers in every European financial pie.

The baron was so impressed by the clever and conscientious

[1] Cf. *The Times,* 23 September 1921.

young clerk at the Anglo-Egyptian Bank, of which he was co-owner that he gave him a recommendation to his brother-in-law, Louis Bischoffsheim, partner of the London finance house of Bischoffsheim & Goldschmidt. From the day of his arrival at their Bishopsgate office, Ernest Cassel never looked back. He started at an annual salary of £200; a year later he was one of the managers. Bischoffsheim sent him to Constantinople where a finance house had got into difficulties. By skilful negotiations with creditors, bankers and lawyers, everyone of them nearly twice the age of the young man sent from London, Cassel rescued the firm from ruin and saved considerable investments Bischoffsheim and other City bankers had made in Turkey. When, in appreciation of this success and other transactions, Bischoffsheim offered him a salary of £500, Cassel replied: 'You mean, of course, £5,000?' and his employer quickly agreed.

At 25, Cassel, an extremely abstemious and thrifty young man, had accumulated from his salary and commissions a tidy fortune of about £50,000. His employers and business acquaintances hinted that he should marry; many wealthy City men would have welcomed him as a son-in-law. But his life, outwardly so successful, suffered from recurring family catastrophes. His mother to whom he was deeply devoted, died in 1874, still in the prime of her life. Within less than a year both his father and his brother Max were dead. His younger sister Minnie, unhappily married in Cologne, and himself were the only surviving members of the family.

Cassel had none of the graces that appeal to women. He was shortish, balding early and already inclined to obesity. He had the nose and fleshy lips of his race. He hated small talk, his mind was preoccupied with making money and he cared little for books, the theatre, games or trivial pleasures. The only relaxation which he permitted himself later in life was, strangely enough, mountaineering, in which he became adept. Ernest Cassel always reached for the peaks – and found them!

When he did decide to marry, it was a surprising decision and a most unexpected choice. He met his bride at one of the rare social functions he attended. She was Annette Maxwell, a frail, shy young girl, from a middle-class Catholic home at Darlington, County Durham. Cassel knew her for only a few weeks when he asked her father for her hand. But, he made it quite clear to Mr Robert Thompson Maxwell that he was not prepared to change his faith. It was only after some hesitation that he was accepted and a quiet wedding was arranged. Cassel marked the event by applying for British naturalisation.

Annette suffered from tuberculosis but the extent of her illness had not been discovered before she married. Eighteen months after the wedding she gave birth to a daughter, Maud, likewise a frail child never to experience a mother's love. Annette Cassel died in 1880, after a marriage that lasted less than three years. Her husband, said to be worth £150,000 at that time, called in famous physicians to try to save his wife's life. This brief, shadowed marriage, revealing to Cassel a love he had never known and was never to know again, transformed him spiritually. In the presence of Annette, his 'pale English rose', he shed the egotism of ambition, the detachment of self-sufficiency. He was melted by her gentleness and deep faith.

When she died in his arms he broke down and could not work for many weeks. Before she died she begged him to become a Catholic. She loved her outwardly forbidding husband and with her abiding faith in an ultimate reunion of souls she was anxious at the thought of losing him for ever. Cassel sacrificed the traditions of his birth and life. Intensely serious about his conversion, he spent six months under instruction of a Jesuit priest, studying Catholic dogma and liturgy, before his baptism and reception. But he kept his conversion secret.

There was to be no second marriage for Ernest Cassel. The devotion he had for Annette he turned with singular intensity upon his motherless child. It was for her that he redoubled his efforts to amass a great fortune. Two or three years later he left Bischoffsheim and began his association with a circle of Jewish bankers on both sides of the Atlantic. One of them was Jacob Schiff, partner in the great banking firm of Kuhn, Loeb & Co., of New York, who became his life-long friend. Cassel saw big opportunities in railroad financing in America. There, in the eighteen-eighties, a fierce battle was being fought out between tycoons such as Collis P. Huntington – who made his first millions in the Californian and Nevada gold bonanzas – and Jay Gould, the notorious New York speculator. The great battles between the Southern Pacific and the Union Pacific were fought not only at green-baized conference tables and by bribery of senators and entire state legislatures, but with private armies clashing in the Rocky Mountains and the deserts of Arizona and New Mexico. Many smaller railway companies failed. Jacob Schiff enlisted Cassel's connections with some of the London banking houses to save the Atchison, Topeka and Santa Fe Railroad Company, and Cassel also helped to reorganise the Louisville-Nashville Railroad. These were but a few of Cassel's enterprises after leaving Bischoffsheim in 1884. Then, at the age of 32 he took an office at 21, Old Broad Street. At the entrance was a small brass plate: 'E. Cassel, First Floor'. This remained his business sign until he retired a multi-millionaire, even though his offices ultimately occupied a multi-storey building. His business methods were never showy – and he always knew how much a junior clerk kept in the petty-cash box.

By 1890, not yet 40 years old, Cassel was one of the members of the 'inner cabinet' in the City of London, a cool, sagacious adviser and a clever manipulator of finance in foreign lands, when the City was the world's undisputed financial centre. No respector of persons, Cassel moved with self-assurance amongst the great moguls of big business. If he was capable of deeper friendship than mere close acquaintance based on similar interests, his demeanour during his working day did not reflect this capacity. He was a masterful man, never indulging in superfluous urbanity or flattery. He was not liked but greatly respected. His interests included railroads in America, tramways and livestock in Argentina, canals, land irrigation, coffee and tin in South America, railways and ore mining in Sweden (he financed and developed the greatest phosphate iron mines in Europe at Graengesberg and built the Oxelosund harbour), railways in the Balkans, banking in Turkey, and the development of the dominions of the Ottoman Empire. He dealt with men of great political power, such as Lord Cromer, that uncrowned ruler of Egypt, last of the Victorian Empire builders and British pro-consuls, himself a hard taskmaster who must have sensed an affinity with that unaffected, hard-headed 'foreigner'.

Lord Cromer's overpowering personality often intimidated men of high rank or great substance; not so Cassel, who stood up to him and treated him on an equal footing. Cromer made him his chief financial adviser for his prodigious development schemes. Much of Britain's political and economic preponderance in the

Middle East before the First World War could be put to Cassel's credit. It was Cassel who negotiated the financing of Cromer's great irrigation schemes in Egypt, the building of the first Asswan and Assuit dams. He founded the Agricultural Bank of Cairo, the National Bank of Turkey, the State Bank of Morocco and introduced many British business, shipping and insurance firms to the Middle East.

While his business interests were ubiquitous and while he also made many of his great deals and profits overseas, Cassel also fostered developments in Britain, considering it his duty to help modernise his country of adoption. He helped to promote the 'Twopenny Tube', the Central London Railway, the most advanced electric Underground, and lost a good deal of money in this enterprise. In 1897 he played a leading part in the amalgamation of the Sheffield firm of Vickers and the Naval Construction and Armament Company and, without making a large profit, gave Britain the great Vickers concern and the modern shipbuilding yards at Barrow-in-Furness.

When he married he lived in a comfortable though unpretentious Bayswater apartment, and later moved to a house at 2, Orme Square nearby. But when the big money began to roll in and his beloved daughter grew up, he bought one of London's fine houses at 48 Grosvenor Square in the heart of Mayfair. And it was here that Cassel suddenly began to acquire and collect the things which had mattered so little to him in the past. He filled the house with fine furniture and *objets d'art*.

Perhaps a little unkindly Benson, who knew him well, said that he bought splendid examples of Old Masters – but he did not care for paintings; he bought the rarest books – but he was not a bibliophile and never looked at them again; he amassed fine collections of English silver, of Italian bronze, of Dresden porcelain – but knew nothing about them. He bought anything that was sufficiently expensive and of testified excellence. But all such things were only the trappings suitable for a very wealthy man, and not the hard-won and intelligent acquisitions of the true collector who does not have his treasures driven to him, but stalks them himself. He became one of the most important clients of Sir Joseph Duveen, the famous art dealer and philanthropist, like Cassel a self-made man of humble Jewish origin. Duveen had come from Holland in 1866 and opened a small second-hand shop in Hull, to become an art-dealer and connoisseur of world renown within 20 years. Cassel, though he knew nothing of art, got shrewd advice from Duveen, which he reciprocated with likewise useful financial tips, and every picture and ornament which Ernest Cassel bought proved a first-class investment.

In 1896 Baron Hirsch died and made Cassel the executor of his vast estate. Hirsch had been an intimate adviser of the Prince of Wales, and Cassel followed him. He not only began to manage the Prince's finances, but became perhaps his closest personal friend. It was a strange friendship between two men of utterly contrasting background, temperament and attitudes to life. The Prince, ten years senior to Cassel, was gay, gregarious, volatile, and enjoyed every moment of his full life, a lover of good food, a connoisseur of beautiful women and of horseflesh, a gambler and sportsman. On the other hand, the banker austere and withdrawn was totally disinterested in the fashionable caprices of the Marlborough House set. Strangely, the Prince and his banker had a striking physical resemblance; on several occasions in the South of France, where both were frequent visitors in later years, Cassel was mistaken for the prince.

The Prince liked foreigners and admired the shrewdness and quick wits of Jewish businessmen, surrounding himself with men such as Baron Ferdinand Rothschild, Alfred de Rothschild, the three brothers Sassoon, Hirsch, and choosing for his personal and confidential physician the brilliant Jewish doctor, Sir Felix Semon – all this to the dismay of Queen Victoria and die-hard Tory politicians. Some biographers of Edward vii have said that his friendship with Cassel arose when the banker was supposed to have met the king's gambling debts. This could not be quite true, because Cassel appeared at Marlborough House only during the last few years of Queen Victoria's reign. Although the Prince of Wales had been a compulsive gambler and notoriously extravagant, thanks to Hirsch's adroit management his finances were in order when he met Cassel, and, in fact, he was the owner of a considerable fortune. On occasions, however, Cassel was called upon to provide quickly liquid funds for the King's interminable and extravagant spending.

But their friendship went much deeper than mere money and credit. Cassel was deeply devoted to his royal friend who was probably the only man outside the Cassel family circle for whom he felt a genuine affection. Perhaps it sprang from a deep, almost subconscious gratitude, for the Heir to the Throne had always treated the 'Jewish upstart' with unwavering courtesy and had made him a close confidant. In 1899, after several earlier efforts, the Prince of Wales persuaded his reluctant mother to make Cassel a Knight of the Order of St Michael and St George – not for his services to the Prince, but to the Queen and her government through his achievements in Egypt.

When in 1901 the Prince of Wales became King Edward VII, Sir Ernest's position at Court and in London Society became as firmly established as it had been for many years in the City and the world of international finance. During his short reign, the king relied on the advice of a small circle of his friends, much more so than of his Ministers and military commanders. Among them were the Portuguese diplomat Marquese de Soveral and Sir Ernest Cassel, two men diametrically different in background, outlook and tastes.

De Soveral, whose swarthy, lean and toothy face and gangling gait gained him the sobriquet of 'Blue Monkey', was a hater of Germany and everything German. While regarded by many as a mere court jester, he greatly influenced the king's anti-German policy. Cassel had never lost his admiration for the country of his birth, for the Kaiser and for the hardworking qualities of the German people. Although he kept aloof from Edward VII's foreign policy manoeuvres, he tried to allay the king's growing hostility to Germany. Soveral disliked Cassel's attempts at reconciling the King with the Kaiser. When Oscar Wilde's *The Importance of Being Earnest* was performed at the St James's Theatre, and the King asked Soveral whether he had seen the play, he replied: 'No, sire, but I have seen the importance of being Ernest Cassel'.

The men and women who revolved around his sovereign, the Duke of Devonshire, an unmistakable English eccentric, Lord and Lady Grey, experts on 'larks' for which the King had a distinct predeliction – such as making apple-pie beds, serving grated soap instead of cheese in sandwiches at royal picnics, or accompanying in shabby clothes one of his women-friends selling violets in Piccadilly Circus – the last 'professional beauties', such as Lady Lonsdale, Consuelo, Duchess of Marlborough, Mrs Cornwallis-West, Lady Paget; great shots, such as Evan Charteris, the son of the Earl of Wemyss, could hardly appeal to Cassel. But with the growing burden of State affairs, Edward VII, too, became more serious-minded and devoted less and less time to the 'larks', which Cassel could never understand. Cassel's position involved social duties he may have disliked, but he carried them out punctiliously and with grave decorum.

Although he knew nothing of horses and was not interested in racing, he associated himself, or rather his money, with Lord Willoughby de Broke for breeding bloodstock. He spent a fortune on his breeding and training establishment at Moulton Paddocks, Newmarket. But despite all the money he spent on the turf his silver-grey and light blue colours won only one classic – his horse Handicapper winning the Two Thousand Guineas in 1901. Immediately after the King's death Cassel retired from the Turf and made a final generous gesture, buying the King's Grafton House property and presenting it to Newmarket in memory of his sovereign who had so often been his guest at Moulton Paddocks.

For many years he wanted to be elected a member of the Jockey Club. Although he had given lavishly to British racing, not even the repeated intervention of the Prince of Wales could secure his admission into this most exclusive of all England's institutions. Even when the Prince became King, his royal wish was disregarded and it was not until 1908 that Sir Ernest Cassel, by then a Privy Councillor, became a member of the Jockey Club.

A man of his wealth and standing was expected to support charities generously. Cassel certainly disappointed no one, even though some of his critics (particularly during the First World War) accused him that his great donations were prompted by some ulterior motives, such as a desire to receive a peerage. This was certainly untrue. A peerage Cassel could have had for the asking. Indeed, King Edward VII repeatedly offered him a barony and later also a viscounty, but Cassel never wanted to enter the House of Lords – not having a son, and never a public speaker.

Cassel gave large sums to charities anonymously. His most munificent donations were for the sick. He had a genuine interest in medical research, which was understandable as he had lost his wife and was to lose his only daughter through the then still terrible scourge of tuberculosis. He built and endowed the great Sanatorium near Midhurst in Sussex, which he named after the late King. Later, he gave £250,000 for another, and he instituted and financed the Papworth Industrial Colony for Consumptives. With Lord Iveagh he paid for 7½ grammes of radium to present to the Radium Institute, and was probably the first private person in Britain to finance cancer research.

After the war he put £500,000 in the hands of trustees for educational purposes including adult education, the study of foreign languages and the establishment of a Faculty of Commerce at London University which later became the London School of Economics. Shortly before his death he gave another £250,000 to found and endow a hospital for nervous disorders at his mansion at Penshurst, Kent. In his last will he made many more charitable bequests, which still benefit a number of foundations.

His constant attendance on his sovereign, and his ever widening circle of the influential and wealthy, compelled Cassel to embark on a much more magnificent way of life than it must have been to his taste. Even so, it was not until 1905 that he moved to Brook House in Park Lane and turned it into one of London's finest mansions. The move was prompted also by his desire to provide his only child, his daughter Maud, with all the luxury money could buy.

The entrance of Brook House was panelled with Verde antico and Jaspis marble from Sicily, alternating with broad strips of semi-precious lapislazuli from Siberia; the five great doors leading into the main hall had magnificent carvings and metal work. The hall and grand staircase were of white Carrara marble, supported by imposing pillars, with hand-wrought gilded balusters and railings. The many doors leading from the wide sweep of the marble gallery were of mirrors, each diamond-etched by Italian craftsmen with designs of scrolls and flowers. A hugh marble ballroom, a dining hall panelled in English oak and seating more than a hundred guests, a library built entirely of cherrywood, with inlaid Wedgwood porcelain cameos along the shelves and lintels, were only some of the 'great rooms'. The library was stuffed with priceless, though unread first editions. Suites of drawing rooms, salons, boudoirs, ran across the entire floor, with windows overlooking Hyde Park and Upper Brook Street.

Altogether there were more than fifty rooms, dozens of bed-rooms, twelve bathrooms, and six separate kitchens with walls lined with white marble. More than 800 tons of Carrara, Luna and Specia marble had been brought from Italy for decoration. Precious antique furniture and countless rich settees, divans and fauteuils crowded the rooms. Bronzes, precious china and silver, jade and *objets d'art* abounded everywhere. The great china collection was housed in rows of cabinets on the first floor; other cabinets were crammed with finest early English silver of the sixteenth, seventeenth and eighteenth centuries, including such priceless pieces as the famous Wolsey beaker, the Bacon cup and the Blacksmith goblet. But often for months, when their owner was abroad, or at one of his country mansions, the cabinets and pedestals stood empty. Cassel kept his treasures in steel cases in strong rooms deep in the cellars. They were carried upstairs only on special occasions, particularly when the King and his gay friends dined beneath some of the world's most valuable paintings. In the dining hall hung four Van Dycks, including the famous portrait of 'The Two Young Stuarts'; on the walls of the salons were great paintings: Sir Joshua Reynolds's portrait of Lady Harewood, a whole collection of early Romneys, Raeburn's famous portrait of the artist's wife, Botticellis, Pre-Raphaelites and fine examples of the early English, German and Flemish schools.

Amid this splendour, Edward vii, irreverently called 'Tum-Tum' by his sycophants behind his back, and 'The Corpulent Voluptuary' by his critics, enjoyed twelve-course meals composed by French and Italian chefs, served with innumerable bottles of vintage champagne and choicest wines and liqueurs, while Cassel – always worried about his diet and digestion – would toy with a little boiled fish, a light soufflé, plus a dry biscuit and a morsel of English cheese.

Into this palace Cassel had brought his sister Minnie, whose marriage at Cologne to a Jewish merchant had ended in separation, and her children Felix and Anne. His sister was a small, plump, sweet-natured woman who was as devoted to her brother as she was afraid of him. She brought up little Maud with the same motherly love she showed Felix and Anne, both older than her delicate niece, 'de poor li'lle shild'.

Auntie Minnie and her children had changed their name to Cassel, following Sir Ernest's wish. The Duchess of Sermoneta who, as a girl and young woman was one of Maud Cassel's closest friends, recalled with affection Mrs Cassel's proverbial spoonerism. 'She would greet the guests with a cheery invitation to "come" their hair and "tidy" their hands before luncheon, and affirm that Cambridge and Newmarket were not more than forty miles away "as de cock crows", or remark that "it is a long worm dat has no turning".'[1] Yet Cassel never failed to arrange for his sister to have a conversation with Edward VII whenever the King came to Brook House; and the King always treated her with great courtesy.

While a single reception might have cost Cassel many thousand pounds, he watched the pennies. Benson told the story how some partridges remained uneaten at a dinner. Next day at luncheon, Cassel sharply inquired: 'What has become of the partridge, it was not given to the servants? They are on board wages!' Luckily the remainder of the partridge dish was discovered on the cold buffet and Cassel was satisfied. During the First World War, when starch was expensive, he gave up wearing his white waistcoats, having heard that it cost eighteen pence to clean and starch them.

But there were no economies in connexion with his family, and particularly with his beloved daughter. Cassel's secret ambition must have been that she should marry into nobility. Both his nephew and his niece did so, very much with his help. Felix – later to become a Baronet and a famous K.C. – married Lady Helen Grimston, the daughter of the third Earl of Verulam. Anne became the wife of a Guards officer, Colonel Albert 'Teddy' Jenkins who, though not titled, belonged to the landed gentry.

In 1901 Maudi Cassel married Wilfrid Ashley, a grandson of the 7th Earl of Shaftesbury. She was beautiful, with a slender, well-proportioned body, but her health was delicate, though nobody thought that she would die of tuberculosis, inherited from her mother, before her thirtieth birthday. Within a year of her wedding she gave birth to a daughter, Edwina. King Edward VII, giving proof of his friendship, was one of the child's godparents. Cassel was overjoyed; if he had wished that his grandchild had been a boy, to whom he could leave his great financial empire, he never showed disappointment and doted on the baby.

[1] Duchess Vittoria Colonna de Sermoneta, *Memoirs,* Hutchinson, London, 1929.

When by 1909 he was told by famous specialists that there was no hope of saving his daughter's life, he almost broke down. He often said he would have given every penny he possessed if he could have bought health for Maudie, and he spent a fortune in desperate attempts to prolong her life. He took her to Egypt and Switzerland, hired entire hotels in the Nile Valley in order to exclude any possible disturbance and noise, bought a fine chateau in the Swiss Alps, and heartbroken watched Maudie resting pale and weak on specially constructed beds in sun-bathed verandahs. Famous doctors from England, Germany and Switzerland were in constant attendance. The only solace he sought was in climbing the Alps. He had been addicted to this, his only exercise, for many years and had become an expert mountaineer. In Switzerland he courageously undertook such difficult climbs as the Finsteraarhorn.

Less than a year before Maud Ashley's death, King Edward VII died on 6 May 1910. To Cassel it was a very personal loss. He had not long returned from Egypt where he had taken his dying daughter for one of her long sojourns. It was a strange twist of Fate that, of all the King's intimates, the financier was to be the last to see him in his dying hour. As it happened, he had an appointment to see the King at Buckingham Palace at 11 a.m. that morning. But this was cancelled by the King's doctor, Lord Davidson, who told Cassel by telephone that the sovereign was too ill to see visitors. However, half-an-hour later Lord Knollys, the King's private secretary, told Cassel on the telephone that the King insisted on seeing him.

Later that day, Cassel wrote to Maud to tell her of that final meeting with Edward VII:

'He looked as if he had suffered great pain, and spoke indistinctly. His kindly smile came out as he congratulated me on having you brought home so much improved in health. He said, "I am very seedy, but I wanted to see you. Tell your daughter how glad I am that she has safely got home and that I hope she will be careful and patient so as to recover complete health". He then talked about other matters, and I had to ask his leave to go as I felt it was not good for him to go on speaking . . . Sir James Reid told me he had dressed on purpose to receive me, and they could not stop him.'

In March 1911 Maud died in her father's arms. For the next few
years Ernest Cassel became almost a hermit. He spent most of his
days alone at Brook House. He hardly saw anybody apart from
members of his family. When war broke out in 1914, Cassel's
world collapsed. Britain burned with hatred of Germany and
everything German, and Cassel, though he retired from business
and public life, was vilified in the Press and by speakers at patriotic
meetings. For years he had been trying hard to improve the
strained relations between Britain and Germany. When in 1908
Kaiser William decreed a bigger German navy, Cassel went to
Hamburg and Berlin and, through mediation of his friend Albert
Ballin, the head of the Hamburg-America Line, and other German
industrialists and bankers, had tried to arrange a naval agreement
between Germany and Great Britain, which the Hague Conference on limitation of naval rearmament had failed to conclude.
Although neither Edward VII, nor the 38-year-old First Lord of
the Admiralty, Winston Churchill, approved of a *rapprochement*
with Germany, the King nevertheless appreciated Cassel's well-
meant efforts for peace. He had made him a Privy Councillor,
awarded him the Grand Cross of the Victorian Order in 1906 and
the Grand Cross of the Order of the Bath in 1909.

But now Cassel had the bitter experience of seeing distinguished
and intelligent people, who had been his friends and whom he
had lavishly entertained and often financially assisted, smearing
him. To many of them he was now a 'Hun', almost a traitor,
and it meant nothing that he had spent his life working for the
greatness and prosperity of his adopted country. With the war all
his vision of British-German co-operation had collapsed. Some
of the war leaders, including Mr Asquith, the Prime Minister,
and Winston Churchill, had remained his friends, even though
they did not declare this publicly. They invited him to become
an economic adviser to the Government, but he refused in the
face of the newspaper attacks which also excelled in accusation
of treachery against Admiral Prince Louis of Battenberg, the
First Sea Lord. Finally, Asquith appealing to his patriotism,
persuaded Cassel to join Lord Reading and Sir Edward Holden
in an Anglo-French mission to negotiate a war loan in the United
States. It was mainly due to Cassel's excellent personal contacts
in Wall Street that the mission returned with an agreement
providing a loan for 500,000,000 dollars.

As soon as Cassel's Government mission became known, the Anti-German League filed a petition in the High Court, demanding that he 'should show cause why he should not be removed from his membership of the Privy Council and have his British naturalisation rescinded'. Sir George MacGill, one of the leaders of the anti-German movement, had succeeded in bringing several such investigations before the courts. The case against Sir Ernest Cassel was heard by Mr Justice Avory, and for several months Cassel had to suffer the indignity of Press comments before at last, in December 1915, the Court's decision was announced that the petition had been dismissed because Sir Ernest Cassel's loyalty to the Crown was beyond question.

Only once did Cassel try to reply to the accusations and abuse. In a letter to *The Times,* in May 1915, he wrote:

'As many other British subjects of German extraction have given public expression to their feelings, my silence might be misunderstood. Nearly half a century of my life has been spent in England, and all my interests – family, business and social – are centred here. All my male relatives of military age are serving with the King's Forces. My unfailing loyalty and devotion to this country have never varied or been questioned, and while affirming this I desire also to express my deep sense of horror at the manner in which the war is being conducted by the German government.'

During the war he gave lavishly to war charities – £220,000 to the National War Relief Fund, £120,000 to the Red Cross, £48,000 to war hospitals. He established a convalescent home for disabled servicemen at his Sandacres estate, provided large finance for the Officers' Families Fund, the Y.M.C.A., the Salvation Army and many other welfare organisations. But the abuse and accusations continued.

When peace came in 1918, Ernest Cassel was 67, had considerably aged and his sturdy health had left him. However, he reopened Brook House and asked his son-in-law, Colonel Ashley – who had remarried – to allow Edwina to act as her grandfather's hostess. Thus the young and attractive girl, unhappy at her step-mother's home, became an accomplished hostess during the two years of her grandfather's Indian Summer. But Sir Ernest did not live long enough to see Edwina's engagement to Lord

Louis Mountbatten. It was a strange twist of Fate that was to unite, as it were posthumously, Ernest Cassel and Louis of Battenberg, both contemporaries, both of German origin, both loyal British subjects, and both assailed as 'Huns' by misguided patriots.

The jingoist attacks had shattered the life of the Battenberg prince. Cassel accepted his misfortune with the philosophical resignation of his race. His happiness had been destroyed much earlier, by a succession of private tragedies.

On 21 September 1921, Miss Stella Underhill, Sir Ernest's secretary for many years, was called to his study by a footman who had found his master slumped over his desk. Ernest Cassel had died alone and lonely.

At that time, Edwina was visiting the Duke and Duchess of Sutherland at Dunrobin Castle. Among the guests was Lieutenant Lord Louis Mountbatten with whom she was in love. But he had left hurriedly a few days later to attend the funeral of his father Admiral of the Fleet the Marquess of Milford Haven – the former Prince of Battenberg. Ernest Cassel and Louis Battenberg had died within ten days of each other. Who would have guessed that the one's granddaughter and the other's son would soon make a historic marriage?

CHAPTER NINE

THE SUPREMO

Admiral of the Fleet
The Earl Mountbatten of Burma

CRITICS of the Earl Mountbatten during his measured, pre-meditated rise to national eminence and international fame, disparaged him as 'a gilded playboy', the meticulous 'Superbo', 'the Viceroy of Scuttle', and a man 'with infinite capacity for minor intrigue'. But even the most bitter of them could not deny his gift for facile accomplishment, his devotion to duty and his panache of authority. So they pointed out that this most gong-hung Insider, born into the Royal Establishment, proud of his kinship with Europe's dynasties since Charlemagne, could have hardly failed whatever he did. In fact, his antecedents were often more a hindrance than a help.

Had he been born a commoner, his vigorous mind, his pro-fessional dedication, his restless ambition, allied to immense charm and extremely good presence, would have carried him to the top: he might have become a prime minister, a great captain of industry, or an international dictator of finance. If, as a military leader he had gained an array of glittering stars and orders, he could have amassed great power and wealth in any other profession.

Oscar Wilde said the British people can forgive everything except genius; some of them can forgive everything except royal brilliance. A distinguished writer on military subjects said on Lord Mountbatten's retirement in 1965 that only an interim verdict on his record could be formed. The Admiral of the Fleet, former Viceroy, Chief of the Defence Staff, Her Majesty's Privy Councillor, Knight of the Most Noble Order of the Garter,

Order of Merit, whose thousand-word *Who's Who* biography is the longest and was exceeded only by that of Winston Churchill, had become a production, a showpiece. Historians will have to sort out reality from the display and judge what he had done for Britain, as Chief of Combined Operations, Supreme Allied Commander in South East Asia, last of the Viceroys of India, rebuilder of the modern Navy and fulcrum of the biggest upheaval in Britain's defence organisation of modern times.

His first energetic action took place appropriately enough at Frogmore House in the grounds of Windsor Castle, where his parents, Prince Louis of Battenberg and Princess Victoria, Queen Victoria's granddaughter, lived when he was born there on 25 June 1900. The old Queen, having inspected her great-grandson immediately after his birth, was driven a month later through the royal gardens in the company of Dr Dalton, the Dean of Windsor, to attend the baby's christening. The podgy yet regal figure, her trembling hand on a silver and ebony stick, sat expectantly whilst a lady-in-waiting took the child from a nurse, glided down the mahoganied salon and presented it to the Queen. She bent over the child, peering with her dim, almost blind eyes. The baby gurgled, shot up a tiny hand and knocked off the Queen's spectacles. Never losing her composure, Queen Victoria had the child, now screaming, handed to the voluble Dr Dalton, who baptised him Louis Francis Albert Victor Nicholas.

How could Queen Victoria, for sixty-three years sovereign of pine and palm, Empress of India, imagine that her great-grandson, born in the sunset of her era, nurtured in its Edwardian afterglow, and maturing in the harsh new age of total war, would fight in two world wars against her own German kinfolk and preside over the dissolution of her Indian realm?

Although his first name was Louis, after his father and grandfather, his parents called him 'Nicky' until the Tsar and his family came to visit them at Heiligenberg. Then everybody joked that there were too many 'Nickies' and his name was changed to 'Dickie'. It remained 'Dickie', affectionately with his family and friends, and as a sobriquet with Cabinet ministers and service chiefs. The boy, taught at home by his strict mother in his early years, was thoughtful, cautious, self-willed, and also precocious for his age, which was only natural as he was reared with his brother George, eight years his senior, and two sisters, Alice who was 15 and Louisa who was 11 when he was born. From early childhood he lived in a cosmopolitan atmosphere. His father was stationed in Malta, was later Director of Naval Intelligence in London, and there were frequent journeys abroad, long stays on the estates in Germany and visits to St Petersburg.

The story is told that his aunt, the Tsaritsa of Russia, asked him what he would like to be when he grew up. 'I haven't quite decided yet,' the little boy replied. 'Perhaps you would like to be a sailor, like your father?' He shook his head: 'No, ships always sink.' 'Well, would you like to be a soldier?' 'No, soldiers always get shot.' The Tsaritsa suggested a commonplace child-like choice: 'An engine-driver, perhaps?' But Dickie did not approve of it either: 'No, the engine might go over the embankment.'

When scolded, he could become moody and sulky. Mrs Crichton, his mother's lady-in-waiting, told the story how he appeared one day with a piece of cardboard on his chest, inscribed with the letters 'I.A.O.', and when asked what this meant, replied: 'It stands for I AM OFFENDED. I shall wear it every time when I am offended.'

His serious schooling began at the age of nine when he was sent to Locker's Park, a preparatory school, which his cousin, Prince Maurice of Battenberg, Princess Beatrice's youngest son, also attended. He showed only modest success in his studies and was bad at football. His father, who had become First Sea Lord, hoped for better things when his son, without great enthusiasm, entered Osborne as a Royal Navy cadet. Life at the Royal Naval College in the Isle of Wight, once a mansion of his queenly great-grandmother, was spartan, with cold plunges at dawn, frugal food and a shilling a week pocket money. He gave little promise of his later brilliant career, was bad at games and something of a disappointment to his parents. They were enormously proud of his brother George, who had passed all examinations with top marks and was already a sub-lieutenant in the Royal Navy, when little Dickie scraped through the College passing out thirty-fifth of a class of seventy-nine. But it was at Osborne that he experienced the biggest emotional shock of his life – and its turning-point. His father, vilely attacked for his German antecedents, had been compelled to resign his post as First Sea Lord soon after the outbreak of the first world war. The news, which shook the

Navy, desolated Dickie. It was said that on the day he heard it, he was seen standing to attention on parade with tears running down his cheeks. At this impressionable age he must have grown almost overnight from a day-dreaming and rather laggard school-boy into a youth determined to vindicate in his life the father who had been so shamefully slandered. When soon afterwards he moved to Dartmouth for a short three-month war-time course, he passed out near the top, showing great dedication to his studies and unexpected tenacity.

Midshipman Prince Louis of Battenberg was posted in July 1916 to H.M.S. *Lion,* the flagship of Admiral Beatty, and later served in H.M.S. *Queen Elizabeth*. When he was ragged by older, ribbonless officers, about the medal ribbon on his breast, which commemorated no greater gallantry than his attendance at the Coronation of King George v, he was not 'offended' any more; his inherent cheerfulness and charm, like his latent capacities, had come to the surface – he had become a good mixer. When in July 1917 his family changed its name to Mountbatten and his father became the first Marquess of Milford Haven, Dickie – now Lord Louis – wrote in a visiting book: 'Arrived Prince Hyde, departed Lord Jekyll'.

If some of his officers sniggered at his ribbon, they had nothing to complain about his work and devotion to duty. When other midshipmen were amusing themselves, he would work on his notes on gunnery, torpedoes, naval strategy, navigation and seamanship. He served in one of the 'sardine tins', submarines of the K.6-class, regarded by many naval officers as death traps. By the time of the Armistice, a sub-lieutenant at 18, he was second-in-command of the P-31, a small, fast patrol boat in the Straits of Dover. At the end of the war the Admiralty, with a surplus of young officers, arranged for some of them to go for a year to universities. Dickie spent two terms at Christ's College, Cam-bridge. If he did not become an intellectual, his outlook certainly broadened. He was the first serving naval officer to be elected to the Union during his first term. Although he had no experience of public speaking, he was chosen to lead a debate against Oxford University. Leading speakers may invite distinguished outsiders to support them, and Lord Louis asked Winston Churchill, then War Secretary in Lloyd George's Coalition Government. Oxford had proposed the motion 'that the time is ripe for a Labour Government'. Lord Louis, later in his life often described as a Labour Party sympathiser, was against it. After several famous politicians had spoken he addressed the President of the Union: 'Sir, in my humble opinion, what previous speakers on both sides have said up to now was tripe!' Churchill afterwards prophetically remarked: 'I trust that he will show as great facility in dealing with admirals on their quarter-decks as with opponents on this platform.'

After he left Cambridge, he accompanied in 1920 his cousin, the Prince of Wales, on a world tour in the battle-cruiser H.M.S. *Renown*. From that time dated his close friendship with the later King Edward viii; Lord Louis was to play an unpublicised but not unimportant role in the abdication crisis of 1936.

The 20-year-old handsome naval officer had become a 'debs' delight', and many a match-making mother sought the royal cousin. But Lord Louis had fallen in love with Miss Audrey James, a beautiful half-American brunette, whose photograph he had seen in the pages of the *Sketch*. He arranged to be introduced to her at a ball at one of the great Mayfair mansions, and after a two-week whirlwind courtship they became engaged. However, after he had sailed away with the Prince of Wales, Miss James, left alone so suddenly, changed her mind, broke off the engagement and soon afterwards married Major Dudley Coats, a kinsman of Lord Glentanar of the millionaire textile family. This led in London Society to the quip that she 'preferred the arms of Coats to a Coat of Arms'.

To forget his wounded pride Lord Louis plunged into the London Season. Among the glittering events was a ball given at Claridge's by the American hostess Mrs Cornelius Vanderbilt. That evening he met Edwina Ashley, the granddaughter of Sir Edward Cassel. In August he accompanied his father on a cruise aboard the *Repulse* and then attended a house-party at the Duke of Sutherland's Dunrobin Castle in Scotland, where he met Edwina again and where the news of his father's sudden death reached him.

Soon afterwards he sailed with the Prince of Wales to India. Edwina Ashley, whose father had died ten days after Lord Louis' father, followed him to Delhi. There, at the Viceregal Lodge, he formally proposed, and the Prince of Wales was the first person to learn of it.

Edwina returned to England alone, Dickie followed several weeks later, in duty bound to complete the tour with the Prince of Wales, which led to Ceylon, Singapore and Japan, before he could return in June 1922 to London for his wedding. The five-month honeymoon was a grand tour of Europe and the United States. Back in England, Lieutenant Lord Louis took up his naval career, while his wife opened Brook House again. They soon became the most-talked-about, written-about and photographed leaders of the 'bright young things' of London's 'Roaring Twenties'.

If Dickie had been a 'gilded playboy' during those years, he did not neglect his service in the Royal Navy. Indeed, he took it very seriously. He spent two years in the battleship H.M.S. *Revenge* in the Mediterranean and with the Atlantic Fleet, his wife accompanying him from port to port. In 1924 Lady Louis gave birth to their first daughter, Patricia; they were reunited in London, and Dickie started on the Long Signal course at Portsmouth, living with his wife and child in a rented house near the base. In 1926 he became Reserve Fleet Signal Officer, was posted to Malta, and soon afterwards promoted Lieutenant-Commander and Signal Officer of the Second Destroyer Flotilla.

In their first home in Malta, the 'Casa Medina', a villa overlooking Sliema Harbour, the Moutbattens lived without ostentation – rather to the surprise of those who imagined that their life would consist mainly of extravagant parties. Dickie devoted much of his leisure to improving his skill at polo. He was not, as some sycophantic biographers said, 'an accomplished polo player'. At Malta some of his brother-officers used to say that he 'looked like a sack of potatoes perched on a pony', but he took great pains to improve his skill, eventually achieving a very high level of competence and elegance, after months of scientific analysis of polo technique, and driving himself hard at practice. Finally, he became such an expert on polo that he wrote – under the pseudonym of 'Marco' – a book on the game which is still regarded a useful textbook.

Lord Louis was always a compulsive worker, with a fanatical attention to detail, a meticulous mind, immense alertness and never failing enthusiasm. At every moment of his naval career he was determined to make himself the unrelenting professional, absorbed, efficient, dedicated. He became a master of the in-

ricacies of naval communications: before he was 30 he produced
series of lectures and a wireless manual which revolutionised
the coding and transmission of signals and became a standard
instructional work. He also compiled still widely used dictionaries
of naval terms in German and French.

After a spell as chief wireless instructor at the Royal Navy
Signals School at Portsmouth he rejoined the Mediterranean
Fleet at Malta in 1931 as its Chief Wireless Officer. He certainly
kept the Fleet telegraphists on their toes, but the remark of a
senior officer, lacking understanding of modern techniques and
envious of Lord Louis' accomplishments, that 'he is a driver not
a leader', was merely malicious. The 'driver' was more popular
with the men of the lower deck he was supposed to drive than
with some of his senior officers.

Like all efficiency experts he wanted to save time: having a
daily schedule of work and play carefully prepared in advance
was not enough. He invented or used many time-saving devices;
he was a pioneer of zip-fronted trousers, invented 'plus-shorts' for
hot-climate uniforms (which came below the knee in those more
decorous days), wore collar-attached shirts, cut out sock-
suspenders by having elastic woven into the tops of the socks,
and devised ingenious shoelaces made of elastic which never
needed untying. Sometimes, perhaps, this gadgetry was gim-
nickry. He devised a dial-like alarm clock outside all bedroom
doors at his home 'Adsdean' at Portsmouth. A twist of a knob
and time was automatically set on the dial, so that the servants –
he had seventeen – knew when to awake the guests. But Dickie,
rather characteristically, had overlooked human foibles. Some of
his guests played jokes with his gadgets, and he and his wife had
a few unpleasant awakenings at dawn; the servants were eventually
told to ignore the dials.

If, in his enthusiasm for technical innovations, he played with
gadgets, he also invented some serious navigational devices. One
made it possible for the officer on the bridge to measure the
correct distance of his ship from one ahead of him. This 'distance
corrector', which some of Lord Louis's critics in the Navy called
'Mountbatten's toy', was after many delays installed in a few
destroyers and proved extremely useful. When he constructed a
new navigational ruler – which the Patent Office later accepted –
the first ironical comment was: 'This is not the first navigational

ruler . . . most naval cadets in their engineering shipwork made
one of brass; ships' courses plotted with those offensive weapons
have been known to be hundreds of miles out.'

Lord Louis had to overcome much obstruction but was rarely
discouraged. In 1937 he heard of an Austrian refugee, Anton
Gazda, who had constructed at the Swiss Oerlikon Works a
naval quick-firing gun. Lord Louis realised that this was a perfect
anti-aircraft gun against dive-bombers. He brought Gazda to
London and introduced him to Admiralty experts. But three
years and 283 meetings were to go by before the Oerlikon gun
was ordered and became one of the most reliable weapons in the
war.

When in 1936 Lord Louis joined the Admiralty Naval Air
Division, the Mountbattens moved to their famous Park Lane
penthouse, which became the scene of great parties. The former
'playboy' had matured, he had become keenly interested in
politics, prompted by Hitler's advent to power and the Spanish
Civil War. His wife was known for her radical views, but Dickie
had to tread cautiously, being a member of the Royal Family
and a serving officer, though he made no secret of his progressive
leanings. He passionately advocated sending British warships
into Spanish ports and 'blowing the Franco fascists off the face
of the earth'. He strongly expressed his hatred of the Hitler regime
and, in advocating this course against Germany and Spain, was
going against the interests of his own family: in Spain the
Republicans had deposed his cousin, Queen Ena; in Germany the
Hitler regime was, at that time, more apt than any other to support
the pretensions of his princely relatives of Hesse and Hanover.

When in later years his conservative critics spoke of the royal
cousin as if he were the Philippe Egalité of the Labour government, derided his liberalism and referred to him as 'the red
prince', they misjudged the motives which moved him. Lord
Mountbatten is far too self-willed, far too imbued with the conviction of his own power of leadership to embrace the doctrines
of any political party. With Thomas Jefferson he could say, 'I
was never the sort of man to submit . . . my opinions to the creed
of any party of men, in religion, in philosophy, or politics, or in
anything else where I was capable of thinking for myself.'[1] His
friends during the last few years before the war included politicians

[1] Cf. Murphy, R., *Last Viceroy,* London, Jarrolds, 1948.

of very different shades – from Anthony Eden, who had rebelled against the Hoare-Laval pact on Abyssinia and the appeasement of Mussolini to 'New Deal' progressive Tories and extreme left-wing Socialists, such as Sir Stafford Cripps.

Lord Louis's promotion to Captain in 1937, a few days before his thirty-seventh birthday, was made by the Admiralty in the normal course of selection among outstanding officers, but caused immediately club gossip of 'favouritism', because some other Commanders usually did not reach this rank before they were 42. In the summer of 1939 Lord Louis was given command of a K-Class destroyer flotilla and put in charge of H.M.S. *Kelly,* a modern destroyer then still under construction at Tyneside. The war was only a few days off when at Chatham Dockyard he addressed the 240 members of the crew, each of whom he had personally chosen from amongst 3,000 applicants who had volunteered to serve in his new ship. He told them:

'In peace time it takes all of three weeks to get a new ship's company together, to let them sling their hammocks and teach them their stations and various duties, to get all the cordite and shells and oil fuel and stores on board, and so on and so forth. Well, you've read your papers and you know that Ribbentrop signed a non-aggression pact with Stalin yesterday. As I see it, that means war next week. So I will give you not three weeks, but three days to get this ship ready to sail.

'None of us will take off our clothes or sling our hammocks, or turn in for the next three days and nights until the job is finished. Then we'll send Hitler a signal saying "The *Kelly*'s ready – you can start your war".'

The 'driver' again? Lord Louis was a keen disciplinarian but he also knew how to treat his men justly and magnanimously. When his ship was damaged in the North Sea by a magnetic mine, one of the stokers panicked and rushed on deck, ready to abandon ship without command. After the *Kelly* had limped back to harbour, Lord Louis had the man put under arrest.

'Do you know what the penalty is for desertion of your post in the face of the enemy?' he asked him.

'Yes, sir – it is death,' the stoker muttered.

'Quite right,' said Captain Mountbatten. 'I will stand your case over and deal with it later.'

Two hours later he addressed the ship's company:

'Out of 240 men on board this ship, 239 behaved as they ought to have, and as I expected them to behave, but one was unable to control himself and deserted his post, and incidentally his comrades in the engine room. I had him brought before me a couple of hours ago, and he himself informed me that he knew the punishment for desertion of his post could be death. You will therefore be surprised to hear that I propose to let him off with a "caution". One caution to him, and a second one to myself, for having failed in four months to impress my personality and doctrine on each and all of you to prevent such incident from occurring.

'From now on I wish to make it clear I expect everyone to behave in the way the 239 did, and to stick to their post in action to the last. I will under no circumstances whatever again tolerate the slightest suspicion of cowardice or indiscipline, and I know from now on that none of you will present me with such a problem.'

The story of the *Kelly* is too well known to need detailed recounting. When she underwent repairs in London Graving Dock, Lord Louis installed a cinema projector aboard, characteristically devising an ingenious arrangement to cut out engine noises and interference, and showed to his crew Chaplin's *The Great Dictator,* inviting the Duke and Duchess of Kent for 'the first night'. Then the *Kelly* took part in the evacuation of Allied forces from Norway and on 9 May 1940 was hit by a German torpedo. Half awash, with her decks at an angle of 45 degrees, her captain tried to bring her back to England, while German aircraft continuously dive-bombed her. The admiral in command of the cruiser squadron sent repeated signals, ordering to 'Abandon ship', and, after Captain Mountbatten ignored them, finally signalled: 'Abandon the *Kelly*, I am going to sink her', to which he was supposed to have received the reply: 'Not while I still have twelve torpedoes with which to sink you if you dare to try'. It took the *Kelly* four days to reach the Tyne, in tow and with the tow-line parting four times, during which Mountbatten, unshaven, soaked, filthy with oil, never slept, himself working one of the anti-aircraft guns.

Many years later, addressing the Military Academy at Dehra

Dun, when he was Governor-General of India, Mountbatten gave a frank, personal account about that journey:

'. . . an enemy E-boat came out of the darkness and opened fire . . . I was alone on the bridge as my damaged ship was being towed back, and the survivors were busy trying to prevent the ship turning over. I ducked behind the bridge screen, a very silly thing to do, for it would not have kept out a rifle bullet. Then I suddenly felt frightfully ashamed and very glad I was alone on the bridge so that no one had seen me duck. I said to myself: "Never again will I permit myself to show when I am afraid".'

When the *Kelly* was under repair for eight months, Mountbatten was leading the destroyer flotilla in other ships, which during operations in the North Sea and Mediterranean were repeatedly engaged with German E-boats, U-boats and the Luftwaffe. At one period they were dive-bombed 47 times in ten days. Eventually, he got his *Kelly* back; she operated from battered Malta and later took part in the evacuation of British troops from Crete. On 21 May 1941 the *Kelly* and other ships were attacked there by a large formation of German bombers. The *Kashmir* was sunk by a 1,000-lb bomb and next was the *Kelly*'s turn. Not one man left the engine room until she had turned turtle, and half of the crew was lost. The survivors, including Captain Mountbatten, were picked up by the *Kipling*. At Alexandria he took leave of his men:

'I have come to say good-bye to the few of you who are left . . . There may be less than half of the *Kelly* [crew] left, but I feel each of us will take up the battle with even stronger heart. Each of us knows twice as much about fighting, and each of us has twice as good a reason to fight. You will all be sent to replace men who have been killed in other ships, and the next time you are in action, remember the *Kelly*. As you ram each shell home into the gun, shout "Kelly!" and so her spirit will go on inspiring us until victory is won.'

His men were proud to have served with him, even though some admirals took a dry view of his methods. When Noël Coward made the famous film of the *Kelly* epic and named it *In Which We Serve*, it was dubbed by some at the Admiralty 'In Which We Sink', and Mountbatten's remark in his farewell speech to the

Kelly survivors that 'There isn't one of you that I wouldn't be proud to serve with again', led to such London clubland gibes as 'There is nobody better to be in a tight spot with and nobody likely to get you into one sooner than Dickie Mountbatten'.

Lord Louis returned to England, was assigned to the command of the aircraft carrier *Illustrious* and went to America to supervise its refitting at Norfolk, Virginia. Although not yet in the war, the United States was rendering great Lend-Lease help. The Chief of the US Naval Staff, Admiral Stark, invited him to visit Pearl Harbour – only three months before the Japanese attack – and on his flight back from Hawaii, Dickie stopped at Los Angeles and Hollywood where he met Walt Disney and another old friend, from the gay pre-war days, Lieutenant-Commander Douglas Fairbanks jun. Dickie's idea to have an emblem designed for the *Illustrious* showing 'Donald Duck' in the uniform of a Royal Navy admiral, standing in a pool, pushing an aircraft carrier with one webbed foot and lifting an aeroplane from the deck with a wing, aroused little enthusiasm at the Admiralty, and the emblem was never displayed. On 10 October 1941 Dickie received a telegram from Churchill: 'We want you home at once for something which you will find of the highest interest'.

His command of H.M.S. *Illustrious* had been suddenly cancelled; in the Admiralty list the letter 'M' was added to his name, which signified 'on secret appointment'. In London the news caused a buzz of speculation and Dickie himself had been left in the dark. It was a climacteric of the war. All Western Europe lay prostrate under Hitler's heel; Yugoslavia and Greece had fallen; in North Africa Rommel had pushed the British almost to the border of Egypt and encircled Tobruk; German troops had poured through the Ukraine into the Crimea and laid siege to Leningrad and Moscow; in the Atlantic grievous British and Allied shipping losses had reached the staggering total of 7,000,000 tons. The 'darkest hours' were still to come: soon Japan was to join the Axis and to conquer Burma, Malaya, the Philippines and all European possessions in the Far East. Yet Churchill never wavered in his determination to turn defensive into attack. The only means to strike back at the Germans in Europe was to retaliate from the air (which Britain with her still small airforce could hardly attempt), to encourage the Resistance by sending secret agents and parachuting arms to the freedom fighters and,

The 2nd Marquess of Milford Haven with his wife, Countess Nadejda Torby, daughter of Grand Duke Michael of Russia, with their two children, David (the present 3rd Marquess) and Lady Tatiana Mountbatten, in 1922.

Lady Louisa Mountbatten (Princess of Battenberg, later Queen of Sweden) with her two brothers, the 2nd Marquess of Milford Haven and Lord Louis Mountbatten (the present Earl).

The 3rd Marquess of Milford Haven with his second wife, Miss Janet Bryce, at their wedding in 1960. He was formerly married to an American divorcée, Mrs Romaine Simpson.

THE SPANISH ROYAL FAMILY
Standing (from left to right): Infante Jaime; a cousin of the King; Infante Alfonso; King Alfonso XIII; Infante Juan; *sitting*: Infanta Beatriz; a niece of the king; Queen Mother Maria Christina; Infante Gonzalo; Queen Victoria Eugenie (Princess Ena of Battenberg); Infanta Maria Christina.

last but not least, by staging coastal raids on Nazi-occupied Europe. To this purpose Churchill had set up the Combined Operations and the Special Operations Executive. Neither had yet succeeded in achieving the minimum tasks set for them. So Churchill offered the post of Chief of Combined Operations to 41-year-old Captain Lord Louis Mountbatten, a post hitherto held by 70-year-old Admiral of the Fleet Sir Roger Keyes, the V.C. hero of Zebrugge. Churchill told Lord Louis:

'Your primary object will be the invasion of Europe, for unless we return to the Continent and beat the Germans on land we shall never win the war. All the other headquarters in this country are thinking defensively. Your job is to be offensive; train for the offensive; work out the craft, the equipment, the tactics, the administration and everything needed to sustain the offensive . . . The South of England is now a bastion against German invasion; you will turn it into the springboard from which to launch our invasion.'

Lord Louis said afterwards: 'I knew at once that he was right. I left the room inspired.' Under Mountbatten's leadership Combined Operations, drawing on scientific resources and technological inventions, employing 'long-haired amateurs' in ill-fitting uniforms from the universities and industry, using unorthodox methods, improvising new equipment, devising novel landing craft, weapons and tactics, training tough men into assault Commandos, became the spearhead Churchill had envisaged for 'setting Europe ablaze', and led to the triumphs of D-Day.

His 'triphibious' forces raided Vaagso, Bruneval, St Nazaire, and with experience bought at grim cost of lives, Dieppe; destroyed in co-operation with SOE the heavy water plant in Norway, thus depriving the Germans of material for their experimental atom bomb production; and accomplished some of the most daring feats of the war.

With his zest for action, his disregard for fossilised Service doctrines, his contempt for indecision and vapidity of chairborne strategists, Lord Louis threw all his energy into an almost impossible task. He used all his diplomacy and charm and – when obstructed almost at every step in the beginning – his ruthlessness in order to achieve the tasks Churchill had set him. Much to the displeasure of some holders of highest military appointments,

Churchill had ordered that the junior Captain should be made an acting Vice-Admiral, Lieutenant-General and Air Marshal and take his seat at the Chiefs of Staff Committee. With his eye for detail, his determination to learn everything at first hand – even foolhardily going down in an experimental one-man 'human torpedo' submarine which leaked – he fostered new devices which his more orthodox colleagues viewed with horrified eyes as products of crazy scientists. Thus he stood at the cradle of such 'impossible' devices as the portable Mulberry harbours, the Pluto underwater oil pipeline from England to Normandy and the close-support rocket-firing ships, without which D-Day could have never been successfully accomplished.

There was a bizarre episode at the Quebec Conference in July 1943, when Lord Louis urged that an invention should be adopted for building gigantic floating airfields of Pykrete, a mixture of ice and wood pulp. Some experts declared that this material was not strong enough. Lord Louis asked General Arnold, Chief of the US Air Force, to chop a block of ordinary ice and one made of Pykrete, and when the general whacked the latter with an axe he jarred his arm badly. Lord Louis pulled his revolver and shattered the ordinary ice block with a single bullet, then he fired into the Pykrete block, narrowly missing Air Chief Marshal Sir Charles Portal. There had been heated discussions during that day, and one of the staff officers waiting outside the conference room exclaimed: 'My God, now they've started shooting each other!'

At Combined Operations Lord Louis's achievements were immense, although he had to battle against opposition all the time. He worked for 18 hours a day, often snatching only a few hours' sleep on a couch in his office, but he somehow found time to visit training establishments, laboratories, and secret workshops, to talk to subalterns and men and to listen to their grumbles and suggestions. He made no less than seventy visits to Commando bases, and he ensured that the training of the three Services was rigorously co-ordinated.

If he encountered opposition from some British 'brass-hats', the American generals and colonels took to him at first sight. They might have expected to find in the royal cousin a phlegmatic, snobbish, polo-playing English aristocrat of the type which bewilders and annoys Americans. Instead, they discovered a man of action, who not only did not despise technology but was ready to adopt any worthwhile 'gadget', and who preferred straight talk to dilly-dallying conferences. Thus Lord Louis achieved the almost impossible: to integrate British and American staff planning. He played a leading part in planning *Operation Torch,* the invasion of North Africa, and *Operation Husky,* the landing in Sicily. When General Eisenhower arrived in England as Supreme Allied Commander, he did not know Lord Louis, but he had heard enough about him from US generals to tell at his first meeting with the Joint Chiefs of Staff that he wanted Lord Mountbatten to be appointed to the Cross-Channel invasion command.

When 'the turn of the tide' had come and emphasis lay upon victory in the Far East, the Americans at once approved Churchill's proposal that Mountbatten should be made Supreme Allied Commander in South-East Asia. Churchill had asked him at the Quebec Conference, during a stroll on the Citadel's battlements, what he thought of the stalemate war against the Japanese.

'They tell me,' Dickie replied, 'the situation out there is in a terrible mess.'

'Well, I want you to go out there,' Churchill said.

Lord Louis thought the Prime Minister had an exploratory mission in mind for him. Diffidently he replied:

'What could I do on a junket like that?'

'I want you to go out there as Supreme Allied Commander. Do you think you could take care of the job?' the Prime Minister asked.

It was for only a moment that Dickie hesitated. 'You know, sir, it's a congenital weakness with me to think I can do anything, but if I am to take the job I must have your assurance that everyone of the American as well as the British Chiefs of Staff support my appointment.'

When he reported to President Roosevelt, the titular Commander-in-Chief of United States Forces told him: 'Your job might have been given to an American, but I rely on you to support our policy in South-East Asia . . .' Thus the 'substantive Captain' Mountbatten became the Supremo, equal to such great American figures as the imperious General McArthur and Admiral King, in command of US Pacific forces.

He faced a task of unprecedented magnitude. His South-East

Asia Command covered a million square miles. The overwhelmingly stronger enemy was experienced in jungle warfare and accustomed to the exacting climate. The Japanese successfully spread the legend of their invincibility among the hundreds of millions of Asians to whom 'colonial' Britain and her American allies could only offer vague promises of reconquest. He had to start from scratch, to train inexperienced troops, to reinvigorate the morale of the 'forgotten' British 14th Army, which had 126 casualties from sickness to each man wounded in combat. He had to support the difficult Chiang Kai-shek, who had very different political aims than his 'white' allies. He had to contend with the personality of General Stillwell, his American deputy, aptly named 'Vinegar Joe', who never grasped Lord Louis's capabilities and regarded him as 'a playboy at war'. Stillwell was quite wrong in his assessment: Lord Mountbatten never played at anything except to win.

He decided to use the same methods to win the loyalty and kindle the enthusiasm of his army as he did when addressing the 240 ratings of the *Kelly* in 1939. He sent a message to all commanding officers: The Supreme Commander is coming and will talk with the troops. No reviews or official inspections. He will talk to the men, informally, standing on a box. Be sure there is a good, strong box accidentally lying around.'

To the men of many nationalities, 'browned-off', often exhausted, sometimes sick from fever, he never pretended to be just one of them. He did not try slap-happy fraternisation, did not tell them he would share their hardships and ordeals in the jungle. He appeared as their 'Supremo', an elegant, crisp, cool figure, in immaculate uniform with rows upon rows of ribbons and insignia showing he was an A.D.C. to His Britannic Majesty: a royal Olympian to lead them to victory. But, from that 'accidentally' found box he knew how to talk to them – and he understood their problems. They called him 'the Superbo', but they knew that despite formidable difficulties they would, at last, have proper supplies, enough 'smokes', canned beer, better hospital and transport arrangements and leave centres. He called from London a brilliant journalist, Frank Owen, who gave them their own newspaper which frankly reported the difficulties, published their grumbles and kept them informed; the best and certainly the only honest army paper of the war. The Supremo told them: 'You have thought of yourselves as the fighters of a forgotten war . . . You're quite wrong about this – the Burma war has not been forgotten, it has never been heard of!' He made sure that from then on a lot was to be heard of the war in the Far East.

Despite fighting the grimmest campaign of the Second World War, the 14th Army which had marched and crawled and fought across 1,000 miles of disease-infested jungle and swamp, reconquered Burma by May 1945. *Operation Zipper,* the biggest-ever planned combined assault, intended to reconquer Malaya before the autumn, was well under way when Japan's might collapsed in the radioactive ashes of Hiroshima and Nagasaki.

The war in the Far East was over, but the problems faced by the Supremo were new and immense. He found himself administering an area the size of Europe, with 128,000,000 people, half-starved, in civil chaos and political unrest. He had to disarm 750,000 Japanese troops, feed them and provide medical treatment, while his first priority was to rescue and care for 200,000 Allied ex-prisoners of war and internees. His wife had already joined him in Delhi and proved an invaluable helper, organising hospitals, camps, rest centres and food distribution.

Succeeding months were occupied with long journeys in the countries within his Command. He became increasingly preoccupied with political affairs, the Labour Government in London had entrusted him with negotiations with the leaders of the resurgent national movements which had emerged after the Japanese occupation. Lord Mountbatten called his new diplomatic experiences 'my political baptism by total immersion'.

Visiting New Delhi in February 1946 he learned from the Viceroy, Lord Wavell, that Pandit Nehru – only recently released from gaol and already talked of as the future Prime Minister of the Dominion of India – intended to visit Indian communities in Malaya. The British military authorities in Singapore, expecting that Nehru would be acclaimed by members of the former Indian National Army (which had been formed by the Japanese and was anti-British), and fearing disturbances, decided to impede Nehru's visit and ordered British Military Police to cordon off many streets. Mountbatten was furious and ordered that Nehru should be treated with every courtesy. He invited the Indian leader to dinner at Government House, which British military and civil leaders reluctantly attended, and then drove with him through the streets. The result was that Nehru dropped all tributes to the members of the disbanded Indian National Army when he later addressed jubilant mass-meetings. Expecting to be cold-shouldered or even arrested, he was extremely pleased about the courtesy he had received.

During this visit an incident occurred which was as significant as it was symbolic. Lady Mountbatten received Nehru on the steps of her Red Cross Indian Rehabilitation Centre. The crowd welcoming Nehru burst through the police cordon and almost trampled Lady Mountbatten underfoot. It was Nehru who rescued her. Out of this incident a friendship grew between the Mountbattens and the Indian leader who within a year became a factor in world politics. This friendship radically changed British-Indian relations.

In June 1946 Lord Mountbatten's post as Supremo in South-East Asia came to an end and he returned to England. There were rumours that Mr Attlee and Ernest Bevin had offered him the post of British ambassador in Washington. But as a member of the Royal Family he could hardly be asked to fill a political or diplomatic post under the Labour Government, even if he was in sympathy with it. In any case, true to the vow he had made as a midshipman, he was determined to return to the Royal Navy. Arrangements were made at the Admiralty to appoint him to the Command of the First Mediterranean Cruiser Squadron.

But already in December 1946 Mr Attlee had approached him with a proposal that was to require all his energy and diplomatic talents. The Labour Government was faced with an intolerable and seemingly insoluble situation in India. Sir Stafford Cripps's mission to establish a united Dominion government had foundered on the bitter hostility between Hindus and Moslems. Local communal clashes were rapidly reaching a dangerous stage and augured an all-out conflict between the warring communities. Failing an agreed solution, the Viceroy (Lord Wavell) was suggesting total evacuation of India by the British civil service and troops. He had already prepared points from which this political Dunkirk of the British Raj was to take place. Such a flight from responsibility was unacceptable to Labour.

'I came to the conclusion that Wavell had shot his bolt, and that I must find somebody else . . . Suddenly I had what I think was an inspiration. I thought of Mountbatten,' Lord Attlee recalled. 'He had an extremely lively, exciting personality. He had an extraordinary faculty for getting on with all kinds of people . . . He was also blessed with a very unusual wife. So I put it to him. Bit of a shock for him, because one of Dickie's great hopes was that he would one day succeed to the position of First Sea Lord from which his father had been most disgracefully thrown out in the anti-German cry at the beginning of the first world war. He didn't want to leave a naval career. But I talked to him and he very patriotically agreed to take on the job . . .'[1]

The King put his influence behind Attlee's pleas; it was not an easy decision to let a member of the Royal Family take on a risky job, 'a hit or miss' in India. Attlee told the King, as he had told Mountbatten, that he thought 'the odds were six to four against success', and that Dickie was going out not to continue the British Raj but to end it. Thus Lord Mountbatten became, with the King's full consent, the British Government's agent to liquidate British rule in India and to bring political independence and self-determination to 450,000,000 people of the sub-continent. It was not even certain whether, after partition, India and Pakistan would remain members of the British Commonwealth; Burma had already opted out. It was the greatest renunciation of imperial and colonial power ever known.

Mountbatten reached Delhi on 22 March 1947. All the rich panoply of the Viceroyalty was displayed two days later at the last Imperial Durbar – the fanfares, the magnificent guards of honour, the unfurling of flags, the royal salutes, the gaudy spleandours of jewel-hung maharajahs. But the new Viceroy, resplendent in his uniform and glittering orders under the blue robe of the Grand Master of the Star of India, warned that the transfer of power must be swift. On his desk stood a calendar, with the date prominently ringed on which the British Raj was to end. He told the Indian people: 'We are a great nation, but we can no longer rule you . . . I shall need the greatest goodwill of the greatest possible number, and I am asking India today for that goodwill.

[1] Lord Francis-Williams, *A Prime Minister Remembers,* London, Heinemann, 1961.

He gained that goodwill from most of them. 'He got on the right side of Nehru and he managed to get a joint Government going for the time being with Jinnah and Nehru and the rest,' Attlee recalled. 'He got on the right side of Gandhi, too, and soon he had all these people talking . . . It took a lot of work and a lot of negotiation. But Mountbatten won, and eventually came the day when we passed the Independence of India Act.'[1]

Where he failed to get goodwill, he behaved – as a commentator put it – with complete ruthlessness, to the point of taking a calculated risk with the lives of minorities on both sides of the partition line. He did not arbitrate between the parties, but bullied them all to achieve the best and quickest compromise he could. He was not a political negotiator: 'He looked and he behaved like a king, carrying out the highest of high acts of State.'

The date of the transfer of power to the new states of India and Pakistan had originally been fixed for June 1948, but the Viceroy had realised that it must take place much earlier if the rising communal tension was not to explode into chaos and massacre that would engulf the entire sub-continent. He recommended to the British Government and the Hindu and Moslem leaders to accept the 14th August 1947, only 145 days after his arrival. On 3 June he announced the details of the partition and transfer and when on the following day he brilliantly expounded the complex plan, without notes and without hesitating for a word to a conference of 200 newspapermen, they spontaneously applauded him.

If Conservative leaders in Britain, including Dickie's old friend Winston Churchill, spoke of scuttling and the 'liquidation of the Empire', the world greeted Britain's abnegation as a great act of wisdom. The distinguished American commentator Walter Lippmann wrote in the *Washington Post:*

'Britain's finest hour is not in the past. Certainly this performance is not the work of a decadent people . . . it is the work of political genius requiring the ripest wisdom and the freshest vigour, and it is done with an elegance and a style that will compel and will receive an instinctive respect throughout the civilized world. Attlee and Mountbatten have done a service

[1] Lord Francis-Williams, op. cit., p. 210.

to all mankind by showing what statesmen can do, not with
force and money, but with lucidity, resolution and sincerity.'

Of course, mistakes were made and insoluble problems remained
in the grand design of partition and independence. Now, almost
twenty years later, with the Kashmir problem having led to an
armed conflict, it is easy to point them out with hindsight. But
in 1947 it was the only and unquestionably the best solution. The
design was that of Attlee and his advisers, 'the elegance and the
style', were Mountbatten's. Shortly before midnight on Independence day, Pandit Nehru told the Constituent Assembly:
'Long years ago, we made a tryst with destiny. Now the time
comes when we shall redeem our pledge, not wholly, or in full
measure, but substantially. At the stroke of the midnight hour,
when the world sleeps, India will awake to life and freedom'.
The next day the Indian Assembly invited Lord Louis Mountbatten to become India's first Governor-General.

The Moslems of the new Pakistan had accused him of bias in
favour of the Hindus and the new Indian State. That might have
been so, but Pakistan's Jinnah had accepted the plan and had
co-operated with the Viceroy, who had devoutly hoped for a
peaceful transfer of power. But almost immediately the sub-
continent was plunged into turmoil. Millions of Hindus, Moslems
and Sikhs began to move from one side of the new boundary
line to the other, pent-up religious hatred was let loose, communal riots broke out, culminating in massacres, panic, starvation
and chaos, with armies of homeless refugees in the grip of mass
hysteria. Lord Mountbatten, bravely helped by his wife, tried to
do all he could to alleviate the misery. By November there were
1,250,000 homeless refugees in India, a large proportion of them
depending on relief work which Lady Mountbatten was organising. Then and later, Lord Mountbatten was bitterly criticised
for having failed to anticipate the disaster, and even for having a
share of responsibility for the massacres. But it was he who had
insisted that any delay in proclaiming independence would have
inevitably led to even worse horrors, and had realised that –
contrary to the opinion of some British politicians – Britain could
not hold India by force. Continued British rule would have meant
a large British army of occupation, possibly four years' National
Service for Britain's young men, and a financial burden which

impoverished Britain could certainly not afford. In any case civil strife could not have been prevented. Years later Mr Attlee, perhaps with the lessons of French Indo-China and Algeria in mind, said: 'The death roll (in India) would have been far higher if we hadn't come out'.

There were many other problems to solve, after Lord Mountbatten had become Governor-General of India. As Viceroy he had been the representative of the King-Emperor, to whom the 565 rulers of Indian states had surrendered only a portion of their sovereignty and with whose Government in London each had a separate and very complicated treaty. It took complex, often devious and frequently frustrating negotiations and manouvres before agreements with the Princes were concluded and India could emerge as the largest parliamentary democracy in the world. It was to a large degree through Lord Mountbatten's skill in conducting these negotiations that – with the exception of the rulers of Hyderabad, Kashmir and Junagahd – agreements were reached to this end. It was Lord Mountbatten's achievement that in most cases the Governments of India and Pakistan treated the Princes fairly and even generously, thus honouring the King-Emperor's historic obligations. No politician could have achieved this, and it was Mountbatten's royal background, his inborn authority and extraordinary personality which made it possible.

There were some amusing episodes. On one occasion the Chief Minister of one of the princely Indian states informed him that he was unable to sign the document because his ruler, the Rajah, was on a visit in America and he could do nothing without his instructions. Lord Mountbatten picked up a glass ball paperweight and said: 'I'll look into my crystal ball and give you an answer'. He paused dramatically and then announced: 'His Highness asks you to sign the Instrument of Accession'. The minister laughed – and signed.

Some months before his appointment as Viceroy Lord Mountbatten was faced with a problem which, in many aspects, was as delicate and difficult than the tasks that awaited him at Delhi. Today it is, of course, well known that Lord Mountbatten and his wife played a decisive role in making possible the marriage between their nephew, Philip, and Princess Elizabeth, the future Queen. King George VI was greatly concerned about the effect on British public opinion of a match between the Heiress to the

Throne and an unknown princeling of German origin. No few
influential advisers at Court expressed grave doubts about the
wisdom of such an engagement.

Subtly the Mountbattens smoothed the way, all the way.
Before the official announcement of his appointment as Viceroy,
Lord Mountbatten took discreet steps to ascertain the reaction
to his nephew's marriage plans.

One morning in February 1947, the house telephone rang on the
desk of Arthur Christiansen, the editor of the *Daily Express*. On the
line was E. J. Robertson, chairman of Beaverbrook Newspapers.

'Chris,' he said, 'can you be free at five o'clock today to come
with me to the Mountbattens for a drink?'

This was a sensational invitation. Lord Beaverbrook had
pursued a feud against the Mountbattens for many years. It had its
origin in a personal clash in which the proprietor of the *Express*
newspapers had felt he had been deadly offended. For years Lord
Louis's and his wife's names were never even mentioned in his
papers. Mr Attlee's decision to entrust him with the transfer of
power in India was violently attacked by the *Express* newspapers
as a betrayal of the British Empire.

Christiansen went with Robertson and John Gordon, the
editor of the *Sunday Express*, to the house in Chester Street, which
the Mountbattens had rented at the end of the war. The three
visitors were shown into a sitting room on the first floor. Lord
Mountbatten, as distinguished in a lounge suit as in an admiral's
uniform, greeted them as though they were old friends, and
Lady Mountbatten beamed graciously.

A fair-haired young man in the uniform of a Royal Navy
lieutenant, who was leaning against the wall in a dim corner of the
room, was unceremoniously introduced by the new Viceroy as
'my nephew Philip'. The conversation which ensued was begun
by Lord Mountbatten, taken over by his wife and resumed by
her husband. The three visitors were being asked to advise the
family on the probable public reaction to nephew Philip taking
out British naturalization papers.

The newspapermen needed a few moments to recover from
their surprise. They were, of course, fully aware of the rumours
about a romance between Lieutenant Philip, Prince of Greece
and Denmark, and Princess Elizabeth, the Heiress Presumptive
to the Throne. They had recorded these rumours in the columns

of their papers. But they had certainly not expected to be consulted on a matter of such portentous significance.

They gave their opinion unanimously. They said that Prince Philip's war service in the Royal Navy gave him a claim to British nationality, quite apart from his blood relations to the Royal Family and his English upbringing. If he was embarrassed by the conversation, Prince Philip showed no sign of it. He remained in his corner, grinning cheerfully from time to time, saying not one word. He was so little part of the gathering at the fireside that when whiskies and sodas were offered, he was not even included in the round.

After an hour the visitors left. Back in his office Arthur Christiansen telephoned Lord Beaverbrook, and told him what had transpired.

'Well, you fellows surprise me,' grated the Proprietor. 'Don't you know yet that the oldest trick in politics is to muzzle the Press by taking it into one's confidence?' He meant that if any of the *Express* group reporters were now to get the news that a naturalization application was afoot for Prince Philip, the editors would have to suppress a big, exclusive story, because the Mountbattens had so artfully confided in the three Beaverbrook executives. It had become impossible for them to betray the confidence.

Apart from muzzling the hostile and unpredictable *Express* group, Lord Mountbatten had, of course, been concerned with wider strategy when discussing the possibility of Prince Philip becoming a subject of the British Crown. In fact, he was taking the first tactical steps towards the announcement of his nephew's engagement to Princess Elizabeth.

There was no criticism of the naturalization proceedings when it was announced in the *London Gazette*; the *Express* papers published the news with polite comments. The advertisement gave the name of the applicant as Lieutenant Philip Mountbatten, and his address as 16, Chester Street, W.1, the family name and the home of his uncle, who had by then departed for New Delhi and the Viceregal palace. From this moment Prince Philip was never out of the public eye, and he showed that he had learned some at least of his uncle's methods of manipulating public opinion. The Mountbatten touch had triumphed once more, with the virtuosity which had worked wonders for the destinies of this extraordinary family for a century.

Despite his exacting duties in India, Lord and Lady Mount-batten attended, of course with all members of the family, the wedding of their nephew to the Heiress to the Throne on 20 November 1947, and were in the foreground of public attention. Another nephew, David, the third Marquess of Milford Haven, was best man at Westminster Abbey.

Lord Mountbatten relinquished his Governor-Generalship of India in June 1948. With his wife he made a long farewell tour of the new Commonwealth – interrupted to attend, barefoot, the funeral pyre of the assassinated Mahatma Gandhi – and then returned to England. Once more there were rumours about great positions being offered to him: Minister of Defence in the Labour Government? Ambassador in Washington or Moscow? Special Commissioner in South-East Asia? But all he wanted was to return to the Royal Navy. 'Thank God, I've finished with politics,' he said to an old friend.

When the former Viceroy of India, now an Earl, Privy Coun-cillor, Knight of the Order of the Garter, was gazetted Rear-Admiral and appointed to the command of the First Cruiser Squadron in Malta, he was 26th in order of precedence there, subordinate to two admirals who had served under him when he was Supremo in South-East Asia. If it was an anticlimax, Earl Mountbatten never gave a hint of it.

In Malta the Mountbattens lived modestly in a villa converted and furnished to their taste. In 1949 Lord Mountbatten was promoted Vice-Admiral and a year later became Fourth Sea Lord, responsible for all administrative planning in the Navy, a post he occupied until his appointment as Commander-in-Chief, Mediterranean Fleet, and then Commander-in-Chief Allied Forces Mediterranean, shouldering the delicate tasks of strategical planning and co-ordinating all Allied naval and air matters and communication lines between the Middle East and the Supreme Allied Headquarters and Nato in Europe.

In 1955, just forty-one years after his father had to resign as First Sea Lord, Earl Mountbatten achieved his life-long ambition to occupy the same position at the head of the Royal Navy. No matter that Britain's Navy was now a shrunken force by com-parison with the great fleets his father had helped to build – the awe-inspiring 'Grey Ambassadors' of the British Empire – or that in the House of Commons they should jest that the Royal

Navy had more chairborne admirals than seagoing ships. There was now one Admiral of the Fleet, in 1956, practical, experienced in many war-time battles, hustling, agile in promoting new ideas. He modernised Britain's new, small Navy through four crucial years, after the political earthquake of Suez.

Despite all opposition, Earl Mountbatten ceaselessly strengthened the position of the Royal Navy in these years, while the Army and the Air Force had to accept cuts in their budgets. He pushed ahead with the development of guided missile ships, aircraft carriers' task forces, Commando ships and, finally, with the *Dreadnought* – a name with a historic ring for a Mountbatten reared in the golden age of Britain's naval expansion – the first Royal Navy nuclear submarine.

In 1959 he was the obvious choice for the new post of the Chief of the Defence Staff. Having allied himself with his friend Professor Solly Zuckerman, the Government's chief scientific adviser on defence matters, he became the Supremo of all defence planning. He had to fight as many battles over the mahogany tables at Whitehall as he had done a quarter of a century earlier as Chief of Combined Operations. Although he was now nearly sixty, he had lost none of his old vigour. With nuclear power having revolutionised political and strategic thinking and created economic problems of fantastic expenditure for armament research and development, traditional conceptions had come to an end, and a single defence system had become vital if Britain was to play a part in a world dominated by great nuclear powers.

As Chief of the Defence Staff and Chairman of the Chiefs of Staff Committee he fostered the plan of a unified defence system and a unified administration. He did not wholeheartedly approve of the conception outlined by Mr Duncan Sandys in 1957. Lord Mountbatten advocated a total merger of the three Services, in which they would have retained their identity only at formation and unit level, while higher organisation and command would have been fused. Bitterly opposed by traditionalists at the War Office, the Air Ministry and even at his 'own' Admiralty, his relations with Service chiefs became often strained; politicians did not go with him all the way. Nevertheless, he succeeded in establishing an overall control of the three Services and in co-ordinating scientific development and strategic planning, with a preponderance of the Navy which he had 'hurled into the modern age', and upon which he based the 'east of Suez defence' to which the Labour Government fully subscribed in 1966. But when he retired from his post this conception received a sharp knock through the disintegration of the Malaysian Federation. It remains to be seen whether his ideas and his reliance on the Navy's carrier task force and guided missile ships were preferable to the more conventional conception of overseas army and airforce bases.

When he retired in 1965, after ten years in Whitehall, he left a deep and lasting imprint of his personality upon Britain's defence organisation and strategic planning. During that time there had been seven Defence Ministers but only one Mountbatten – always formidable, imperious, unwilling to accept advice from anyone but a few chosen, but always dedicated. He had been, at times, dispraised and even lampooned for being almost naïvely self-centred and possessive. A service chief complained that 'he'd go on for hours, trying to work out how many guns ought to salute the Chief of the Defence Staff'. Bitter quips were made about his efforts to add the ranks of Field Marshal and Marshal of the Royal Air Force to that of Admiral of the Fleet; he was called Pooh-Bah, Lord High Everything, and it was said that 'Dickie does everything for an audience of one'. His references to 'my Navy', or 'my witch-doctor' (about Professor Zuckerman) were regarded as fatuous, even if they had to be expected from a Mountbatten, so imbued with his near-regal authority.

On the eve of Lord Mountbatten's retirement a commentator aptly summed up these feelings: 'Saying good-bye with a formal profusion of regrets, Whitehall breathes more freely. It turns thankfully from a decade of tension and turbulence in the Service departments unparalleled since Trenchard's days. Sleep sound, air marshals and others: the Hound of the Battenbergs will not run tonight.' Whether the silence which descended upon the moors of Whitehall benefited Britain's defence remains another question.

Earl Mountbatten's more recent years have been crowded, quite apart from his exacting work as Chief of Defence, not to speak of his presidency of almost a score of official and voluntary organisations, his seats at 26 councils and committees, and his membership of twelve clubs. In 1963 he made a 25,000-mile goodwill tour of Mexico and a dozen South American countries, picking up many more glittering Orders and Stars to add to his cascade. He rarely missed a family occasion abroad – whether the wedding of his nephew, King Constantine of Greece, or happy events in the families of his nieces in Germany – and somehow managed to snatch a day off to relax with his daughters and their families in their homes, or at Broadlands.

In 1965, shortly before his retirement, Mr Harold Wilson asked him to head a mission to several Commonwealth countries to seek agreement on a new basis for immigration to Britain. It was a delicate task, for deepening social criticism and political controversy over coloured immigrants had caused much resentment in several Commonwealth countries. If he did not succeed in accomplishing agreement, he at least allayed the anxieties about a growing 'colour-bar' trend in the United Kingdom.

On his retirement he was awarded the Order of Merit, a rare distinction outside the narrow circle of great statesmen and luminaries of science and literature. He was made Governor of the Isle of Wight, a position his royal aunt, Princess Beatrice, had held for many years. He moved to Broadlands, within easy commuting distance by helicopter of the Isle of Wight he was to govern.

But few people believed that, at 65, either his desire for service or his usefulness to the nation was at an end, still less that his influence at the heart of Britain's rule would wane. It may well be that when these lines leave the printing presses, Earl Mountbatten may occupy yet another high office.

His position had been without precedent. He never forgot his royal origin, but he could afford to act as a democrat and even a radical, and he voiced the political conscience of the British people when proclaiming the independence of India. Outwardly very much a member of the Establishment, imperious about precedence, fussy about dignities, beaver-like about protocol, he was nevertheless a man of progress, of the scientific, and therefore the social, revolution. During his half-century of service to Britain, true to his family's motto 'In Honour Bound', he was sustained by a devout but never sentimental patriotism. Whatever his foibles and faults, he gave his rich talents and energy unsparingly and he deserved well of our nation.

CHAPTER TEN

THE GREAT HEIRESS

Edwina Ashley
Countess Mountbatten of Burma

THE life of Edwina Ashley, the Countess Mountbatten of Burma, was poised on a paradox. Born into luxury, heiress to her grand-father's millions, the leader of the 'Gay Set' in the 1920s and 1930s, in later years she championed the underprivileged and was known for her radical opinions, passionately held and tenaciously argued.

Some of her conservative friends were convinced that she was a Communist. One day when she was driven in her Rolls Royce to a State function at Buckingham Palace, wrapped in the velvet robe of a Dame Grand Cross of the Order of the British Empire, with the gold chain of the Royal Victorian Order, and a sparkling tiara on her head, a passer-by peered through the open window of the car when it stopped at traffic lights and exclaimed: 'I see, so that's what a Communist looks like!'

Lady Mountbatten was, of course, never a member of the Communist Party, or even the Labour Party, but she had often expressed admiration for, and agreement with, Socialist tenets. When, after her death, Lord Attlee was asked by a journalist whether he thought that Lady Mountbatten had been a com-munist, he sucked his pipe and replied: 'I do not know, but she was very, very Left.'

How, asked her friends, could a woman of at least partly blue blood and immense wealth, who for many years had been featured as the best-dressed and most extravagant lady of London Society, be a leveller, a Socialist? Was it not paradoxical that living in palaces, waited upon by scores of servants, moving among Royalty, she should champion the underdogs? Some observers tried to explain it by saying that she had tried to model herself after her paternal great-grandfather, the seventh Earl of Shaftesbury, the great Victorian social reformer who rescued the boy chimney sweeps and shortened the hours of toil in the factories and mills of the Industrial Revolution. Some said that she had inherited the mercurial temperament from Sir Ernest Cassel whose origin was in a Frankfurt ghetto. But Lord Shaftesbury had been an exceptional figure in the long lineage of the Ashleys, Coopers and Shaftesburys whose ancestry went back to the Plantagenet kings and Henry viii; and Cassel had all his life been an admirer and supporter of the privileged ruling classes.

The reasons for Lady Mountbatten's radical views and social conscience must be sought in her own personal experiences. She was born with a golden spoon in her mouth, but her childhood had not been carefree. Sir Ernest Cassel's wife Annette, his 'pale English rose', died only three years after their marriage. Her only daughter Maud had inherited her weak lungs, and for twenty years her father lived 'in a paroxysm of frenzied endeavour to provide her with the background and riches' he was no longer able to give to his wife. Beautiful, frail, with the mysterious aura of the consumptive, Maudie had many suitors. Almost at the zenith of his fortunes, Sir Ernest must have wished a great marriage for his daughter, although he would probably have relented had she chosen a poor man.

He could hardly wish for a better match when, at 21, Maudie fell in love with Wilfrid William Ashley, Lord Shaftesbury's grandson. Twelve years older than Maudie, a Major in the Grenadier Guards after Harrow, Sandhurst and Oxford, Wilfrid Ashley was a tall, handsome man with a distinct gift for oratory which predestined him for politics, the House of Commons and Cabinet office. Although he had little money, he was related to every great family in the land, and from his grandmother, the wife of Lord Palmerston, had come to him the fine Broadlands estate at Romsey in Hampshire – which the first Viscount Palmerston had purchased in 1736 from the St Barbe family who had lost their fortune in the South Sea Bubble – and 8,000 acres with Classiebawn Castle in County Sligo in Ireland.

It was easy for Sir Ernest Cassel to arrange for his son-in-law to have unhampered possession of these estates. The wedding of

Maud Cassel and Wilfrid Ashley in January 1901, attended by King Edward VII and members of the Royal Family, was a great occasion for London Society. When, ten months later, on 28 November, Maudie gave birth to her first child, a girl, Sir Ernest was overjoyed and begged the King to become the godfather. Edward VII immediately consented; he must have been titillated by the link of the old blood of the Shaftesburys with that of his friend Cassel.

The girl was baptised Edwina Cynthia Annette, her first name chosen in honour of her royal godfather. She remained Sir Ernest's only grandchild for five years, until the arrival of her sister Mary.[1] When Edwina, a plump, blue-eyed, fair-haired baby, became a little older, her grandfather insisted that she be brought to his house at least once a week, and he was a frequent visitor to her nursery at the Ashley homes, at nearby Bruton Street and at Broadlands.

After the birth of her second daughter Maud Ashley's health began rapidly to fail. For some time she acted as the hostess at her father's palatial Brook House while her husband, who had become Tory M.P. for Blackpool in 1906, was busy with politics. Soon the seal was set on Maud Ashley's expectation of life; in the following five years tuberculosis tightened its hold on her fragile constitution. But Cassel refused to accept the doctors' verdict. He spent the last few years of his daughter's life almost constantly in her company; he even neglected his business and took her for long rest cures to Egypt and Switzerland, but it was all in vain.

With an invalid mother and a father preoccupied at the House of Commons and by gentlemanly pursuits of hunting, shooting and fishing, Edwina's childhood years were lonelier than they should have been. Not that her mother's illness cast a perpetual gloom over the family. Maud Ashley had her father's strong will and keen intellect, but they were tempered by a sense of humour and a genuine interest in people, both of which he lacked. There was nothing self-pitying about the feverish young woman on the chaise-longue: she never lost either courage nor gaiety. She asked her friends to visit her daily, and even during the last years of her life great dinners and parties were held at Broadlands. The

[1] Mary Ashley married in 1927 Captain Alec Cunningham-Reid, M.P., her father's Private Parliamentary Secretary.

King and Queen Alexandra came, and amongst the guests were such remarkable figures as F. E. Smith (Lord Birkenhead), the young Cabinet Minister Winston Churchill, recently married to lovely Clementine Hozier, Nancy Astor, young Prince Yusoupov (who some years later put Rasputin to death). The Aga Khan was one of Maudie's regular bridge partners.

Her two little girls were brought to her each afternoon. Maudie Ashley would tell them fairy stories and delight them with poems she herself had written and illustrated with pretty ink drawings for them. There were glittering events in the life of little Edwina, but every year her mother spent many months abroad, and when she died Edwina was approaching the age when a girl needs a mother most.

With Broadlands, the magnificent mansion in gardens laid out by Capability Brown, with prolonged visits to her grandfather's splendid homes, Edwina could hardly be called a deprived child. But the void created by the loss of her mother was not adequately filled. She and her sister Mary were looked after by Auntie Grannie, Sir Ernest Cassel's soft-hearted Jewish sister; but the old lady was in poor health and soon retired to Bournemouth. Edwina's closest childhood friend was her cousin Marjorie, the daughter of Cassel's niece, Mrs Anne Jenkins. In the words of this cousin – the later Countess of Brecknock – 'Edwina's father, though a charming person, was ill-suited to look after two small children, with the result that they spent a good deal of their time with their grandfather and my grandmother . . . or with my parents, or more often than not, alone with governesses and nurses . . . Edwina never had the sort of real home and family life which children enjoy.'[1]

Colonel Ashley, M.P. married again when Edwina was 13. His second wife was a divorcée who, before her second husband was raised to the peerage, insisted on the prefix 'Honourable', although she was born plain Miss Muriel Emily Spencer, the daughter of a Herefordshire vicar. She had been married to Rear-Admiral Lionel Forbes-Sempill, a younger son of Lord Sempill and derived her noble prefix from that marriage. The second Mrs Ashley became an elegant and mundane hostess, greatly concerned with beautifying Broadlands – then not yet crammed with Sir Ernest Cassel's treasures – and after the outbreak of the

[1] The Countess of Brecknock, *Edwina Mountbatten*, London, Macdonald, 1961.

First World War she was preoccupied with arranging entertainment for officers on leave from the trenches.

Remaining childless, she did not care for her step-daughters, and certainly not for Edwina who had grown into a thin, leggy girl, whom her step-mother thought precocious and too serious-minded. The Hon. Mrs Ashley hardly concealed her dislike of the girl's 'foreign blood', and the ill-feelings were mutual. Edwina constantly schemed escapes from her unhappy home and regarded it as a deliverance when she was sent to a boarding-school at Eastbourne. Mrs Ashley had chosen a smallish and 'strict' school, and later decreed that Edwina be sent to a domestic science training school at Aldeburgh in Suffolk, while she later graciously allowed her younger step-daughter Mary to go to a fashionable finishing school for young ladies in Switzerland.

Edwina's schooling was somewhat erratic, and she hated every moment at the domestic science training establishment. Most of the pupils came from middle-class homes and the future heiress to the Cassel millions was forced to get up at 5 a.m., to scrub floors, clean flues in winter, and wash greasy pots. Food, if only because of wartime rationing, was frugal, dormitories and washing facilities spartan. Her vacations at home brought no happy relief. There was no love between her and her step-mother, neither could the growing-up girl establish an emotional or intellectual contact with her father.

Colonel Ashley, who had seen gallant service in France, became in 1918 a Member of Parliament for Fylde, Lancashire, and later represented Christchurch, the constituency near his Broadlands estate. He was ultra-conservative in his views, not only on politics, but on traditions, family life and the education and upbringing of daughters. A really crusty Tory, he was haunted by fears of a Socialist revolution, and he bombarded *The Times* with interminable letters, denouncing the Labour Party and the trade unions and warning that they were bent on establishing the dictatorship of the proletariate. 'Reds' to him included not only Socialists but Lloyd George and William Beveridge. Having been Minister of Transport in Baldwin's cabinet during the General Strike, he was raised in 1932 to the peerage as Lord Mount Temple and held office under Chamberlain. He became a great admirer of Hitler and the Nazi doctrine, and as the President of the Anti-Socialist Union and chairman of the notorious

Anglo-German Fellowship was feted in 1936 in Berlin by Rudolf Hess, Ribbentrop and Goebbels. He enthusiastically supported Chamberlain's Munich policy. Although in February 1938 he was still writing letters to *The Times* praising the Nazis as a bulwark against Bolshevism, it must be said to his credit that by the end of that year he saw the light: he resigned from the chairmanship of the Anglo-German Fellowship when the anti-Jewish atrocities in Germany and Austria had shocked everybody in Britain. Perhaps, somewhat belatedly, he had remembered that he had been a Jew's son-in-law.

Edwina was seventeen at the end of the 1914–18 war, during which her life had almost been cloistered. The only happiness and freedom she had known were during holidays at Classiebawn Castle in Ireland where she could run wild, riding, swimming and playing with all the animals on the estate. Her affection went to horses, dogs, cats, piglets or lambs, and her preference for the companionship of animals rather than people was very marked. Her grandfather, himself lonely and abused during the war, must have noticed the unhappiness of the young girl who had grown to look so touchingly like his beloved Maudie. He asked Edwina's father to allow her to join him at Brook House. Although Colonel Ashley disapproved of a 17-year-old girl entering the great world, his wife did not object to her stepdaughter leaving her home.

Almost overnight Edwina's life was transformed from a near-Cinderella existence into that of a glittering round of the hostess at her grandfather's mansions. Her task was pleasant but not easy. There were, of course, housekeepers and butlers to command an army of servants. But Sir Ernest, imperious and exacting, soon expected his granddaughter to plan and preside over the great receptions and dinners. At first she was overwhelmed and had to fight her natural reticence before she could welcome and entertain, in the manner expected of her, the members of Europe's top society who had returned to Brook House after the war. Although she would not admit it, she was often bored by the conversations which usually centred around politics, finance and big business.

Sir Ernest had arranged a coming-out ball for her in 1920, and it was a red-letter event of the London Season. As the principal debutante of the year, she was in the centre of attention for months. This was heady wine for a girl who had had a lonely childhood and lately moved only in the company of people much older than her. She had become a most desirable match and was pursued by young guardees and impecunious aristocrats and their mammas. She was caught up in a whirl of balls, soirées, dinners, first nights, race meetings, country-house weekends, sporting and charitable functions. Now a splendid butterfly emerged from a drab chrysalis: Edwina's shyness had disappeared and it was a poised, elegant, self-confident Miss Ashley whose photographs filled the glossy magazines.

In the early summer of 1921, Mrs Cornelius Vanderbilt, the American millionairess, gave a charity ball at Claridge's. Everybody who was anybody was there, and the hostess introduced to Edwina a tall, slim young naval officer, deeply tanned from his world tour with the Prince of Wales. Lieutenant Lord Louis Mountbatten, one-and-a-half-year older than Edwina, had a classic profile, immense charm, was gay, danced superbly and talked intelligently. He was very different from the chinless wonders swarming around Edwina. By the time the ball finished, Sir Ernest Cassel's granddaughter was already half in love with Queen Victoria's great-grandson.

During the following weeks she waited impatiently to meet Dickie Mountbatten again. But it was not until August that they met during Cowes Week. Slacks and jerseys were the order of the day, and sailing the only topic of conversation. But in the evening there were parties and balls, and Edwina was seen dancing with Dickie every night, until tongues began to wag. Mrs Vanderbilt, determined to act as a matchmaker, invited the two young people with some other friends for a cruise aboard her yacht to the Belgian and French coasts. In September they met again in Scotland, at the castle of the Duke of Sutherland. There Dickie learned of his father's sudden death and hurried to London. Ten days later Edwina received a telegram informing her that her grandfather had died. Neither the former First Sea Lord, nor the great financier ever knew of Dickie's and Edwina's romance. One wonders whether either or both would have approved.

In October 1921 Dickie had to leave on another tour of India and the Far East with the Prince of Wales. He asked Edwina to come to Delhi, and they eagerly discussed the plan. The Viceroy, Rufus Isaacs the Earl of Reading, had been a close friend of Sir Ernest Cassel and he would welcome her as a guest. But after her grandfather's death Brook House was closed, and Edwina had, unhappily, moved back to Broadlands. When she mentioned that she would like to visit India, her father and step-mother were shocked at the suggestion that a young girl should travel alone around the world.

Edwina had been left the bulk of her grandfather's fortune – more than £6,000,000, equal to about £25,000,000 at the present value of money – but her inheritance was bound by complex trust provisions and, in any case, she could not benefit before her 21st birthday, or on her marriage. For the time being her allowance was only £300 a year, by October she had spent her 'pocket money' and was so poor that she could not afford a passage to India. In despair she turned to Auntie Grannie who, after many admonitions and warnings of the dangers to a young girl, gave her £100, with the understanding that a chaperon went with her. Edwina hurried to a shipping office, scanned the passenger list of the next India-bound liner, found the name of a single lady and asked her to be her chaperon. She reached Bombay in a second-class inner cabin, with still enough money to travel to Delhi in a third-class compartment crowded with twenty 'natives'.

The discomfort was quickly forgotten through the happiness of her reunion with Dickie at the Viceregal Lodge, where Lord and Lady Reading warmly welcomed her. But Dickie's duties as A.D.C. to the Prince of Wales took almost all his time, and they could only snatch an hour now and then to be alone. They told the Prince of Wales that they wanted to marry and the Prince immediately sided with them. Together they composed a telegram to King George V, begging for his support and also asking for his formal consent, necessary because Lord Louis Mountbatten was, at least in theory, in the line of the succession to the Throne. The Prince of Wales sent another personal and long telegram to his father and, although they hardly dared to hope for it, the King wired his consent and congratulations even before Colonel Ashley did.

The engagement was announced at a party given by the Viceroy just before Dickie had to leave Delhi to accompany the Prince of Wales on further travels in the Far East. Edwina returned, unchaperoned, to England, making the journey on board a cargo boat. At Broadlands she found her father rather annoyed, but he could hardly oppose the King.

The wedding at St Margaret's, Westminster, on 18 July 1922 was the biggest event of the Season. On her marriage Edwina had come into an income of £60,000 a year – even after tax it was an amount that would be worth £100,000 today – and the trustees released a substantial advance. She went on a shopping spree, buying everything that took her fancy, and the fashion editors and gossip writers filled their columns with near-delirious descriptions of the 'glamorous lingerie' and 'ravishing confections' of her trousseau. At the wedding ceremony the future King Edward VIII was the best man, towered over by bride and bridegroom. The crowds in Parliament Square were able to see a throng of European royalty and foreign ambassadors bedecked in sparkling tiaras, resplendent uniforms and heavy gold braid: a gathering that seemed to be the entire Debrett and Alamanach de Gotha come to life. The Russian relatives were represented by the thinned ranks of the Romanov grand dukes and grand duchesses who had escaped Bolshevik firing-squads, and the German, Greek, Danish and Spanish royal relations were there.

The bride wore a gown of frosted silver, her seven bridesmaids included the four Greek princesses, sisters of the later Duke of Edinburgh. It was, of course, a naval wedding, and with an early touch of Mountbatten showmanship, the limousine in which the newly-married couple left the church was drawn by a gun crew of twenty-five blue-jacks. For the reception, attended by King George V and Queen Mary with the entire Royal Family, Brook House had been transformed into a garden of white lillies, giant delphiniums and bowers of orange blossoms, with all the priceless Cassel treasures, old masters, fine silver, porcelain, bronzes, jade and gems on display. It would have gladdened his heart if he could have seen the 1,600 guests thronging the salons and galleries.

The honeymoon lasted for five months, its itinerary drawn up by Dickie like a naval manœuvre. After a secret but brief stay at Broadlands, Dickie and Edwina began a grand tour of Europe, visiting Mountbatten relations – the Grand Duke of Hesse at Wolfsgarten, some of the expatriate 'Greeks' in Paris, the King and Queen of Spain at the palace of Santander. After a brief return to Britain and a visit to the Duke of Sutherland's Dunrobin Castle, which held memories of their early romance, Dickie and Edwina embarked in the *Majestic* for the United States.

When the ship docked in New York, newspaper reporters gave the couple a third-degree grilling. Even now – as Princess Margaret's and Lord Snowdon's visit in November 1965 showed – nothing excites Americans more than foreign royalty; it certainly did to a degree bordering on mass-hysteria forty-odd years earlier. The Mountbattens were mobbed wherever they went, and they went everywhere, taking American hospitality and American ballyhoo in their stride. They were gossipped about with endless inaccuracy in the newspapers and glossy magazines. Dickie was made into a figure straight from P. G. Woodhouse's Jeeves stories, was never referred to as Lord Louis but as 'the Prince', and remarks ascribed to him were heavily laced with words like 'ripping', 'topping' and 'divine' which he never used. He was described as the inventor of 'fad games played by English nobility', one of which, called 'Decameron', was apparently played by a number of English 'sports' who had in a ballroom to spot a lady with a mole on her *décolleté* and shout 'Yoo hoo, Decameron!' to score points.

Edwina – 'the Princess' – was quoted as starting every sentence with "'pon my soul', and saying, when asked about American 'flappers': 'I'll see to it that my husband won't meet any'. Atrocious stories about her and Dickie's romance, alleging an 'elopment to India', filled newspaper columns *ad nauseam* and Edwina's 'multi-million fortune' was multiplied a few times and made, in dollars, into a truly astronomic figure. Dickie and Edwina had hoped to see something worthwhile in America, and he was particularly interested in technological progress. But they were unable to escape the all-enveloping American hospitality, and the millionaire-hostesses of the 'Four Hundred' vieing with each other to arrange balls and dinners, some at the cost of 100,000 dollars, with the 'English royals' as the centre of attraction. When they tried to escape, and went with a few friends to a Broadway theatre or cabaret, or travelled West to see Indian reservations and cowboys, stories appeared under headlines such as 'Prince and Princess Vanish', or 'Prince Home With The Milkman'.

They travelled across America in a private train, followed by reporters at every step. When they went to see the Grand Canyon and the Niagara Falls, they were the guests of State governors and senators, and the President of the Niagara Falls Power

Company acted as their guide with a battalion of technicians. Already in New York they met the stars of the entertainment world; Jerome Kern brought the complete troupe of Ziegfield Girls to a dinner in their honour. In Hollywood they were entertained by Sam Goldwyn and Cecil de Mills, stayed at Mary Pickford's and Douglas Fairbanks' magnificent 'Pickfair'; Charlie Chaplin was their guide through the studios and made a very funny private film, with himself, Dickie and Edwina in the leading parts.

When they returned to England after their fantastic American tour, Edwina had been infected with the dazzle in which America's wealthy élite lived. While Dickie resumed his naval career, she opened Brook House and party followed party.

It was an era when Britain – and most of Europe – sought and found an antidote to the strains left by the First World War; the age of conquering jazz, cropped hair, over-the-knee skirts, Kate Meyrick and 'wicked' London night clubs, fast Hispano-Suiza cars and pink gin; the age of so-called 'decadent' novels, such as Michael Arlen's (which nowadays would not raise the eyebrow of a bishop's maiden aunt), of cocktail party flirts, 'lounge lizards' and nightly amusements defined as 'irregular movement from bar to bar'. Young ladies of Society had little butterflies and flaming hearts tattooed on their thighs and attended 'Night-time Day Parties', sleeping all day, arriving at the party at 10 p.m. for 'breakfast', having 'lunch' at 2 a.m., playing tennis by moonlight, dancing until the morning – and so to bed. It was an era of which a later satirist said:

> Vice on the stage was all the rage
> When Noël Coward and sin came in . . .

The Mountbattens were young, gay, very wealthy and well-connected. They represented the prototypes produced by that era, and they accepted the leadership of the 'wild set' with gusto. One of their biographers justly remarked that, nevertheless, they were two exceptional people whose basic strength of character was not debased by an atmosphere which corrupted and wrecked many weaker natures. Even though they almost regularly returned home 'with the milkman', or entertained their friends at 'Arabian Nights' at Brook House, Dickie still assiduously devoted himself to his service with the Royal Navy, completed during those wild years the Long Signal course, became an expert in Wireless Telegraphy and an instructor at the Naval Signal School at Portsmouth. When he served at Portsmouth, Edwina rented a mansion, 'Adsdean', some twenty miles from the city and, although she kept seventeen servants there and entertained friends, she and her husband lived unostentatiously, even though 'Adsdean' became a base for the fashionable round of Ascot, Cowes and Goodwood.

Like her husband, Edwina possessed seemingly inexhaustible energy and stamina. If she herself made some play about her extravagance and provided gossip columnists and Society photographers with good reasons for acclaiming her as the most elegant woman in London, she also began to find time for serious interests. Aware of her sketchy education, she became an avid reader and was soon engrossed in books on history, biography and travels. She also became a regular theatregoer, choosing Shaw or Wilde rather than Cochran revues, and showed more than a flitting interest in good music and modern art.

Perhaps not yet noticeably to herself she began to take interest in social problems and wanted to discover how 'the other half' lived. There was in her character that streak of loneliness which had been so typical of her grandfather's life. While for years stories of her great parties, her fashionable dresses and hair styles, her mastery of dancing steps and the Mountbatten showmanship filled the gossip columns, it seems that she was happiest in riding breeches, or sweater and tartan skirt, at 'Adsdean', and later in Malta, playing with her animals, swimming, or spending a few hours alone with a good book.

Her first daughter was born on 14 February 1924 and baptized Patricia Edwina Victoria. The Prince of Wales and Lady Patricia Ramsay, the granddaughter of Queen Victoria, were her godparents. For the christening the Mountbattens invited, beside their royal relatives, Mary Pickford and Douglas Fairbanks. It was the year of the British Empire Exhibition; London was thronged with foreign visitors, and the Mountbattens were now constantly in the company of the Prince of Wales and his 'Palace set'. A private preview at Brook House of Mary Pickford's and Fairbanks's film 'The Thief of Bagdad' was attended by a very select audience: Lord Louis's cousin the Queen of Spain, the King and Queen of Rumania, the Prince of Wales, of course, and his two younger brothers, Prince Henry and Prince George.

The same year the future King Edward VIII went to America and asked Dickie and Edwina to accompany him. American millionaires visiting London or Paris bid £1,000 for a cabin on the *Berengaria* in order to sail together with 'Prince Charming' and the Mountbattens. There was the already familiar round of great parties in New York and, after their return to London, Edwina gave a ball at Brook House for the coming-out of her sister Mary, which was followed by a series of other great parties, until Edwina suddenly tired of it all. She had become conscious of a nagging desire to do something worth while. 'I decided to travel across the world on my own,' she told a friend, who replied: 'Edwina, you must be crazy! What are you looking for? You've everything one can desire.' Edwina shrugged; she could not answer the question, she did not know why she wanted to leave her husband, her baby daughter, her life of luxury, much less what she was seeking.

She packed one suitcase and went to Russia, across Siberia to China and then to the South Sea, sailing in a fifty-ton cargo boat between Polynesian islands and being lost to the world for four months, until Dickie thought that she had been drowned or had met with a fatal accident. She was away for many months, returning home by way of the Pacific and the United States. It was the first of her many subsequent strange and long retreats from glamour and frivolity.

Later she went with her husband to Malta, where he was posted as Fleet Wireless Officer to Admiral Sir Roger Keyes. The comparatively quiet life there was interrupted by visits to London, and the couple's attendance at the wedding of Edwina's sister Mary to Captain Alec Cunningham-Reid, M.P., Colonel Ashley's P.P.S. In the spring of 1929, when Dickie was Signal Officer to the Second Destroyer Flotilla, Edwina was expecting her second child. Dickie's ship put in at Gibraltar, Edwina met him there and they went to Tangier for a week-end. Bad weather prevented their return by the excursion steamer and Dickie chartered an open launch to get back on time to his duties. Edwina insisted on going with him and the crossing was very rough. Although unwell, Edwina decided to motor alone to Barcelona where Dickie was to join her a few days later.

When Dickie arrived at the small hotel near Barcelona, he found his wife in labour. She greeted him with: 'I think it's coming today'. He inquired what or who was coming. 'The baby, of course. It didn't care for the rough sea trip', Edwina replied. Dickie was aghast: 'But it's six weeks ahead of schedule', he protested, always a stickler for correct timekeeping.

The baby, however, was ready to make its debut and the only doctor whom Dickie was able to find in a hurry was an ear-and-throat specialist who lived near the hotel. Dickie telephoned for help to his cousin, Queen Ena, at the royal palace of Madrid. But the queen was away and King Alfonso personally took the call. He promised to send immediate assistance, and the Governor of Barcelona was ordered to find an obstetrician, doctors, a midwife and nurses. Somehow the Governor must have misunderstood the order, because he sent along a Royal Guard of Honour, complete with brass band. The child was safely delivered by a Catalan matron to the accompaniment of martial music beneath the hotel windows. It was another girl, and the Mountbattens went for her christening to London. She was named Pamela Carmen Louisa – Carmen was added in memory of the rousing marches played at her birth – and her sponsors were the King of Spain and Prince George later Duke of Kent.

The new baby joined her five-year-old sister in the nurseries of Brook House, and Casa Medina in Malta, with their mother often away. By 1931 Edwina Mountbatten was off again on one of her sensational world tours. Her cousin, Lady Brecknock, who accompanied her on some of these travels, said:

> 'Throughout these years, Edwina's assistance to her husband in his career and interests was invaluable and her happiness at his achievements was very sincere. But in spite of this and her busy life, there was still a vast amount of unused energy left which created a restlessness, an urge to accomplish something in her own right. The desire for achievement found an outlet in travel.'[1]

Some people had said that Edwina and Dickie, both strong-willed and self-contained, 'got on each other's nerves', when they were together for a longer spell of time, and that this was the real

[1] The Countess of Brecknock, op. cit., p. 5.

reason for Edwina's frequent disappearances from home. This might have been so, but tales that their married life was not as happy as it outwardly appeared are untrue. Obviously, with two people of such extraordinary personalities, there must have been clashes of temperament, but whenever they parted, whether for a few weeks or months, they fretted for each other's company, and after every reunion they were visibly blissfully happy. Some present-day foreign observers believe to have detected a parallel in the relations between the Queen and the Duke of Edinburgh.

Her travels covered all Europe. In 1931 she went to the West Indies and Mexico, a few months later, with her sister-in-law, the Marchioness of Milford Haven, she set off to Palestine, Syria, Transjordan, Iraq and Persia, travelling by aircraft, car, on horseback, by mule and joining camel caravans across deserts. She was away for many months, but soon after her return home she was planning new journeys to far-away corners of the world, her wanderlust never sated.

Despite her wealth, with growing taxation the money value of her income had been greatly reduced and Edwina found the cost of maintaining and staffing Brook House – more than £17,000 a year – a heavy burden. In 1933 she sold the Cassel palace to the banking firm of Coutts & Co.; it was pulled down and in its place rose a tall block of apartments. The agreement provided, however, for a two-storey penthouse for the Mountbattens, designed to Edwina's and Dickie's own plans. The upper floor had two large suites for the owners, with several guest rooms and bathrooms. The five large reception rooms had soundproof partitions which could be rolled into the main walls to form a ballroom and a cinema to seat 150 people. The lower floor included a nursery wing, drawing rooms, servant quarters, kitchens and a long gallery. A private lift shot from the ground level to the seventh floor in four seconds. The penthouse was luxuriously decorated and furnished with the help of Mrs Joshua Cosden, a fashionable New York designer. It was symbolic of the rich, film-set world of the Mountbatten circle, the world of speed-boats, polo, fast cars, caviare and sable. But Lord and Lady Mountbatten lived there for only three years; the penthouse was not ready for occupation until 1936, and was closed, never to be used again, after the outbreak of the war. Even during those three years Edwina spent only short stays there, being often away on her travels.

It was said that Edwina decided to put an end to the ostentation of Brook House, fruit and symbol of Sir Ernest Cassel's Empire-wide financial dominance, appalled by the social injustice of which she had become aware on her travels The misery and disease she saw among the peons in South America, or the squalor and exploitation of the Middle East had deeply touched her heart. The dole queues, the hunger marches and the stony-hearted response of the ruling class during the Recession in Britain in the 1930s must have filled her with a sense of personal guilt. But if this was true, it was characteristic of her divided personality that her new Park Lane penthouse was hardly less magnificent than her grandfather's palace, and that she took care that most of the Cassel treasures were moved from Brook House into her new home.

However, it is true that at about that time the Mountbatten circle had undergone a significant metamorphosis. Edwina, and even more so her husband, were still very much part of the Establishment, they still moved in the 'exotic society', supposedly decadent because unconventional, and in the 'americanized' Fort Belvedere Set around the Prince of Wales and Mrs Simpson. But at the penthouse new friends had begun to arrive. Edwina continued to entertain international celebrities, but amongst them were left-wing politicians and intellectuals, refugees from Spain, Jews from Germany and Austria, and above all Liberal and Labour leaders despising Baldwin's and Chamberlain's politics. Amongst them were such extreme left-wing figures as Sir Stafford Cripps and the stormy petrel from Ebbw Vale, Aneurin Bevan.

Already in 1936, when she was in Malta, where Dickie was serving with the Mediterranean Fleet, she had been outraged by Mussolini's attack on Abyssinia. Although she was still giving great parties there – at one in the big hall of the Polo Club 300 guests danced after dinner and watched a film featuring Fred Astaire dancing the Carioca – she wanted to do something which would prove her opposition to Italian fascism. While in London politicians talked of Sanctions against the Italian agressor and, in fact, secretly worked on appeasing Mussolini, Malta had been mobilised and special broadcasting stations were established to relay BBC bulletins. Edwina volunteered to be one of the radio

Lady Louis Mountbatten (later
Countess Mountbatten
of Burma) with her father,
Lord Mount Temple and
her elder daughter,
Patricia (now Lady
Brabourne) in 1931.

The wedding of Lord Louis Mountbatten and Edwina Ashley on
18 July 1922. The wedding group at Sir Ernest Cassel's Brook House,
with the Prince of Wales (later King Edward VIII, Duke of Windsor)
as Best Man. Among the bridesmaids are Prince Philip's four sisters
the Princesses Margarita, Theodora, Cecilia and Sophia of Greece

The Supremo.
Lord Louis Mountbatten,
Commander-in-Chief,
South-East Asia Command
in 1944.

Lady Louis Mountbatten as
Superintendent-in-Chief of
the St John Ambulance
Brigade during the war.

announcers and spent four months reading the news bulletins and official comments, and although of course she was unable to express her own, much stronger views, she felt that she had, at least, made some contribution against fascism.

She had begun to be interested in, and to understand, ways of thought and feeling very different from those of the complacent, hare-brained society in which she had spent her youth, and from which she was now gradually turning away. It is uncertain whether what moved her at that time was merely the realisation that the times were growing too stern for frivolity and the empty social round, or a deepening and genuine curiosity about the lives and needs of the grey masses so remote from the chic world of etiolated vowels, pink champagne and silk-quilted bedrooms, a curiosity that was finally to produce a genuine conviction for the need of social and political change.

During her husband's service in Malta, she had been several times and for long periods travelling the world. Once again she went to the South Seas; one of her journeys she had made aboard a copra trading schooner, signing on as a member of the crew. She visited Australia and Canada, and in 1937 spent several months in Africa, from where she brought her lion cub Sabi, which became her inseparable companion. When the cub grew up and a friend anxiously inquired whether it was not dangerous to have it about the house, Edwina replied: 'He could never become as savage as some human beings.' She was appalled by the news coming from Nazi Germany and wrote in December 1938 – significantly to her father: 'It is such a ghastly nightmare, the Jewish question! I am glad to say that I have been able to help some individuals, as well as sending donations. I have set up one refugee in London, and have sent one to America last week, but there is so little one can do. It makes one despair!'

In 1938, after Munich, in a Britain preparing at a tortoise-pace for the inevitable war, Edwina realized that much would depend on individual effort, and how much there was to do in such little time to alleviate the threatening human misery. While her father still preached appeasement, she suddenly cut short all her Society engagements and enlisted in the Women's Voluntary Service, an organisation composed in London mainly of suburban house-wives. She chose nursing and civil defence, arranged at her penthouse meetings attended by overawed middle-class women, and in these incongruous surroundings were given first-aid lectures and dressing lessons. She took such a passionate interest in every detail that some of her fashionable women friends whom she had coerced into attending thought she was really overdoing it: 'Edwina is so intense about rolling people up in miles of bandages, and she behaves as if bombs were dropping on our heads', they said.

She must have been soon disillusioned about those phoney war preparations and decided on yet another escape. Early in 1939 she set off on her last pre-war voyage, this time to Malaya and Burma, hoping to reach China and to see for herself something of the horrible results of Japan's attack. From Rangoon she travelled to Lashio, a point on the new Burma Road, which the Chinese had begun to build in order to secure a supply road from India. She accepted great hardship, travelled at first by lorries and finally on mules over rough mountain tracks, lived on hard biscuits and rice, and was horrified to discover that the 70,000 coolies, men, women and children who build the road lived on a wage of 30 cents a day.

After she returned to England by way of Hanoi and Saigon, it was not long until the bombs began to drop on London. She enlisted as a trainee nurse at Westminster Hospital, spent six months emptying bedpans and, overcoming sickening repulsion at the sight of blood and suffering, helped to dress hideous wounds. A few weeks before the outbreak of the war her father, Lord Mount Temple, died and she inherited the family estates of Broadlands and in Ireland. Many of her noble friends had hurriedly evacuated themselves to safe places in the country, some had gone to Canada. Edwina did not even give a thought to the then still comparative safety of Broadlands which she had turned into a war hospital. She had joined the St John Ambulance Brigade and, while her husband was in command of the *Kelly*, took charge of all St John units helping in air raid precaution service in the worst affected areas of London. Night after night she visited the shelters in the blazing, shattered streets of the East End. She saw horror and death at close quarters for the first time in her life, and at last she had a mission. Through her work and influence with the authorities, conditions in the verminous, rat-ridden shelters were soon greatly improved; she organised food supplies, cared for the old and the children, spent nights in the crypts of churches and Underground stations which served as shelters, and joined the undaunted Cockneys in their sing-songs.

After Dickie had almost been drowned in the *Kelly* and was appointed to the command of the carrier *Illustrious* – then under refitting in America – Edwina joined him for a few weeks in New York. She had been asked to go to the United States on a mission organised by the American Red Cross for Britain's War Relief. She visited many cities, and it was at least partly through her efforts that American donations, amounting to many million dollars, were collected and sent to Britain. Her war-work was described in great detail in various books and articles and it may be sufficient to mention that she did not spare herself, nor did she limit her efforts to the usual Royalty round of hospital visits, inspections and bazar openings. Edwina Mountbatten was the moving spirit in organising many important relief schemes, and particularly in establishing and equipping highly trained nursing and welfare teams which rendered valuable service after D-Day in France and liberated Western Europe.

Shortly after D-Day, General Eisenhower invited Edwina to tour military hospitals in liberated parts of France. She went to the shattered towns of Bayeux, Caen, Amiens, and arrived in Paris soon after its liberation. She enlisted the help of Allied military authorities to provide supplies for French civilians. Later she insisted on going to the Low Countries where heavy fighting was still in progress. On a flight to Nijmwegen – shortly before the Allied parachute drop at Arnhem – the pilot, trying to avoid Luftwaffe fighters, flew over German lines at a height of 400 feet. The 'plane was attacked by anti-aircraft guns and Edwina had a narrow escape from death. One of the engines received a direct hit and fire seared the face of an assistant sitting next to her.

Lord Mountbatten had become the Supremo of South East Asia Command and he asked his wife to join him in Delhi. On 9 January 1945 she arrived in Karachi and was now in her real element, organizing rest centres and visiting 172 hospitals of the 'forgotten' 14th Army. She travelled across India, through Burma and into China, where she visited, with her husband, Marshal Chiang-Kai-shek at Chunking. With a handful of assistants she performed miracles of organisation. Most of the hospitals and dressing stations lacked elementary equipment, there was a dire shortage of doctors, nurses, medical supplies, beds and blankets. Edwina saw surgical operations performed by the light of torches, and wounded men brought from the battle line to be bedded on straw. After a few weeks she went to London, saw Churchill, had some stormy interviews with the War Secretary and the Minister of Health, and succeeded in persuading them to send several teams of doctors, nearly 500 nurses, and medical supplies to SEAC.

Then she returned to the Far East. The war against Japan was almost at its end. There was no organisation to cope with the fantastic problem of half-a-million sick, starved and maltreated Allied ex-prisoners and internees. Lord Louis told her: 'I want you to look after them, wherever they are, and help to get them out as soon as you can. I want you to use your own initiative, you can appeal to any of my military commanders, but I can accept nothing less than an all-out effort.'

Edwina Mountbatten used very unorthodox methods. She bullied and begged, pestered generals and air marshals, and it was due to her work and insistence that it took only a few weeks to recover tens of thousands of ex-prisoners from 230 Japanese horror camps, to rehabilitate them and bring them home. She saw terrible sights in the horror camps of 'the railway of death', in Malaya, Siam, Burma, Indo-China, Java and Borneo. She accepted great hardships, travelled by jeep, aircraft and boat, went for many days without a bath, shared rough quarters, but in the end she succeeded in rescuing countless men and women. At Nako Nayok Camp in Siam she found her 28-year-old nephew Harold Cassel, Auntie Grannie's grandson, whom the family believed dead since he was reported missing in Malaya in 1942. He was sick and emaciated like the rest, and his hair had turned white.

By the time Edwina returned to England at the end of 1945, she had travelled across sixteen countries, from Assam to the Philippines and the Netherlands East Indies. It would be banal to say that she was now a 'changed woman'. She had long since begun to take a passionate interest in social and political problems. The human suffering she had witnessed, whether in bomb-scarred London, or the ravaged countries of the Far East, had greatly influenced her outlook as she faced the post-war world of 1945.

In Britain there was now a Labour Government, bent upon creating the Welfare State, transforming sectors of the economy into public ownership, and proclaiming the desirability of an egalitarian society. Edwina Mountbatten agreed with these principles. When she was asked whether she would have liked to go into politics, if this were possible, she replied: 'We are all politicians at heart. All thinking people are. Only I have no aspirations or ambitions, but simply a desire to serve people. I am concerned with politics insofar as they further the cause of the people, by raising the standards of health, education, housing and social welfare in general.'[1] If it was perhaps a guarded statement, it showed her sympathy for a socialist society.

But those who later tried to claim her as a 'comrade' misunderstood her real motives. Although she was endowed with an almost masculine power of thinking clearly and logically, she was moved by emotions and a feminine compassion for the suffering and dispossessed masses, rather than by a conscious process of political and economic reasoning.

She was neither a rebel nor a hot-head. She was greatly pleased and proud when honours and decorations were showered upon her husband, and gratified when the King bestowed upon herself the exalted rank of a Dame Commander of the Royal Victorian Order. She attended Victory festivities and receptions at Buckingham Palace in splendid robes and regalia, and proudly wore her uniform of Superintendent-in-Chief of the St John Ambulance Brigade, with gold braid and elaborate badges, which Dickie had specially designed for her.

But she did not return to her penthouse, and persuaded Dickie to rent a modest house in Chester Street as their London *pied-à-terre,* spending such leisure as she had at Broadlands, with the children and her beloved animals. In February 1946 she once again went to the Far East, where Lord Mountbatten was still in command of SEAC. She took her daughter Patricia with her, who served in the WRNS, joined her father's staff and later became engaged to Lord Brabourne, one of his A.D.C.s.

Soon Edwina was once more engrossed in welfare work. It was at that time that her friendship with Pandit Nehru, who had emerged as the leader of the new India, began. She had much in common with him. Handsome, brilliant, the son of an ancient

[1] Cf. Masson, M., *Edwina,* London, Hale, 1958, p. 242.

Brahmin family, he had spent his youth in luxury and had returned from Harrow and Cambridge to become the champion of the exploited peasantry: 'this liberal-minded product of Western education, this believer in democracy and socialism, who had crystallised into the classic type of Indian hero – the rich youth who renounces the pleasures of the world to devote himself to poverty and asceticism for the public weal.' Edwina admired him, and in some way, she must have envied him for the choice he had made. Had she been a man, she might have chosen a similar road. But she was the wife of a royal cousin and, whatever the radical and humanitarian tenets she now embraced, she knew her place was at her husband's side.

She went with Dickie on a long tour, visiting the rulers and governments of the countries liberated from Japanese occupation, met General McArthur, the King of Nepal, went to Bangkok, Kashmir, Singapore, and also visited Australia and New Zealand, where she was greatly feted and officially thanked for her work on behalf of the ex-prisoners from the two Dominions. In June 1946 Lord Mountbatten relinquished his Far East command, returned with Edwina to London and reverted to his rank of Rear-Admiral. He was determined to resume his naval career, asked for a posting in Malta, and Edwina full-heartedly supported him in this decision.

After a period of leave Dickie attended the Senior Officers' Technical Course at Portsmouth, although there was little the instructors could teach the former Chief of Combined Operations and ex-Supremo. At their home in Chester Street there was now a regular guest – Lieutenant Prince Philip of Greece. And there were intimate and unpublicised dinner parties, attended by the King and Queen, and Princess Elizabeth. Soon rumours sprang up of a romance between the Princess and Lord Mountbatten's nephew.

It was later said that Lady Mountbatten had played an active and even conspiratorial role in bringing Princess Elizabeth and Prince Philip together. This was not the case, although she fully supported her husband in his efforts to smooth away certain difficulties, knowing that it was Dickie's heart's desire to see his nephew married to the Heiress Presumptive to the Throne. But there was no need for any 'conspiracy'; the King and Queen fully approved of their daughter's romance; their only concern being that the engagement should not provoke oppugnancy in some quarters of the British public because of Prince Philip's German ancestry. There was no need, nor an opportunity for Edwina to intervene, and in any case, her relations with the Royal Family were delicately balanced. The King and Queen liked and admired her, particularly for her selfless war work. But they were somewhat overawed by her intellectual qualities and her unconventional nature; and they were at times disconcerted about the radical views she openly expressed.

Edwina always wanted to help people, and she was eager to do so in this case, for she was very fond of both Princess Elizabeth and Philip. But she wisely kept aloof when the matter was discussed within the royal family. The wedding of her daughter Patricia to Lord Brabourne in October 1946 was attended by the King and Queen, and Princess Elizabeth and Princess Margaret were two of the bridesmaids. Philip had, of course, been invited, but on Lady Mountbatten's suggestion he did not join the wedding group when photographs were taken. Although by then the King had already given his consent to his daughter's engagement, it was felt wise to avoid unwelcome publicity which a picture would have caused, showing Philip and Princess Elizabeth side by side at a formal occasion.

A few weeks before Dickie was to take up his new command in Malta, Mr Attlee asked him to accept the office of Viceroy of India. Like her husband, Edwina was aware of the magnitude of the task and responsibilities that awaited them. Lord Mountbatten's achievement in accomplishing the seemingly impossible task of the transfer of power from the British Raj to an independent democratic regime led by Indian nationalists, is now part of Britain's proud history. The part his wife played – quite apart from her subsequent magnificent welfare work during and after the chaos and massacres of communal strife – was quite remarkable.

The Mountbattens arrived in March 1947 in Delhi as the representatives of the King Emperor; they had to observe the ancient pomp and traditions this high office carried. The Viceroy was still the autocratic ruler over 200 million Hindus, 100 million Moslems and Sikhs, 50 million members of the Depressed Classes, and 80 million inhabitants of the Princely States. He had a Court much more splendid than the King in England.

Edwina had to preside over a household that in addition to an army of personal servants, butlers, footmen and maids, employed a regiment of chefs, cooks, kitchen-boys, butchers, bakers, launderers, washerwomen, tinmen, carpenters, polishers, painters, plumbers, lift-boys, tailors, barbers, sweepers, chauffeurs, coachmen, ricksha-boys, elephant-boys, grooms, stable-boys, seventeen ball-boys and caddies and, last but not least, musicians of the Viceregal orchestra. Two 'chicken cleaners' were kept busy plucking 150 chickens consumed every day by the household. The gardens – their upkeep cost £25,000 a year – were tended by 350 gardeners. At an official banquet 100 liveried servants waited at the tables.

Her experience as her grandfather's hostess at Brook House stood Edwina in good stead. During their fifteen-month stay in India, the Mountbattens entertained 41,205 guests – an unprecedented number in the history of the Viceroyalty – over 7,000 at luncheons, more than 8,000 at dinners, and more than 25,000 at garden parties and receptions. Lord Mountbatten had told Mr Attlee that he and his wife were determined 'to meet not only Indian leaders and British officials but ordinary people on much less formal terms than had been the case with previous Viceroys'. He wrote to the Prime Minister: 'Although it is our intention to observe the protocol necessary to uphold the position of Viceroy and Vicereine, my wife and I wish to visit Indian leaders . . . and Indian people in their own homes and unaccompanied by staff, and make ourselves easier of access than protocol appears to make possible.' Edwina certainly put this into practice. Particularly concerned with the emancipation of Indian women, she founded and organised many new institutions. The Indian Nursing Council and training scheme which produced thousands of direly needed nurses owe their existence to her.

Much of the goodwill Lord Mountbatten gained in India for his mission – and for Britain – was due to his wife's efforts. If, in the words of Mr Attlee, 'Mountbatten got on the right side of Nehru and Gandhi', Edwina succeeded in making genuine friends of these and other Indian leaders. When in July 1947 she and her husband celebrated their Silver Wedding, she received this note from the Mahatma:

'Dear Sister, so you are celebrating the silver jubilee of your wedding amid a shower of congratulations and good wishes. Let me add mine to them. I hope that your joint career here will blossom into citizenship of the world.'

Edwina visited Gandhi in his bare room, and in a symbolic gesture sat with 'the Saint' on the floor, watching him working his spinning wheel. Another time a historic Press photograph was taken, unawares, of Gandhi walking with his hand on Edwina's shoulder. Such spontaneous marks of courtesy and friendship made an immense impression on the Indian people.

When Partition came, followed by the horror of communal riots, massacres, aimlessly fleeing refugee hordes, burning villages and overflowing hospitals, Edwina threw herself into relief work, heading an Emergency Council, travelling thousands of miles in conditions of peril and misery, to bring help to the starving, sick and homeless. An experienced observer of the Indian scene, Norman Cliff, wrote of the Vicereine at the time:

'To the disabled and heartbroken there came not a grand lady standing in the distance, but a mother and nurse who squatted in the midst of the dirty and diseased, took their soiled and trembling hands in hers and spoke quiet words of womanly comfort . . .'

And at the last State function at Delhi, Pandit Nehru, who had fought the British Raj most of his life and had spent many years in prison, addressed this Englishwoman thus:

'The gods or some good fairy gave you beauty and high intelligence, and grace and charm and vitality – great gifts – and she who possesses them is a great lady wherever she goes . . . But they gave you something that was even rarer than those gifts – the human touch, the love of humanity, the urge to serve those who suffer and who are in distress . . . Wherever you have gone you have brought solace, and you have brought hope and encouragement. Is it surprising, therefore, that the people of India should love you and look up to you as one of themselves? Hundreds of thousands have seen you personally in various camps and hospitals, and hundreds of thousands will be sorrowful at the news that you have gone . . .'

Despite the troubled times and her untiring relief work, Edwina had rushed to England in November 1947 to make arrangement at

Broadlands for the stay there of Princess Elizabeth and Prince Philip, who had expressed their wish to spend part of their honeymoon at the Mountbattens' estate. Dickie and Edwina attended, of course, the Royal Wedding on 20 November, but soon afterwards returned to India. Then, in June 1948 their mission came to an end. They returned to London, and in October Dickie took up his naval appointment as Rear-Admiral in command of the First Cruiser Squadron in Malta.

The former Vicereine, who had been made a Dame Grand Cross of the Order of the British Empire, was now a 'junior wife' giving precedence at official functions to the wife of the Commander-in-Chief and the wives of senior admirals. The Mountbattens lived quietly in Malta in a rented house; their old home, the Casa Medina, had been long since converted into flats. There were, however, festive occasions. Prince Philip the Duke of Edinburgh, arrived to take up his appointment as First Lieutenant in H.M.S. *Chequers*, a destroyer stationed in Malta, and was joined for a prolonged spell by his young wife, Princess Elizabeth. Uncle, aunt, nephew and niece were almost constantly together, and a bond of great affection developed between them.

After their return from India Lord and Lady Mountbatten were compelled to consider their financial situation. Edwina was, of course, still a wealthy woman. But her annual income – £60,000 at the time of her marriage in 1922 – had been reduced by heavy taxation to a mere £4,500 a year. In India the Mountbattens had spent vast sums of money from their own pocket to finance the hospitality at the Viceregal palace, the many travels and, above all, Edwina's relief and welfare schemes. The Viceroy's allowance of £13,000 covered but a fraction of this expenditure. On the advice of her lawyers Edwina decided to draw on the capital left to her on trust by her grandfather. This well-invested capital had, in fact, greatly increased over the thirty years since the bequest. But to obtain a capital sum from a trust fund a special bill had to be passed by Parliament. The necessary legislation could have been achieved by a so-called 'Private Bill', usually passed without a debate as a matter of form.

But after the bill was passed without difficulties in the House of Lords, a group of Conservative M.P.s blocked its passage through the House of Commons. It was a political move, a revenge against the man who had 'liquidated the Indian Empire'.

Edwina immediately asked her lawyers to withdraw the bill. Eventually, the Labour Government introduced the Married Women (Restraint Upon Anticipation) Bill designed to alleviate the antiquated law which restrained women from anticipating income from trust property. When the bill was debated, Mr Woodrow Wyatt, Labour M.P. for Birmingham-Aston, said in the House of Commons:

'The reason there is so much opposition by the Tories is not on the merits of the Bill but is based on political and personal animosity against a member of the House of Lords who was a very fine Viceroy, who carried through a policy in which he believed and in which the Conservative Party did not believe. This is the way they are attempting to pay him out. The Conservatives have taken this despicably underhand action against a member of their own social class because they feel in some way he had betrayed them.'

The bill was passed by a substantial majority and became law, benefiting not only Lady Mountbatten, but many other women in a similar position. Incidentally, a good slice of the capital she thus obtained was soon used to finance her many welfare schemes. When in 1950 Lord Mountbatten became the Fourth Sea Lord, Edwina realised that their old *pied-à-terre* in Chester Street could not be used as a permanent London home and she found a more spacious house in Wilton Crescent. While Dickie was once again preoccupied with his duties at the Admiralty, Edwina set off on new travels. For the St John Ambulance Brigade and the Red Cross she visited hospitals and welfare centres in Tanganyika, Kenya and Uganda, and in response to urgent invitations from her friends went to India and Burma.

Her last decade was as busy as all her life had been. In 1952 Lord Mountbatten was appointed C.-in-C. of the Allied Mediterranean Command, and once again went with his wife to Malta. When, some months later, the Argostoli area in Greece was shattered by an earthquake, Edwina immediately went there, heading Red Cross teams and organising the Greek Relief Fund. In Malta she founded and chaired a dozen welfare organisations. She also travelled widely, visiting with her husband Turkey, Italy, France and also paying visits to President Tito of Yugoslavia and the

Emperor Haile Selassie at Addis Ababa. On President Eisenhower's invitation the Mountbattens also went to the United States. Eventually, they returned to London on Dickie's coveted appointment as First Sea Lord.

In the meantime, Edwina had organised relief work for the Allied troops in Korea and, as one would expect, went twice to Korea when the war there was at its height, visiting field hospitals near the battle lines. A never tiring world traveller, she journeyed during these years also to Australia, New Zealand, Canada and the West Indies, combining as always leisure with social service. She had taken a very special interest in the Save the Children Fund and worked for it on a world-wide scale.

In 1960, a few days after the wedding of her younger daughter, Pamela, who had for a number of years assisted her mother in her welfare work, Lady Mountbatten set off on another long journey. She went to Cyprus, where the prolonged insurrection against British rule had caused much suffering, and opened a nurses' training centre for which she had collected the funds. Then she visited her beloved India for a brief holiday, and travelled on to Malaya and Singapore for an inspection of St John and Red Cross establishments and nursing centres. On 18 February she arrived in North Borneo. Two days later she died there in her sleep, ten months before her 60th birthday.

Sir Arthur Bryant, the distinguished historian, had written this epitaph for Edwina Mountbatten:

'Endowed with rare good looks and charm, a vast fortune and dazzling inheritance, and blessed by a brilliant and happy marriage, she was consumed by a passionate desire to alleviate human suffering and a resolve, pursued with wonderful vitality and courage, to put that desire into practice . . . Her dedication to the service of the poor and distressed arose from an intensely affectionate heart and profound sense of compassion.

'Edwina Mountbatten was so much more than a brilliant social personality or a figurehead of the "Establishment" . . . No one who did not come into contact with her in her work for others can have any conception of her immense, widespread power for good. It is hard to reckon the sum total of the service she gave, because no one except herself can ever have

known just how many activities of mercy and social better-
ment she aided and encouraged and how much, by personal
intervention, she did for each . . . Whenever her help was
needed it was given, quietly and, usually even before it was
asked, with unfailing good sense, tact and understanding . . .
She was never too busy, never spared herself, and nothing
ever seemed too humble for her attention. She used her great
possessions to alleviate the misery and sufferings of humanity,
but she did not merely give her wealth; she gave herself.

'When the present can be seen in perspective, she will be
recognised as one of the wisest, noblest women of our time.
Her personal intervention of love and mercy in the terrible
Punjab massacres will be remembered in Indian history long
after the passions that accompanied Partition have been forgotten. She was the antithesis of a Mrs Jellaby or a blue-
stocking. She was like a sword of love, and that sword "at
the service of the pilgrims".'

CHAPTER ELEVEN

THE GREEK PRINCESS

Alice of Battenberg,
Princess Andrew of Greece

THE Battenberg family produced three notable women. Only one of the sons of Prince Alexander of Hesse gained a minor throne, and this with tragic results. But in the second generation the Battenbergs entered Europe's royal dynasties in strength, through two of Alexander's sons marrying descendants of Queen Victoria. It is remarkable that of the five sons and three daughters of Louis and Henry all the girls were destined to places in history which none of their brothers achieved: one became the Queen of Spain, the other married the later King of Sweden, the third became the wife of a Greek prince and mother-in-law of the Queen of England.

During the rainy summer of 1965, amongst the Queen's guests at Balmoral Castle was an old lady who had only shortly before celebrated her eightieth birthday: Princess Andrew of Greece, the mother of Prince Philip, the Duke of Edinburgh.

Age and adversity had engraved furrows upon her once beautiful face, but her figure was still erect, her poise faultless and imperious as that of most of her family. Much of her life she had spent in exile, often beset by money worries. For many years she led a self-imposed ascetic life, bordering on eccentricity, wearing a nun's rough habit and devoting herself to charitable work at the monastery of a Greek-Orthodox religious Order she had founded. 'My mother's life is her own business', Prince Philip once curtly told a gossip column reporter. Princess Alice's life had always been her own business, mostly a difficult one.

Yet in her youth she wore tiaras, lived in the pomp of palaces, knew gaiety and romance. She was Queen Victoria's great-granddaughter, born on 25 February 1885 at Windsor Castle, where also her mother and her grandmother had been born. In 1965, at Balmoral, she could tell her grandchildren of the festivities at Queen Victoria's Diamond Jubilee – the last surviving member of the Royal Family who attended it as a girl of twelve. Her family albums showed her as a baby in the old Queen's lap, as a little girl with her still young great-aunt, Princess Beatrice, with her aunt the Tsaritsa of Russia, and also with her little brother Louis, who became the Earl Mountbatten of Burma.

Her parents were Princess Victoria of Hesse – the daughter of Grand Duke Louis IV who had married Queen Victoria's second daughter – and Admiral Prince Louis of Battenberg, the later Marquess of Milford Haven. Her mother was a woman of strong character, clear mind and singleness of purposes: she often used to say: 'I should have been the man in the family'. Some of her children, particularly Alice and Louis, had inherited these qualities. Alice's christening at Darmstadt was the occasion on which Queen Victoria gave her formal consent to the engagement of her youngest and favourite daughter, Beatrice, to Prince Henry of Battenberg, the newly-born girl's uncle.

Alice was a Maid of Honour when all the Battenbergs attended the Coronation of King Edward VII in 1902. It was only one of the many great royal functions of her childhood: she had been already a bridesmaid when the Duke of York (later King George V) married Princess Mary of Teck, and she had attended the wedding of her aunt, Alix of Hesse, to the later Tsar Nicholas II of Russia.

Her father was often away at sea with the Royal Navy, and Princess Alice with her mother and her younger sister Louisa used to stay for long spells at Heiligenberg, which Prince Louis had inherited from his father, Prince Alexander of Hesse. In a corner of the large terraced gardens stood a tiny wooden cottage where the little princesses played under the eyes of their English nannie at being housewives, sweeping the floor, washing their dolls' clothes and baking cakes and scones in a miniature oven. Alice was a pretty girl, with golden hair and large dark eyes which had a far-away look, caused perhaps by her deafness from which she suffered from childhood. Later the two sisters attended lessons at the 'school for young ladies' at Darmstadt, run by

Fraulein Texter who was very proud of being related to Goethe, where Alice's young aunt Alix of Hesse (the last Tsaritsa) had also received her education.

She was 17 when she met her future husband. Among the Coronation guests in 1902 was the fourth son of King George 1 of the Hellenes, 20-year-old Prince Andrew of Greece, called Andrea by his family. A son of the German-Danish prince, who had been elected to the Greek throne after a revolution, and Grand Duchess Olga of Russia, he lived at a Court which, according to his brother Christopher, was a Tower of Babel: 'My parents spoke German to one another and English to us children, except to my brother Andrea, who flatly refused to speak anything but Greek; we spoke Greek in the nursery and schoolroom; my sister-in-law Marie Bonaparte (brother George's wife) spoke French to everybody; my brother Nicholas' wife, Grand Duchess Helena spoke Russian.'[1] When Danish, German, British and Russian relations visited the Greek royal family, conversation was even more polyglot.

There was a gap of fourteen years between Andrew and his eldest brother, Constantine, and his two other brothers were much older, too. He thus escaped the Spartan discipline his father, who had spent his youth in the Danish navy, insisted upon. Even so, Andrew was not pampered; he was 'hiked out of bed at six in the morning for the detested cold bath tub and a simple breakfast', lessons were from 7 to 9, then, after reporting to his stern papa, lessons again, physical exercise and gymnastics supervised by German instructors, lunch, a visit to his mother's drawing room, lessons again and so to bed at 7.30. At the age of 14 his routine was probably even more inflexible when he became a cadet at the Athens military school, drilled by German officers. There the fair-haired, slight boy became friendly with a fellow-pupil, Theodore Pangalos. Years later Pangalos was a leader of the revolution which ousted the royal family; the friendship must somehow have endured, because Pangalos spared Andrew's life when in 1922 he stood before a revolutionary tribunal.

It was no wonder that Prince Andrew later became a lover of all good things in life, even if he could rarely afford them. When

---

[1] Prince Christopher of Greece, *Memoirs,* London, Right Book Club, 1938.

Princess Alice of Battenberg met him he was a tall, handsome young man, sporting a monocle, an excellent horseman and a gay talker, given to practical jokes. He must have swept the quiet young girl off her feet. Her own childhood and adolescence were spent between the puritanical households of Queen Victoria and the provincialism of Darmstadt.

Their whirlwind romance was encouraged by Andrew's father, but at first looked upon with misgivings by Alice's family. Andrew's niece, Princess Alexandra of Greece (later the wife of King Peter of Yugoslavia) recalled in her memoirs how she had been told of Edward VII, running his podgy fingers through Alice's soft golden ringlets, remarking that no throne in Europe was too good for her, and raising an eyebrow at an unpromising match to a younger son of the new and impecunious royal house of the Hellenes. Yet the demure princess got round her parents and the King and, after Andrew had spent some months at Heiligenberg to become better acquainted with Alice's family, he received their consent.

The engagement was officially announced on 5 May 1903, and on the following evening at a dinner given at Marlborough House by the Prince and Princess of Wales (the later King George V and Queen Mary) King Edward and Queen Alexandra and members of the Battenberg, Greek and Danish families drank toasts to the young couple. The *Daily Express* revealed that 'the match had originally met with strong opposition from the bride's relatives owing to the bride's and bridegroom's lack of money, but Prince Andrew wooed his love boldly and would not be discouraged'. The newspaper could also disclose that all was well: 'Love triumphed at last over considerations of prudence, and it is stated that several imperial and royal relatives have between them generously contributed sufficient funds to enable the young couple to start life without excessive financial sorrows. A wedding present from the Tsar of £100,000 was the largest contribution.' The British Byron Society sent their congratulation, declaring that 'a further bond of union between Albion and Hellas has been forged', and the Greeks celebrated the occasion by a dynamite outrage against the Sultan's palace in then still Turkish-occupied Salonika.

Europe's royalty flocked to the wedding on 8 October 1903 at Darmstadt. King Edward VII had decreed that his niece must be married with Protestant rites, whatever other forms the Greek family required. To comply with German laws, Alice and Andrew had in the morning to go through a civil marriage before the local registrar. Then, at 3 p.m. the wedding procession entered the Protestant Castle Church, where Dr Petersen, head of the Consistorial Council of the German Evangelical Church, solemnized the marriage, with 'Peace Be With You' as his sermon text.

The procession proceeded to the Russian Orthodox Church on the Mathildenhöhe where the Russian Archpriest Janitchev, assisted by Greek priests, performed yet another marriage ceremony. The Tsar had brought to Darmstadt the St Petersburg Imperial Choir, eighty strong, for the two-hour ceremony. There was a slight hitch when, because of her deafness, Alice misunderstood the questions which the Archpriest muttered into his luxuriant beard. To the first – whether she desired to take Andrew as a husband – she replied 'No', and to the second – whether she had promised her hand to someone else and whether there was an impediment, she firmly said 'Yes', and only when Prince Christopher standing behind her nudged her sharply, did she correct herself.

Tens of thousands had come from all over Hesse to cheer the newly-weds through the streets. The list of guests assembled for the family dinner at the grand-ducal palace recalled the gatherings at Heiligenberg of emperors and kings who, three decades earlier, came to consult Prince Alexander of Hesse on Europe's political intrigues. It also showed how the golden Battenberg thread ran through Europe's reigning dynasties. The father of the bride, Rear-Admiral Prince Louis, on a brief leave from his duties as Britain's Director of Naval Intelligence, could welcome a truly regal party: Queen Alexandra (representing King Edward VII, who was unable to attend), with her daughter Princess Victoria, Princess Beatrice, Tsar Nicholas II and Tsaritsa Alix with their four daughters, the King and Queen of Greece, parents of the bridegroom, four of their sons and daughters with their wives and husbands, the family of the Grand Duke of Hesse, Prince Henry of Prussia, brother of the German Kaiser, a throng of Russian grand-dukes, German, Danish and French princes, Austrian archdukes, and the bride's entire Battenberg family, including a little boy of three in the arms of a nannie, the present

Earl Mountbatten, whose sister's wedding was his very first official function.

To make the dinner as informal as possible, court officials and adjutants were excluded, and after the dessert the servants were sent away, Grand Duke Ernest of Hesse and the bridegroom's brothers acting as waiters. Prince Christopher afterwards recalled a contretemps with his eccentric aunt, Duchess Vera of Wurttemberg (a grand-duchess of Russia and sister of his mother) who was small and dumpy, irresistibly funny and always wore her hats and even tiaras secured by elastic bands to her round, fat, spectacled face'. The family and guests gathered at the door throwing rice at the bridal pair when they set off for the honeymoon. 'Somebody knocked off poor Aunt Vera's spectacles which were smashed on the stone steps. Unable to see clearly, but guessing that my brother George was to blame – because he always teased her unmercifully – she dealt a mighty box on the ear of the person standing immediately behind her. Unfortunately it was not George, for he had taken care to slip out of range, but the British Admiral Mark Kerr, who was the recipient of it'.[1]

The admiral, a close friend of the bride's father, had given a somewhat different account of the incident: the Duchess did not box his ear but 'pulled her hat off and started to hit me over my head with it'. He also recalled how the Tsar led the chase after the couple with the tiaraed and bestarred guests armed with 'good luck' bags of rice and white satin slippers: 'As Prince Andrew and Princess Alice came in the carriage under the lights, it appeared to the German detectives that something unusual was happening, for the paper bags must have looked like bombs and the satin shoes gleaming under the searchlight appeared very like daggers. Thereupon they shouldered their umbrellas and joined the rush. The Emperor of Russia went straight for the backs of the people, who were anxiously awaiting the passing of the royal carriage. Putting his head down, he rammed them, gradually pushed his way through the six files of human beings . . . and reached the street at the moment when the carriage was going by, with Princess Alice bowing her acknowledgements to the crowd. At this moment she received the contents of a full bag of rice, which the Emperor had carried, in her face, followed by a satin shoe. Casting dignity aside, she caught the shoe . . . and

[1] Prince Christopher, op. cit.

hit the Emperor on the head with it . . . which so overcame him that he remained in the middle of the road, shrieking with laughter.' The Tsar had nothing to fear: there were no assassins in Darmstadt. Admiral Kerr observed that 'everyone was sky-larking about, it was more like a Bank Holiday on Hampstead Heath than a royal ceremonial'.[1]

When, after their honeymoon, the young couple went to Athens to set up home, they were soon confronted with the sober facts of life. They lived at first with Prince Andrew's family at the Old Palace which was 'excessively uncomfortable'. There was only one bathroom, and no one had ever been known to take a bath in it, for the taps would scarcely run, and if they did, emitted a trickle of water in which the corpses of cockroaches floated dismally. In winter the cold was unbearable and 'the wind whistled down the corridors and curled like a lash in and out of the lofty salons'; the palace was heated by a few ornamental china stoves and lit by oil-lamps. Nevertheless, the younger members of the royal family put the state rooms to good use: the huge ballroom and long passages served for roller-skating and cycling, and even King George sometimes joined his sons in playing shuttlecock in one of the large halls, to keep warm.

The first years of Andrew's and Alice's married life were happy and carefree; two daughters, Margarita and Theodora, were born in quick succession. The Tatoi summer palace in the pine forests north-east of Athens, where the king had built several small houses for members of his family, provided greater comfort. Princess Alice and her small daughters enjoyed happy weeks at the Tatoi farms, watching the cows being milked and helping with making butter and cheese, or feeding poultry.

The young couple were particularly close to Andrew's older brother Nicholas, who was married to the Russian Grand Duchess Helena and had three daughters, Olga (the later Princess Paul of Yugoslavia), Elizabeth (the later Countess Törring-Jettenbach), and little Marina (the later Duchess of Kent), who was the same age as Theodora. An English nannie, Miss Roose, had nursed the three little girls, later joined Princess Alice's family and, eventually, looked after Prince Philip. A firm friendship developed between Alice and Helena, although one can hardly imagine two young women so entirely different in appear-

---

[1] Kerr, M., *Prince Louis of Battenberg*, London, Longmans, 1934.

ance, temperament, outlook and upbringing: Alice, fair, quiet, serious-minded, deeply religious, and with simple tastes; Helena, dark, beautiful, vivacious, brought up in the luxury of the St Petersburg Court, loving gaiety and parties, wrapped in costly sable furs, ordering her dresses in Paris, and owning magnificent jewellery. Her daughter, Marina, who married the Duke of Kent in 1934, inherited her mother's sophistication.

The two princesses learned Greek together and spent holidays with their families at Corfu, but while Helena often travelled abroad and attended festivities in St Petersburg, Alice soon began to take interest in charitable organisations, often mixing with ordinary Greek people. She spent many hours every week at the School of Greek Embroidery, at first learning the intricate colourful patterns of this traditional folk-craft, and later helping the school's founder, Lady Egerton, wife of the British envoy, in instructing Greek girls. Little she knew that one day this hobby would provide a source of income in exile.

There were visits to relatives in England, Germany and Russia; in London Princess Alice and her daughters usually stayed at her father's house in Spring Gardens behind Admiralty Arch, and on one such occasion Britain's first women's magazine[1] fatuously reported: 'The prettiest princess in Europe is said to be Princess Alice of Greece, the elder daughter of that popular naval officer, Prince Louis of Battenberg. She is the first cousin of the young Queen of Spain, whom she strongly resembles, but she has the advantage of Queen Victoria Eugenie of Spain in good looks for she has a better figure, the Spanish queen having a very short neck, a feature which characterised her grandmother, our late Queen.'

For almost forty years King George 1 of the Hellenes had ruled Greece in comparative peace, surviving alike the shocks of Balkan politics and the rivalries of the Great Powers. In 1898, however, prodded by nationalist leaders who clamoured for a union with Crete and Thessaly, he had embarked upon a war against Turkey, which brought military defeat and political and economic disaster to Greece. On his accession he had chosen for his dynasty the motto: 'My strength is in the love of my people', but both the love of his impoverished subjects and his own strength had waned. Real power now lay in the Military League,

[1] *Home Notes,* London, 24 September 1908.

led by young officers, such as Pangalos and Plastiras, who later
became the leaders of the revolution. They compelled the king to
curtail his prerogatives and, by 1909, with republicanism growing
and tacitly supported by prime minister Venizelos, the League
forced all the king's sons to relinquish their army and navy
commissions. 'I feel as though living on the top of a volcano', the
the king used to tell his sons, and there were many occasions
when the royal family waited, with bags packed, ready to leave
the country in one of the British warships lying at Piraeus.

The alliance between Serbia, Bulgaria and Greece against
Turkey, which in 1912 led to the first Balkan War, temporarily
united the Greek people, particularly after the victories over the
Turks and the occupation of Janina and Salonika. But Greece
soon quarrelled with her northern neighbour, Bulgaria, over
territories in Macedonia. On 18 March 1913 King George was
being cheered by the Greek population of liberated Salonika
when a Macedonian Greek shot him dead in the street. Described
as 'a tool of the Bulgars', the assassin more likely belonged to
one of the Greek anti-royalist secret societies.

Ascending a tottering throne, his son Constantine found the
country allied with Serbia and Rumania against Bulgaria in the
Second Balkan War. Although it ended in victory, Greece had
now hostile neighbours both to the north and south, and both
flirting with Germany and Austro-Hungary. Across the Aegean
the Young Turk revolution triumphed under Enver Pasha who
had called in German officers to reorganise the Turkish army. It
was only natural that Constantine, married to the sister of the
German Kaiser, became inclined the same way, although his
ministers and people looked towards Britain and France for
protection.

At the outbreak of the First World War the Greek royal
family found themselves in an extremely difficult position, divided
in their personal sympathies. Prime Minister Venizelos wanted
Greece to side with the Western Allies, and offered to support
British and French operations by sending Greek troops against
Turkey. Constantine opposed it; Venizelos resigned and set up
at Salonika a revolutionary committee against the king, proclaiming alliance with Britain and France. For a time, relying on loyal
troops in Athens and leaning on pro-German politicians, King
Constantine was able to maintain his regime in the capital,

despite demonstrations, attacks on his palace, and the firing of the royal residence at Tatoi. But when French troops landed in Salonika, and the Allies recognised Venizelos' committee as the *de facto* government, Constantine had no choice but to resign. The last days of his reign in December 1916 were packed with drama. British and French warships appeared off Piraeus, threatening to bombard Athens. A French cruiser, mistaking an order, opened fire. It lasted for only half-an-hour, but several shells fell in the garden of the royal palace.

Princess Alice at the time was working at the embroidery school, and she drove at top speed through the shellfire to the palace 'in a fever of anxiety for her daughters'. Although a shell had exploded in front of their nursery windows, she found them unhurt and took them – the youngest Sophie was a baby of two – to the house of her brother-in-law, Prince Nicholas. There they remained huddled together with Nicholas's two older girls and little Princess Marina until the Allies landed and order was restored. The Allies took Constantine and other members of his family into exile, but prevailed upon Venizelos to make his younger son, Alexander, king.

The ambiguous conduct of the deposed king, and particularly of his Prussian wife, Queen Sophie, led to a vendetta in the British Press. Neither Prince Andrew, who held no German sympathies, nor even his wife Princess Alice, born at Windsor Castle and with a father and two brothers serving in the Royal Navy, were spared the 'hate campaign' conducted in Britain against Germany and everything German. Her father had already been forced to leave the Admiralty, but by 1917 the anti-German blast was turned full scale upon 'the German Greeks'.

Under the title 'How Prince Andrew of Greece Repays Our Hospitality', the *Daily Mail* published on 10 May his photograph, in which he wore a bowler and carried an umbrella, in the company of Colonel Metaxas. The accompanying article stated that 'Prince Andrew had been scheming with Colonel Metaxas, formerly of the Greek general staff and a prominent member of the Germanophile group, who had smuggled out information from Greece to Berlin, disclosing Allied troop movements'.

The newspaper alleged that 'proof that the Greek princes have been intriguing behind the Allies back is provided by letters intercepted by the British Secret Service'. Ex-Crown Prince

George, Andrew's brother, was accused of having been 'the leader of pro-German irregulars and the organiser of ambushes against Allied troops'. Later, several London newspapers alleged that Prince Andrew had been involved in deals between King Constantine's prime minister Gounaris and Colonel Metaxas and the former German ambassador in Athens, Count Mirbach, and the Kaiser's emissary Baron von Schenk, who 'had paid substantial sums of money to stir up trouble against the Allies in Greece'.[1]

Of the exile-life in Switzerland which Prince Andrew, his wife and their daughters shared with the Greek royal family, his brother Christopher wrote: 'We lived in Switzerland for the next three years, spending our summers in Zurich and Lucerne, and our winters at St Moritz. It was . . . a hand-to-mouth existence with its daily worries over ways and means. Our private incomes were stopped and we had to depend on borrowed money . . . Just when we were wondering where in the world the next quarter's rent was coming from, someone always stepped into the breach . . . As political exiles we were regarded as dangerous and suspicious characters and our friends could only visit us in the strictest secrecy, for we were subject to a rigid espionage[2] and had all our correspondence censored.'[3]

At Athens young King Alexander was virtually a prisoner in his palace. At the end of the World War, Venizelos, banking on Lloyd George's support, attacked the Turks in Anatolia, but despite their recent defeat the Turks worsted the Greek army. During the campaign King Alexander died at the age of 27; officially he was said to have been bitten by his pet monkey, other reports blamed a blood disease. Venizelos called a general election, hoping to proclaim the republic but, because of the people's dissatisfaction with the Anatolian adventure, he was heavily defeated. A plebiscite, held in spite of Allied warnings, surprisingly resulted in almost unanimous vote to recall ex-king Constantine, whereupon Britain and France withdrew all support from Greece.

With Constantine, Prince Andrew and his family returned to Athens. The king, anxious to reassert his popularity, decided to

---

[1] *Daily Mail*, 9 and 10 May 1917.
[2] Apparently by the British Secret Service.
[3] Prince Christopher, op. cit., pp. 147 ff.

continue the war against the Turks 'until final victory'. Prince
Andrew commanded an army corps in Anatolia while Princess
Alice had gone with their daughters to Corfu, where on 10 June
1921 she gave birth to her fifth child and only son – Prince
Philip.[1]

As she waited in Corfu for news from her husband, Greece
was in turmoil. The army had suffered crushing defeats; the
volatile Greeks, only yesterday cheering the king, turned once
more against the monarchy and the country was on the brink of
revolution. Princess Alice was in constant fear for her husband's
life. Already on 4 April 1921 the Turks had announced that
'Prince Andrew of Greece, Commanding General of the Greek
2nd Corps, had died of wounds near Broussa', but this was
quickly denied in Athens. In September 1921 Princess Alice
heard that her father, Admiral the Marquess of Milford Haven,
had suddenly died, and she went with her children to London
to attend the funeral. In July 1922 she and her children made
another brief visit to England for the wedding of her brother,
Lord Louis Mountbatten to Edwina Ashley. But anxious to be
near her husband she soon returned to Corfu.

After the defeat of the Greek army by Mustapha Kemal, the
founder of the new Turkey, and the massacre at Smyrna where
thousands of Greeks were killed in scenes of horror, burnt alive
or drowned, a revolution in Athens, led by Generals Gonatis,
Plastiras and Pangalos swept King Constantine from the throne.
Under pressure from London and Paris the revolutionary leaders
agreed to make his son, George, king, but he was a ruler in name
only, and until the proclamation of the republic on 1 May 1923
remained a puppet in the hands of the military dictatorships.

In October 1922, relieved from his command, Prince Andrew
was with his family in Corfu. Officers of the revolutionary committee arrived and told him that he was needed in Athens. He was
put aboard a destroyer which sailed to the mainland and, after
being kept prisoner for sixteen days, he was formally indicted
for high treason together with other 'royalist traitors' – three
former premiers, several ministers and the Commander-in-Chief
of the Greek army – blamed for the disastrous outcome of the
war. Death sentences were likely, and Alice sent frantic appeals
to her Mountbatten brothers in London, to King George V, to

[1] See *infra* page 247.

her cousin Ena's husband, King Alfonso of Spain, and to the Pope.

Andrew's brother, Prince Christopher, married to an American millionairess, had spent the turbulent years before the revolution abroad. Now he returned to Athens in an attempt to help to save his brother's life. 'No one was allowed to go near Andrew, except his valet', he recalled. 'Guards kept strictest watch and confiscated all letters and parcels. Finally I hit on the expedient of writing a letter on cigarette paper, rolling it tightly and putting it with cigarettes into his valet's case. Andrew answered it with a short note, full of courage, but . . . I knew that he had no longer any hope of regaining his freedom. He had just had a conversation with his former school-fellow, Pangalos, now Minister of War and instigator of his trial, that left him small grounds for optimism.

' "How many children have you?" Pangalos had asked suddenly, and when my brother told him, he shook his head: "Poor things, what a pity, they will soon be orphans!" '[1]

The first trial of the 'royalist traitors' took place on 13 November, and the former prime-minister Gounaris and five other accused were executed by a firing squad next morning. Prince Andrew and five generals were facing trial on 2 December, and expected a similar fate. However, Princess Alice's appeals did not remain unheard. Her brother Dickie had seen King George v and conferred with Bonar Law. But the Foreign Secretary, Lord Curzon, was in Geneva at a meeting of the League of Nations, and much time was lost before a rescue plan was devised. Diplomatic intervention would, the British statesmen confidently expected, save Prince Andrew's life, but the question was how to spare him long imprisonment. Lord Curzon decided to call in the British Secret Service and summoned to Geneva Commander Gerald Francis Talbot, at one time British naval attaché in Athens. He was asked to get Prince Andrew, Princess Alice and their five children out of Greece.

Commander Talbot travelled under an assumed name and in disguise from Italy to Athens where he arrived on 28 November, three days before the trial. He saw the Prince and then had a long talk with General Pangalos. On the following Saturday the trial took place in the Parliament building. All accused, except Prince

[1] Prince Christopher of Greece, op. cit., p. 175.

Andrew, were sentenced to death and subsequently shot. The verdict on the prince was imprisonment, deprivation of rank and titles and banishment for life. Talbot had arranged to abduct Prince Andrew immediately after the trial, but this proved unnecessary – General Pangalos – Minister of War and co-dictator – came late that night to the prison and drove the Prince and Talbot to Phalerum, where a Royal Navy destroyer, H.M.S. *Calypso*, was lying at anchor. His wife was waiting for him aboard the British warship.

While crowds demonstrated in Athens in celebration of the traitors' executions, the *Calypso* steamed off to Corfu where the five children were taken aboard. The journey continued to Brindisi and Talbot accompanied the rescued family to Rome, where Prince Andrew and his wife had an audience with the Pope and expressed their thanks for the help given by the Holy See. A few days later they were reunited in Paris with Prince Christopher and his wife who, with their American connections and money, left Greece unmolested.

Commander Talbot had gone ahead to London to make his report, and on arrival was told to go to Lord Stamfordham, the King's private secretary. At Buckingham Palace he was led to a drawing room; King George v entered and took a sword from his equerry. Little was said, Talbot was told to bend a knee, the King touched his shoulder with the sword, and when he arose – the most surprised man in the world – he was Sir Gerald Talbot, K.C.V.O.

The Greek royal family, its property confiscated, was dispersed in exile. When Prince Andrew arrived with his wife and five children in London he was almost penniless. Princess Alice had to depend on help from her British relatives, which her husband was unwilling to accept. In any case, contribution from the Mountbatten brothers was modest: George (the second Marquess of Milford Haven) inherited the title but little money from his father; his wife, the daughter of Grand Duke Michael of Russia, had lost her fortune to the Bolsheviks; Dickie (Lord Louis Mountbatten) lived affluently, but beside his service pay his income was affected by the complex trust provisions of his wife's Cassel inheritance. So Princess Beatrice, Queen Victoria's 67-year-old daughter and Henry of Battenberg's widow, took it upon herself to look after 'the Greeks', particularly after

King George V said he would 'not pay for any extravagance Andrea might indulge in'.

Help soon came from Prince Andrew's brothers. Prince Christopher and his rich wife had rented Spencer House in St James's Place and there 'the Greeks' lived for a time. Later Prince Andrew and Princess Alice were his guests in America and on cruise in his yacht from Canada to Palm Beach. During their parents' absence, the four girls and little Philip stayed with their grandmother, the Dowager Marchioness of Milford Haven at her grace-and-favour residence at Kensington Palace. Then came the turn of *la tante Bonaparte,* Princess Marie Bonaparte, a great-granddaughter of Napoleon's brother Lucien. She had married another of Andrew's brothers, Prince George of Greece. Her father, Prince Roland Bonaparte gained wealth by marrying Marie Blanc, the daughter of the founder of the Casino of Monte Carlo. At one time *la tante Bonaparte* was regarded with some embarrassment by her royal relations, owing to her Casino connections, and because she had become an ardent disciple of Siegmund Freud and an amateur practitioner of psychoanalysis. But now her offer to help was eagerly accepted.

She put a suite of rooms at her Paris palais near the Bois de Boulogne at the disposal of Prince Andrew and his family. This eased but did not solve his problem; it involved servants and upkeep he could ill afford. The family moved, therefore, into a gamekeeper's lodge in the grounds of a big country house Marie Bonaparte owned at St Cloud. Life was difficult in the shoe-size house, and Prince Andrew could hardly be blamed for not feeling happy in his new uncomfortable home, where money worries never left him.

The four girls were sent for prolonged visits to relatives in Germany. They stayed with Andrew's sister-in-law, ex-Queen Sophie of Greece, at Pankau on the Baltic, and with the Hesse family in Darmstadt. The former queen, whose husband ex-King Constantine had died in exile in Palermo in 1923 and whose brother, the ex-Kaiser, was in exile in Holland, maintained lively contacts with all her relations and, eventually all the daughters of Andrew and Alice married German princes.

In Paris, Princess Alice, left only with her son Philip, opened a boutique called 'Hellas' in the Faubourg St Honoré, in partnership with an aristocratic French woman. At first they sold Greek embroidery and lace, made under Princess Alice's expert eye. Later the shop also dealt in antiques, Prince Christopher and his American wife and Prince George and Marie Bonaparte helping to provide wealthy customers. Princess Alice did not, as some magazine stories later suggested, have to spend nights at needle-work to eke out a living; but constant work, her separation from her children – even Philip left home when he was only seven and was sent to England – and the estrangement from her husband, who went to live in Monte Carlo, had undermined her spirit and health.

Within one year, in 1930 and 1931, all her daughters married. The first was Sophia, the youngest and only sixteen; her marriage to 30-year-old Prince Christopher of Hesse illustrated the complex intertwining of Mountbatten destinies. Christopher was the youngest brother of Prince Maximilian of Hesse who, as a lieutenant in the Prussian Death's Head Hussars, was 19 when he was fatally wounded in an engagement with British cavalry in Flanders on 12 October 1914. At a British field hospital at Bailleul he told an army doctor that he was a great-grandson of Queen Victoria, and gave him a locket to send to his mother in Germany. The British doctor promised to do so. Prince Maxi-milian died within a few hours and three days later the doctor was killed when a German shell hit the field hospital. The locket with a note by him was sent to his widow in England, who forwarded it to Queen Mary; it eventually reached Princess Margaret of Hesse, the boy's mother, through Princess Louisa of Battenberg, Princess Alice's sister.

Princess Christopher of Hesse – Cri, as he was called by his family – may have never forgiven the British for killing his brother in battle. In 1933, three years after his marriage, he became an ardent Nazi and a high-ranking S.S. officer on Himmler's staff in Berlin. It was a grave embarrassment to the Mountbatten family that the husband of Lord Louis' niece should have taken this course. It became even worse when Prince Cri volunteered during the war for the Luftwaffe, and as a pilot took part in the *Blitz* air raids on London. He was killed when shot down on a bombing raid in Italy, leaving Sophia a widow at 29 with four small children and a fifth born posthum-ously in 1944. She later married Prince Georg of Hanover and has three more children from her second marriage. Her husband, a son of the Duke of Brunswick and Cumberland, was in direct descent of the Hanoverian kings of England; in 1961 his brother Prince Ernst August successfully claimed British nationality, even though the Master of the Rolls remarked that 'it seems an extraordinary thing that a man who fought against this country can come along and say that he was a British subject; if he is right he would appear to have committed high treason during the war.'

Princess Alice's eldest daughter, Margarita, married Prince Gottfried von Hohenlohe-Langenburg, a grandson of Prince Alfred of Edinburgh, and thus another great-grandson of Queen Victoria. Her second daughter, Theodora, became the wife of Margrave Berthold of Baden, and with her husband, who worked at his father's famous Salem school, later took special interest in the education of her little brother Prince Philip. The third daughter, Cecilia, married the Hereditary Grand Duke Georg Donatus of Hesse. Though periodically reunited with her daughters, Princess Alice lived during the 1930s alone, undergoing treatment in nursing homes. She regained her composure and health and eventually returned to Greece after monarchy was restored in 1935 and her nephew, King George II, returned to his throne in Athens.

She lived quietly in a small apartment near the Kolonaki Square in the centre of Athens, with a companion, Madame Socopol, and a maid. There, her son Philip – still at Gordonstoun and swotting for his entrance examinations for Dartmouth naval college – and some of her daughters visited her. Her niece, Princess Alexandra of Greece, recalls: 'I can see Aunt Alice continually glancing at the clock . . . when Philip was expected. To welcome him on these comparatively infrequent occasions a large meal was always prepared . . . I would find myself in the overcrowded rooms, crammed with old-fashioned furniture and well stocked with signed photographs of innumerable Battenbergs . . . Aunt Alice has rarely abandoned the religious costume she has worn for many years. Long before she founded her own nursing order on the isle of Tinos, she experimented with suitably austere costumes, oblivious of any quiet amusement she caused. Not that Aunt Alice lacked a sense of humour. At one time she loved to frequent a cinema that showed old classic silent films, chiefly for the joy of lip-reading . . . Once Aunt Alice described one of the big scenes in, I think, von Stroheim's

Greed. In the midst of a passionate love scene, the hero was really telling the heroine that he was being evicted for not paying his rent. These glimpses of real life from the movies were all the more comical for Aunt Alice's explosive method of blurting them out'.[1]

Her serene life was shattered in November 1937 by a family tragedy. Her daughter Cecilia with her husband Georg Donatus of Hesse and their two young sons were flying to London for the wedding of the Grand Duke's brother Prince Louis – who had served on Ribbentrop's staff in the German embassy – to the Hon. Margaret Geddes. In the mist outside Ostend the aircraft struck a factory chimney and all the passengers and crew were killed. The tragedy contributed to Princess Alice's decision to withdraw altogether from public life. Always deeply religious, she devoted herself to nursing.

During the war she remained in Athens when the Greek royal family was evacuated by British warships to Crete and later to Egypt. She tended wounded Greek soldiers, and after the Italians and Germans occupied Greece she was left unmolested and continued her hospital work. She was able to stay in touch with her daughters in Germany, whose husbands were serving in the German forces, and also to write sporadically to Prince Philip, who was sailing with the British Royal Navy.

In 1947, when Greece was torn by fratricidal strife and Communist revolts, she left her work only for a brief while to attend her son's marriage to Princess Elizabeth. For the festivities she discarded her nun's grey habit and wore a Paris dress and hat. Then she returned to Athens, and for years her life was fulfilled by her hospital work with the Greek Orthodox Order of Nursing Sisters she had founded, and of which she was the Mother Superior. Only rarely did her patients learn that the kind, deaf old Sister was a royal princess and the mother-in-law of the Queen of England.

In recent years Princess Alice visited her children and grandchildren in Britain and Germany more frequently. She had handed over the administration of her Order and the nursing school at the convent of Psychico to younger women she had trained. But when in 1961 it was suggested to her that she should

[1] Queen Alexandra of Yugoslavia, *A Family Portrait*, London, 1960, Hodder & Stoughton.

settle down in London, she did not accept the Queen's offer of a grace-and-favour apartment at Hampton Court. She said she did not desire a settled home, wanted to travel and also to continue her charitable work in Greece.

She took great interest in her twenty grandchildren. A special affection developed between her and Prince Charles and Princess Anne, although in her austere appearance, and with her serious ways, she was very different from their beloved 'Grannie', the Queen Mother, who – according to Prince Philip – 'was terribly spoiling the children'. Prince Philip calls his mother 'our family's genealogist and chronicler'. She would spend hours in telling Prince Charles and Princess Anne of a life of hardship and adventure so very different from that they knew of their mother's surely-established Royal Family. There were, however, also lighter moments. Prince Philip sometimes found his mother busily running his eldest son's electric railway – when Prince Charles was still small – or going with the boy through his stamp collections and explaining to him the events of world history, so often mirrored in old postage stamps.

During her visit in 1965 Princess Alice knew fresh happiness in playing with her youngest grandsons, Prince Andrew and Prince Edward. She remarked that in future she would spend much more time in Britain to be near them. She was also a frequent guest of her brother, Earl Mountbatten, and his daughters and families, particularly at Broadlands, and through marriages of her German grandchildren she had become a great-grandmother, paying regular visits to the homes of her daughters and their families. At the age of 80 she had discarded her nun's habit for ordinary if severely-cut clothes, and after a lonely, often adverse and sorrowful life, which spans an amazing stretch of history from Queen Victoria to the era of space flights, she had found a new happiness in her large family of Battenberg lineage.

Prince Philip with his sisters, Princess Margarita of Hohenlohe-Langenburg, Princess Sophia of Hanover and Princess Theodora of Baden, during his visit at Salem Castle in Germany in 1946. His fourth sister, Princess Cecilia of Hesse, was killed with her husband and two sons in an aircrash in 1937.

Lady Brabourne (Patricia Mountbatten) with her husband and her cousin, Prince Philip, in 1947.

Prince Philip at the age of
13 months at the wedding
of his uncle Lord Louis
Mountbatten (the present
Earl) in London in 1922.

The Queen (as Princess
Elizabeth) and
Lieutenant Philip
Mountbatten, RN,
after the announcement
of their engagement in
July 1947.

CHAPTER TWELVE

PRINCE PHILIP OF GREECE

IN A tumbledown Corfiot villa, lost among 25,000 rose trees, Prince Philip, the only son of Alice of Battenberg and Andrew of Greece, came into the world on an old dining table covered with white cloth. The baby, destined to be the husband of Her Most Excellent Majesty Elizabeth the Second, by the Grace of God, of the United Kingdom of Great Britain and Northern Ireland and of Her other Realms and Territories Queen, Head of the Commonwealth, Defender of the Faith, reached England and exile in an orange box – for the British warship, which rescued him, his parents and sisters from Greek revolutionaries, had no cot aboard.

For centuries the Ionian island of Corfu, guardian of the Adriatic straits, fascinated mediaeval conquerors and modern royalty. A scene of the Odyssey, it came under Byzantine, Sicilian, Neapolitan, Venetian, Turkish, Napoleonic and, for seven years, Russian rule. Britain occupied the island after Waterloo, taught the natives the moral precepts of cricket, and restored it to Greece in 1863.

Among the conquerors and rulers who built palaces on the island was Empress Elizabeth of Austria, who tried to vie with her deranged cousin, King Ludwig II of Bavaria, in creating bizarre palaces. On Corfu she had built an edifice entirely of white marble, which she dedicated to Achilles and named Achilleon. She also built a smaller, fake Greek temple, on the crown of the hill, consecrated not to any Athenian deity but to her favourite German-Jewish poet Heinrich Heine. This slight to the classical Olympus was offset by rows of white marble statues of Greek gods and goddesses, peering through dark bowers of laurel and cypress trees.

After Empress Elizabeth had been assassinated by an Italian anarchist, Kaiser William II – whose vulgar taste had often shocked Queen Victoria – acquired the Achilleon and made it one of his summer palaces. There, between 1906 and 1914, he dreamed his dreams of a German Kingdom of Jerusalem. When four years later he fell from his throne, grew a beard and fled into exile to Holland, his palace on Corfu became just another memory of his boastful glory. The Achilleon was given to the Greek king, as part of Germany's war reparations. The park had become a wilderness of decay, the marble pillars and statues stood dirty and crumbling. Lush vegetation had swept over the rose bushes and lawns and thorns had enveloped the marble stairways and arenas.

By 1919 the King of the Hellenes had other worries than to restore the palace of Corfu. Yet Corfu, blessed with a wonderful climate, could never be anything but beautiful. It rose in dark green majesty from the blue sea, serene and untouched by the holocaust which had swept Europe for four years and was still smouldering in the war between Greece and Turkey.

A few hundred yards from the Achilleon stood a mansion, 'Mon Repos', a villa built in Regency style in 1832 by Sir Frederick Adams for his Corfu-born wife. For half a century it had housed a succession of British governors, and later became a summer house of the Greek royal family. It gave the woman who was bearing her fifth child a peaceful refuge.

Alice of Battenberg, Princess Andrew of Greece, had gone with her daughters to Corfu while her husband was in command of a Greek army corps fighting the Turks in Anatolia. Athens was in turmoil but there was peace and beauty at Corfu. What little could be done at 'Mon Repos' to prepare for the royal confinement was seen to by the princess' Scottish housekeeper, Mrs Agnes Blower, whose husband was the gardener and odd-job man. The old house was dilapidated and crammed with Victorian furniture and junk left behind sixty years earlier by its British official tenants.

Alice of Battenberg had borne her husband four daughters, and, waiting for her fifth child, she prayed that it would be a boy. She wrote to her brother Dickie in London: 'If the child will be a boy, he will be sixth in succession to the Greek throne ... As things are today, with Alex[1] dead, Tino (King Constantine) threatened by Venizelos, and George[2] and Andrea[3] unacceptable, my son if God wills could become one day the king, if monarchy prevails.'

Mrs Agnes Blower, living in 1962 at the age of 92, in an old folks' home in Peterborough recalled the evening when the child was born on 10 June 1921.

'They didn't live like Royals,' she said. 'Everything at the villa was very primitive. There was no electricity, no gas, no running hot water and no proper heating. We had a few un-trained peasant girls to help, and two unwashed footmen who were rough fellows. When the princess and the four girls wanted a bath, water had to be heated in big pails on the old coal stove in the kitchen and then carried in buckets upstairs ... Of course, they were as poor as church mice.'

It was a difficult birth. Princess Alice had suffered from the nervous strain caused by the events in Athens during her pregnancy. The local doctor was not particularly familiar with modern gynaecology. He decided that he might well need an operating table of some sort, and when Princess Alice began her labour, she was carried from her bedroom to the dining room downstairs and there, on the table, covered with an embroidered table cloth, the child was born.

The princess had, however, two devoted women by her side. Mrs Blower busied herself in the kitchen, cooking some wholesome dishes so that Princess Alice should pick up strength again. And there was a motherly English nannie, Miss Roose – 'Roosie' to the family – who had in succession nursed the three daughters of Prince Nicholas of Greece: Marina, the present Princess Marina, Duchess of Kent, Olga, the wife of Prince Paul of Yugoslavia, and Elizabeth, Countess Törring.

Nannie Roose, although used to looking after foreign princely children, had a strong English suspicion of everything foreign and was no respector of persons. She was one of those dedicated English spinsters who regard a baby's life as more important

---

[1] King Alexander, see *supra* p. 238.
[2] Prince George had renounced his rights to succession.
[3] Her husband.

than any consideration of high birth. A few weeks before the birth she demanded certain supplies from London. Lord Louis obliged by sending them in a British warship. From then on Philip was fed on English baby food, washed with English soap and dressed in Scottish woollens. Mrs Blower well remembered the year the new baby spent at 'Mon Repos'.

'He was a plump and healthy baby and he had a wonderful appetite. He had to be weaned early and there was no clean cow milk available on the island, where the natives used goats' milk. But when he was a little older I soon put a stop to his being fed on those messy foreign dishes which the Greek cook concocted, and instead, I made for him nourishing rice and tapioca puddings and good wholesome Scots porridge . . .'

The boy, born seven years after his youngest sister, would have had a princely baptism had he been in Athens or in Britain, with the Greek, German and Danish princes and all the Mount-battens clustered around the font. But on remote Corfu, with his father absent, the baptism took place without much ceremony. He was christened Philip, after the second name of his uncle, the hapless King Alexander of Greece.

Within three months of Philip's birth, Princess Alice received two messages at 'Mon Repos'. One was from her brother Dickie, conveying the news that their father, Admiral the Marquess of Milford Haven, had died of heart failure; the other was from Athens, informing her of the defeat of her husband's army on the banks of the river Sakharia.

Princess Alice decided to take her children to London when she went to her father's funeral in September 1921. Although only 36, the princess was prematurely aged, greying and very deaf. The girls were Margarita, 16, Theodora, 15, Cecilia, 10, and chubby, 7-year-old Sophie, called 'Tiny'. Baby Philip travelled with them under the watchful eyes of nannie 'Roosie'. After the funeral, Princess Alice proudly showed off her new baby to her mother, Princess Victoria of Hesse (the Dowager Marchioness) and all the other members of the family who had assembled at Netley Abbey. After a few weeks 'the Greeks' returned to Corfu, where Princess Alice hoped to be reunited with her husband.

The first year in Philip's life was austere. His nursery, shared with his nannie, was a small, sparsely furnished room, with the wallpaper peeling off.

'The little boy did not have many toys. Not even a teddy bear,' said Mrs Blower forty years later. 'I sat with him on the old carpet and we played with red, white and blue bricks, roughly hewn from some old pieces of timber by a young gardener. Philip was a lively little lad, and when he got tired of building castles he ran around banging an empty tin with a stick. His favourite toy was his nannie's pin cushion. He would sit quietly in his cot for hours pulling the pins and needles out and pushing them in again. I always worried that he would hurt himself.' Apparently he never did; at a very early age he showed his inclination for mechanics and method.

In July 1922 the entire family attended the wedding of Lord Louis Mountbatten to Edwina Ashley. While his four sisters acted as bridesmaids, in white and blue dresses of Greek national colours, little Philip was left with his nannie at Kensington Palace, where the family were guests of Alice's mother. Wedding festivities over, the 'Greek relations' hurriedly returned to Corfu because of grave news arriving from Athens. A few months later Philip's father was a prisoner of the revolutionary regime, facing trial for his life. Eventually, rescued by the British Secret Service, Prince Andrew and his wife were taken aboard a British cruiser to Corfu. The warship picked up Philip, his four sisters and nannie Roosie at Corfu. The weather at sea was bad and the captain ordered that an orange box should be padded to receive baby Philip instead of the dangerous bunk; since during the hurried departure his cot had been left behind at 'Mon Repos'.

With the abolition of the Greek monarchy – the king and members of his family had been sent into exile on 19 December 1923 – Prince Andrew was now without Greek nationality. He decided to revert to the Danish nationality of his grandfather, and rather than call himself a Prince of Schleswig-Holstein-Sonderburg-Glücksburg he chose the title of a Prince of Denmark and Greece. The Danish embassy issued him and his family with passports. In London the exiles stayed at Marlborough House as guests of their Danish-born great-aunt, Queen Alexandra. It was there, and later on the creaking floors of Kensington Palace, where his grandmother, the Dowager Marchioness of Milford Haven, had a grace and favour apartment that Philip first learned to walk.

During the next few years life for Philip's parents was difficult. When they lived in Paris, as guests of Prince George of Greece and his wife, *tante Bonaparte,* Philip was soon the only one of the five children to remain at home. His sisters were sent to relatives in Germany. At the age of six he became a pupil at the American Country School *The Elms,* at St Cloud, for the children of wealthy Americans residing in France. The fees were high but they were paid by Philip's uncle, Prince Christopher in New York. Philip's first teacher, Mr Donald MacJannet, remembers him as 'a rugged, boisterous boy, but always remarkably polite; he was full of energy, got along well with other children, wanted to learn to do everything himself and asked at one time to be shown how to wait at table . . .'

When he was in Paris and his mother was busy at her boutique, Philip was in the care of his old nannie 'Roosie', who had loyally remained with Princess Alice. The nannie accompanied him on visits abroad during his vacations, which were spent with his father's sister-in-law, ex-Queen Sophie of Greece (a sister of Kaiser William II) at Pankau on the Baltic, or with his father's niece, Queen Helen of Rumania, at the palace of Sinaia in the Transylvanian Alps, where he first met his cousin, King Michael of Rumania.

His mother taught him to speak English when he was still a little tot; mixing with his many German relatives he acquired fluency in that language, and from his father a smattering of Greek; he soon also learned fluent French. But during his school-days at *The Elms* he began to speak with a slight American drawl, imitating some of his class-mates. Princess Alice complained about it in her letters to her brothers in London, and George Milford Haven suggested that she should send Philip to him. He could then join his own son, David, who was two years older, at the prep-school at Cheam.

Philip was brought to London in 1929 when he was eight years old and spent three years at the famous Cheam school. He is remembered there as a likeable boy though not particularly brilliant. The only prize he ever won was for French, a language in which his previous residence in Paris gave him a marked advantage over his English school-fellows. During the holidays he was sent from one relation to another, but mostly stayed with uncle Milford Haven and his wife Nada, daughter of Grand Duke

Michael of Russia, at their country house at Holyport near Maidenhead. Although as a little boy he had visited on a few occasions his other uncle, Lord Louis Mountbatten – it was said that Philip was so shy with uncle Dickie that he used to hide under his bed at Brook House – it was only later that he became a regular visitor at Dickie's and Edwina's Broadlands estate.

Some biographers of Prince Philip have suggested that he was interested in a naval career from the earliest years. This is not true, though at one time Lord Louis did suggest to his sister that Philip be entered at the Dartmouth naval college. It was after the Marquess of Milford Haven, having resigned his commission in the Royal Navy and gone into business, offered to send Philip to an English public school that his schooling was finally decided. Philip's sister, Theodora, decisively intervened over his further education when the time came for him to leave Cheam.

She had married in 1931 Berthold, the son of Prince Max of Baden. This German prince had been the Kaiser's last Reich-Chancellor in October 1918. In a desperate attempt to save his throne, William II had called upon Prince Max, known for his liberal views, to appeal to President Wilson, Lloyd George and Clémenceau for 'an armistice with honour'. By then mutinies had broken out in the German navy and army, and the prince, realising that only the removal of the Kaiser and his Prussian militarist clique could prove to the Allies his own desire for peace and a democratic regime in Germany, proclaimed on 9 November 1918 the abdication of the Kaiser, without informing him beforehand. However, Prince Max's honest attempt had come too late. He handed the government to the leaders of the German Socialists, who proclaimed the republic and offered surrender to the Allies.

Abused by German nationalists as 'the Red Prince', Max of Baden retired from politics and devoted himself to the idea of 're-educating' the new German generation. He believed that 're-education' should start with the young people of the upper-classes, in order to create a new German democratic intelligensia, free from the overweening, boastful, militaristic spirit of the 'Junkers'. He wanted to provide a new élite for a new Germany. Related through his own marriage to English royalty, this idealist manque had often visited Britain and was deeply impressed by the public school system, something he came to regard as the real secret of British Imperial power.

The idea of a 'democratic élite' was not entirely his own. He had met some years earlier a German-Jewish educationist, Dr Kurt Hahn, who had devised a strange and particularly Teutonic brand of 'supermanship' through education. While they were progressive in the German sense, Hahn's ideas were very remote from any concept of equality of opportunity and a classless society. He wished to replace the spirit of Prussian militarism with a new idea of 'devoted and dutiful patriotism', to imbue what he termed 'the élite of enlightened leaders'. Prince Max offered Dr Hahn his large and gloomy Castle Salem near Lake Constance as a home for the school for the new-type 'supermen'. There, during the 1920s, Dr Hahn built up Salem School, from which later Gordonstoun was to emerge, though somewhat modified.

Dr Hahn's curriculum placed the greatest importance on self-reliance: his boys had to discover themselves, to learn to accept success or failure philosophically, to suppress personal desires for the benefit of the team. Emphasis was placed on the virtues of almost monastic renunciation, 'self-contemplation' and periods of silence. But since all this could produce physical weaklings, the boys had to undergo the most exacting physical training, engage in heavy agricultural and construction work, and all in all lead a thoroughly Spartan life. The spirit of adventure was encouraged through climbing, tough marches, swimming, and sailing. Formal education was given a very low place. The normal subjects were taught, but neither Salem, nor later Gordonstoun, has ever produced a noted scientist, writer, artist or technician.

The founder's concept at Salem was to breed modern 'princes' of Machiavelli's kind, and the school's main appeal was to parents who hoped that their sons would become leaders in politics and diplomacy, or in industry and commerce where lay Germany's best chances of revival. But for the Nazi regime Salem might have produced a new generation of enlightened German leaders. Significantly, in the Hitler Youth the same aims were pursued though in a different way. In present-day Germany the Salem ideals are followed in a number of new and highly-selective boarding-schools. By segregation and its insistence on its pupils being 'superboys', Salem, probably against the wishes of its founder, turned out arrogant young men. This and the 'superboy' aspect is very noticeable in Prince Philip's character, accentuated as it is by the inherent hauteur of the Battenberg family.

Princess Theodora was enthusiastic about Salem for Philip, and his uncles George and Dickie visited the school to see for themselves. They decided to send the boy for a year or two, Lord Louis remarking that it would be good initial training before the boy went to Dartmouth as a Royal Naval cadet. Philip, aged 11, reached Salem for the winter term of 1932–33. There were about 100 pupils; in addition to boys from wealthy and aristocratic families, Dr Hahn admitted at reduced fees a small number of boys from middle class homes as a sort of leavening.

Soon after Philip arrived at his new school Hitler came to power and Dr Goebbels, his Minister for Public Enlightenment, ordered the arrest of the headmaster of Salem, who was now described as 'a decadent Jewish corrupter of German youth'. The school, however, remained open for a time. Prince Max of Baden appointed his son, Prince Berthold (the husband of Philip's sister Theodora) as the new headmaster and he was allowed to carry on. For a while some of the Nazi 'ideologists' toyed with the idea of making Salem a sort of high academy for the Hitler Youth. After some months, during which Hahn's masters ran the school on the old lines, defying Nazi control, Salem was closed.

Prince Philip's period at Salem was stormy, and he added to the troubles. With his English upbringing he had little respect for the new Nazi movement and its posturings. One day a jack-booted S.S. officer stormed into Prince Berthold's study to demand severe punishment for a fair-haired boy who had that day been watching storm troopers giving the Hitler salute to the Swastika flag as it was being hoisted in the market square of nearby Uberlingen. The boy had asked in a loud voice whether all those men with upraised arms were in urgent need of 'being excused'! Prince Berthold tried to explain that the schoolboy was a Danish prince who knew of no other reason for raising an arm like that. Philip's remark was typical of those that were later to make the Duke of Edinburgh famous throughout the world. It was hastily decided to send Philip back to England.

Dr Hahn, released from prison on the intervention of powerful friends, had gone to London some time earlier and had been welcomed by men such as Lord Tweedsmuir (the author John Buchan and later Governor-General of Canada), Lord Allen of Hurtwood and Mr Claude Elliott, then headmaster of Eton. They helped him found a 'New Salem' in the home of the Gordon-Cummings family on the bleakly beautiful shores of the Moray Firth a few miles from Elgin. Philip now went to Gordonstoun, which had at least one great attraction for its boys. It was near the sea and was ideal for playing 'cops and robbers'. However, Dr Hahn had rather different ideas. Before breakfast the boys had to run 400 yards slowly and on their toes, they skipped during the mornings and did physical exercises in the afternoons and evenings. Four times a week the academic studies were suspended for 45 minutes of running, jumping and javelin throwing, and time was daily given to agricultural tasks or woodwork. Food was frugal, beds were hard, the rule was cold baths summer or winter, there was no 'tuck shop' and clothing was of the simplest. The austerity of those days has been greatly changed in recent years, and Prince Charles did not share all the hardships his father experienced.

On arrival at Gordonstoun Philip was greeted by 'Chewey', Mr Chew, then deputy headmaster and later successor to Dr Hahn, with a few words of welcome. One of Gordonstoun's principles was that a boy must learn the ropes himself. The 'Trust System' now ruled Philip's life. Every evening he had to mark a chart on which he had to affirm that he had not broken any of the unwritten (and sometimes as yet unknown) rules. If he felt that he had, the details must be entered: failing to take a second cold shower, eating sweets, walking instead of running. The masters did not inspect these 'confessional' charts, and the boys were expected to pay the penalty with a bad conscience if they lied or betrayed the Trust System.

Misdemeanours known to the masters were, however, dealt with by 'Punishments One to Six' accordingly. The first five consisted of walks of different lengths early in the morning and within a given time. Number Six meant an interview with the headmaster. The punishment walks were in fact quite severe, because they had to be completed before the boy started the usual daily mile run at seven a.m. It meant that a boy had to rise before six a.m., take his cold shower, make his bed, tidy his

locker, walk a mile in well under 15 minutes if the punishment
was a three or four-miles stretch, and be back for seven a.m.
to start all over again. Understandably no boy liked Gordonstoun
when first he arrived, and Philip was no exception, but gradually
he and the others came to accept the regime. Gordonstoun of
course strongly coloured Prince Philip's attitude to life and
people. The basic Battenberg zest for adventure and activity was
here channelled into a determination to do all things well and to
expect that others did so also. Many years later, when addressing
a distinguished audience he extolled 'great men with an all-
consuming passion for work and their achievements', adding:
'It will be a sad day if we ever fail to produce that kind of
dedicated men'. Prince Philip likes speedy, factual results, he
regards purely intellectual pre-occupations with ill-concealed
boredom, some times even with contempt.

It was the Gordonstoun boy who, when thrown at polo,
immediately remounted and played on with a broken finger, and
on another occasion with bruised ribs and strained leg. Certainly
the school made an excellent athlete of him and he is today fitter
than most men ten years younger. His years at Gordonstoun,
where he became 'Room Leader', then 'Guardian' and finally
'Head Boy', convinced him that this was the hardening system he
wanted for his son Charles, who had spent his childhood in
much greater comfort. Philip became a 'superboy' at Gordonstoun
by his sheer dedication and not by his rank, which in those days
counted for little in any event. There was not much time to
demonstrate intellectual abilities. One biographer recorded that
he was very interested in Shakespeare and 'took a leading part'
in a performance of *Macbeth*. Prince Philip must have chuckled
if he read this remark. He did take part in *Macbeth* certainly, the
part of Donalbain. When in July, 1963, with the Queen he was
host to his cousin King Paul of Greece and Queen Frederika,
there was a party at Lancaster House after a gala performance
of *A Midsummer Night's Dream* at the Aldwych Theatre. At the
party Prince Philip recalled his own debut as an actor. 'It was not
an exacting part,' he said with a grin. 'I had just one line to say:
"What is amiss?" when I entered just after Duncan's murder!'
His son, Prince Charles, definitely outdid him: in November
1965 he acted with great success at Gordonstoun in the title role
of *Macbeth*. Significantly Prince Philip's best subjects at Gordons-

toun were those which were to serve him well in his new, genuine interest in seamanship. He was adept in mathematics and geography.

In deference to the British seafaring tradition, Dr Hahn had decreed that all his boys must be trained in sailing. He engaged as instructor Commander Lewty, a retired Royal Navy officer, and the school had several sailing boats and later a schooner. At first the boys sailed in the Scottish lochs, then the best, including Philip, were allowed to put to sea aboard the schooner for journeys as far as the Outer Hebrides and the coast of Norway. The commander reported on Philip: 'He is a cheerful shipmate, very conscientious in carrying out both major and minor duties, thoroughly trustworthy and unafraid of dirty and arduous work'.

Of all his adult male relatives Philip knew well only his uncle George, the Marquess of Milford Haven, who was like a second father to him. But he hero-worshipped uncle Dickie. His mother had told him that it was uncle Dickie who had saved their lives during the Greek revolution, and Philip knew that Lord Louis, the handsome, dashing naval officer, had come top of eighty cadets at Dartmouth, had served under Admiral Beatty and had seen a real naval battle in the Great War. Now he was in command of the destroyer *Daring*, an A.D.C. to the Prince of Wales, an accomplished polo player, the husband of a most attractive woman, and a man-of-the-world whose name and picture appeared almost every day in newspaper columns and glossy society magazines.

By the age of 14 or 15 Philip was determined to emulate his uncle. But Lord Louis, preoccupied with his naval duties and his social round, took at first only a vague if kindly interest in his nephew. Lord Louis did not like that 'funny school' in Scotland, and when during a holiday stay at Broadlands Philip shyly asked him whether he would advise him to choose a naval career, uncle Dickie immediately and enthusiastically agreed.

At first it was thought that Philip should enter the Greek Navy. After the restoration of the monarchy in Greece in November 1935, Constantine's eldest son, George, who had been king for 15 months in 1922–23, returned to Athens from his eleven years' exile. Philip's father, Prince Andrew, also returned from France and suggested that his son should go to the Greek Nautical College. But neither Philip, who had become acclimatized to

Britain, nor his English uncles liked this idea. Philip's study was now decorated with pictures of British warships and photographs of uncle Dickie cut from magazines. He opened his heart to Lord Louis and was told: 'Of course, Philip, you must go to Dartmouth. You aren't an old Greek and it's the Royal Navy for you and not some leaky Greek boat!' Lord Louis arranged for Philip to take his exams at Gordonstoun and then to sit for the Special Entry at Dartmouth, so that no accusation of untoward influence could be made.

During Philip's last year at Gordonstoun he had been called twice to Dr Hahn's study to receive sad news from the headmaster. In 1937 his sister Cecilia, her husband, her two sons and her mother-in-law perished in an air crash during a flight from Germany to London. Less than a year later his uncle George, the Marquess of Milford Haven died of cancer at the age of 46. In 1938 Philip was sent to live with Mr and Mrs Mercer at Cheltenham. Mr Mercer was a naval coach and he tutored Philip for the Dartmouth examinations.

As the boy was leaving Gordonstoun, Dr Hahn sent a confidential report to the Admiralty: 'Prince Philip is universally trusted, liked and respected. He has the greatest sense of service of all the boys in the school. He is a born leader, but will need the exacting demands of a great service to do justice to himself. His best is outstanding; but his second best is not good enough. Prince Philip will make his mark in any profession where he will have to prove himself in a full trial of strength'. Whatever one might think of some of Dr Hahn's educational methods, this report showed a remarkable insight into Prince Philip's character.

The result of the Special Entry examination at Dartmouth was not particularly distinguished. Philip was little above the half-way mark in the order of those who passed. But he had been in a disadvantageous position. Most of the boys who outshone him had been to naval cadet schools, while Philip entered at the late age of nearly 18 from a 'civilian' school. Some of his friends, including his cousin David (third Marquess of Milford Haven) who was already a Sub-Lieutenant in the Royal Navy, offered an intriguing explanation of Philip's low listing. A few weeks before he sat for the exam he went to Venice for a visit to the widowed Princess Aspasia of Greece and her daughter Alexandra (later the wife of King Peter of Yugoslavia). Alexandra was the same age as Philip and there was some reason to believe that Princess Aspasia had ideas of a match between the two young people. Philip very definitely had no such thoughts. In her memoirs Alexandra wrote: 'Philip was interested in canals, gondolas, sailing, good food . . . and girls – in that order'.[1] Suddenly transferred from the austerities of Gordonstoun Philip made the most of the occasion.

'Philip would lie in bed until eleven or twelve o'clock. Gordonstoun must have utterly exhausted him. Then he would come down demanding a full English breakfast of eggs and bacon from our Italian cook. Afterwards came lunch and then Philip was ready for every possible exploit. He was delighted that I had a speedboat and he went off in it alone, leaving me stranded, for hours at a time. Venice, too, proved the occasion of probably the first and only time Philip ever got drunk. At Gordonstoun he had to promise abstinence from alcohol . . . Released from this vow, Philip had to have a night out. Lord and Lady Melchett[2] were giving a party at one of the fishermen's tavernas that had become fashionable at Torcello . . . Before he knew what was happening, the Italian wine unexpectedly went to my cousin's head. He began to make us all laugh by dancing about the terrace like a young faun, a very handsome and graceful faun, I must admit. Then he began swinging from the pergola. It went beyond a joke, for the pergola collapsed bringing the vine down with it, and Philip disappeared under the greenery. The enraged proprietor and his daughters – and a rueful, suddenly sobered Philip – cleaned up the mess. Happily, the Melchetts did not mind paying for the damage. I am sure they realised that a young man's intoxication on a Venetian evening was just as explosive as the chemicals from which their family fortune was founded.'

It must have been disappointing for Alexandra that her cousin did not pay much attention to her. She quizzically recalls the 'blondes, brunettes and redheads' Philip impartially squired. 'Then, gradually, one girl in our group began to stand out a little more than the others,' the princess noted, and this seems to have been Philip's first love at the age of 17½. One night he came home very late, having taken his girl friend for a moonlight trip in

[1] Ex-Queen Alexandra of Yugoslavia, op. cit.
z Lord Melchett, the 2nd baron, was the son of the German chemist Dr Ludwig Mond, who founded the I.C.I. concern.

Alexandra's motorboat. Alexandra recalls that next morning he 'sheepishly' explained: 'We had trouble with the sparking plugs . . .'

More nightly trips down the canals followed and Alexandra teased her cousin about it. But, she says, Philip did not like to be teased: 'I am afraid that when he began taking his girl friend out in my speedboat while I stayed at home, we had a most uncousinly row.' It was perhaps not only because he borrowed the boat too often. Queen Alexandra also disclosed in her memoirs that 'there was talk that we might get engaged when we are older,' and she might have felt pangs of jealousy when Philip so brashly neglected her. But his romantic moonlit nights and the high life at Venice finished soon with the end of the summer and Philip returned to the Mercers' modest home at Cheltenham to continue swotting for his Dartmouth exams.

CHAPTER THIRTEEN

LIEUTENANT PHILIP
MOUNTBATTEN, R.N.

IN MAY, 1939 Philip, Prince of Greece and Denmark, put on for the first time the uniform of a Royal Naval cadet. His course at Dartmouth was brief, for a few months later the war began. But he crammed an astonishing number of activities into that time. He took part in various sports competitions, and excelled on the squash court, and when the College took part in the Devonport Athletic Championships his javelin throw of 140 feet 10 inches put Dartmouth well ahead of all competitors, being only 30 feet short of the Royal Navy's senior championship standard. Philip also greatly improved his cricket at Dartmouth, a sport that had been neglected at Gordonstoun.

22 July 1939 was a fateful day for Prince Philip. King George VI and Queen Elizabeth visited the Royal Naval College, accompanied by Princess Elizabeth who was 13, and Princess Margaret who was 9. In many newspaper and magazine stories, and even in some memoirs of retired Court officials, it has been said that Prince Philip had been a childhood playmate of the Princesses. In fact, Philip had met his uncle Bertie and aunt Elizabeth perhaps only two or three times on formal occasions, but he had hardly ever even seen the Princesses. When the Royal visit was announced, the Dartmouth cadets were ordered to smarten themselves up and Philip was told that he had been chosen as one of the escorts for the little Princesses.

Philip was in a bad mood even before this news came. He had recently been punished for some minor breach of discipline and had to dig a slit trench and then put in a few hours of solitary drill. To make it worse, this was on Saturday, 10 June, his 18th birthday, when he had hoped to get a leave pass and have a birthday party at the home of uncle Dickie.

The royal yacht *Victoria and Albert* dropped anchor at Dartmouth in the morning, and among the group of naval officers was Captain Lord Louis Mountbatten who, a trifle anxiously, looked down the line of cadets drawn up on the jetty, to spot a sullen-faced Philip, entirely unamused at the prospect of attending all day on two small girls. But the programme was abruptly changed when the Queen was told that seven cadets were in the College sick bay with mumps. The Queen ordered that the two Princesses must not attend the church Service or mix with any of the cadets to avoid a risk of infection. The royal party went at once to the house of Captain (later Admiral Sir Frederick) Dalrymple-Hamilton, the commanding officer.

The Captain had two daughters and a son, whose model electric railway had been laid out on the floor of the drawing-room to entertain the princesses. Philip was told to operate the railway. Though he tried hard to amuse them the two little girls were thoroughly bored. Princess Elizabeth said she wanted to go for a walk and was told she could not. So they ate ginger biscuits and drank enormous quantities of lemon and orange squashes. Philip had no experience of playing with small girls, all his sisters were much older than he. He suggested a game of croquet. This, too, was a failure, and Princess Elizabeth repeatedly asked, 'When are we going home?'

For want of a better idea Philip now took them through the College grounds, showing them the swimming pool and playing fields. But the princesses demanded to see 'the boys' rooms'. Philip, remembering the Queen's order, had a great deal of trouble persuading the lively and determined 'Lilibet' that she must stay outside. That night the King gave a dinner aboard the royal yacht to which all officers and Captain-Cadets were invited. Though Philip was only a junior cadet, uncle Dickie had secured an invitation for him. Much to Philip's relief the two little princesses had gone to bed long before his arrival on board. That was the first, and for a long time the last occasion, on which Prince Philip met his future wife.

Six weeks later Britain was at war. Philip worked intensely at Dartmouth. Uncle Dickie twice visited him and impressed on him that he must pass out really well, otherwise it might be difficult to get him a commission in the Royal Navy in war-time, because of his foreign nationality. In the winter of 1939–40, both Greece and Denmark, whose nationalities Philip could claim, were still neutral countries. There was no need for Lord Louis to have any qualms. Philip passed out as the best Special Entry cadet of his term and was awarded the King's Dirk. He also won the Eardley-Howard-Crockett prize. With the prize went a book-token to the value of £2. Significantly the Prince of Greece and Denmark selected a book on strategy by Captain Lidell Hart, entitled *The Defence of Britain*.

In January 1940, he was posted as a midshipman to the battle-ship *Ramillies,* stationed at Colombo, to escort transports of the first Australian contingents to the Mediterranean. It is characteristic of Philip that when his ship berthed at Australian ports he did not join the young officers at social rounds and cocktail parties, but eagerly inquired how he could reach the nearest cattle station. There, on his shore-leaves, he roamed the Queensland countryside in the saddle, sharing the life, if sometimes only for a few days, with rough 'jackaroos'.

When *Ramillies* arrived in the spring of 1940 at Alexandria, the Lords of the Admiralty conferred with Buckingham Palace and the Foreign Office. Lord Halifax, then Foreign Secretary, advised that Philip should be transferred to a ship that was not engaged on warlike duties. Philip was still a 'neutral citizen', apart from being a foreign prince, and it was considered imperative that there should be no danger of his being taken prisoner by the Germans. Midshipman Philip was posted to the East Africa Station and joined the complement of H.M.S. *Kent* at Cape Town. Later he was transferred to H.M.S. *Shropshire* stationed at Durban. Apart from being engaged on some uneventful patrol duties in the Indian Ocean, he enjoyed the hospitality and gay life of the British-minded community of Durban.

Denmark was invaded by the Germans on 9 April 1940, and on 28 October Hitler attacked Greece. Philip, Prince of Greece and Denmark, was no longer a neutral. Nevertheless, his position was delicate. All his sisters were married to Germans; one of his brothers-in-law, Prince Christopher of Hesse, 'the Nazi Cri', who had been for years an ardent supporter of Hitler and was an S.S. Sturmführer on Himmler's Gestapo staff, had joined the

Luftwaffe and taken part in air attacks on Britain. His other brothers-in-law, though not sharing Prince Christopher's enthusiasm for the Nazis, were German officers.

In South Africa, Philip read how the ill-equipped Greek army had beaten superior Italian forces. He wrote to Lord Louis beseeching him for a posting with an active naval unit. The message did not reach Lord Louis until many weeks later, when he had returned from the stricken voyage of the *Kelly*, but Philip had also written to the First Sea Lord, Admiral Sir Dudley Pound, requesting a 'real' posting. He was at last sent to the Mediterranean Fleet and joined H.M.S. *Valiant*.

The Greeks were still bravely fighting in the mountains when Philip went ashore in the Piraeus and had a brief meeting with his cousin, King George II of the Hellenes, and his family in Athens. But by the end of April 1941, the Greek resistance was finally broken by the German panzers and dive-bombers and the king, his family and the Greek government were taken to Crete, where the Royal Navy had landed Marines and Commonwealth troops. H.M.S. *Valiant* was one of the British warships to escort the Greek exiles to Alexandria. Philip had hoped that his mother, who had left France for Athens at the outbreak of the war would be with the Greek royal party. However Princess Alice, preoccupied with her religious and charitable activities, decided to remain in Greece to look after the wounded. His family was now completely scattered: his mother in Athens, his father in Monte Carlo, his three sisters in Germany. Philip had only infrequent news from any of them, sent through neutral Sweden, where his aunt Louisa Mountbatten was the wife of the Crown Prince.

Some weeks before escorting the Greek royal party, Philip had his baptism of fire in the battle of Cape Matapan which so decisively altered the balance of naval power in the Mediterranean. Three of Italy's heavy cruisers and two destroyers were sunk, the battleship *Vittorio Veneto* and several other warships were heavily damaged, without a single loss to the Royal Navy. Midshipman Philip was in charge of one section of the searchlight controls on *Valiant*. It was a very modest role, and it astonishingly prompted Admiral Sir Charles Morgan to write in his despatches:

'Thanks to Midshipman Prince Philip's alertness and appreciation of the situation, we were able to sink in five minutes two eight-inch-gun Italian cruisers.'

This mention in despatches caused huge amusement in the Royal Navy and much embarrassment for Philip, even though the jokes were at the admiral's expense. It hardly seemed probable that the absence of Midshipman Philip and his searchlight would have stopped the Royal Navy from sinking the Italian cruisers *Zara* and *Fiume*. Philip himself never made any claim to the achievement ascribed to him by Admiral Morgan. Nevertheless his cousin, the King of Greece, hearing of Philip's first naval battle, sent him the Greek War Cross of Valour, which was the first decoration he ever received. Queen Alexandra recalled that when later she congratulated Philip in Cairo on his first gallantry award, 'he just shrugged his shoulders'.

After Philip's participation in the rescue of the Greek Royal Family there was quite a reunion of the Moutbattens at Cairo. With the Greek royalties had also arrived Princess Aspasia and her daughter Alexandra, while Lord Louis Mountbatten and David Milford Haven were on shore-leave. At Shepheard's Hotel, Philip discussed his future with uncle Dickie. Lord Louis told him that he was returning to Britain to take command of the aircraft carrier *Illustrious*. He promised Philip to arrange for him a posting to England to take a course and secure promotion. For a few weeks, while waiting for this, Philip had a pleasant leave in Cairo. Ex-queen Alexandra recalls: 'Now we were all three – with Philip and David – together again, ready to do the town. We went out to a swimming pool or beach and splashed happily in the sun. Philip had contrived to get hold of an absurdly small car. I found my two cousins handsome and attractive beaux. I liked David's lazy smile and Philip's broad grin . . . We went out to the Gezira Club, explored the old bazaars . . . or in a chatty mood went to Groppi's for tea.'[1]

Philip made the journey back to Britain aboard a troopship on a fantastic roundabout route: from Alexandria to Cape Town, across the South Atlantic to Puerto Rico, on to Halifax to take aboard Canadian troops and then in convoy to Britain. During the journey, the Chinese stokers deserted at Puerto Rico, and Philip, with other midshipmen and ratings, was ordered to

[1] Ex-Queen Alexandra of Yugoslavia, op. cit.

'volunteer' for stoking. His trimmer's certificate is still among his proud souvenirs. In England he attended an officers' training course but was not promoted until February 1942, though he was then given nine months' seniority as a sub-lieutenant, because of the good results of his examinations.

During the winter of 1941–42 Philip received his first invitation to Buckingham Palace. He had already been invited before to the homes of other members of the Royal Family, particularly by his cousin, Princess Marina, with whom he had shared nannie 'Roosie'. He spent many week-ends at the Duke and Duchess of Kent's home at Iver. His aunt Nada, widow of his uncle George Milford Haven, presented him to Queen Mary.

That very exacting and outwardly so straitlaced old lady took an immediate liking to the young officer. Philip completely charmed her, although she did not generally approve of 'wild young men'. Philip became a regular caller at Marlborough House. The truth was that Queen Mary, who for two generations had been the model of respectability and the arbiter on dignity and etiquette for the whole Royal Family, was fond of extremely risqué stories. Usually they were provided by General Sir Arthur Slogett, who had been director-general of the Royal Medical Corps in the First World War, and became her consulting physician and trusted friend. At Court he was nicknamed 'Naughty Arthur'. The late Sir Philip Gibbs, the distinguished journalist, novelist and friend of Queen Mary, recalled that most of the stories 'Naughty Arthur' used to tell to the queen 'made my hair curl'. Prince Philip was delighted to tell her some of the un-bowdlerized jokes he had picked up in the Navy, and was commended by Queen Mary as a 'very bright and agreeable young man'.

With this distinctly unusual success at Marlborough House, Philip now qualified to be received at Buckingham Palace and at Sandringham. He was, however, warned to be on his best behaviour when meeting King George VI and Queen Elizabeth. Neither shared Queen Mary's fondness for piquant tales. At first his visits to Buckingham Palace were formal. He was invited with other family members, or with young serving officers of the aristocracy, when there was a tea party or a dance for the young princesses.

In blacked-out London he was now squiring some of the most

beautiful girls who in peace time would have been keenly sought-after debutantes. He was a frequent guest at the 400-Club and the Savoy, where young officers on leave and members of the upper-crust dined and danced during the winter of 1941, in spite of the disastrous news from the Far East.

The gay interlude was soon over. After a course at the naval gunnery school at Whale Island, Philip was posted to the Rosyth Station, and became the youngest sub-lieutenant in the Royal Navy, as 'Number Two' aboard H.M.S. *Wallace,* a flotilla leader of destroyers, covering East Coast convoys. At 20 he was responsible for the discipline, service routine and physical fitness of a fairly large complement of sailors. Between convoy duties in the North Sea and the perilous 'E-boat alley', Philip had an opportunity of visiting the Royal Family at Balmoral.

Ex-Queen Alexandra recalled that Princess Elizabeth told her that Philip's name was not at the time on the Palace mailing list for Christmas and Birthday cards. Elizabeth herself made a point of having this put right and sent him a greeting card, showing portraits of the King, Queen and two princesses, signing it 'Lilibet'. While it is unlikely that Philip was at that time seriously interested in the 16-year-old princess, she began to take a girlish interest in her handsome 'Greek cousin'. Philip looked so much like uncle Dickie, whom she adored, and he seemed to follow in his heroic footsteps.

Lord Louis Mountbatten, now an acting Rear-Admiral, was appointed Chief of Combined Operations by Mr Churchill. The Prime Minister had been an old and intimate friend of Lord Louis's father, and had known Edwina from babyhood, having been a friend of her grandfather, Sir Ernest Cassel. The year 1942, memorable for the raids by Combined Operations on St Nazaire and Dieppe, which Lord Louis had planned and executed, was uneventful for his nephew. However, the first shot fired in anger from Philip's destroyer *Wallace* brought down a raiding Heinkel, and Philip also experienced a few skirmishes with German E-boats. In May 1943 *Wallace* was sent to the Mediterranean, in preparation for the Allied invasion of Sicily. H.M.S. *Wallace* was a leaky old ship, badly in need of repair, and after helping to cover the landing of Canadian troops on Sicily she limped into Malta for refitting. Philip returned to England and remained for several months on home stations.

Practically everyone who was in close contact with the two young people, particularly ex-queen Alexandra who in her memoirs made no secret of her affection for Philip, believes that the Prince seriously began to take notice of 'Lilibet' at Christmas, 1943, when she and Margaret staged the pantomime *Aladdin* at Windsor Castle. Apart from members of the family, only nine guests were invited, but Philip was among them and Princess Elizabeth asked him to take a part in the play. He refused. He was, however, amused at some of the distinctly 'corny' jokes in the otherwise carefully-edited pantomime in which Princess Elizabeth appeared as the Principal Boy, complete with tights, while 13-year-old Princess Margaret played the Princess. Some of the dialogue went thus:

Widow Twankey:	There are three acres and one rod.
Princess:	Please! We don't want anything improper!
Widow Twankey:	And there is a large copper in the kitchen.
Princess:	Oh well, we'll soon get rid of him . . .

During that time Philip lived in an attic of uncle Dickie's house, 16, Chester Street, Belgravia. In spring, 1944, he was promoted Lieutenant, RN and appointed 'Number One' to the new destroyer H.M.S. *Whelp*, which sailed for the Far East in May. His ship later joined the 27th Destroyer Flotilla under Admiral Sir James Somerville and took part in the final operations against Japan. During a shore leave at Sydney Philip wrote in the Guest Book of the Governor General, Lord Gowrie: 'Whither the storm carries me I go a willing guest'. In fact, Philip was practically finished with storms. He had grown his famous golden beard, and in Sydney he was a tremendous success with the ladies. But it was to Princess Elizabeth that some time during the spring of 1945 he sent at her request his photograph, beard and all, with the brief yet meaningful inscription: 'To Elizabeth, Philip'. Now a regular correspondence developed, though it does not appear that King George and Queen Elizabeth showed any enthusiasm about it.

Their anxiety was understandable. At 19 Princess Elizabeth had become the world's most eligible girl. She had been accompanying her mother on many functions and undertaking official engagements of her own, and while it was still not done to discuss escorts and boy friends of the Heiress Presumptive, the reticence of the gossip writers was abandoned when she appeared in the stalls of the Globe Theatre with Margaret and two good-looking officers of the Household Cavalry, instead of accompanying her parents to the Royal Box, or being chaperoned by a Lady in Waiting. From that moment Princess Elizabeth began to occupy a prominent place in the gossip columns. The Hon. Mrs Wills and Captain John Wills of the Life Guards took her to her first supper-restaurant, and afterwards she danced till the early hours with Guards officers. The dances were the Bolero and the Samba, of which the *Evening Standard* remarked, 'These Latin-American dances are not widely known in this country, though they are now being increasingly danced in the West End'.

By January 1946 it was reported that Princess Elizabeth would soon have a suite of her own at Buckingham Palace as well as a country house. The reports were denied. The Princess, extremely keen on horses from babyhood, delighted the racing world with the increasing interest she began to take in the Turf. As the Season revived after the war, she was constantly seen in the company of handsome Guards officers at dances and race meetings.

Some weeks before she celebrated her 20th birthday in April, a journalist, permitted to visit her study at Buckingham Palace, described the room overlooking the Mall: 'Furnished in Victorian style, it has several easy chairs but the centre-piece is a business-like desk where the Princess writes her private letters and also attends to her growing official correspondence.' Apparently the Princess always inspected her daily mail 'because she was an avid stamp collector'. Her 'small but carefully-selected library of books' did not indicate any strong literary taste. There were many books on horses and riding, twelve volumes of Shakespeare, some Robert Louis Stevenson and the works of the Brontë sisters. There was a 'well-thumbed' edition of *The Swiss Family Robinson*, a book about the Scottish Highlands . . . and all the *Just William* books.

At that time the public speculated as to whom the Princess would marry, a problem very much in the minds of the King and Queen and their advisers. There was a worrying absence of acceptable suitors. Of course, there were plenty of German princelings, but the very idea of a marriage to a German relative was out of the question so soon after the war. None of the

Danish or Norwegian princes was of suitable age or standing, and the Heiress Presumptive could marry only a Protestant.

If King George VI was pondering over his daughter's marriage plans, the Mountbattens and 'the Greeks' were already thinking and working hard on behalf of Philip. They had long since abandoned any idea of a marriage between Philip and Alexandra; indeed, she was now the wife of Peter of Yugoslavia, who hoped one day to return to his throne in Belgrade. When King George II of the Hellenes visited London he made a tactless remark in the hearing of several people. To Elizabeth's father he said: 'It was a pity Philip and Alexandra did not get "hitched up", but it might be for the best. How nice it would be if we could re-unite our families and countries through Lilibet and Philip'.

At first, though visibly embarrased, King George VI said nothing, but the Greek king went brashly on: 'It seems Lilibet is in love with Philip, and I know that he adores her'. Usually so self-controlled, King George VI scowled with anger. He clearly resented this surprising frontal attack in public. For a moment he glanced across at his daughter sitting on the far side of the room, chatting and laughing with two young guests. He turned back to George of Greece and said slowly, with his slight stammer: 'Philip had better . . . not think any . . .more . . . about it at present . . . They are both too young.'

Of course, there was far more to it all than the couple's youth. As a father King George VI was not opposed to the match, and Queen Elizabeth apparently now favoured it. Philip could not be dismissed offhand as a suitor. Lord Mountbatten had recently suggested that Philip should become a naturalized British subject, and had reminded the King of Queen Victoria's interest in the Battenbergs, mentioning the marriage of Victoria's favourite daughter Beatrice to Henry of Battenberg. He took the point no further; all he had suggested was that the King should approve of Philip's British naturalization in order to regularize his position in the Royal Navy. The King had several private talks with Mr Churchill, the Leader of the Opposition (who was in favour) and then with the Prime Minister, Mr Attlee, Lord Jowitt, the Lord Chancellor, and Mr Chuter Ede, the Home Secretary, discussing with them the political and constitutional problems arising from a possible engagement of the Heiress to the Throne to a Greek prince.

There were many problems. Greece was in the throes of a civil war; the Communists were openly supported and armed by the Soviet Union, the royal regime in Athens precariously survived only because of the presence of 100,000 British troops, and the British intervention was causing international tension. The Labour Party and Mr Attlee's cabinet were divided over Greece; 86 Labour left-wing backbenchers had published a statement expressing their 'profound sense of horror at what was happening in Greece', and accusing the Greek royal government of 'barbaric atrocities' and 'persecution of democratic leaders'. A marriage of Princess Elizabeth to a Greek prince, however personally removed from Greek politics, might have been unpopular. Through the difficult summer of 1946, while the likelihood of an engagement between Elizabeth and Philip was accepted in informed political circles, both Buckingham Palace and Downing Street were in full agreement that the less said about it the better.

Uncle Dickie, before becoming Viceroy of India, engaged in some delicate and cautious diplomacy among his personal friends who were Labour cabinet members. Philip was seeing Elizabeth regularly, though their meetings remained strictly unpublicized. Ex-king Peter and Alexandra had a house at Sunningdale with a private gate into Windsor Great Park. Philip often stayed with them, and as often, but most discreetly, met Elizabeth for walks and rides in the Park. He also met her at 'Coppins', the home of Princess Marina, the widowed Duchess of Kent. Then, on 19 August 1946, the name of Prince Philip appeared for the first time in the pages of King George vi's Game Book at Balmoral and was mentioned in the Court Circular. He was the youngest of five guests invited to accompany the king for grouse shooting over Tomboddies and Blairglass.

It was at Balmoral that Philip proposed and was accepted. Several years later the Queen revealed in an unguarded moment that this took place 'beside some well-loved loch, the white clouds sailing overhead and the curlew crying'. King George, however, laid it down that a formal announcement must be deferred for at least six months. In any case, a Royal visit to South Africa and Rhodesia was planned for the winter, and the two princesses were to accompany their parents.

However, the royalist Athens newspaper *Hellenicon Aema,*

mouthpiece of the Greek Court, was able to publish in September 1946 the story of the 'impending announcement of the betrothal of Princess Elizabeth to Prince Philip of Greece'. While British newspapers were desperately trying to obtain from Buckingham Palace confirmation or denial of this sensational story, the Press of the rest of the world was splashing the news across the front pages. There was little doubt that the 'leak' had been officially inspired by the Greek king, or his prime minister, in the hope that a link between the British and Greek royal families would strengthen the precarious position of the Greek regime. There was virtual panic at Buckingham Palace, and after consultations with Mr Attlee and Mr Churchill the reports were officially denied, or rather the answer was left open, for a typically ambiguous statement was made: 'No engagement of Her Royal Highness has been announced'. Of course, nobody ever said that it had.

While the Royal Family were on their trip to South Africa and Rhodesia, the reports of their journey replaced rumours of the engagement, but behind the scenes in London top-level conferences and delicate exchanges of views continued nonstop. King George vi had a meticulous regard for both the privileges of, and restrictions on, the British monarchy. The crisis caused by his brother's love affair with Mrs Simpson, which had precipitated him on to the throne, was still a horror in his mind, and the term is not exaggerated. The peril into which the throne had been placed in 1936, and the deep cleavage of opinion it had caused among the British people, had made an everlasting impression on the king. He well knew that the British people and the world were divided on the Greek question, and he dreaded the thought of his beloved daughter becoming the centre, even the target, of a political and constitutional controversy. For Philip to remain a Greek prince would certainly mean just this.

Before the King went to South Africa, he had many conferences with his advisers and elder statesmen, particularly with Winston Churchill. The situation was complicated by the fact that in December 1946 Mr Attlee had approached Viscount Mountbatten to become Viceroy of India, and help the Labour Government to establish full self-government there, or, as opponents of this policy put it, to become 'the grave-digger of the Indian Empire'.

At first, Lord Mountbatten declined. According to one of his biographers, the reason for this initial refusal was that 'he had taken a personal decision to apply his talents to the naval service, and there he wished to remain'.[1] Less kindly disposed observers have put forward the theory that the real reason for Lord Mountbatten's hesitation was that he wanted to make sure that all the obstacles to the betrothal of his nephew were removed before he embarked for New Delhi. That Lord Mountbatten had been the driving force in organising the match between Princess Elizabeth and Prince Philip is undisputable. John W. Wheeler Bennett, in his biography *King George VI*[2] wrote that 'as far back as 1944, four years before Elizabeth's marriage, Lord Mountbatten was urging his nephew's desire . . .'

During his African visit, the king was kept informed on developments. Mr Attlee and Lord Jowitt, the Lord Chancellor, had hit on an apparently happy solution. If Prince Philip would renounce his Greek nationality and all his dynastic rights and privileges in the Greek Royal House, become a British subject and assume a different name, this would remove him from the arena of political controversy. Indeed, such a gesture could be conveniently interpreted as an implied criticism of the current regime in Greece, and an indication that Philip wished to have no part in it whatsoever. Thus Mr Attlee expected to placate any opposition to the match within his own party and make it acceptable to British public opinion.

In great secrecy preparations were made along those lines, without Prince Philip himself being particularly consulted. It was left to uncle Dickie to inform him of the progress that was being made on his behalf, such as the interview with the *Express* editors.

Mr Attlee felt that despite the renunciation of his Greek title, and even after his British naturalization, there was no reason why Philip should not retain the title of a Prince, if only the Danish one. Otherwise, on his marriage he would have to be created a Peer of the Realm, since it was unthinkable that the Heiress to the Throne should marry a commoner. Two senior officials of the College of Heralds, entrusted with the research, suggested that Prince Philip should take the title of 'Prince of Oldcastle' –

[1] Brian Connell in *Manifest Destiny*, Cassell, 1953.
[2] London, Macmillan, 1958.

a translation of the German name of the Dukes of Oldenburg, ancestors of the Danish Royal family of Schleswig-Holstein-Glücksburg-Sonderburg. This was not at all to the liking of uncle Dickie, who in the depth of his heart hoped that the husband of the future Queen would incorporate the name of Mountbatten into his title.

It was the Socialist Home Secretary, Mr (later Lord) Chuter Ede, once a humble schoolteacher and well-known for his commonsense and dry wit, who surprisingly came to Lord Mountbatten's aid. He persuaded King George VI that there was nothing undignified in the suggestion that Prince Philip should assume the maiden name of his mother. 'It is certainly grander and more glittering than Oldcastle,' he told the King and won the day. There was still some talk of making Philip an earl or marquess before the official announcement of the betrothal, but now it was he who rejected the idea. He said he preferred to be known as Lieutenant Philip Mountbatten, RN, although he had to accept the prospect of becoming a duke before leading his bride to the altar.

On 18 March 1947, while the royal family was still in South Africa, a month before Princess Elizabeth's 21st birthday, the *London Gazette* published a list of over 800 naturalizations granted by the Home Office. Some of the names were of Jewish refugees from Germany, others of Poles who had fought during the war with the British troops. One name was that of Prince Philip. It cost Lieutenant Mountbatten £10 2s. 6d. Ten pounds covered the registration duties, the half crown was the Commissioner of Oaths' fee for administering the oath of allegiance of the new British subject 'to His Majesty King George VI and his Heirs and Successors . . .'

Prince Philip's carefree courtship time was now over, for the naturalization announcement led the newspapers to watch his every move. After the Balmoral visit he had been posted to H.M.S. *Royal Arthur* near Corsham in Wiltshire, so that he could be nearer London. While the Royal Family was in Africa, he spent the bitter winter of 1947 in the miserable Nissen huts and prefabricated buildings of the camp. Philip and his fellow officers found refuge in the *Methuen Arms,* playing skittles and drinking beer. Even here reporters found him, and soon there were stories about his letters to Princess Elizabeth. He had dropped the subterfuge of sending them via one of her ladies-in-waiting, and now boldly addressed them to 'H.R.H. The Princess Elizabeth, Buckingham Palace; To be forwarded'. Somebody at the post office mentioned to the reporters letters for Prince Philip arriving regularly from South Africa.

When, one day, Philip was seen by a reporter in front of a jeweller's shop in Bond Street, a newspaper published the story under the banner headline: 'Is Philip buying the ring?' He was not. In fact, the engagement ring he eventually put on his bride's finger had been fashioned from an old one which his mother had given him, although at the Princess's wish, a new square diamond was inserted into a modern setting.

The royal family returned from Africa in the middle of May. Philip was now given extended leaves from Corsham, was seen frequently with Princess Elizabeth in London's West End restaurants and night clubs, but always accompanied by some of the Royal friends. Their visit to a play at the Aldwych Theatre, entitled *The Hasty Heart*, obviously invited more newspaper stories. One paper conducted an 'opinion poll' in which people were asked if they approved of the marriage of Princess Elizabeth to Prince Philip. The result was that 87 per cent voted in favour, only a few disagreed and the rest said 'Don't know'.

At last, on 10 July 1947, after the scattered members of the Mountbatten family and the heads of governments of the Commonwealth had been informed, Buckingham Palace issued the long awaited official announcement:

'It is with the greatest pleasure that the King and Queen announce the betrothal of their dearly beloved daughter The Princess Elizabeth to Lieutenant Philip Mountbatten, RN, son of the late Prince Andrew of Greece and Princess Andrew (Princess Alice of Battenberg), to which union the King has gladly given his consent.'

The Battenbergs in the third generation of their fantastic history were on the threshold of their greatest triumph. It came not so much with the wedding of Philip Mountbatten to Princess Elizabeth, but with the Princess' unexpectedly early accession to the throne. When Elizabeth II inherited the crown in the bizarre circumstances of a tree-top house in a Kenya game reserve, she was a Mountbatten by marriage.

For two months, from 6 February to April 1952, she was a Queen of England of the 'House of Mountbatten'. This glory for the Mountbatten family was historic but constitutionally short-lived. To everyone's surprise, and to the consternation of Philip's relatives, the Queen decided to change the family name to Windsor, her 'maiden name'. On the considered advice of her Prime Minister – Mr Winston Churchill – the Queen issued a proclamation on 9 April 1952, declaring in Council 'her Will and Pleasure' that she and her children and her descendants, other than female descendants who marry, 'shall bear the name of Windsor'.

Philip Mountbatten had been raised to high rank already on the eve of his wedding. At a private investiture at Buckingham Palace, George VI touched his prospective son-in-law with a sword and invested him with the Most Noble Order of the Garter. When Sir Philip Mountbatten rose, the King created him Duke of Edinburgh, Earl of Merioneth and Baron Greenwich.

His dukedom revived a title extinct since the death in 1900 of Queen Victoria's son Prince Alfred, who had been a close friend of Prince Louis of Battenberg, Philip's grandfather. Eight days before the ceremony, the king had given the Order of the Garter to his daughter, to ensure her seniority over her husband in the list of the highest order of chivalry.

Between the announcement of the betrothal and the wedding at Westminster Abbey on 20 November 1947, the newly created Duke of Edinburgh had to cope with a host of worrying matters. Firstly, there was the constitutional problem of the bridegroom's religion. As a member of the Greek royal family, he was baptized after his birth in Corfu in the rites of the Greek-Orthodox Church. He was now quietly received into the Church of England. Then, there was the matter of his finances. Lieutenant Mountbatten had lived on his Service pay, helped to some extent by an allowance from his uncle Dickie. There was also a little money from the estate of his father, the late Prince Andrew. His father's finances were, however, in a somewhat complicated state. As the son of the late King George I of the Hellenes he had been entitled to estates in Greece. A long drawn out probate case had to be settled, which included a litigation, although a purely formal one, conducted on behalf of 'Prince Andrew of Greece, deceased' by the executors, the London solicitors Rehder &

Higgs, against Prince Philip of Greece. The settlement before a judge in the Chancery Division gave Philip only modest funds.

Philip's dreary days at the Corsham hutments were now over. He moved to Kensington Palace as a guest of his 74-year-old grandmother, Princess Victoria, Dowager Marchioness of Milford Haven, where his mother, Princess Andrew of Greece, had also arrived. His valet, who subsequently published his memoirs in America, remarked that 'the young Navy officer brought all his worldly belongings in two suitcases', and 'did not even have a pair of proper hairbrushes'. After his marriage the Duke of Edinburgh could at least look forward to the Royal Navy allowance for a lieutenant's wife, amounting at that time to £4 7s. 6d. a week.

Fortunately, it was not all as bad as that. The king had sent a message to Parliament 'relying on the liberality and affection of his faithful Commons', and Mr Herbert Morrison (the late Lord Morrison of Lambeth), the Leader of the House, set up a Select Committee to examine the financial provisions for the Heiress Presumptive and her husband on their marriage.

The Commons did not show, however, unanimous 'liberality and affection'. By thirteen to five votes the Select Committee eventually approved an arrangement by which the Duke of Edinburgh was to receive a special annuity of £10,000, in addition to an increased annuity of £50,000 for Princess Elizabeth, all payments subject to Income Tax. Because of the economic situation in 1947, and Sir Stafford Cripps' austerity policy, the sum of £10,000 for Philip was regarded as 'adequate', although the House of Commons had voted a century earlier an annuity of £30,000 for Prince Albert on his marriage to Queen Victoria, a sum worth ten times more in purchasing power. Moreover, 'in order to ease the burden on the taxpayers, King George VI voluntarily surrendered £100,000 from the Civil List savings made during the war. This amount alone was sufficient to pay the Duke of Edinburgh's allowance for ten years. On the other hand, the House of Commons did vote a credit of £50,000 for the renovation and furnishing of the home allocated to the newly-married couple: Clarence House hitherto had a single bathroom hidden in a dark cupboard.

Philip was able to make one small saving. He did not have to buy a wedding ring. A nugget of Welsh gold arrived as a gift

Uncle and nephew: Earl
Mountbatten of Burma and
Prince Philip, Duke of
Edinburgh, at Malta.

Admiral of the Fleet Earl Mountbatten of Burma, as First Sea Lord.

The Royal Family at Frogmore House, Windsor (the birthplace of
Earl Mountbatten of Burma). Descendants in the male line who
are not princes will bear the name of Mountbatten-Windsor.

from the people of Wales. It was large and Princess Elizabeth said at once: 'It's big enough for two rings. We can save a piece for Margaret'. It was saved, but it was not used for some years.

Before the wedding ceremony, Philip held the traditional 'stag party'. It took place at the Dorchester Hotel, and the court reporters of the daily newspapers were invited, a somewhat strange decision ascribed to Earl Mountbatten. On the wedding morning there were long descriptions of the 'hilarious incidents'. In fact, however, the press reporters were not invited to Philip's real bachelor party. The first and 'official' stag party ended shortly after midnight after a respectable display of 'hilarity', and the press reporters hurried to Fleet Street to write their stories. Only then did Uncle Dickie invite a small and selected group of male relatives to the famous penthouse on the top floor of the hotel. There Philip celebrated his last night as a bachelor with his cousin David Milford Haven who was his best-man, young King Michael of Rumania, on his last visit as a king from behind the Iron Curtain, and few close friends, unwatched and unembarrassed.

Early in the morning a pale, tired Royal Navy officer was driven in a small, inconspicuous car, to Kensington Palace, passing on the way many thousands of people lying on the pavements, waiting to see the Royal Wedding procession that day. No one even turned a head as the car with the most famous bridegroom of the century went through London's misty November morning.

CHAPTER FOURTEEN

THE NEW GENERATION

THE Queen's loyal subjects, propping up their newspapers against their breakfast marmalade jars on 9 February 1960, were puzzled over a Royal Declaration issued from Buckingham Palace.

It announced the Queen's decision that her descendants – other than her children and the children of her sons, entitled to the style of Royal Highness and the title of Prince and Princess – would bear the name of Mountbatten-Windsor. The announcement came a few days before the birth of the Queen's third child, a son to be named Prince Andrew, after the Duke of Edinburgh's father. The new Declaration thus reversed the Queen's decision announced on 9 April 1952, which had restored the name of Windsor to all her descendants. A Buckingham Palace spokesman cryptically explained: 'The Queen has always wanted to associate her husband's family name with their descendants; she has had this in mind for a long time and it is close to her heart.'

The official announcement was couched in archaic language and was not easy to understand, but the newspapers explained, with the help of experts on royal genealogy and constitutional law that, in fact, only some of the great-grandchildren of the Queen and Prince Philip would bear the imposing new dynastic name.

One writer ingeniously explained that the first 'Royal Mountbattens' would probably not appear before the year 2000. If Prince Charles, the Prince of Wales, married in 1969 at the age

of 21 – which the writer believed unlikely – and a year later had
a son, who would also marry at 21, in 1991, and he had two
sons, then the second grandson of Prince Charles in, say 1995,
would be the first Hon. Mountbatten-Windsor. Even this would
happen only if Prince Charles had not by then ascended the
throne, otherwise all the king's younger sons would have royal
titles, such as Duke of York or Duke of Cambridge. However,
in the twenty-first century, there would be some 'Royal Mountbatten-Windsors', because the grandsons of the younger sons
of the Queen – Prince Andrew and Prince Edward – would
bear this name without a royal predicate and would not be
entitled to the style of Royal Highness.

The new Declaration, providing for the name of Mountbatten
to be linked with that of Windsor from the third generation
onwards, produced some critical comments in the British Press.
While the *Daily Telegraph* stated that 'it was the normal practice
of the Queen's subjects that a child uses the name of his father's
family, and this personal wish, natural in an expectant mother,
had become stronger than ever . . .', views expressed in some
newspapers were less kind. The *Daily Mirror* described it as a
'Curious Decision', and asked: 'Is the decision prudent? If it is
prudent is it necessary? If it is necessary, is it well timed?',
reminding its readers that 'it is only fifteen years after the second
world war against Germany that the British nation are abruptly
informed that the name Mountbatten, formerly Battenberg, is
to be joined willy nilly with the name of Windsor, formerly
Hanover.' Even more unkindly, the *Mirror*'s leader writer quoted
the Queen's much criticised speech, back in October 1958 during
the visit of the German Federal President in London, when she
said 'the connection between my family and the old states of
Germany goes back for many generations'.

Some newspapers were quick to infer, either by innuendo or
question, that the whole idea was not really the Queen's but that
of Earl Mountbatten of Burma, known for his concern to
perpetuate his name in history. After asking whether the Prime
Minister and the Cabinet 'were merely informed, or did they
agree?', the *Daily Mirror* declared that 'Earl Mountbatten was
fully aware of what was going on', while the *Daily Mail* wrote
that the announcement 'which will hyphenate the newly-forged
Mountbatten name indissolubly to the British Crown, can have

brought profounder gratification to no one more than Earl
Mountbatten, son of Prince Louis of Battenberg, whose name
did not then ring sweetly in British ears, and uncle of Prince
Philip . . . certainly the most controversial figure in this forcefully
successful family.'

The *Daily Express* – at that time distinctly unfriendly to
Earl Mountbatten – followed the official announcement with a
dramatic 'disclosure':

'While he has sat in his office in Whitehall and pondered
the problems of defence, or the Navy, or whatever high
position he happened to be holding, one spectre has always
confronted Earl Mountbatten of Burma: that his family name
should finally die out. For he himself has two daughters now,
both married . . . and he has a nephew who is the Marquess
of Milford Haven. And another who holds perhaps the greater
honour and responsibility than any other member of his
ancient family – Prince Philip. Small wonder then that Lord
Mountbatten, whose devotion to his heritage is little short of
fanatical, has for many years nursed a secret ambition. That one
day, the name of the ruling house of Britain might be Mountbatten . . . Within the conclave of the family, Lord Mountbatten
has raised the matter more than once: suggested that even if
the name of Windsor be retained, the name of Mountbatten
might also be included.

'Prince Philip himself was less concerned than his uncle in
the future of the name, though he took pains to see that the
Prince of Wales should know of his heritage. He sent over to
German genealogists to secure a complete family tree for
Prince Charles to see. Through all this, the Queen remained
steadfast in one respect. She could never see the name of
Windsor, chosen by her grandfather, abandoned by the royal
house. On the other hand, she sympathised with her husband's
feelings – and more particularly with the overtures of his
uncle. So, the compromise. Her descendants – though not
those who stand in direct line to the Throne – shall carry the
name Mountbatten-Windsor . . . Will Lord Mountbatten be
a happier man in his office this morning? I suspect so. Though
he may well be dreaming still of things that might have
been.'

The *Daily Express* writer, revealing his inside information of what had been happening 'within the conclave of the family', added that Lord Mountbatten had 'found there is no male line to carry on the family name'. It did not need much finding. In fact, Lord Mountbatten had made provision, many years before the Queen's declaration, that not only his name but also his earldom, viscounty and barony should not become extinct.

When he was created a Viscount on 23 August 1946 a 'Special Remainder' was incorporated into his Letter Patent, whereby 'in default of heirs male of his body', his title should go 'to his elder daughter and the heirs male of her body, and to every other daughter successively in order of seniority of age and priority of birth, and to the heirs male of their bodies'. This provision was also included in the Letter Patent when Lord Mountbatten was created an Earl of the United Kingdom and Baron Romsey on 23 October 1947. Such 'remainders' had been granted by the Sovereign on previous occasions. In simple language it means that on Lord Mountbatten's death, his elder daughter, Lady Patricia, married to the 7th Baron Brabourne, would become a Countess Mountbatten in her own right, even though she might not use the title nor take the seat in the House of Lords. As she is the mother of five strapping sons, there can be no doubt that on her death there will be an heir to the grandfather's titles, and that another Earl Mountbatten of Burma sometime in the twenty-first century will bear the proud name. No doubt he will have some 'Royal' Mountbatten-Windsors as his contemporaries.

So long as Earl Mountbatten is alive – and at the time of writing, although past his 65th year, he enjoys excellent health and undiminished vigour – he is generally regarded as 'the' Mountbatten, the head of the ebullient family which during three generations had moved close to the very centre of the Establishment. But, in fact, he is not the head of the family, but only of its junior line, or, in the parlance of genealogists, the 'secundo-geniture'.

In 1917, when the 'English' Battenbergs changed their name to Mountbatten, there were only five male members who assumed it: Admiral Prince Louis of Battenberg, the former First Sea Lord, his two sons, 25-year-old Prince George and 17-year-old Prince Louis (the present Earl), and the two surviving sons of the late Prince Henry of Battenberg and Princess Beatrice, Prince Alexander and Prince Leopold. There was also still alive the fourth son of Prince Alexander of Hesse, Prince Francis Joseph von Battenberg, then 56 years old and married to the daughter of King Nicholas of Montenegro. He lived abroad, kept the name of Battenberg until his death in 1924, and, his marriage having remained childless, the Battenberg line became extinct. There was also living a son of the late Prince Alexander (Sandro) von Battenberg, the former ruler of Bulgaria. But hapless Sandro, after his abdication, the end of his romance with the German Emperor's granddaughter, and his subsequent marriage to the opera singer Johanna Loisinger, had renounced his family name and called himself Count Hartenau; his only son, Assen, was legally no more a Battenberg.

Within days of the 'English' Battenbergs becoming Mountbattens, King George v created the family's head, Admiral Prince Louis, a Marquess of Milford Haven; his elder son George received the courtesy title of Earl of Medina, while his younger son became Lord Louis Mountbatten. Likewise, the elder son of the late Henry of Battenberg was made the Marquess of Carisbrooke, his younger brother became Lord Leopold Mountbatten. With Leopold's death in 1922, eventually only one sole male member remained to carry on the family's name – Lord Louis, the present Earl, if one disregards the fact that his nephew Philip used it temporarily after abandoning his royal titles of Greece and Denmark, before becoming the Duke of Edinburgh.

The senior line, or 'primogeniture', of the Marquesses of Milford Haven is today represented by third and fourth generations. The elder son of the first Marquess, George, died in 1938, leaving two children, Lady Elizabeth Tatiana, born in 1917, and David, born on 12 May 1919, who inherited the title in 1938, and who is the present head of the Mountbatten family. A schoolfellow of Prince Philip at the Cheam prep, he chose like his father and grandfather the naval career, and passing out from Dartmouth became a Midshipman in 1937. At the outbreak of the war he was a Sub-Lieutenant on H.M.S. *Kandahar,* went through the Signals Course, became a Flotilla Signal Officer, later saw war service with the British Pacific Fleet, and was a Staff Signal Officer in the Far East during the final stages of the war against Japan, winning a D.S.C. and an O.B.E. After the war he served with the Naval Air Arm, and in 1947 was his cousin Philip's best man at his wedding to Princess Elizabeth.

A year later her retired from the Royal Navy and went into business, working for an American company and living in the United States. His marriage in 1950 to a beautiful young American divorcée, Mrs Romaine Dahlgren Simpson (no relation to the Duchess of Windsor) caused surprise in London Society. The young Marquess, so closely related to the royal family, had been a very eligible bachelor and was expected to make a great marriage in the British aristocracy or plutocracy. His American marriage ended in 1954 in a Mexican divorce. His former wife – 'Doddy' to her friends – has since been often in the news as a sought-after fashion model, the organiser of charities and a smart Manhatten hostess.

After his divorce, the Marquess returned to London where he acquired various business interests. At that time his name was linked with that of the Hungarian-born film star Eva Bartok, who introduced him to a 'spiritual group', called Pak Sabuh, presided over by an Indian mystic and holding séances at a house in Kingston-on-Thames. For more than three years the Marquess' friendship with Eva Bartok and his attendances of the Puk Sabuh rituals nurtured the gossip columns. In December 1957 the *Daily Mail* reported that 'the 38-year-old Marquess of Milford Haven and Miss Bartok would marry soon'.

When Miss Bartok shortly afterwards gave birth to a daughter, she was besieged by reporters, but refused to disclose the name of her child's father. The Marquess refused to confirm or deny his marriage plans, but his mother told the Press that her son 'would certainly not marry Miss Bartok'. In turn, the Marquess issued a statement that he 'had not told his mother that he did not intend to marry Miss Bartok', and he referred to the uncertainty of his legal position regarding his Mexican divorce.[1] Then Miss Bartok stated that she and the Marquess 'intend to marry soon'.[2] In October of that year the Marquess filed a petition in the High Court, asking that his Mexican divorce in 1954 should be declared valid in Britain. This revived reports of his impending marriage to the Hungarian film-star. However, on

[1] *Daily Telegraph*, 27 January 1958.
[2] *Daily Mail*, 20 May 1958.

22 October 1958, Miss Bartok formally announced that she would marry the wealthy Indian Prince Shiv, and that she and the Marquess of Milford Haven 'had come to the parting of the ways three months ago'.[1] In December it was reported that the Marquess had lost his case in the High Court, and that after lengthy hearings and several adjournments his El Paso divorce decree was not confirmed. At that time he was a frequent escort of a beautiful London fashion model, 20-year-old Miss Liese Denz. But on 11 November 1959 he told newspaper reporters that this friendship had ended.[2] Early in 1960 a new legal process to obtain a validation of the El Paso divorce was successful and his marriage to Doddy Dahlgren Simpson was finally dissolved according with British law.

In the late autumn of 1960, the Marquess announced his engagement to 22-year-old Miss Janet Bryce, another beautiful model, whose British father had been a wealthy New York stockbroker until his death eight years earlier. The bride had spent her childhood in the Bahamas and in Bermuda, where her family owned estates, and she came to England at the age of 19. The gossip column years between the Marquess' appearance as the best man at the Royal Wedding in 1947 and his engagement to Miss Bryce in 1960, did not endear him at Court. This might have accounted for the fact that neither the Queen nor the Duke of Edinburgh attended his wedding on 17 November 1960 at St Andrew's Church, Hampstead. Instead, at the same hour, Prince Philip was visiting the Employment Exchange at Holloway, two miles away.

Nevertheless, the reception at Claridge's was a great if somewhat unconventional occasion. Royal lustre was provided by the presence of the bridegroom's aunt, the Queen of Sweden. Earl Moutbatten was, of course, among the 500 guests, who included such diverse personalities as Lord and Lady Astor, Mr Charles Clore, fashion designer Hardy Amies, ace-jockey Lester Pigott and 'the king of gamblers' Mr John Aspinall, together with a throng of newspaper reporters, who were not disappointed. Some of them commented that it was a 'Knees-up Wedding', with dancing at the reception to the music of jazz pianist Cliff Hall, specially imported from New York for the occasion.

[1] *Daily Mail*, 22 October 1958.
[2] *Daily Express*, 11 November 1959.

On 6 July 1961 it was announced that a son was prematurely born to the Marchioness of Milford Haven. He was baptized George (after his paternal grandfather), Ivor (after his mother's uncle, Mr Ivor Bryce, a Holywood film producer) and Louis (after his great-uncle, the Earl Mountbatten). At birth the baby had become the Earl of Medina. In 1963 a second son was born and given the first name of Ivor, with Alexander and Michael to follow. Little Ivor is now the only other Lord Mountbatten.

Turning to the descendants of Henry of Battenberg and Princess Beatrice, and thus in direct line from Queen Victoria, only their eldest son, Alexander – the later Marquess of Carisbrooke[1] – and their daughter Ena – Queen Victoria Eugenie of Spain – married and had children. The Marquess married in 1917 Lady Irene Denison, daughter of the 2nd Earl of Londesborough, and had only one child, Lady Iris Victoria Beatrice Grace Mountbatten, born in 1920.

Brought up so near the British Throne, spending her girlhood holidays at Windsor and Sandringham, visiting her aunt at the Spanish Court and her royal German relations, a trainbearer to Queen Elizabeth at King George VI's Coronation in 1936, she was expected to marry one of her princely relatives, or into British or foreign nobility. But Lady Iris betrayed already as a young girl the unpredictable Mountbatten temperament as well as Mountbatten talents. At the age of 19 she fell in love with a handsome 31-year-old Irish Guards officer, Captain Hamilton Keyes O'Malley and, despite family misgivings, married him in February 1941 at a quiet war-time wedding. The marriage was, however, not happy and ended in divorce in 1946. Lady Iris resumed her maiden name of Mountbatten by deed poll and went to America. There she tried several careers – modelling, song writing, working in a New York department store, commentating on television.

Then, in 1957, she married Mr Michael Kelly Bryan, a well-known guitarist, but this marriage lasted for only a few months. A son, Robin Alexander, was born at Christmas 1957, some months after the marriage was dissolved by an Alabama court. Lady Iris had become estranged from her royal cousins; she had neither been invited to the wedding of the King's daughter to Prince Philip, nor to the Queen's Coronation, which was attended

[1] See *supra* page 119.

by the entire adult and adolescent Mountbatten brood, including the German and Greek relatives. Her second marriage had been omitted from Burke's Peerage, the explanation being that she had not obtained the Sovereign's consent, and, as she was affected by the Royal Marriage Act, doubts existed whether the American marriage was valid in Britain. Yet, privately, she kept in touch with her family and paid her first visit to London in 1956 after seven years of absence, when her mother was on her death bed.

Stories about Lady Iris's life in America continued to appear in newspapers on both sides of the Atlantic – how she was managing New York night club singers; how her son Robin was being brought up with a tame cheetah; how she was faced with a bill for £600 for the upkeep of her mastiff 'Butch'. In December 1965, at the age of 45, Lady Iris Mountbatten – she had abandoned both her married names of O'Malley and Bryan – often unaccountably described in American gossip columns as 'Prince Philip's Favourite Cousin', announced that she had married for the third time. The bridegroom was Mr Bill Kemp, a Canadian actor and television announcer, a widower with a 10-year-old daughter, Sharon. He told reporters: 'I had known Lady Iris for twelve years; her son and my daughter used to play together. We shall live in Toronto and Iris plans to work in public relations.' As the Marquess of Carisbrooke had made no provision for a 'Special Remainder' of his title, young Robin Bryan has no chance of ever becoming a Peer of the Realm. With the death of his grandfather the marquessate of Carisbrooke had become extinct. The children and grandchildren of Queen Ena of Spain are 'semi-Battenbergs', too. They have been mentioned elsewhere in this book.

Much closer to the family fold are, of course, Prince Philip's sisters, the 'Greek princesses' who had all married German Princes. Theirs is a large and flourishing side-line of the Battenberg-Mountbatten tribe. Prince Philip had, over the years, acquired nineteen nephews and nieces and, at a rather early age, is also a great-uncle several times over. To enumerate them all would make a long catalogue of German names. Several of his nephews and nieces are frequent visitors to Buckingham Palace and the Royal country homes; one was Prince Charles's schoolfellow at Gordonstoun. Since 1962 the two older children of the

Queen have paid with their father several private visits to their German cousins, and the Queen met several of them during her State Visit in Germany in 1965.

Prince Philip's eldest sister, Princess Margarita, became a widow at the age of 55, when her husband, Prince Gottfried Hermann von Hohenlohe-Langenburg, died in May 1960. The present head of the family is her eldest son, Prince Kraft Alexander Ernst Louis, born in 1935, and she has three other sons, two of them twins born in 1944, and a daughter, named Beatrice, born in 1936.

The second sister, Princess Theodora, lost her husband, Margrave Berthold of Baden, when she was 57 in 1963. Of retiring disposition, she lives with her eldest son Margrave Max (born in 1933) in the baroque splendour of Schloss Salem, a few miles from the Lake of Constance. She has another son Louis and a daughter, Margarita, married to Prince Tomislav of Yugoslavia.

The third sister, Cecilia, wife of Grand Duke Georg Donatus of Hesse, had lost her life with her husband and their two small sons in the tragic aircraft crash in 1937;[1] her baby daughter, Jeanne Marina, had been left behind, but she died at the age of three in 1939.

The fourth of the 'Greek princesses', Princess Sophia, believed to be Prince Philip's favourite sister, produced eight children from her two marriages, the first to Prince Christopher of Hesse, known as 'the Nazi Cri', because he was an S.S. Standartenfuhrer (Colonel) and adjutant of Gestapo chief Heinrich Himmler. During the war he joined the Luftwaffe, and having taken part in bombing raids on London was shot down by an R.A.F. fighter in Italy on 7 October 1943. From this marriage Princess Sophia had five children, two sons and three daughters. The eldest boy was named Karl Adolf; his second name, which he does not use anymore, was chosen in honour of the Führer.

The close link between the German Battenberg descendants and the Royal Family can be judged from the fact that Prince Karl came in October 1965 to London to tell his uncle Philip of his engagement to the young Hungarian Countess Yvonne Szapary. The 28-year-old Hesse prince had been partly educated in Britain, and his uncle later arranged for him to attend an estate management course with the Council of the Duchy of Cornwall,

[1] See *supra* page 245.

of which the Duke of Edinburgh is the head; the income from the Duchy's estates goes, since the times of the Black Prince in the fourteenth century, to the Sovereign's eldest son, the Prince of Wales. Prince Karl of Hesse had inherited from his father the magnificent Castle of Kronberg near Frankfurt, where his mother and some of his brothers and sisters now live. At one time there were rumours that Prince Karl would marry Princess Alexandra of Kent. He was her frequent escort in the early 1960s, before her marriage to Mr Angus Ogilvy.

Prince Karl's sister, Christina Margarete, born in 1933, had also lived in Britain for several years, had been a regular visitor of the Royal Family and at the Mountbatten home at Broadlands. She was married to Prince Andrej of Yugoslavia, the brother of ex-king Peter, but this marriage was dissolved in 1962. For some years she lived with her two children on a Berkshire farm, and in 1962 married the London painter, Mr Robert Flores van Eyck, an exponent of modern art and sixteen years her senior. From her second marriage she has also two children, Prince Philip's great-nieces. When she and her husband were househunting, the Mountbatten family came to their aid: Lady Pamela Hicks, Earl Mountbatten's younger daughter, put at their disposal the Hickses' country house at Britwell Salome in Oxfordshire.

Princess Sophia had remarried in 1946. Her second husband is Prince Georg Wilhelm of Hanover, closely related to the Royal Family through the Hanoverian Georges. From this marriage Princess Sophie has three more children, two boys and a girl. Being the youngest of Prince Philip's sisters, she is still an attractive woman. Two of her children, Prince Welf and Prince Georg Paul, are of the same age as the Prince of Wales and Princess Anne, while the youngest girl was born in 1954. Sophia is closest to Prince Philip, and accompanied by some of her children visits the Royal Family regularly. Prince Philip, too, has paid many private visits to her home in Germany. In December 1960 he persuaded her to be his passenger on a flight from Frankfurt to Turin when he piloted the aircraft. The flight was a bad weather adventure, with unscheduled landings at Zurich and Nice, but Prince Philip expertly managed to avoid disaster.

In April 1962, five days after his return from his memorable tour of South America, Prince Philip took his eldest son on his first visit to the German Battenberg cousins. While his father

was piloting the scarlet four-engine Heron aircraft, Prince
Charles sat behind him in the cockpit. Since then Prince Charles
and Princess Anne have visited and welcomed their cousins
on many occasions. In the winter of 1963 the Prince of Wales
spent a ski-ing holiday at Tarasp in Switzerland with his cousin
Prince Ludwig of Hesse, Cecilia's brother-in-law. On another
occasion his father took him for boar-hunting to the estates of
the Hanover relatives. Many of these German cousins were
regularly entertained by Earl Mountbatten at Broadlands and in
the homes of his daughters.

Thus, we finally turn to the branch of the Mountbatten family
which is regarded as the genuinely British one – the family of
Earl Mountbatten of Burma, whose eldest grandson will one
day inherit his name and titles – and what will remain of the
Cassel millions and treasures.

Both the daughters of the Earl's marriage to Edwina Ashley
are married. The childhood of Patricia and Pamela Mountbatten
was spent in the splendour of Brook House, the comfort of
'Adsdean' and Casa Medina in Malta, the magnificence of Broadlands and the serenity of the Irish estates. But when they were
still quite young, war overshadowed the happiness of their
family life. When Lord and Lady Mountbatten were on war
duties, they were parted from their daughters for many months
and even years, and saw them only during brief leaves.

In war and peace, however, it was a happy family, and the two
girls were brought up by their sophisticated and progressively-
minded parents less conventionally than most of their class.
Obviously their parents were deeply concerned with their
education. The girls were put to war-work; their father maintaining that it was their duty as members of the Royal Family,
their mother believing that they should serve humanity. Patricia
joined the Women's Royal Naval Service as a rating, was trained
as a signaller at Portsmouth, shared many hardships of war
service with girls from humbler homes, and eventually was
commissioned with the rank of a Third Officer (equivalent to a
Sub-Lieutenant in the Royal Navy) and went to Delhi, and later
to Singapore, where she served on her father's staff.

At that time Patricia met Captain John Ulick Knatchbull, who
had become the 7th Baron Brabourne on the death of his brother
Norton. His brother had been a Lieutenant in the Grenadier

Guards, was wounded during the Allied invasion of Italy and taken prisoner; during the transport to a P.o.W. camp, he escaped from the train despite his wounds, was recaptured and shot by the Germans in September 1943.

Lord Brabourne, who is the same age as Patricia, had joined the Coldstream Guards on leaving Eton, fought in Malaya, was severely wounded and eventually became one of Lord Mountbatten's A.D.C.s at SEAC. At one time part of his duties was to assist Lady Mountbatten with her welfare work, and he became almost a member of the family. It was only natural that the two young people were drawn together and fell in love with each other. Their engagement was announced in January 1946 in Singapore, and the following October Patricia Mountbatten and Lord Brabourne were married at Romsey Abbey by the Archbishop of Canterbury. Patricia's bridesmaids were Princess Elizabeth, Princess Margaret, Princess Alexandra of Kent and her sister Pamela.

Despite post-war austerity, the wedding reception at Broadlands was a splendid occasion, attended by 1,300 guests, including the entire Royal Family headed by King George VI, who proposed the bride's and bridegroom's health. Two special receptions were held for the farmers, estate workers and tenants both from Broadlands and the bridegroom's estates at Mersham-le-Hatch in Kent, brought by special train, and for 500 citizens of Romsey. Lord Mountbatten must have been gratified by his elder daughter's marriage to a scion of an ancient and noble family, which had held land in Kent at the times of Edward II, and had owned the Mersham estates since 1485. Many of Lord Brabourne's ancestors had rendered distinguished service to king and country; there had always been a Knatchbull in the House of Commons since the eighteenth century; several had been Cabinet ministers, and one a Governor of Bombay and Bengal who, curiously enough, had been one of Earl Mountbatten's predecessors as acting Viceroy of India in 1938. Another kinsman was Sir Hughe Knatchbull-Hugessen, British ambassador in Turkey during the war, who became best known through the 'Cicero' spy affair at the Ankara embassy, Patricia, who, like her sister, had been a girlhood friend of the two Royal princesses, inherited from her mother not only her good looks and elegant figure, but also her dedication to public service. Because of the war and her war service she had missed the social round of a debutante, but she seemed not to have regretted it. She is a devoted wife and mother of a large family, but she nevertheless takes a prominent part in the community life in Kent, and has quietly done much good work in various social and charitable organisations. After the war Lord Brabourne became a film producer and his company had made some remarkable films, including *Sink the Bismarck* in 1959 and *H.M.S. Defiant* in 1961, sagas of sea battles which must have pleased his father-in-law.

At the time of writing the Brabournes have seven children. The eldest, Norton Louis Philip, born in 1947, is a godson of Prince Philip, and the heir to the barony of Brabourne as well as to the earldom of Mountbatten. His younger brother, Michael John Ulick, born in 1950, is a godson of the Queen. Two boys are twins, born in 1964, and there is another boy, Philip Ashley, and two girls, Joanna Edwina and Amanda Patricia.

Earl Mountbatten's younger daughter, Pamela, married when she was 31, comparatively late considering that she must have been a sought-after match. She had remained a close friend of the Queen and Princess Margaret, was a bridesmaid to the Queen, and for several years her Lady-in-Waiting. She accompanied her on that memorable visit to Kenya in 1952 during which King George VI died, and was also with the Queen and Duke of Edinburgh during their Commonwealth tour in 1953 and 1954. She is a wealthy woman, having received at birth a considerable legacy under the will of her great-grandfather, Sir Ernest Cassel.

During the war, as a schoolgirl, she joined the Girl Guides on her mother's suggestion, and for many years, as far as her Court duties permitted it, took an active interest in youth club organisations. In 1955 she became the first Commandant of the Girls' Nautical Training Corps. The announcement on 2 November 1959 of her engagement to Mr David Hicks caused surprise. Many people failed to understand that the choice of her heart had fallen upon a handsome, young and talented interior decorator then not yet well known. Even newspaper reporters found it difficult to discover further details about Mr Hicks' family and background, apart from the facts that his father, dead for many years, had been a London stockbroker and that his mother lived in Belgravia. In fact, David Hicks was a brilliant young designer who had made a name in architectural circles and had established a prosperous studio, working for many wealthy clients.

London Society might have expected a more spectacular marriage for Lady Pamela, but her parents, as well as her royal cousins, knowing of her discreet romance and her great happiness, certainly approved of her choice. Her wedding took place on 13 January 1960 at Romsey Abbey, and 1,200 guests were invited to the reception at Broadlands. The Queen, expecting the birth of her third child, was unable to attend, but all the other members of the Royal Family were there, led by Queen Elizabeth the Queen Mother. It was a harsh wintry day, with a blizzard raging, but this did not prevent the occasion from being one of the biggest gatherings of the whole Mountbatten tribe, led by the bride's aunt, the Queen of Sweden. Princess Anne was one of the bridesmaids, others included two German nieces of Prince Philip, who toasted the newly-married couple.

When the great party assembled among the splendour of the Cassel treasures, to admire the display of 900 wedding presents, including a pair of aquamarine pendant ear-rings from the Queen, the lights suddenly failed. The weather was to blame for the power failure, but Earl Mountbatten soon organized with military precision a procession of footmen carrying five-branched candelabra, and the reception went on by the romantic light of candles.

For Lady Mountbatten it was the last happy family occasion. Five days afterwards she left for North Borneo and a month later she was dead, thousands of miles away from her loved ones. Lady Pamela – in 1966 the mother of two children, a girl named Edwina and a baby-boy, Ashley, whose godfathers are Prince Philip and the King of Sweden, prefers life in the country. She and her husband bought a fine eighteenth-century mansion, Britwell, near Watlington in Oxfordshire, and they also have a town house in London's Knightsbridge, next door to the Brabournes.

Earl Mountbatten of Burma, after his retirement from the Ministry of Defence, had put up his London house for sale and had gone to live at Broadlands. Between his travels, on fine summer days, this still youthful grandfather and great-uncle can enjoy there a muster of his family's new generation, whose ages range from near-twenty to babyhood, all of them handsome and gifted – like all Mountbattens; a family which includes the future British Sovereign. Will Earl Mountbatten, all through his incredibly busy life so greatly concerned with the destinies of his family, be satisfied with the serenity of an Indian Summer? It would be surprising if this champion of a thousand causes should feel that his restless mind and untamed energy would find a sufficient outlet in pottering in his gardens.

When on that November night of 1851 at sleepy Darmstadt the Grand Duke of Hesse decided to make 'the little Polish orphan' a Countess of Battenberg in order to preserve decorum, who could have foreseen the tempestuous and majestic progress of her descendants?

Her sons established a family destined to become one of the most coherent and influential in many centres of power, to hold sway over many great and mighty figures of history, and to flourish beyond its founders' dreams. Its members were tangled with the toy kingdoms and vanished principalities of old Germany, the emergence and twilight of the German Reich, the downfall of the Second French Empire, the tortuous Eastern Question, the age-long, seemingly immortal reign of Queen Victoria, the maritime ascendancy of the British Empire and its transformation into a multi-racial Commonwealth. They stood at the fulcrum of Europe's balance of power, witnessed the glories and the decline of Tsardom, the see-saw fortunes of Greek royalty, the collapse of the Spanish monarchy. They played distinguished and gallant parts in two World Wars, and they remained on the world stage as the vast-beyond-imagining drama of social, political, economic and strategic revolution unrolls before our own eyes.

A century ago the few names of the obscure family deserved but a paragraph in the pages of the Almanach de Gotha. Within the century the extraordinary family grew into a mighty clan whose interlinked circles continue to encompass many centres of power. Its members share the vigour and tenacity of purpose so characteristic of the Battenberg and Mountbatten heritage.

Genealogical table of the Battenberg and Mountbatten Family

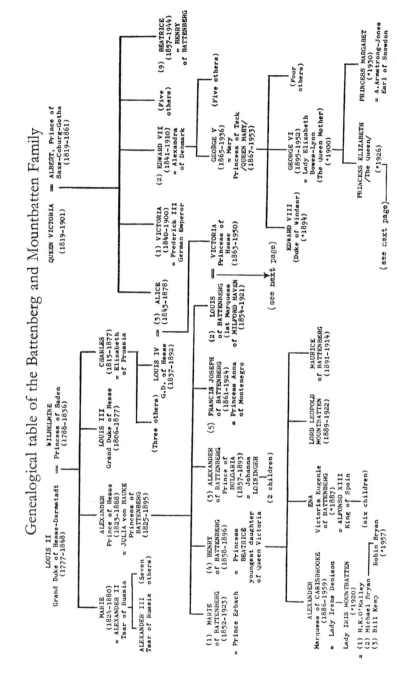

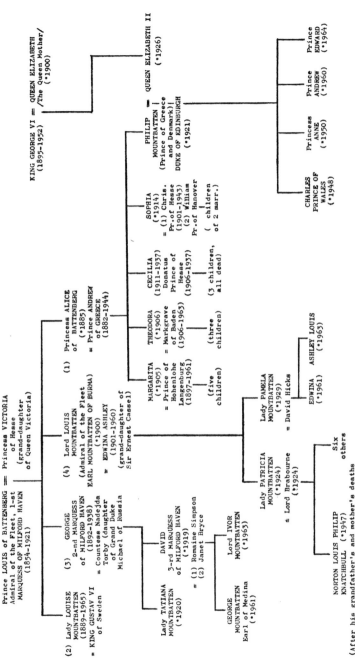

Prince LOUIS of BATTENBERG ═══ Princess VICTORIA
Admiral of the Fleet, 1-st   of Hesse
MARQUESS OF MILFORD HAVEN   (grand-daughter
(1854-1921)   of Queen Victoria)

(2) Lady LOUISE   (3) GEORGE   (4) Lord LOUIS
    MOUNTBATTEN   2-nd MARQUESS   MOUNTBATTEN
    (1889-1965)   of MILFORD HAVEN   (Admiral of the Fleet
= KING GUSTAV VI   (1892-1938)   EARL MOUNTBATTEN OF BURMA)
  of Sweden   = Countess Nadejda   (*1900)
                           Torby (daughter   = EDWINA ASHLEY
                           of Grand Duke   (1901-1960)
                           Michael of Russia)   (grand-daughter of
                                                           Sir Ernest Cassel)

(1) Princess ALICE
    of BATTENBERG
    (*1885)
  = Prince ANDREW
    of GREECE
    (1882-1944)

DAVID
3-rd MARQUESS
of MILFORD HAVEN
(*1919)
= (1) Romaine Simpson
  (2) Janet Bryce

Lady TATIANA
MOUNTBATTEN
(*1920)

GEORGE
MOUNTBATTEN
Earl of Medina
(*1961)

Lord IVOR
MOUNTBATTEN
(*1963)

Lady PATRICIA
MOUNTBATTEN
(*1924)
& Lord Brabourne
(*1924)

Lady PAMELA
MOUNTBATTEN
(*1929)
= David Hicks

MARGARITA
(*1905)
= Prince of
  Hohenlohe
  Langenburg
  (1897-1961)

(five
children)

THEODORA
(*1906)
= Markgrave
  of Baden
  (1906-1963)

(three
children)

CECILIA
(1911-1937)
Donatus
Prince of
Hesse
(1906-1937)

(3 children,
all dead)

SOPHIA
(*1914)
= (1) Chris.
  Pr.of Hesse
  (1901-1943)
  (2) William
  Pr.of Hanover

(children
of 2 marr.)

NORTON LOUIS PHILIP
KNATCHBULL (*1947)

Six
others

EDWINA
(*1961)

ASHLEY LOUIS
(*1963)

(After his grandfather's and mother's deaths
he will be 2-nd EARL MOUNTBATTEN OF BURMA)

PHILIP
MOUNTBATTEN
(Prince of Greece
and Denmark)
DUKE OF EDINBURGH
(*1921)

KING GEORGE VI ═══ QUEEN ELIZABETH
(1895-1952)   /The Queen Mother/
                    (*1900)

═══ QUEEN ELIZABETH II
    (*1926)

CHARLES
PRINCE OF
WALES
(*1948)

Princess
ANNE
(*1950)

Prince
ANDREW
(*1960)

Prince
EDWARD
(*1964)

SELECTED BIBLIOGRAPHY

ADLER, C., *Jacob H. Schiff*, London, Heinemann, 1929.

ALEXANDRA OF YUGOSLAVIA, *Prince Philip, A Family Portrait*, Hodder, 1959.

PRINCESS ANDREW OF GREECE, *Towards Disaster*, London, 1930.

ANONYMOUS, *Uncensored Recollections*, London, Lippincott, 1924.

ARTHUR, G., *King George V*, London, Cape, 1929.

BEAL, E., *Royal Cavalcade*, London, Stanley Paul, 1939.

PRINCESS BEATRICE, *A Birthday Book*, London, Smith Elder, 1881.

BENSON, E. F., *As We Are*, Longmans, London, 1932.

BENSON, E. F., *King Edward VII*, London, Longmans, 1933.

BENSON, E. F., *The Kaiser and English Relations*, London, Longmans, 1936.

BENSON, E. F., *Daughters of Queen Victoria*, London, Cassell, 1939.

BISMARCK, O., *Gedanken und Erinnerungen*, Leipzig, 1905 and 1921.

BOLITHO, H., *King Edward VIII*, London, Eyre & Spottiswoode, 1937.

BRECKNOCK, COUNTESS OF, *Edwina Mountbatten*, London, Macdonald, 1961.

BUCHANAN, M., *Queen Victoria's Relations*, London, Cassell, 1954.

CALVERT, A. F., *The Spanish Royal Wedding*, Taunton, Privately, 1906.

CAMPBELL-JOHNSON, A., *Mission with Mountbatten*, London, Hale, 1951.

PRINCESS CHRISTIAN, *Alice, Grand Duchess of Hesse*, London, Murray, 1885.

PRINCE CHRISTOPHER OF GREECE, *Memoirs*, London, Right Books Club, 1938.

CHURCHILL, W. S., *World Crisis*, London, Butterworth, 1923.

CHURCHILL, W. S., *The Second World War,* London, Cassell, 1948–52.

CONNELL, B., *Manifest Destiny,* London, Cassell, 1953.

CORTI, E. C., *Unter Zaren und Gekronten Frauen,* Salzburg, 1936.

CORTI, E. C., *Furst Alexander von Bulgarien,* Vienna, 1939.

CORTI, E. C., *The Downfall of Three Dynasties,* London, Methuen, 1934.

CORTI, E. C., *The English Empress,* London, Cassell, 1957.

COWLES, V., *Edward VII and His Circle,* London, Hamish Hamilton, 1956.

DALWIGH, K. F. R., *Tagebucher* (edit. W. Schussler), Frankfurt, 1921.

DOWNSHIRE, J. P., *Prince Philip, Duke of Edinburgh,* London, Yates, 1950.

DRANDNER, A. G., *Le Prince Alexandre de Bulgarie,* Paris, 1884.

EMDEN, P. H., *Jews in Britain,* London.

EMDEN, P. H., *Behind the Throne,* London, Hodder & Stoughton, 1934.

ENGLE-JANOSI, *Graf Rechberg,* Munich, 1927.

EPPSTEIN, V., *Furst Bismarck's Entlassung,* Berlin, 1920.

ERBACH-SCHÖNBERG, PRINCESS MARIE ZU, *Reminiscences,* Allen & Unwin, 1925.

ERBACH-SCHÖNBERG, PRINCESS MARIE ZU, *Aus Stiller und Bewegter Zeit,* Frankfurt, 1921.

PRINCE FRANCIS JOSEPH (OF BATTENBERG), *Die Volkswirtchaftliche Entwicklung Bulgariens,* Leipzig, 1891.

FRANCIS-WILLIAMS, *A Prime Minister Remembers,* London, Heinemann, 1960.

EMPRESS FREDERICK, *Letters* (Edit. by Sir F. Ponsonby), London, Macmillan, 1929.

FRIEDJUNG, K., *Der Kampf um die Vorherrschaft in Deutchland,* Vienna, 1924.

GILLIARD, P., *Le Tragique Destin de Nicholas II,* Paris, Payot, 1921.

GLASER, R., *Furst Alexander von Bulgarien,* Bensheim, 1901.

GOLOWINE, F., *Alexander von Bulgarien,* Vienna, 1896.

GORMAN, J. T., *George VI,* London, Foyle, 1937.
GRAHAM, E., *The Queen of Spain,* London, Hutchinson, 1929.

HAMMOND, B. and J. L., *Lord Shaftesbury,* London, Constable, 1923.
HAUPT, H., *Hessische Biographien,* Darmstadt, 1920.
HAUPT, H., *Quellen zur Hessischen Geschichte,* Darmstadt, since 1913.
HEP, A., *Ferdinand de Bulgarie Intime,* Paris, 1931.
HISTORICAL COMMISSION OF THE STATE OF HESSE, *Publikationen,* since 1920.
HODGETTS, B. E., *The Court of Russia,* London, 1908.
HOLMAN, D., *Lady Louis,* London, Odhams, 1952.
HORSTENAU-GLAISE, E., *Kaiser Franz Joseph,* Vienna, 1930.
HOUSMAN, L., *Happy and Glorious,* London, Cape, 1945.
HUHN, V., *Aus Bulgarischer Sturmzeit,* Leipzig, 1886.

KERR, M., *Louis of Battenberg,* London, Longmans, 1934.
KLAEBER, E., *Furst Alexander von Bulgarien,* Dresden, Heinrich, 1904.
KNIGHT, A. E., *Victoria, Her Life and Reign,* London, Partridge, 1897.
KOCH, A., *Furst Alexander,* Darmstadt, 1887.
KOLLER, O., *Bismarck Literatur,* Berlin, 1896.
KRAUS, E., *Die Abenteuer des Grafen zu Erbach,* Frankfurt, 1897.

LAFERTE, V., *Alexandre II, Details sur sa vie intime et sa mort,* Paris, 1883.
LEE, G. A., *The Royal House of Greece,* London, Ward, Lock, 1948.
LEE, S., *Queen Victoria,* London, Smith Elder, 1902.
LEE, S., *King Edward VII,* London, Macmillan, 1927.
LEPSIUS, J., MENDELSSOHN-BARTHOLDY, A., and THINNER, F. (Edit.) *Die Grosse Politik der Europaeischen Kabinette,* 1871–1914, Berlin, 1922/27.

MCCLINTOCK, M. H., *The Queen Thanks Sir Howard,* London, Murray, 1945.
MAINE, B., *Edward VIII, Duke of Windsor,* London, Hutchinson, 1957.
MARCKS, E., *Otto von Bismarck, Ein Lebensbild,* since 1915.

PRINCESS MARIE LOUISE, *My Memoirs of Six Reigns,* London, Evans, 1956.

MARTIN, T., *Queen Victoria As I Knew Her,* Oxford, Blackwood, 1908.

MASSON, M., *Edwina,* London, Hale, 1958.

MAUROIS, A., *King Edward VII and His Times,* London, Cassell, 1933.

MERES, H. J., *A Sermon Preached after the Funeral of Prince Henry of Battenberg,* London, 1896.

MORLEY, J., *The Life of William Ewart Gladstone,* London, Lloyd, 1908.

MOUNTBATTEN OF BURMA, EARL, *Time Only to Look Forward* (Speeches), London, Kaye, 1949.

MOUNTBATTEN OF BURMA, EARL, *Relations Tables,* New Delhi, Viceregal Press, 1947.

MURPHY, R., *Last Viceroy,* London, Jarrolds, 1948.

PRINCE NICHOLAS OF GREECE, *My Fifty Years,* London.

NICOLSON, H., *King George VI,* London, Constable, 1952.

NOGRI, *Bismarck,* Saggio storico, Milan, 1884.

PALEOLOGUE, M., *La Romance Tragique de Alexandre II,* Paris, 1924.

PEACOCK, M. D., *The Duke of Edinburgh,* London, Phoenix House, 1961.

PETKO-LEONOV, R., *Geheime Dokumente der Ostpolitik,* Berlin, 1883.

PONSONBY, F., *Recollections of Three Reigns,* London, Eyre & Spottiswoode, 1957.

PRINCESS RADZIWILL, C., *Nicholas II,* London, Cassel, 1931.

PRINCESS RADZIWILL, C., *The Empress Frederick,* London, 1934.

REDLICH, J., *Kaiser Franz Joseph,* Berlin, 1928.

SARA, M. E., *The Life and Times of Princess Beatrice,* London, Stanley Paul, 1945.

SCHAEFFER, D., *Bismarck,* Berlin, 1917.

Schnepfenthal Festschrift zur 100. Jahresfeier, Schnepfenthal, 1884.

SCHNURER, F., *Briefe des Kaisers Franz Josephs,* Munich, 1932.

SCHUSSLER, W., *Das Leben des Freiherrn Karl Friedrich von Dalwigk,* Frankfurt, 1920.

SENCOURT, R., *King Alfonso,* London, Faber, 1942.

SERMONETA, DUCHESS COLONNA V., *Memoirs,* London, Hutchinson, 1929.

SOBOL, L. N., *Der Erste Furst von Bulgarien,* Liepzig, 1886.

STEARNS, F., *The Life of Prince Otto von Bismarck,* London, 1900.

STEINER, J. W. C., *Geschichte des Grossherzogtums Hessen,* Darmstadt.

STRACHEY, L., *Queen Victoria,* London, Chatto & Windus, 1921.

THOMPSON, B., *The Allied Secret Service in Greece,* London, 1924.

QUEEN VICTORIA, *Letters.* London, John Murray, 1907–1932.

QUEEN VICTORIA, *Leaves from the Journal,* London, Smith Elder, 1869.

QUEEN VICTORIA, *More Leaves from the Journal,* London, Smith Elder, 1884.

QUEEN VICTORIA, *Letters.*

PRINCESS VICTORIA OF PRUSSIA, *My Memoirs,* London, Grayson, 1929.

WILLIAM II, *Aus Meinem Leben,* Leipzig, 1927.

WINDELBAND, W., *Bismarck und die Grossmachte* 1879–1888, Leipzig, 1926.

YUSUPOV, J., *Avant l'Exil,* Paris, 1952.

ZANCADA, P., *Bodas Reales,* Madrid, 1906.

INDEX

INDEX

* Children of Princess Sophia of Greece.   † Children of Princess Cecilia of Greece.

* Children of Princess Margarita of Greece.